LOEB CLASSICAL LIBRARY

FOUNDED BY JAMES LOEB 1911

EDITED BY

JEFFREY HENDERSON

BEDE

II

LCL 248

BEDE

HISTORICAL WORKS

ECCLESIASTICAL HISTORY OF
THE ENGLISH NATION
BOOKS IV–V

LIVES OF THE ABBOTS

LETTER TO EGBERT

WITH AN ENGLISH TRANSLATION BY

J. E. KING

HARVARD UNIVERSITY PRESS
CAMBRIDGE, MASSACHUSETTS
LONDON, ENGLAND

First published 1930

LOEB CLASSICAL LIBRARY® is a registered trademark
of the President and Fellows of Harvard College

ISBN 978-0-674-99273-3

Printed on acid-free paper and bound by
The Maple-Vail Book Manufacturing Group

CONTENTS

BAEDAE HISTORIA ECCLESIASTICA GENTIS ANGLORUM HISTORIA ABBATUM EPISTOLA AD ECGBERCTUM

HISTORIAE ECCLESIASTICAE ELENCHUS CAPITUM

LIBER IV

ELENCHUS CAPITUM

ELENCHUS CAPITUM

LIBER V

ELENCHUS CAPITUM

ELENCHUS CAPITUM

THE VENERABLE BEDE

THE FOURTH BOOK OF THE

ECCLESIASTICAL HISTORY OF THE ENGLISH NATION

DE VENERABILIS BAEDAE

HISTORIAE ECCLESIASTICAE GENTIS ANGLORUM

LIBER QUARTUS

CAP. I

Ut defuncto Deusdedit, Vighard ad suscipiendum episcopatum, Romam sit missus: sed illo ibidem defuncto, Theodorus archiepiscopus ordinatus, et cum Hadriano abbate sit Brittaniam missus.

ANNO memorato praefatae eclipsis et mox subsequentis pestilentiae, quo et Colman episcopus unanima catholicorum intentione superatus ad suos reversus est, Deusdedit sextus ecclesiae Doruvernensis episcopus obiit pridie Iduum Iuliarum; sed et Erconberct rex Cantuariorum eodem mense ac die defunctus, Ecgbercto filio sedem regni reliquit, quam ille susceptam per novem annos tenuit. Tunc cessante non pauco tempore episcopatu, missus est Romam ab ipso simul et a rege Nordanhymbrorum Osuio, ut praecedente libro paucis diximus, Vighard presbyter, vir in ecclesiasticis disciplinis doctissimus, de genere Anglorum, petentibus hunc ecclesiae Anglorum archiepiscopum ordinari: missis pariter

[1] July 664 till May 669, when Theodore reached Canterbury.

THE VENERABLE BEDE

THE FOURTH BOOK OF THE ECCLESIASTICAL HISTORY OF THE ENGLISH NATION

CHAPTER I

How after the death of Deusdedit Wighard was sent to Rome to be made bishop : but upon his dying in that same place Theodore was ordained archbishop and sent to Britain with abbot Hadrian [664–669].

In the year recorded of the foresaid eclipse and pestilence that soon after followed, in which also bishop Colman, overcome by the general sentence of the catholics, returned home to his countrymen, Deusdedit the sixth bishop of the church of Canterbury died the 14th day of July; moreover, Earconbert king of Kent died the same month and day, and left to his son Egbert the throne of his kingdom, which he received and held by the space of 9 years. At that time, the bishopric being vacant a great while,[1] Wighard, priest, a man well learned in the disciplines of the Church, an Englishman born, was sent to Rome by Egbert as well as by Oswy king of the Northumbrians (as we have briefly mentioned in the foregoing book), they being desirous for him to be ordained archbishop of the Church of the English : and at the same time presents were sent to the

apostolico papae donariis, et aureis atque argenteis vasis non paucis. Qui ubi Romam pervenit, cuius sedi apostolicae tempore illo Vitalianus praeerat, postquam itineris sui causam praefato papae apostolico patefecit, non multo post et ipse et omnes pene qui cum eo advenerant socii, pestilentia superveniente deleti sunt.

At apostolicus papa, habito de his consilio, quaesivit sedulus quem ecclesiis Anglorum archiepiscopum mitteret. Erat autem in monasterio Niridano[1] quod est non longe a Neapoli Campaniae, abbas Hadrianus, vir natione Afir, sacris literis diligenter imbutus, monasterialibus simul et ecclesiasticis disciplinis institutus, Graecae pariter et Latinae linguae peritissimus. Hunc ad se accitum Papa iussit episcopatu accepto Brittaniam venire. Qui indignum se tanto gradui respondens, ostendere posse se dixit alium, cuius magis ad suscipiendum episcopatum et eruditio conveniret, et aetas. Cumque monachum quemdam de vicino virginum monasterio, nomine Andream, pontifici offerret, hic ab omnibus qui novere dignus episcopatu iudicatus est. Verum pondus corporeae infirmitatis, ne episcopus fieri posset, obstitit. Et rursum Hadrianus ad suscipiendum episcopatum actus est: qui petens indutias, si forte alium, qui episcopus ordinaretur ex tempore posset invenire.

Erat ipso tempore Romae monachus Hadriano notus, nomine Theodorus, natus Tarso Ciliciae, vir et saeculari et divina literatura, et Graece instructus

[1] For *Hiridano*, Pl.

apostolic pope, of great store of plate, both silver and gold. And being arrived to Rome in the time that Vitalian was over the apostolic see thereof, and having declared the cause of his coming to the said apostolic pope, no long time after both Wighard himself and almost all his company, which had come with him, were surprised of a pestilence and destroyed.

Whereupon the apostolic pope having taken counsel thereon inquired diligently whom he might send for archbishop over the churches of the English. Now there was in the monastery of Niridan, not far from Naples in Campania, an abbot, Hadrian, an African born, a man accurately learned in the sacred writings as well as trained in monastical and ecclesiastical discipline, and right skilful in the Greek as well as the Latin tongue. This man being called to the pope was willed of him to take the bishopric upon him and travel unto Britain. But he answering that he was no meet man for so high a degree, said that he could point out another which both for his learning and his age were better fit for undertaking the bishopric. And when he presented to the pope a certain monk belonging to a neighbouring monastery of virgins, called Andrew, this man was of all that knew him esteemed worthy of the bishopric. Yet the burden of a weak and sickly body made it impossible that he should be appointed bishop. And Hadrian, being required again to take it upon him, desired certain days of respite, if haply in time he could find another to be ordained bishop.

At this very time there was in Rome a monk of Hadrian's acquaintance, named Theodore, born at Tarsus in Cilicia, a man well learned both in profane and divine literature and in the Greek and Latin

et Latine, probus moribus, et aetate venerandus, id est, annos habens aetatis sexaginta et sex. Hunc offerens Hadrianus pontifici, ut episcopus ordinaretur obtinuit: his tamen conditionibus interpositis, ut ipse eum perduceret Brittaniam, eo quod iam bis partes Galliarum diversis ex causis adiisset; et ob id maiorem huius itineris peragendi notitiam haberet, sufficiensque esset in possessione hominum propriorum: et ut ei doctrinae cooperator existens, diligenter adtenderet ne quid ille contrarium veritati fidei, Graecorum more, in ecclesiam cui praeesset, introduceret. Qui subdiaconus ordinatus, quatuor exspectavit menses, donec illi coma cresceret, quo in coronam tonderi posset; habuerat enim tonsuram more Orientalium sancti apostoli Pauli. Qui ordinatus est a Vitaliano papa anno Dominicae incarnationis sexcentesimo sexagesimo octavo, sub die septima Kalendarum Aprilium, Dominica. Et ita una cum Hadriano, sexto Kalendas Iunias Brittaniam missus est. Qui cum pariter per mare ad Massiliam, et deinde per terram Arhelas pervenissent, et tradidissent Iohanni archiepiscopo civitatis illius scripta commendatitia Vitaliani pontificis, retenti sunt ab eo, quousque Ebrinus maior domus regiae copiam pergendi quoquo vellent tribuit eis. Qua accepta Theodorus profectus est ad Agilberctum Pariseorum episcopum, de quo superius diximus, et ab eo benigne susceptus, et multo tempore habitus est. Hadrianus perrexit primum ad Emme Senonum,

---

[1] Slaves of his own, which would save cost.

[2] Perhaps because of the Monothelite controversy. Bright, p. 220.

[3] Who shaved the whole head. They also wore beards.

[4] Clothaire III.

tongues, in manners and conversation virtuous and for age venerable, being, that is, then 66 years old. Him Hadrian presented to the pope, and obtained that he was ordained bishop: yet with these conditions first made, that Hadrian should himself conduct him into Britain, because having twice before travelled into the parts of France for divers matters, he had therefore more experience in accomplishing this journey, and was sufficiently provided with men of his own:[1] and that assisting him always in teaching, he should give diligent eye that Theodore enduced not after the manner of the Greeks[2] anything contrary to the true faith into the Church now subject unto him. And Theodore, being ordained sub-deacon, tarried four months until his hair should be full grown, that it might be shorn into the shape of a crown, for before he had the tonsure of the holy apostle Paul after the manner of the Easterns.[3] And he was ordained of Vitalian, the pope, in the 668th year of the Lord's incarnation, the 26th day of March, upon a Sunday. And so on the 27th of May in the company of the abbot Hadrian he was directed to Britain. And when together they had arrived to Marseilles by sea, and after by land to Arles, and had delivered to John the archbishop of that city the letters of commendation from Vitalian the pope, they were held back there by him until that Ebroin, mayor of the king's[4] palace, gave them safe-conduct to pass and go whithersoever they would. Which being granted them, Theodore took his journey to Agilbert bishop of Paris, of whom we have spoken before, and was very friendly received of him and kept there a long time. Hadrian went his way first to Emme bishop of Sens, and after to

et postea ad Faronem Meldorum episcopos, et bene sub eis diutius fuit: coegerat enim eos imminens hiems ut ubicumque potuissent quieti manerent. Quod cum nuntii certi narrassent regi Ecgbercto, esse scilicet episcopum quem petierant a Romano antistite in regno Francorum, misit illo continuo Raedfridum praefectum suum ad adducendum eum: quo cum venisset, adsumpsit Theodorum cum Ebrini licentia, et perduxit eum ad portum cui nomen est Quentauic, ubi fatigatus infirmitate aliquantisper moratus est; et cum convalescere coepisset, navigavit Brittaniam. Hadrianum autem Ebrinus retinuit, quoniam suspicabatur eum habere aliquam legationem imperatoris ad Brittaniae reges adversus regnum, cuius tunc ipse maximam curam gerebat. Sed cum nihil tale illum habere vel habuisse veraciter comperisset, absolvit eum, et post Theodorum ire permisit. Qui statim ut ad illum venit, dedit monasterium beati Petri apostoli, ubi archiepiscopi Cantiae sepeliri, ut praefatus sum, solent. Praeceperat enim Theodoro abeunti domnus apostolicus, ut in dioecesi sua provideret, et daret ei locum in quo cum suis apte degere potuisset.

Faro bishop of Meaux, and rested in their care a good space: for winter was at hand, and had driven them to abide quietly in such convenient place as they could get. Now when sure messengers had brought word to king Egbert, that certes the bishop whom they [1] had desired of the pope of Rome rested in the kingdom of the Franks, he sent thither straightway Redfrid his reeve to bring him on: who, when he came thither, took Theodore with the leave of Ebroin and brought him to the port that is named Quentawic,[2] where Theodore being vexed with sickness continued a space; and as soon as he began to recover health again, he sailed to Britain. But Ebroin with held back Hadrian, suspecting that he had some embassy of the emperor [3] to the kings of Britain, against the realm [4] whereof at that time he had himself the special charge. But, when he found indeed that he had no such thing nor had had, he let him go and suffered him to come after Theodore. Who as soon as Hadrian came to him, gave him the monastery of the blessed Peter the apostle, where, as I have said before, the archbishops of Kent are wont to be buried. For the apostolic lord had required Theodore at his departure to provide and give Hadrian a place in his province,[5] where he and his company might be able to live together commodiously.

[1] Oswy and Egbert.
[2] Étaples on the Canche.
[3] Constans II, then at Syracuse.
[4] Of the Franks.
[5] Union of dioceses (*parochiae*) under an archbishop, Pl.

CAP. II

Ut Theodoro cuncta peragrante, Anglorum ecclesiae cum catholica veritate, literarum quoque sanctarum coeperint studiis imbui : et ut Putta pro Damiano Hrofensis ecclesiae sit factus antistes.

PERVENIT autem Theodorus ad ecclesiam suam secundo postquam consecratus est anno, sub die sexto Kalendarum Iuniarum, Dominica; et fecit in ea annos viginti et unum, menses tres, dies viginti sex. Moxque peragrata insula tota, quaquaversum Anglorum gentes morabantur, nam et libentissime ab omnibus suscipiebatur atque audiebatur, rectum vivendi ordinem, ritum paschae celebrandi canonicum, per omnia comitante et cooperante Hadriano disseminabat. Isque primus erat in archiepiscopis, cui omnis Anglorum ecclesia manus dare consentiret. Et quia literis sacris simul et saecularibus, ut diximus, abundanter ambo erant instructi, congregata discipulorum caterva, scientiae salutaris quotidie flumina irrigandis eorum cordibus emanabant: ita ut etiam metricae artis, astronomiae et arithmeticae ecclesiasticae disciplinam inter sacrorum apicum volumina suis auditoribus contraderent. Indicio est quod usque hodie supersunt de eorum discipulis, qui Latinam Graecamque linguam aeque ut propriam in qua nati sunt, norunt. Neque unquam prorsus ex quo Brittaniam petierunt Angli, feliciora fuere tempora; dum et fortissimos Christianosque habentes

[1] Albinus is mentioned as one, p. 5.

[2] Bede wrote a treatise *de arte metrica*.

[3] Studies connected with the calendar, into which astronomy would enter.

CHAPTER II

How, when Theodore travelled through all the country, the churches of the English along with catholic truth began to be instructed also in the study of Holy Writ; and how Putta was made bishop of the church of Rochester in the room of Damian [669].

Now Theodore came to his church the second year after his consecration, on the 27th day of May, being Sunday; and continued in the same twenty-one years, 3 months and 26 days. And soon he travelled over all the island, wheresoever the English tribes dwelled, for all men did most gladly receive him and hear him; and having with him the company and help of Hadrian in all things, did sow abroad the right rule of living and the canonical manner of celebrating Easter. And he was the first archbishop unto whom all the whole Church of the English did consent and submit themselves. And because both he and Hadrian, as we have said, were fully learned in profane as well as in holy literature, they gathered a company of scholars [1] unto them, and streams of wholesome knowledge did daily flow forth to water their hearts: so that along with the volumes of the sacred writings, they did withal instruct their hearers in the sciences of metric,[2] astronomy and algorism.[3] The proof whereof is, that even to this day some of their scholars yet living have as good knowledge of the Latin and Greek tongues as of their own in which they were born. Neither was there ever since the English first came to Britain, any time more happy than at that present; when they both had most valiant and Christian kings and were feared of all

reges cunctis barbaris nationibus essent terrori, et omnium vota ad nuper audita caelestis regni gaudia penderent, et quicumque lectionibus sacris cuperent erudiri, haberent in promptu magistros qui docerent. Sed et sonos cantandi in ecclesia, quos eatenus in Cantia tantum noverant, ab hoc tempore per omnes Anglorum ecclesias discere coeperunt: primusque, excepto Iacobo de quo supra diximus, cantandi magister Nordanhymbrorum ecclesiis, Aeddi cognomento Stephanus fuit, invitatus de Cantia a reverentissimo viro Vilfrido, qui primus inter episcopos qui de Anglorum gente essent, catholicum vivendi morem ecclesiis Anglorum tradere didicit.

Itaque Theodorus perlustrans universa, ordinabat locis opportunis episcopos, et ea quae minus perfecta repperit, his quoque iuvantibus corrigebat. In quibus et Ceadda episcopum cum argueret non fuisse rite consecratum; respondens ipse voce humillima: "Si me," inquit, "nosti episcopatum non rite suscepisse, libenter ab officio discedo: quippe qui neque me umquam hoc esse dignum arbitrabar; sed obedientiae causa iussus subire hoc, quamvis indignus consensi." At ille audiens humilitatem responsi eius, dixit, non eum episcopatum dimittere debere; sed ipse ordinationem eius denuo catholica ratione consummavit. Eo autem tempore quo defuncto Deusdedit, Doruvernensi ecclesiae episcopus quaere-

---

[1] Gregory's missionaries brought his mode of chanting. The Irish system of chanting is not known.

[2] Cf. III. 20.

[3] The biographer of Wilfrid.

[4] But the English bishops Ithamar, Thomas, Boniface, Deusdedit, Damian were all predecessors of Wilfrid.

[5] Chad had been appointed to the see of York and consecrated by Wini and two British bishops.

barbarous nations, and the desires of all were wholly bent to the late joyful tidings of the kingdom of heaven, and if any desired to be instructed in the reading of Holy Scripture there lacked not masters ready to teach them.

Moreover, too the tunes of singing in church, which until then were only known in Kent,[1] from this time on began to be learned through all the churches of England: and the first master of song in the churches of Northumberland (except James [2] whom we spake of before), was Eddi,[3] surnamed Stephen; who was called from Kent by Wilfrid, a man most reverend, which first among the bishops that were of the English nation did learn to deliver the catholic manner of life [4] to the English churches.

And thus Theodore, viewing over and visiting eachwhere, did in convenient places ordain bishops, and with their assistance did also amend those things which he found to come short of perfectness. And among other also when he reproved bishop Chad for that he was not duly consecrated [5]; Chad made most humble answer and said: "If you know that I have taken the office of a bishop not in due order, I am ready with all my heart to give up the same: for neither did I think myself ever worthy thereof; but for obedience' sake being so commanded I did agree, although unworthy to take it upon me." Whereon Theodore hearing that humble answer, said that Chad ought not to give up the office of bishop; but did himself complete Chad's ordination anew after the catholic manner.[6] Moreover, at that time in which after the death of Deusdedit a bishop was

[6] Probably when Chad was made bishop of Mercia.

batur, ordinabatur, mittebatur, Vilfrid quoque de Brittania Galliam ordinandus est missus: et quoniam ante Theodorum rediit, ipse etiam in Cantia presbyteros et diaconos, usquedum archiepiscopus ad sedem suam perveniret, ordinabat. At ipse veniens mox in civitate Hrofi, ubi defuncto Damiano episcopatus iam diu cessaverat, ordinavit virum magis ecclesiasticis disciplinis institutum et vitae simplicitate contentum, quam in saeculi rebus strenuum, cui nomen erat Putta; maxime autem modulandi in ecclesia more Romanorum, quem a discipulis beati papae Gregorii didicerat, peritum.

CAP. III

Ut Ceadda, de quo supra dictum est, provinciae Merciorum sit episcopus datus: et de vita et de obitu et sepultura eius.

Eo tempore provinciae Merciorum rex Vulfheri praefuit, qui cum mortuo Iarumanno, sibi quoque suisque a Theodoro episcopum dari peteret, non eis novum voluit ordinare episcopum; sed postulavit a rege Osuio, ut illis episcopus Ceadda daretur, qui tunc in monasterio suo, quod est in Laestingae, quietam vitam agebat, Vilfrido administrante episcopatum Eboracensis ecclesiae, necnon et omnium Nordanhymbrorum, sed et Pictorum, quousque rex Osuiu imperium protendere poterat. Et quia moris erat eidem reverentissimo antistiti, opus evangelii magis ambulando per loca, quam equitando perficere;

[1] Chad was a Northumbrian.

sued for, ordained, and sent for the church of Canterbury, Wilfrid also was sent from Britain to France to be ordained: and as he returned before Theodore came, did himself also ordain priests and deacons in Kent until the time that the archbishop came to his see. But Theodore at his coming shortly after to the city of Rochester where the bishopric had been now long vacant by the death of Damian, did ordain there a man better skilled in the ecclesiastical discipline and more given to plain sincerity of life than politic in worldly affairs, whose name was Putta; moreover, he was specially cunning in chanting in church after the Roman use, which he had learned of the blessed pope Gregory's scholars.

CHAPTER III

How Chad afore mentioned was given to be bishop to the province of the Marchmen; and of his life, death and burial [669–672].

At that time was Wulfhere king of the Marchmen, who after the death of Jaruman desired also of Theodore to have a bishop given to him and his; but Theodore would not ordain a new bishop for them, but required of king Oswy that Chad [1] should be given them for bishop, who at that time lived quietly in his monastery at Lastingham, and Wilfrid ruled the bishopric of the church of York and also of all the Northumbrians, and moreover of the Redshanks as far as king Oswy's lordship did reach. And because the same most reverend bishop Chad was wont to do the work of the Gospel more walking afoot, where he went, than on horseback, Theodore willed him to ride whensoever there came occasion of a

iussit eum Theodorus ubicumque longius iter instaret, equitare, multumque renitentem, studio et amore pii laboris, ipse eum manu sua levavit in equum, quia nimirum sanctum esse virum comperit, atque equo vehi quo esset necesse, compulit. Susceptum itaque episcopatum gentis Merciorum simul et Lindisfarorum Ceadda, iuxta exempla patrum antiquorum, in magna vitae perfectione administrare curavit: cui etiam rex Vulfheri donavit terram quinquaginta familiarum, ad construendum monasterium in loco qui dicitur Adbaruae, id est, Ad Nemus, in provincia Lindissi, in quo usque hodie instituta ab ipso regularis vitae vestigia permanent.

Habuit autem sedem episcopalem in loco qui vocatur Lyccidfelth, in quo et defunctus ac sepultus est; ubi usque hodie sequentium quoque provinciae illius episcoporum sedes est. Fecerat vero sibi mansionem non longe ab ecclesia remotiorem; in qua secretius cum paucis, id est, septem sive octo fratribus, quoties a labore et ministerio verbi vacabat, orare ac legere solebat. Qui cum in illa provincia duobus annis ac dimidio ecclesiam gloriosissime rexisset, adfuit superno dispensante iudicio tempus, de quo loquitur Ecclesiastes, quia, "Tempus mittendi lapides, et tempus colligendi." Supervenit namque clades divinitus missa, quae per mortem carnis, vivos ecclesiae lapides de terrenis sedibus ad aedificium caeleste transferret. Cumque plurimis de ecclesia eiusdem reverentissimi antistitis de carne

---

[1] Barton-on-Humber, or more probably Barrow in Lincolnshire.

[2] Eccles. iii. 5.

[3] From the quarry to the building; cf. 1 Peter ii. 5.

longer journey; and when Chad strongly resisted for the desire and love that he had of godly travail, Theodore himself did lift him on horseback with his own hands, knowing him indeed to be a holy man, and so compelled him to ride whither need required. Chad accordingly, being made bishop of the Marchmen as much as of Lindsey, did diligently govern the same after the example of the ancient fathers in great perfection of life: and king Wulfhere also gave unto him the land of 50 households to build a monastery in the place that is called Adbarwae, that is By the Wood,[1] in the province of Lindsey, where until this day the steps of monastical life which Chad established there do yet remain.

Now he had the see of his bishopric in the place which is called Lichfield, where he died also and was buried; in which place until this day continueth the see of the bishops that succeed also in that province. He had indeed made himself not far from the church an abode somewhat withdrawn, in which, as often as he was at leisure from the business and ministry of the word, he was wont to pray and read more apart with a few, that is to say, seven or eight brethren. And when he had governed the church most worthily in that province two years and a half, by the appointment of judgment from on high, that time came which Ecclesiastes speaketh of,[2] that "There is a time to cast stones and a time to gather them together." For there came upon him a plague sent from God, which by the death of the flesh should remove the live stones of the Church from their earthly places [3] to the heavenly building. And when very many members of the church of the same most reverend bishop had been taken away from the flesh,

subtractis, veniret hora ipsius ut transiret ex hoc mundo ad Dominum; contigit die quadam ut in praefata mansione forte ipse cum uno tantum fratre, cui vocabulum erat Ouini, commoraretur, ceteris eius sociis pro causa opportuna ad ecclesiam reversis. Erat autem idem Ouini monachus magni meriti, et pura intentione supernae retributionis mundum derelinquens, dignusque per omnia, cui Dominus specialiter sua revelaret arcana, dignus cui fidem narranti audientes accommodarent. Venerat enim cum regina Aedilthryde de provincia Orientalium Anglorum, eratque primus ministrorum, et princeps domus eius. Qui cum crescente fidei fervore saeculo abrenunciare disponeret, non hoc segniter fecit; sed adeo se mundi rebus exuit, ut relictis omnibus quae habebat, simplici tantum habitu indutus, et securim atque asciam in manu ferens, veniret ad monasterium eiusdem reverentissimi patris, quod vocatur Laestingaeu. Non enim ad otium, ut quidam, sed ad laborem se monasterium intrare signabat. Quod ipsum etiam facto monstravit: nam quo minus sufficiebat meditationi Scripturarum, eo amplius operi manuum studium impendebat. Denique cum episcopo in praefata mansione pro suae reverentia devotionis inter fratres habitus, cum illi intus lectioni vacabant, ipse foris quae opus esse videbantur, operabatur. Qui cum die quadam tale aliquid foris ageret, digressis ad ecclesiam sociis, ut dicere coeperam, et episcopus solus in oratorio loci

and when his own hour was come to pass out of this world to the Lord; it happened on a certain day that he chanced to be staying in the aforesaid abode and had no one but one brother with him, whose name was Owin, all the rest of his fellows being returned to church, as the cause and hour required. Now this same Owin was a monk of great deserving, and one that forsook the world with pure intent and hope of reward from above, a man for all points worthy that the Lord should in special wise reveal to him His secrets, and worthy that to his words the hearers might give credit. For he had come with queen Ethelthryth from the province of the East English, and was the chief of her thanes, and governor of her house. Who, for the great zeal of faith that increased in him, determining to renounce the world, did accomplish the same, not negligently, but in such sort unclad himself of worldly matters, that, forsaking all that he had, being clothed but with plain and poor apparel and bearing an axe and hatchet in his hand, he came to the monastery of the same most reverend father, called Lastingham. For he signified that he was entering the monastery not for ease, as some do, but to travail. Which very thing he shewed also in his doing: for the less apt he was for the study of the Scriptures, the more diligent and painful he was to work with his hands. In short, his reverence and devotion were such, that the bishop accepted him for one of his brethren to accompany him in the foresaid abode, where, while they within were occupied in reading, he without did those things which seemed necessary to be done. And on a certain day, as he was doing some such thing abroad, his fellows being gone to church, as I began to say, and the bishop

lectioni vel orationi operam daret, audivit repente, ut postea referebat, vocem suavissimam cantantium atque laetantium, de caelo ad terras usque descendere: quam videlicet vocem ab euroaustro, id est, ab alto brumalis exortus, primo se audisse dicebat, ac deinde paulatim eam sibi adpropiare, donec ad tectum usque oratorii in quo erat episcopus, perveniret: quod ingressa, totum implevit atque in gyro circumdedit. At ille dum sollicitus in ea quae audiebat animum intenderet, audivit denuo, transacto quasi dimidiae horae spatio, ascendere de tecto eiusdem oratorii idem laetitiae canticum, et ipsa qua venerat via ad caelos usque cum ineffabili dulcedine reverti. Qui cum aliquantulum horae quasi adtonitus maneret, et quid haec essent sollerti animo scrutaretur, aperuit episcopus fenestram oratorii, et sonitum manu faciens, ut saepe consueverat, si quis foris esset, ad se intrare praecepit. Introivit ille concitus, cui dixit antistes: "Vade cito ad ecclesiam, et hos septem fratres huc venire facito; tu quoque simul adesto." Qui cum venissent, primo admonuit eos ut virtutem dilectionis et pacis, ad invicem et ad omnes fideles servarent: instituta quoque disciplinae regularis, quae vel ab ipso didicissent et in ipso vidissent, vel in patrum praecedentium factis sive dictis invenissent, indefessa instantia sequerentur. Deinde subiunxit diem sui obitus iam proxime instare. "Namque hospes," inquit, "ille amabilis, qui fratres nostros visitare solebat, ad me

---

[1] Angel of death.

being alone in the oratory of the place, occupied in reading or prayer, this Owin heard suddenly, as he after told, a most sweet noise of voices singing and rejoicing come down from heaven to the earth: the which voice, he said, he first heard beginning from the south-east, that is, above the region of the winter sunrise, and then by little and little drawing near him, until it came up to the roof of the oratory where the bishop was: and there it entered, filling it within and compassed it all round about. Whereat giving mind earnestly to mark the thing that he heard, he did again, as it were after the space of half an hour, hear the same joyful song go up from the roof of the same oratory and return up to the heavens the very same way that it came, with unspeakable sweetness. And as he mused some hour's space and was as it were astounded, devising deeply in his mind what this might be, the bishop opened the oratory window and, as he often used to do, made a noise with his hand, and bade some man come in to him, if there were any without. Owin entered in straightway, to whom the bishop said: "Go to the church quickly, and cause these seven brethren to come hither: do thou also come with them." And when they were come, first he warned them to keep among themselves and toward all the faithful folk the virtue of charity and peace: also with unweary continuance to follow the rules of regular discipline, which they had either learned of him and seen in him, or found in the doings or sayings of the former fathers. Next did he tell them, moreover, that the day of his departing was already very nigh at hand. "For that lovely guest," [1] quoth he, "who was wont to visit our brethren, hath vouchsafed this day to

quoque hodie venire, meque de saeculo evocare dignatus est. Propter quod revertentes ad ecclesiam, dicite fratribus ut et meum exitum Domino precibus commendent, et suum quoque exitum, cuius hora incerta est, vigiliis, orationibus, bonis operibus praevenire meminerint." Cumque haec et huiusmodi plura loqueretur, atque illi percepta eius benedictione, iam multum tristes exissent, rediit ipse solus qui carmen caeleste audierat, et prosternens se in terram: "Obsecro," inquit, "pater; licet aliquid interrogare?" "Interroga," inquit, "quod vis." At ille: "Obsecro," inquit, "ut dicas quod erat canticum illud laetantium quod audivi, venientium de caelis super oratorium hoc, et post tempus redeuntium ad caelos?" Respondet ille: "Si vocem carminis audisti, et caelestes supervenire coetus cognovisti, praecipio tibi in nomine Domini, ne hoc cuiquam ante meum obitum dicas. Re vera autem angelorum fuere spiritus, qui me ad caelestia quae semper amabam ac desiderabam praemia vocare venerunt, et post dies septem se redituros, ac me secum adducturos esse promiserunt." Quod quidem ita ut dictum ei erat, opere completum est. Nam confestim languore corporis tactus est, et hoc per dies ingravescente, septimo, ut promissum ei fuerat, die postquam obitum suum Dominici corporis et sanguinis perceptione munivit, soluta ab ergastulo corporis anima sancta, ducentibus, ut credi fas est, angelis comitibus aeterna gaudia petivit. Non

come to me also and call me out of this world. Wherefore go your ways to the church again, and speak unto the brethren, that with their prayers they both commend unto the Lord my departure, and remember also with watching, praying and good works to prevent their own departing, the hour whereof is uncertain." And when he spake these and more like words, and that the brethren had taken his blessing and were now come forth very heavy and sad, Owin that only had heard the heavenly song came in again, and casting himself flat on the ground said: "I beseech you, father, may I be bold to ask you a question?" "Ask what you will," quoth he. Then quoth the other: "I pray you tell me what was that song which I heard of that joyful company descending from heaven upon this oratory, and after a time returning to heaven again?" The bishop answereth and saith: "If thou hast heard the voice of the song and understood the coming of the heavenly company, I command you in the name of the Lord to tell no man hereof before my death. Now they were indeed angelic spirits, which came to call me to the heavenly rewards which I always loved and longed for, and after seven days they have promised to come again and take me with them thither." The which was indeed fulfilled as it was told him. For straightway he was taken with a faintness of body, which daily grew more grievous upon him, and the seventh day (as it had been promised him), after he had first strengthened his departing with the receiving of the body and blood of the Lord, his holy soul being loosed from the prison of the body was carried and led (as we may well believe) of the company of angels to the joys everlasting. And it is no marvel if he

autem mirum si diem mortis, vel potius diem Domini laetus aspexit, quem semper usquedum veniret, sollicitus exspectare curavit.

Namque inter plura continentiae, humilitatis, doctrinae, orationum, voluntariae paupertatis, et ceterarum virtutum merita, in tantum erat timori Domini subditus, in tantum novissimorum suorum in omnibus operibus suis memor, ut sicut mihi frater quidam de eis qui me in Scripturis erudiebant et erat in monasterio ac magisterio illius educatus, vocabulo Trumberct, referre solebat, si forte legente eo vel aliud quid agente, repente flatus venti maior adsurgeret, continuo misericordiam Domini invocaret, et eam generi humano propitiari rogaret. Si autem violentior aura insisteret, iam clauso codice procideret in faciem, atque obnixius orationi incumberet. At si procella fortior, aut nimbus perurgeret, vel etiam corusci ac tonitrua terras et aera terrerent; tunc veniens ad ecclesiam sollicitus orationibus ac psalmis, donec serenitas aeris rediret, fixa mente vacaret. Cumque interrogaretur a suis, quare hoc faceret; respondebat: "Non legistis, quia 'intonuit de caelo Dominus, et Altissimus dedit vocem suam. Misit sagittas suas, et dissipavit eos, fulgura multiplicavit, et conturbavit eos?' Movet enim aera Dominus, ventos excitat, iaculatur fulgura, de caelo intonat, ut terrigenas ad timendum se suscitet, ut corda eorum in memoriam futuri iudicii revocet, ut superbiam eorum dissipet, et conturbet audaciam, reducto ad mentem tremendo illo tempore, quando ipse caelis

---

[1] Ps. xviii. 13, 14.

gladly beheld the day of death, or rather the day of the Lord, which day he did always carefully look for till it should come.

For among his manifold merits of abstinence and lowliness, of preaching, of prayer, of wilful poverty and all other virtues, he was so far humbled to the fear of the Lord, so much mindful of his latter end in all his works, that (as a certain brother named Trumbert was wont to tell, one of them that taught me in the Scriptures and was brought up in Chad's monastery and government) if perhaps, while he was reading or doing some other thing, there rose any sudden greater blast of wind, by and by would he call on the mercy of the Lord and beseech Him to have pity on mankind. But and if there came a gust yet more vehement, then would he shut up his book and fall down on his face and set himself more fervently to prayer. But if a stronger storm or blustering shower continued long, or also that lightning and thunder did make both the earth and air to shake for fear; then would he go to church and earnestly set his mind to prayer and saying of psalms, until the air waxed clear again. And his companions asked him why he did so. "Have ye not read," answered he, "that 'the Lord thundered from heaven and the Most High uttered His voice. He sent out his arrows and scattered them: He multiplied lightnings and troubled them'?[1] For the Lord moveth the air, raiseth up winds, shooteth out lightnings, thundereth from heaven, to stir up the creatures of the earth to fear Him, to call again their hearts to the remembrance of the judgment to come, to overthrow their pride and confound their boldness, and thus to bring back to their minds that terrible time, when the

ac terris ardentibus, venturus est in nubibus in potestate magna et maiestate ad iudicandos vivos et mortuos. Propter quod," inquit, "oportet nos admonitioni eius caelesti, debito cum timore et amore respondere; ut quoties aere commoto, manum quasi ad feriendum minitans exerit, nec adhuc tamen percutit, mox imploremus eius misericordiam, et discussis penetralibus cordis nostri, atque expurgatis vitiorum ruderibus, solliciti ne unquam percuti mereamur, agamus."

Convenit autem revelationi et relationi praefati fratris de obitu huius antistitis etiam sermo reverentissimi patris Ecgbercti, de quo supra diximus, qui dudum cum eodem Ceadda adulescente, et ipse adulescens in Hibernia monachicam in orationibus et continentia, et meditatione divinarum Scripturarum vitam sedulus agebat. Sed illo postmodum patriam reverso, ipse peregrinus pro Domino usque ad finem vitae permansit. Cum ergo veniret ad eum longo post tempore, gratia visitationis, de Brittania vir sanctissimus et continentissimus, vocabulo Hygbald, qui erat abbas in provincia Lindissi, et ut sanctos decebat, de vita priorum patrum sermonem facerent, atque hanc aemulari gauderent, intervenit mentio reverentissimi antistitis Ceadda; dixitque Ecgberct: "Scio hominem in hac insula adhuc in carne manentem, qui cum vir ille de mundo transiret, vidit animam Ceddi fratris ipsius cum agmine angelorum descendere de caelo, et adsumta secum anima eius, ad caelestia regna redire." Quod utrum de se

heavens and the earth shall burn, and Himself come down upon the clouds with great power and majesty to judge the quick and the dead. And therefore," quoth he, "it behoveth us with due fear and love to make answer to His warning from heaven; that, as oft as He troubleth the air and stretcheth out His hand as He were threatening to strike, and nevertheless smiteth not yet, we straightway call upon His mercy, and bolting out the very bottom of our hearts and casting out the refuse of sin, do carefully provide that we never deserve to be smitten."

Furthermore, with the revelation and report of the foresaid brother concerning the death of this bishop, the words also of the most reverend father Egbert, of whom we spake before, do well agree; which Egbert, at the time when the same Chad was a young man and himself of like age too, did once together with him in Ireland straitly lead a monastical life in prayers, abstinence and study of the holy Scriptures. But Chad being afterwards returned to his country, Egbert abode there still as a pilgrim for the Lord's sake unto the end of his life. When then a long time after there came to visit him from Britain a most holy and virtuous man, named Hygbald, who was an abbot in the province of Lindsey, and they talked together, as becometh holy men to do, of the life of former fathers, and gladly would wish to follow the same, they fell upon mention of the most reverend bishop Chad; and Egbert said: "I know a man yet remaining in the flesh in this island, who, when Chad passed out of the world, did see the soul of his brother Cedd with a company of angels descend from heaven, and take up his soul with them and return again to the heavenly realms." Which vision whether Egbert

an de alio aliquo diceret, nobis manet incertum, dum tamen hoc quod tantus vir dixit quia verum sit esse non possit incertum.

Obiit autem Ceadda sexto die Nonarum Martiarum, et sepultus est primo quidem iuxta ecclesiam sanctae Mariae; sed postmodum constructa ibidem ecclesia beatissimi apostolorum principis Petri, in eandem sunt eius ossa translata. In quo utroque loco, ad indicium virtutis illius, solent crebra sanitatum miracula operari. Denique nuper phreneticus quidam, dum per cuncta errando discurreret, devenit ibi vespere, nescientibus sive non curantibus loci custodibus, et ibi tota nocte requiescens, mane sanato sensu egressus, mirantibus et gaudentibus cunctis, quid ibi sanitatis Domino largiente consequeretur, ostendit. Est autem locus idem sepulcri tumba lignea in modum domunculi facta coopertus, habente foramen in pariete, per quod solent hi qui causa devotionis illo adveniunt, manum suam immittere, ac partem pulveris inde adsumere: quam cum in aquas miserint atque has infirmantibus iumentis sive hominibus gustandas dederint, mox infirmitatis ablata molestia, cupitae sospitatis gaudia redibunt.

In cuius locum ordinavit Theodorus Vynfridum, virum bonum ac modestum, qui, sicut praedecessores eius, provinciis Merciorum et Mediterraneorum Anglorum et Lindisfarorum episcopatus officio praeesset: in quibus cunctis Vulfheri, qui adhuc supererat, sceptrum regni tenebat. Erat autem Vynfrid de clero eius cui ipse successerat antistitis, et diaconatus officio sub eo non pauco tempore fungebatur.

meant to be seen of himself or of some other, it remaineth to us uncertain, yet when so worthy a man as he said that it was true, the thing cannot be uncertain to us.

Now Chad died the second day of March and was buried first by Saint Mary's church; but afterward, when the church of Peter, the most blessed chief of the apostles, was built in the same place, his bones were removed thither. In both which places, in token of his virtue, often miracles of healing are wont to be wrought. In short, of late a certain man that had a frenzy and ran up and down wandering everywhere, came thither at an evening, by the ignorance or negligence of them that kept the place, and remained there all the night, and in the morning came out well in his wit, and declared to the wonder and joy of all men what soundness of mind by the gift of the Lord he got there. Now the same place of the sepulchre is covered with a wooden tomb made like a little house, having a hole in the wall, at which they that come thither for devotion's sake are wont to put in their hand and take to them some of the dust therefrom: the which they put into water and then give it to taste to sick beasts or men, whereby the grief of their sickness is anon taken away, and they will return to their joyful desired health.

In the place of Chad, Theodore ordained Wynfrid, a virtuous and sober man, to rule and have the office of bishop, as his predecessors had before him, over the provinces of the Marchmen and Middle English and of the men of Lindsey: in all which countries Wulfhere (who yet lived) did hold the crown and sceptre. Moreover, Wynfrid was of the clergy of that bishop whom he had succeeded, and executed the office of deacon under him no small time.

CAP. IV

Ut Colman episcopus, relicta Brittania, duo monasteria in Scottia, unum Scottis, alterum Anglis, quos secum adduxerat, fecerit.

INTEREA Colmanus, qui de Scottia erat episcopus, relinquens Brittaniam, tulit secum omnes quos in Lindisfarnensium insula congregaverat Scottos: sed et de gente Anglorum viros circiter triginta, qui utrique monachicae conversationis erant studiis imbuti. Et relictis in ecclesia sua fratribus aliquot, primo venit ad insulam Hii, unde erat ad praedicandum verbum Anglorum genti destinatus. Deinde secessit ad insulam quandam parvam, quae ad occidentalem plagam ab Hibernia procul secreta, sermone Scottico Inisboufinde, id est, insula vitulae albae, nuncupatur. In hanc ergo perveniens, construxit monasterium, et monachos inibi, quos de utraque natione collectos adduxerat, collocavit. Qui cum invicem concordare non possent, eo quod Scotti tempore aestatis quo fruges erant colligendae, relicto monasterio per nota sibi loca dispersi vagarentur; at vero hieme succedente redirent, et his quae Angli praeparaverant, communiter uti desiderarent: quaesivit Colmanus huic dissensioni remedium, et circumiens omnia, prope vel longe, invenit locum in Hibernia insula, aptum monasterio construendo, qui lingua Scottorum Mageo nominatur; emitque partem eius non grandem, ad construendum ibi

---

[1] Lindisfarne.
[2] Or *Vaccae albae*, Inisboffin, off the coast of Mayo.
[3] Mayo.

CHAPTER IV

How bishop Colman leaving Britain made two monasteries in the land of the Scots, one for the Scots, the other for the English whom he had brought with him [667].

In the meantime Colman, who was a Scottish bishop, left Britain and took with him all the Scots that he had gathered together in the isle of Lindisfarne: moreover, about 30 Englishmen, and all of either race were brought up in the exercises of monastical life and conversation. And leaving in his own church [1] certain brethren, he came first to the isle of Hy, from whence he had been sent to preach the word to the English nation. Afterward he departed to a certain little isle which lieth on the west side, out of a good way from Ireland, and is called in the Scottish tongue Inisboufinde, that is to say, Whitecalf Isle.[2] Into which he came and built a monastery, and placed the monks there, which he had brought with him and gathered of both nations. And. since they could not agree together (for that the Scots in summer-time, when harvest was to be got in, would leave the monastery and go wander abroad in places of their acquaintance, but of a truth, when winter approached, would come again and require to enjoy in common the things that the Englishmen had provided and laid up): Colman, seeking remedy for this discord and viewing all places far and near, found a place in the island of Ireland meet for the building of a monastery, called in the Scottish tongue Mageo [3]; and of that ground he bought a small parcel to build a monastery thereon

monasterium, a comite ad cuius possessionem pertinebat: ea conditione addita, ut pro ipso etiam qui eis locum commodaret, consistentes ibi monachi Domino preces offerrent. Et constructo statim monasterio, iuvante etiam comite ac vicinis omnibus, Anglos ibidem locavit, relictis in praefata insula Scottis. Quod videlicet monasterium usque hodie ab Anglis tenetur incolis. Ipsum namque est quod nunc grande de modico effectum, Muigeo consuete vocatur, et conversis iamdudum ad meliora instituta omnibus, egregium examen continet monachorum, qui de provincia Anglorum ibidem collecti ad exemplum venerabilium patrum sub regula et abbate canonico, in magna continentia et sinceritate proprio labore manuum vivant.

CAP. V

De morte Osuiu et Ecgbercti regum; et de synodo facta ad locum Herutforda, cui praesidebat archiepiscopus Theodorus.

ANNO Dominicae incarnationis sexcentesimo septuagesimo, qui est annus secundus ex quo Brittaniam venit Theodorus, Osuiu rex Nordanhymbrorum pressus est infirmitate, qua et mortuus est anno aetatis suae quinquagesimo octavo. Qui in tantum eo tempore tenebatur amore Romanae et apostolicae institutionis, ut si ab infirmitate salvaretur, etiam Romam venire, ibique ad loca sancta vitam finire

---

[1] A.S. *gesith*, member of a king's *comitatus* or war-band.

[2] Roman Easter and tonsure.

of the count[1] that possessed the same: upon this condition withal, that the monks there abiding should make prayer to the Lord also for the lord of the soil who let them have that place. And the monastery being forthwith erected by the help also of the count and all such as dwelled thereby, Colman placed the Englishmen there, the Scots being left in the foresaid island. The which monastery indeed unto this day is holden of English occupiers. For it is the selfsame which is now customably called Muigeo, being much enlarged of that it was at first, and (all things being long since brought to a better order[2]) hath in it a notable company of monks gathered from the country of the English; who live therein after the example of the worthy old fathers, under a rule and canonical abbot, in great abstinence and singleness of heart by the labour of their own hands.

CHAPTER V

Of the death of the kings Oswy and Egbert; and of the synod made at Hertford, at which the archbishop Theodore was president [673].

In the 670th[3] year of the Lord's incarnation, which is the second year after that Theodore came to Britain, Oswy king of Northumberland was taken with a grievous sickness, whereof also he died the 58th year of his age. Who at that time bare such love to the Roman and apostolic rule, that if he might have escaped his sickness, he purposed also to go to Rome[4] and there end his life at the holy

[3] Should, it seems, be 671: Pl. II. 211.
[4] As other early kings did, some of whom became monks.

disponeret; Vilfridumque episcopum ducem sibi itineris fieri, promissa non parva pecuniarum donatione, rogaret. Qui defunctus die decima quinta Kalendarum Martiarum, Ecgfridum filium regni heredem reliquit: cuius anno regni tertio Theodorus cogit concilium episcoporum, una cum eis qui canonica patrum statuta et diligerent et nossent, magistris ecclesiae pluribus. Quibus pariter congregatis, diligenter ea quae unitati pacis ecclesiasticae congruerent, eo quo pontificem decebat animo, coepit observanda docere. Cuius synodicae actionis huiusmodi textus est:

"In nomine Domini Dei et Salvatoris nostri Jesu Christi, regnante in perpetuum, ac gubernante suam Ecclesiam eodem Domino nostro Jesu Christo, placuit convenire nos, iuxta morem canonum venerabilium, tractaturos de necessariis ecclesiae negotiis. Convenimus autem die vigesima quarta mensis Septembris, indictione prima, in loco qui dicitur Herutford. Ego quidem Theodorus, quamvis indignus, ab apostolica sede destinatus Doruvernensis ecclesiae episcopus; et consacerdos ac frater noster reverentissimus Bisi Orientalium Anglorum episcopus: quibus etiam frater et consacerdos noster Vilfrid Nordanhymbrorum gentis episcopus per proprios legatarios adfuit. Adfuerunt et fratres ac consacerdotes nostri, Putta episcopus Castelli Cantuariorum quod dicitur Hrofescaestir, Leutherius episcopus Occidentalium Saxonum, Vynfrid episcopus provinciae Merciorum. Cumque in unum convenientes iuxta

---

[1] The first English provincial council or synod, according to Nicene rules. Bright, p. 240.

places; and to entreat bishop Wilfrid to be his guide in his journey, promising no small present of money. But he died the 15th day of February, and left Egfrid his son inheritor of his realm; in the third year of whose reign Theodore gathered a council of bishops [1] along with many teachers of the Church, such as loved and understood the canonical statutes of the fathers. Who being assembled together, he began with that mind that became a bishop to teach such things to be observed as were convenient for the unity and peace of the Church. Of which synodical proceeding the record is as follows:

"In the name of the Lord God and our Saviour Jesus Christ, the same our Lord Jesus Christ reigning for ever and governing his Church, it seemed good unto us to assemble ourselves together according to the custom prescribed by the ancient canons, to treat of necessary affairs of the Church. Moreover, we met together on the 24th day of the month of September, in the first indiction, at the place which is called Herutford.[2] To wit, I, Theodore, although unworthy, appointed by the apostolic see bishop of the church of Canterbury; and our fellow-priest and brother the most reverend Bisi bishop of the East English; with whom also was present our brother and fellow-priest Wilfrid bishop of the Northumbrian people by his proper delegates. There were present also our brethren and fellow-priests, Putta bishop of the Kentish Castle called Rochester, Lothere bishop of the West Saxons, and Wynfrid bishop of the province of the Marchmen. And when we were all assembled together and seated each one

[2] Hertford.

ordinem quique suum resedissemus: 'Rogo,' inquam, 'dilectissimi fratres, propter timorem et amorem Redemptoris nostri, ut in commune omnes pro nostra fide tractemus: ut quaeque decreta ac definita sunt a sanctis et probabilibus patribus, incorrupte ab omnibus nobis serventur.' Haec et alia quamplura quae ad caritatem pertinebant, unitatemque ecclesiae conservandam, prosecutus sum. Cumque explessem praelocutionem, interrogavi unumquemque eorum per ordinem, si consentirent, ea quae a patribus canonice sunt antiquitus decreta, custodire. Ad quod omnes consacerdotes nostri respondentes dixerunt: 'Optime omnibus placet, quaeque definierunt sanctorum canones patrum, nos quoque omnes alacri animo libentissime servare.' Quibus statim protuli eundem librum canonum, et ex eodem libro decem capitula quae per loca notaveram, quia maxime nobis necessaria sciebam, illis coram ostendi, et ut haec diligentius ab omnibus susciperentur, rogavi."

"Primum capitulum, 'Ut sanctum diem paschae in commune omnes servemus Dominica post quartam decimam lunam mensis primi.'

"Secundum, 'Ut nullus episcoporum parochiam alterius invadat, sed contentus sit gubernatione creditae sibi plebis.'

"Tertium, 'Ut quaeque monasteria Deo consecrata sunt, nulli episcoporum liceat ea in aliquo

[1] The order in which the prelates are named is not quite easy to explain. Bright, p. 241.

[2] Collection of ancient canons made by Dionysius Exiguus at the beginning of the sixth century. Bright, p. 243.

in order[1]: 'I beseech you,' say I, 'most dearly beloved brethren, for the fear and love of our Redeemer, that we all unite in taking counsel together for our faith: that whatever hath been decreed and appointed of holy and approved fathers may be kept unspotted by all of us.' These things I went on with, and very much else that pertained to the preservation of charity and the unity of the Church. And, when I had made an end of the prefatory address, I demanded of each of them in order, whether they agreed to keep those things which have been canonically decreed of the fathers of old time. Whereto all our fellow-bishops answered and said: 'It pleaseth us all very well that all things which the canons of the holy fathers have appointed, we do also all heartily and readily observe the same.' And straightway did I bring forth unto them the said book of canons,[2] and out of the said book I shewed before them ten articles which I had noted in divers places, because I knew them to be most necessary for us, and I besought them that the same might be received and kept diligently of them all."

"First article, 'That we all in common do keep the holy day of Easter on the Sunday after the fourteenth moon of the first month.'[3]

"Second, 'That no bishop shall intrude into another's diocese,[4] but be contented with the charge of the people committed unto him.'

"Third, 'That whatever monasteries have been consecrated to God, it shall be lawful for no bishop to

[3] Of the Jewish year, *i.e.* Nisan (green ears). Levit. xxiii. 5.
[4] *Parochia* also means *parish* as early as 506, Pl. II. 212.

inquietare, nec quicquam de eorum rebus violenter abstrahere.'

"Quartum, 'Ut ipsi monachi non migrent de loco ad locum, hoc est, de monasterio ad monasterium, nisi per dimissionem proprii abbatis: sed in ea permaneant obedientia quam tempore suae conversionis promiserunt.'

"Quintum, 'Ut nullus clericorum relinquens proprium episcopum, passim quolibet discurrat, neque alicubi veniens absque commendatitiis literis sui praesulis suscipiatur. Quod si semel susceptus noluerit invitatus redire, et susceptor et is qui susceptus est excommunicationi subiacebit.'

"Sextum, 'Ut episcopi atque clerici peregrini contenti sint hospitalitatis munere oblato; nullique eorum liceat ullum officium sacerdotale absque permissu episcopi in cuius parochia esse cognoscitur, agere.'

"Septimum, 'Ut bis in anno synodus congregetur; sed quia diversae causae impediunt, placuit omnibus in commune, ut Kalendis Augustis in loco qui appellatur Clofeshoch, semel in anno congregemur.'

"Octavum, 'Ut nullus episcoporum se praeferat alteri per ambitionem; sed omnes agnoscant tempus et ordinem consecrationis [1] suae.'

"Nonum capitulum in commune tractatum est, 'Ut plures episcopi, crescente numero fidelium, augerentur;' sed de hac re ad praesens siluimus.

[1] For *congregationis*, Pl.

---

[1] Forsaking secular life.

[2] Not certainly identified. Probably near London.

trouble them in any wise, nor violently take from them aught that is theirs.'

"Fourth, 'That the monks themselves shall not pass from place to place, that is to say, from monastery to monastery, unless by the leave of their own abbot: but shall continue in the obedience which each did promise at the time of their conversion.'[1]

"Fifth, 'That none of the clergy forsaking his own bishop shall run up and down where he list, nor, when he come anywhither, shall he be received without letters of commendation of his prelate. And if that he be once received and refuse to return being summoned, both the receiver and he that is received shall incur excommunication.'

"Sixth, 'That bishops and clerks when travelling abroad be content with such hospitality as is freely offered to them; and that it be lawful for none of them to execute any office of a priest without the permission of the bishop in whose diocese they are known to be.'

"Seventh, 'That the synod be assembled twice in the year; yet because of divers inconveniences it seemed good to all in common that we should assemble once in the year on the first day of August in the place which is called Clofeshoch.'[2]

"Eighth, 'That no bishop shall set himself above another out of ambition; but that all shall acknowledge the time and order of their consecration.'

"In the ninth article it was generally entreated, 'That the number of bishops should be increased as the number of believing folk waxeth greater,' but hereof at this point we said nothing.[3]

[3] Theodore could not carry his suffragans along with him here. Bright, p. 247.

"Decimum capitulum pro coniugiis, 'Ut nulli liceat nisi legitimum habere connubium. Nullus incestum faciat, nullus coniugem propriam, nisi, ut sanctum evangelium docet, fornicationis causa, relinquat. Quod si quisquam propriam expulerit coniugem legitimo sibi matrimonio coniunctam, si Christianus esse recte voluerit, nulli alteri copuletur; sed ita permaneat, aut propriae reconcilietur coniugi.'

"His itaque capitulis in commune tractatis ac definitis, ut nullum deinceps ab aliquo nostrum oriatur contentionis scandalum aut alia pro aliis divulgarentur, placuit ut quaeque definita sunt unusquisque nostrum manus propriae subscriptione confirmaret. Quam sententiam definitionis nostrae Titillo notario scribendam dictavi. Actum in mense et indictione supra scripta. Quisquis igitur contra hanc sententiam, iuxta decreta canonum, nostra etiam consensione, ac subscriptione manus nostrae confirmatam, quoquo modo venire eamque infringere tentaverit, noverit se ab omni officio sacerdotali et nostra societate separatum. Divina nos gratia in unitate sanctae suae Ecclesiae viventes, custodiat incolumes."

Facta est autem haec synodus anno ab incarnatione Domini sexcentesimo septuagesimo tertio, quo anno rex Cantuariorum Ecgberct mense Iulio obierat, succedente in regnum fratre Hlothere, quod ipse annos undecim et menses septem tenuit. Bisi autem episcopus Orientalium Anglorum, qui in praefata synodo fuisse perhibetur, ipse erat successor Bonifatii, cuius supra meminimus, vir multae sancti-

"The tenth article concerning marriages, 'That no one be allowed to have any but a lawful marriage. Let no one commit incest, let no one forsake his own wife, except, as the holy Gospel teacheth, for the cause of fornication. But if any man put away his own wife being lawfully united to him in wedlock, if he will be a right Christian man, let him be joined to none other; but let him so continue as he is, or else be reconciled to his own wife.'

"And thus these articles being in common treated of and appointed, that no offence of contention should rise from any of us hereafter, or they be published in divers manners, it seemed good that each of us should confirm all these things that were appointed, subscribing thereto with his own hand. Which ordinance of our appointment I dictated to Titil'us the secretary to write out. Given the month and indiction above written. Whosoever, therefore shall endeavour to go about any wise to do against this ordinance prescribed according to the decrees of the canons, and confirmed also with our consent and subscribing of our hands, let him know himself to be excluded from all office of priesthood and from our fellowship. The grace of God keep us safe, living in the unity of His holy Church."

Now this synod was held the 673rd year from the incarnation of the Lord, in which year Egbert king of Kent had died in the month of July, and his brother Lothere succeeded him in the kingdom, the which he enjoyed 11 years and 7 months. Moreover, Bisi bishop of the East English, who is said to have been present in the foresaid synod, a man of much holiness and devotion, was himself successor to Boniface, of

tatis et religionis. Nam Bonifatio post decem et septem episcopatus sui annos defuncto, episcopus ipse pro eo, Theodoro ordinante, factus est. Quo adhuc superstite, sed gravissima infirmitate ab administrando episcopatu prohibito, duo sunt pro illo, Aecci, et Baduuini, electi et consecrati episcopi: ex quo usque hodie provincia illa duos habere solet episcopos.

CAP. VI

Ut deposito Vynfrido, Saexuulf episcopatum eius acceperit, et Earconuald Orientalibus Saxonibus sit episcopus datus.

Non multo post haec elapso tempore, offensus a Vynfrido Merciorum episcopo per meritum cuiusdam inobedientiae, Theodorus archiepiscopus deposuit eum de episcopatu post annos accepti episcopatus non multos; et in loco eius ordinavit episcopum Sexuulfum, qui erat constructor et abbas monasterii quod dicitur Medeshamstedi, in regione Gyrviorum. Depositus vero Vynfrid rediit ad monasterium suum quod dicitur Adbaruae, ibique in optima vitam conversatione finivit.

Tunc etiam Orientalibus Saxonibus, quibus eo tempore praefuerunt Sebbi et Sigheri, quorum supra meminimus, Earconualdum constituit episcopum in civitate Lundonia: cuius videlicet viri et in episco-

[1] Acci to Dunwich, Badwin to Elmham for Norfolk, Pl.

whom we have made mention above. For when Boniface was dead, after he had been bishop 17 years, this man was made bishop in his place, being ordained thereto by Theodore. This Bisi yet living, but grievously vexed with sickness, in such sort that he could not execute the office of a bishop, two other for him, Acci and Badwin, were chosen and consecrated bishops[1]: from which time unto this day that province is wont to have two bishops.

CHAPTER VI

How Wynfrid was deposed and Sexwulf took his bishopric, and Earconwald was given for bishop to the East Saxons [675].

No long time after these things were done, Theodore the archbishop, being offended with Wynfrid bishop of the Marchmen for a certain crime of disobedience, deposed him[2] of his bishopric not many years after he had received the same; and in his place ordained Sexwulf for bishop, who was the builder and abbot of the monastery that is called Medeshamstead[3] in the country of the Gyrwas. But Wynfrid being deposed returned to his monastery which is named Adbarwae, and there ended his life in virtuous conversation.

At that time also when Sebbi and Sighere, of whom we spake before, ruled the East Saxons, Theodore appointed over them Earconwald to be their bishop in the city of London: the life and conversation of

[2] The reason is not given, but may have had to do with the question of division of dioceses. Bright, p. 256.

[3] Peterborough.

patu, et ante episcopatum vita et conversatio fertur fuisse sanctissima, sicut etiam nunc caelestium signa virtutum indicio sunt. Etenim usque hodie feretrum eius caballarium, quo infirmus vehi solebat, servatum a discipulis eius, multos febricitantes vel alio quolibet incommodo fessos sanare non desistit. Non solum autem subpositi eidem feretro vel adpositi curantur aegroti, sed et astulae de illo abscissae atque ad infirmos adlatae, citam illis solent adferre medelam.

Hic sane priusquam episcopus factus esset, duo praeclara monasteria, unum sibi, alterum sorori suae Aedilburgae construxerat, quod utrumque regularibus disciplinis optime instituerat. Sibi quidem in regione Sudergeona, iuxta fluvium Tamensem, in loco qui vocatur Cerotaesei, id est, Ceroti Insula; sorori autem in Orientali Saxonum provincia, in loco qui nuncupatur In Berecingum, in quo ipsa Deo devotarum mater ac nutrix posset existere feminarum. Quae suscepto monasterii regimine, condignam se in omnibus episcopo fratre, et ipsa recte vivendo et subiectis regulariter et pie consulendo praebuit; ut etiam caelestia indicio fuere miracula.

which man indeed, both when he was bishop and before he was bishop, is reported to have been most holy, as also even now the signs of mighty heavenly works do well declare. For until this day his horse-litter, wherein he was wont to be carried when he was sick, being kept by his scholars, ceaseth not to cure such as have agues or are wearied by any other infirmity. Moreover, not only sick parties that are put under or laid by the said litter be so healed, but also the chips that are cut off from it and brought to sick folk are wont to bring them speedy remedy.

This man had indeed, before he was made bishop, builded two goodly monasteries, one for himself, the other for his sister Ethelburga,[1] and had established them both very well in regular discipline. That which was for himself was in the Country of Sudergeona,[2] by the river of Thames at the place that is called Cerotaesei,[3] that is to say, Isle of Cerot; while that for his sister was in the province of the East Saxons at the place that is named In Berecingum,[4] where she should be able to be a mother and nurse of women devoted to God. And after she had taken upon her the rule of the monastery, she behaved herself in all things as became the sister of the bishop her brother, both for her own right way of life, and godly guiding of them that were under her charge in monastical rule; as also was well proved by miracles from heaven.

[1] Not the daughter of king Anna, I. p. 363.
[2] Surrey.
[3] Chertsey.
[4] Barking.

CAP. VII

Ut in monasterio Bericinensi, ubi corpora sanctimonialium feminarum poni deberent, caelesti sit luce monstratum.

In hoc etenim monasterio plura virtutum sunt signa patrata, quae et ad memoriam aedificationemque sequentium, ab his qui novere, descripta habentur a multis: e quibus et nos aliqua Historiae nostrae Ecclesiasticae inserere curavimus. Cum tempestas saepe dictae cladis late cuncta depopulans, etiam partem monasterii huius illam qua viri tenebantur, invasisset, et passim quotidie raperentur ad Dominum: sollicita mater congregationis, qua hora etiam eam monasterii partem, qua ancillarum Dei caterva a virorum erat secreta contubernio, eadem plaga tangeret, crebrius in conventu sororum perquirere coepit quo loci in monasterio corpora sua poni et cimiterium fieri vellent, cum eas eodem quo ceteros exterminio raptari e mundo contingeret. Cumque nihil certi responsi, tametsi saepius inquirens, a sororibus accepisset, accepit ipsa cum omnibus certissimum supernae provisionis responsum. Cum enim nocte quadam expletis matutinae laudis psalmodiis, egressae de oratorio famulae Christi, ad sepulcra fratrum, qui eas ex hac luce praecesserant, solitas Domino laudes decantarent, ecce subito lux emissa caelitus, veluti linteum magnum venit super

---

[1] The yellow pest.
[2] Double monasteries were in that day to be found in Spain and France as well as Britain: Mayor and Lumby, p. 316.
[3] Matins before daybreak.
[4] Cf. Acts x. 11.

CHAPTER VII

How it was shewed by a light from heaven in what place the bodies of the nuns should be buried in the monastery of Barking [? 664].

For in this monastery many signs of mighty works were wrought, which for the memory and edifying of the after-comers are also kept of many men, being written down of them that knew the same: some of the which too we have been forward to put in our Ecclesiastical History. When the tempest of the calamity so often mentioned,[1] storming abroad over all the country, had also fallen upon that part of this monastery where the men did live,[2] and daily one or other was carried off to the Lord: the mother of the community, in the hour when the same visitation reached also to that part of the monastery, in which was the company of the handmaids of God set apart from the dwelling-place of the men, began carefully in the convent of the sisters oftimes to ask, in what place about the monastery they would have their bodies to be laid and a burial-ground made, against such time as it should happen them to be caught away with the same destruction as the others were. And when she had gotten no certain answer, although she often asked them, she received herself and all the rest withal a most certain answer of the providence from above. For upon a certain night, after the singing of the psalms of early morning praise[3] was done, as the handmaids of Christ went forth of the chapel and did sing their accustomed praises to the Lord at the graves of the brethren that were gone out of this life before them, behold, suddenly a light sent from heaven like a great sheet[4] came upon them,

omnes, tantoque eas stupore perculit, ut etiam canticum quod canebant tremefactae intermitterent. Ipse autem splendor emissae lucis, in cuius comparatione sol meridianus videri posset obscurus, non multo post illo elevatus de loco, in meridianam monasterii partem, hoc est, ad occidentem oratorii secessit, ibique aliquandiu remoratus et ea loca operiens, sic videntibus cunctis ad caeli se alta subduxit; ut nulli esset dubium, quin ipsa lux quae animas famularum Christi esset ductura vel susceptura in caelis, etiam corporibus earum locum in quo requietura, et diem resurrectionis essent exspectatura, monstraret. Cuius radius lucis tantus exstitit, ut quidam de fratribus senior qui ipsa hora in oratorio eorum cum alio iuniore positus fuerat, referret mane, quod ingressi per rimas ostiorum vel fenestrarum radii lucis, omnem diurni luminis viderentur superare fulgorem.

CAP. VIII

Ut in eodem monasterio puerulus moriens, virginem quae se erat secutura, clamaverit; utque alia de corpore egressura, iam particulam futurae lucis aspexerit.

Erat in eodem monasterio puer trium circiter, non amplius, annorum Aesica nomine, qui propter infantilem adhuc aetatem in virginum Deo dedicatarum solebat cella nutriri, ibique meditari. Hic praefata

and strake them with so great a trance, that for very fear also they left off their song that they sang. Moreover, the selfsame brightness of the light sent from above, to which in comparison the sun at midday might seem but dark, being not long after lifted up from that place, went away to the south part of the monastery, that is to say, to the west end of the chapel, and there abiding a while and covering those places withdrew itself to the heights of heaven; so plain to all their sights that none of them all doubted but that the very light, which should lead and in the heavens receive the souls of Christ's handmaids, did also shew a place for their bodies to rest in and abide the day of resurrection. And so bright was the ray of this light, that a certain elderly man, one of the brethren, who at that very hour had been set with another younger man in their chapel, reported in the morning, that the beams of light entering in through the chinks of the doors and windows did seem to pass all brightness of the daylight.

CHAPTER VIII

How a little boy dying in the same monastery called by name upon a virgin that should follow him; and how another virgin on the point of her departing from the body did see already a small part of the light to come [? 664].

There was in the same monastery a little boy of about three years old, not more, named Esica, which because of his age, being yet a very infant, was wont to be brought up in the house of the virgins dedicated to God and con his lesson there. This child being

pestilentia tactus, ubi ad extrema pervenit, clamavit tertio unam de consecratis Christo virginibus, proprio eam nomine quasi praesentem alloquens, " Eadgyd, Eadgyd, Eadgyd "; et sic terminans temporalem vitam, intravit aeternam. At virgo illa quam moriens vocabat, mox in loco quo erat, eadem adtacta infirmitate, ipso quo vocata est die de hac luce subtracta, et illum qui se vocavit ad regnum caeleste secuta est.

Item quaedam ex eisdem ancillis Dei cum praefato tacta morbo, atque ad extrema esset perducta, coepit subito circa mediam noctem clamare his quae sibi ministrabant, petens ut lucernam quae inibi accensa erat, exstinguerent: quod cum frequenti voce repeteret, nec tamen ei aliquis obtemperaret, ad extremum intulit: " Scio quod me haec insana mente loqui arbitramini; sed iam nunc non ita esse cognoscite: nam vere dico vobis, quod domum hanc tanta luce impletam esse perspicio, ut vestra illa lucerna mihi omnimodis esse videatur obscura." Et cum ne adhuc quidem talia loquenti quisquam responderet, vel adsensum praeberet, iterum dixit: " Accendite ergo lucernam illam, quam diu vultis; attamen scitote quia non est mea: nam mea lux, incipiente aurora, mihi adventura est." Coepitque narrare quia apparuerit sibi quidam vir Dei qui eodem anno fuerat defunctus, dicens quod adveniente diluculo perennem esset exitura ad lucem. Cuius veritas visionis cita circa exortum diei puellae morte probata est.

taken with the foresaid plague, when he came to his last moment, cried out three times upon one of the virgins consecrated to Christ, speaking to her, as if she were present, by her own name, " Eadgyth, Eadgyth, Eadgyth "; and therewithal ending the temporal life entered into life eternal. But that virgin which he called at his death, straightway in the place where she was, being taken with the same sickness, the very same day that she was so called was taken out of this life, and followed him that called her to the kingdom of heaven.

Also a certain one of the same handmaids of God, being taken with the said disease and now brought to her last point, began suddenly about midnight to cry out to them that attended her, desiring them to put out the candle that was there burning: and when she ofttimes called and so desired them, and yet none of them would do as she bade them: " I know," put she in at the last, " that ye think me thus to speak as if I were not in my right mind; but now at this time know ye that it is not so: for I tell you truly that I see this house filled with so great a light that that candle of yours seemeth to me altogether dim." And when none of them did even yet answer unto these sayings of hers nor follow her bidding: " Well," quoth she again, " let that candle burn as long as ye list; but yet know ye well that the same is not my light: for my light is to come to me when the morning beginneth." And she began to tell that a certain man of God appeared unto her, which had died the same year, and said to her, that when the morning light drew near, she should depart hence to the everlasting light. The truth of which vision was proved by the speedy death of the maiden about the break of day.

CAP. IX

Quae sint ostensa coelitus signa cum et ipsa mater congregationis illius e mundo transiret.

Cum autem et ipsa mater pia Deo devotae congregationis Aedilburga esset rapienda de mundo, apparuit visio miranda cuidam de sororibus, cui nomen erat Torctgyd, quae multis iam annis in eodem monasterio commorata, et ipsa semper in omni humilitate ac sinceritate Deo servire satagebat, et adiutrix disciplinae regularis eidem matri existere, minores docendo vel castigando curabat. Cuius ut virtus iuxta apostolum in infirmitate perficeretur, tacta est repente gravissimo corporis morbo, et per annos novem pia Redemptoris nostri provisione multum fatigata: videlicet ut quicquid in ea vitii sordidantis inter virtutes per ignorantiam vel incuriam resedisset, totum hoc caminus diutinae tribulationis excoqueret. Haec ergo quadam nocte incipiente crepusculo, egressa de cubiculo quo manebat, vidit manifeste quasi corpus hominis, quod esset sole clarius, sindone involutum in sublime ferri, elatum videlicet de domo in qua sorores pausare solebant. Cumque diligentius intueretur quo trahente levaretur sursum haec quam contemplabatur species corporis gloriosi, vidit quod quasi funibus auro clarioribus in superna tolleretur, donec caelis patentibus

[1] 2 Cor. xii. 9.

CHAPTER IX

What signs were shewed from heaven when also the mother herself of that company departed from the world.

Now when Ethelburga also, the godly mother herself of the holy professed company, should be taken out of the world, a wonderful vision appeared to one of the sisters whose name was Tortgyth; the which had now many years continued in the same monastery, and was herself always diligently occupied in serving God with all humility and sincerity, and set herself to be forward in helping the said mother to keep regular discipline with instructing or correcting the younger sort. The virtue of which woman, that it might, as the apostle saith,[1] be made perfect in weakness, she was suddenly taken with a very grievous sickness of body, and was therewith sore tormented by the space of nine years through the merciful provision of our Redeemer: surely to the end that whatsoever spot of defiling sin had through ignorance or negligence remained among her virtues, it might all be melted out by the furnace of long tribulation. This woman then on a certain night, when the daylight began a little to appear, as she went out of her chamber that she abode in, saw plainly as it were a corse, brighter than the sun, wound up in muslin and carried upward, being taken indeed from the house in which the sisters were wont to rest. And as she diligently marked what it should be that drew upwards this vision of the glorious body which she beheld, she saw that it was lifted up on high as it were by cords brighter than gold, until it was taken into the open heavens

introducta, amplius ab illa videri non potuit. Nec dubium remansit cogitanti de visione, quin aliquis de illa congregatione citius esset moriturus, cuius anima per bona quae fecisset opera, quasi per funes aureos levanda esset ad caelos: quod revera ita contigit. Nam non multis interpositis diebus, Deo dilecta mater congregationis ipsius, ergastulo carnis educta est; cuius talem fuisse constat vitam, ut nemo qui eam noverit, dubitare debeat quin ei exeunti de hac vita caelestis patriae patuerit ingressus.

In eodem quoque monasterio quaedam erat femina sanctimonialis, et ad saeculi huius dignitatem nobilis et in amore futuri saeculi nobilior: quae ita multis iam annis omni corporis fuerat officio destituta, ut ne unum quidem movere ipsa membrum valeret. Haec ubi corpus abbatissae venerabilis in ecclesiam delatum, donec sepulturae daretur, cognovit, postulavit se illo afferri, et in modum orantium ad illud adclinari. Quod dum fieret, quasi viventem adlocuta, rogavit, ut apud misericordiam pii Conditoris impetraret se a tantis tamque diutinis cruciatibus absolvi. Nec multo tardius exaudita est: nam post dies duodecim et ipsa educta ex carne temporales adflictiones aeterna mercede mutavit.

Cum vero praefata Christi famula Torctgyd tres adhuc annos post obitum dominae in hac vita teneretur, in tantum ea quam praediximus infirmitate

and could be seen of her no longer. And when she thought upon the vision she doubted no whit but some person of that company should die shortly, whose soul should be lifted up to heaven by the good works it had done, even as by golden cords. Which thing happened so indeed. For not many days after, the mother of that company, for the love that God bare her, was taken out of the prison of the flesh; whose life was certainly such that no man which knew it ought to doubt but that the entering into the heavenly country was open unto her, upon going out of this life.

There was also in the same monastery a certain holy nun, both noble for the dignity of this world and more noble in the love she had of the world to come: the which was many years so bereft of all use of her body, that she was not able of herself to move one single limb. This nun, when she knew that the body of the venerable abbess was brought into the church, until it should be buried, desired that she might be carried thither, and laid by the same, bowed down as folk do at their prayers. And this being done, she spake to the abbess as if she had been alive, and desired her to obtain of the mercy of the pitiful Creator, that she might be rid of so great and so long torments. And not long after her petition was heard: for twelve days after, she was herself also taken out of the body and received everlasting reward in change of her temporal sufferings.

Now when Tortgyth, the foresaid handmaid of Christ, had her life prolonged yet three years after the death of the abbess, she was so far pined away with the sickness that we spake of before, that the

decocta est, ut vix ossibus haereret, et ad ultimum, cum tempus iam resolutionis eius instaret, non solum membrorum ceterorum, sed et linguae motu caruit. Quod dum tribus diebus et totidem noctibus ageretur, subito visione spiritali recreata, os et oculos aperuit; aspectansque in caelum, sic ad eam quam intuebatur visionem, coepit loqui: "Gratus mihi est multum adventus tuus, et bene venisti": et hoc dicto, parumper reticuit, quasi responsum eius quem videbat, et cui loquebatur, exspectans. Rursumque quasi leviter indignata subiunxit: "Nequaquam hoc laeta ferre queo." Rursumque modicum silens, tertio dixit: "Si nullatenus hodie fieri potest, obsecro ne sit longum spatium in medio." Dixit; et sicut antea, parum silens, ita sermonem conclusit: "Si omnimodis ita definitum est, neque hanc sententiam licet immutari, obsecro ne amplius quam haec solummodo proxima nox intersit." Quibus dictis, interrogata a circumsedentibus, cum quo loqueretur: "Cum carissima," inquit, "mea matre Aedilburge." Ex quo intellexere quod ipsa ei tempus suae transmigrationis in proximum nuntiare venisset. Nam et ita ut rogabat, transacta una die ac nocte, soluta carnis simul et infirmitatis vinculis, ad aeternae gaudia salutis intravit.

skin and bones did scant cleave together, and at last, the time of her release being now at hand, she could not only stir none of all her limbs but could not move her tongue. In which case as she continued three days and as many nights, suddenly being relieved with a ghostly vision, she opened her mouth and eyes; and looking up to heaven began thus to speak to the vision that she saw: "Thy coming to me is very joyful, and thou art welcome": and when she had so said, she held her peace a little, as it were abiding for an answer of him whom she saw and spake to. And again as it were a little angerly she added: "I can by no means gladly suffer this." And again holding her peace a little, she spake the third time and said: "If it cannot by any means be to-day, I beseech thee that the meantime be not long delayed." Wherewith holding her peace a little, as she had done before, she ended her talk thus: "If it be so fully appointed, and that this judgment may not be changed, I beseech thee that there be no more but only this next night between." After which words, being demanded of them that sat about her, with whom she was speaking: "With my most dear mother Ethelburga," quoth she. Whereby they understood that she had come in person to bring Tortgyth word that the time of her passing hence was nigh. For even as she made request, after one day and one night passed, she was delivered at once of the bonds of the flesh and of her sickness, and entered into the joys of eternal salvation.

CAP. X

Ut ad cymiterium eiusdem monasterii orans caeca lumen receperit.

Successit autem Aedilburgi in officio abbatissae devota Deo famula, nomine Hildilid, multisque annis, id est, usque ad ultimam senectutem eidem monasterio strenuissime, in observantia disciplinae regularis, et in earum quae ad communes usus pertinent rerum providentia praefuit. Cui cum propter angustiam loci in quo monasterium constructum est, placuisset ut ossa famulorum famularumque Christi quae ibidem fuerant tumulata, tollerentur, et transferrentur omnia in ecclesiam beatae Dei genitricis, unoque conderentur in loco: quoties ibi claritas luminis caelestis, quanta saepe fragrantia mirandi apparuerit odoris, quae alia sint signa ostensa, in ipso libro de quo haec excerpsimus, quisque legerit, inveniet.

Sane nullatenus praetereundum arbitror miraculum sanitatis, quod ad ipsum cymiterium Deo dicatae congregationis factum idem libellus refert. Erat quippe in proximo comes quidam, cuius uxor ingruente oculis caligine subita, tantum per dies eadem molestia crebrescente gravata est, ut ne minimam quidem lucis alicuius posset particulam videre. Cui dum aliquandiu caecitatis huius nocte clausa maneret, repente venit in mentem, quia si ad monasterium delata virginum sanctimonialium,

[1] Probably a life of St. Ethelburga, Pl.
[2] A.S. *gesith.*

CHAPTER X

How at the burial-ground of the same monastery a blind woman praying recovered her sight.

Now in the office of the abbess Ethelburga there succeeded a handmaid dedicated to God, by name Hildilid; the which many years, that is until extreme old age, governed the same monastery exceeding diligently, in the keeping of regular discipline, and in providing the things that appertained to the general use. This woman, because of the straitness of the place wherein the monastery was built, thought good to have the bones of the servants and handmaids of Christ, which were in that same place, taken up and removed all to the church of the blessed mother of God, and there buried in one place: in which place how often the brightness of the heavenly light appeared, how often and how great was there a fragrant odour of a marvellous sweet savour, and what other signs were there shewed, whoso will read shall find in that very book [1] out of which we have taken these things.

Truly methinks I must in no case let pass a miracle of healing, which (as the same book declareth) was wrought at the burial-ground itself of the community dedicated to God. For there was thereby a certain count [2] whose wife had a sudden darkness come over her eyes, the grief whereof daily increasing she was so far troubled therewith that she could not see even any smallest little bit of light. This lady remaining some space shut up in the night of this blindness, it came suddenly to her mind that if she were brought to the monastery of the holy

ad reliquias sanctorum peteret, perditam posset recipere lucem. Nec distulit quin continuo, quod mente conceperat, expleret. Perducta namque a puellis suis ad monasterium, quia in proximo erat, ubi fidem suae sanationis integram se habere professa est, introducta est ad cymiterium: et cum ibidem diutius flexis genibus oraret, nihilo tardius meruit exaudiri. Nam exsurgens ab oratione, priusquam exiret de loco, petitae lucis gratiam recepit: et quae famularum manibus adducta fuerat, ipsa libero pedum incessu domum laeta reversa est; quasi ad hoc solummodo lucem amitteret temporalem, ut quanta sanctos Christi lux in caelis, quae gratia virtutis possideret, sua sanatione demonstraret.

CAP. XI

Ut rex eiusdem provinciae Sebbi, in monachica vitam conversatione finierit.

Eo tempore praeerat regno Orientalium Saxonum, ut idem etiam libellus docet, vir multum Deo devotus, nomine Sebbi, cuius supra meminimus.[1] Erat enim religiosis actibus, crebris precibus, piis eleemosynarum fructibus plurimum intentus; vitam privatam et monachicam cunctis regni divitiis et honoribus praeferens, quam et olim iam, si non obstinatus coniugis animus divortium negaret, relicto regno subiisset.

[1] III. 30.

virgins and made petition at the relics of the saints, she might recover her lost sight. And she made no delay to fulfil straight that which she had conceived in her mind. For being led by her maids to the monastery (being hard by adjoining), where she declared she had full belief to be healed, she was brought unto the burial-ground: and as she prayed there for a space upon her knees she was thought worthy to have her request heard forthwith. For rising up from her prayer, before she went out of the place she recovered the benefit of the sight that she sought: and she that had been led thither by the hands of waiting-maids returned home joyfully, walking freely on her feet by herself; so that it might seem that she lost the light of this world only for this end, that she might shew by her healing how great the light and what grace of mighty working is that Christ's saints have in heaven.

CHAPTER XI

How Sebbi king of the same province ended his life in monastical conversation [664–694].

At that time, as also the foresaid book sheweth, there reigned over the East Saxons a man very devout and godly, named Sebbi, of whom we made mention above.[1] For he was very much given to exercises of religion, to often prayer and to charitable alms deeds; esteeming the solitary and monastical life before all the riches and honours of a kingdom, which kind of life too he had taken long before and given up his kingdom, had not the self-willed mind of his wife refused to separate from

Unde multis visum et saepe dictum est, quia talis animi virum, episcopum magis quam regem ordinari deceret. Cumque annos triginta in regno miles regni caelestis exegisset, correptus est corporis infirmitate permaxima, qua et mortuus est: ammonuitque coniugem, ut vel tunc divino se servitio pariter manciparent, cum amplius pariter mundum amplecti, vel potius mundo servire non possent. Quod dum aegre impetraret ab ea, venit ad antistitem Lundoniae civitatis, vocabulo Valdheri, qui Erconualdo successerat; et per eius benedictionem, habitum religionis quem diu desiderabat, accepit. Attulit autem eidem et summam pecuniae non parvam, pauperibus erogandam, nil omnimodis sibi reservans; sed pauper spiritu magis propter regnum caelorum manere desiderans.

Qui cum ingravescente praefata aegritudine, diem sibi mortis imminere sensisset, timere coepit homo animi regalis, ne ad mortem veniens tanto adfectus dolore, aliquid indignum suae personae, vel ore proferret vel aliorum motu gereret membrorum. Unde accito ad se praefato urbis Lundoniae in qua tunc ipse manebat, episcopo, rogavit ne plures eo moriente quam ipse episcopus et duo sui ministri adessent. Quod dum episcopus libentissime se facturum promitteret, non multo post idem vir Dei, dum membra sopori dedisset, vidit visionem consolatoriam, quae

him. And therefore many men thought and often said that a man of such a nature was more meet to be made a bishop than a king. And when this soldier of the heavenly kingdom had passed 30 years upon the throne, he was seized with a very grievous sickness of body whereof too he died: and he admonished his wife that even then they should wholly give themselves both together to serve God, whereas they could no longer enjoy or rather serve the world together. Which thing when with much ado he obtained of her, he came to the bishop of the city of London, named Waldhere, who had succeeded Earconwald; and at his hand and blessing received the habit of religion, which he had so long desired. Moreover, he brought to the same bishop also no small sum of money to be bestowed upon the poor, keeping back nothing in any way for himself; but rather desiring to remain poor in spirit for the kingdom of heaven's sake.

And when he perceived the day of his death to be at hand, because the foresaid sickness grew on still upon him. for the princely haut courage that he had, he began to fear lest on coming to die, through the bitter pangs of the same, he might either utter with his mouth, or by motion of other of his limbs do something that were not meet for his person. And therefore summoning to him the foresaid bishop of the town of London, where he himself then continued, he desired him that at his departing there should be no more present but the bishop himself and his two chaplains. Which thing when the bishop promised most gladly to do, not long after, the same man of God after setting his limbs to rest saw a comfortable vision of a sort to take from him

omnem ei anxietatem memoratae solicitudinis auferret; insuper et qua die esset hanc vitam terminaturus, ostenderet. Vidit enim, ut post ipse referebat, tres ad se venisse viros claro indutos habitu; quorum unus residens ante lectulum eius, stantibus his qui secum advenerant comitibus, et interrogantibus de statu eius quem languentem visitare venerant, dixit quod anima eius, et sine ullo dolore, et cum magno lucis splendore esset egressura de corpore: sed et tertium exinde diem quo esset moriturus insinuavit. Quod ita utrumque ut ex visione didicit completum est. Nam die dehinc tertio completa hora nona, subito quasi leviter obdormiens, sine ullo sensu doloris emisit spiritum.

Cuius corpori tumulando praeparaverant sarcofagum lapideum: sed cum huic corpus imponere coepissent, invenerunt hoc mensura palmi longius esse sarcofago. Dolantes ergo lapidem in quantum valebant, addiderunt longitudini sarcofago quasi duorum mensuram digitorum. Sed nec sic quidem corpus capiebat. Unde facta difficultate tumulandi, cogitabant aut aliud quaerere loculum, aut ipsum corpus, si possent, in genibus inflectendo breviare, donec ipso loculo caperetur. Sed mira res, et non nisi caelitus facta, ne aliquid horum fieri deberet, prohibuit. Nam subito adstante episcopo, et filio regis eiusdem ac monachi Sighardo, qui post illum cum fratre Suefredo regnavit, et turba hominum non modica, inventum est sarcofagum illud congruae

all care of the foresaid fear; moreover, too, one that shewed him on what day he should end this life. For he saw (as after he reported himself) three men come to him arrayed in bright apparel; and one of them (while his fellows that came with him stood by and asked how the sick man did whom they had come to visit) sat before his bed and said that his soul should depart from the body both without pain and with great light and brightness: farther also he declared unto him that the third day after was the day whereon he was to die. Both which things were fulfilled in like manner as he learned by the vision. For the third day ensuing, when the ninth hour was finished, suddenly as if fallen into a soft sleep he gave up the ghost without feeling any grief at all.

And whereas for the burial of his body they had prepared a coffin of stone, when they began to lay his body in it, they found it to be longer than the coffin by the quantity of an hand-breadth. They hewed therefore in the stone as much as they might, and made it longer than it was, about two fingers' breadth. But yet it could not receive the body not so neither. Whereupon because of the distress of burying him they were minded either to look for another coffin or, if they might, to shorten the body itself by bowing it at the knees, until it should be received in the coffin that they had. But a wonderful thing happened and not without working from heaven, the which prevented that any of these means should be taken. For suddenly (the bishop standing by and the son of the same king and monk, Sighard, which after him reigned, with his brother Swefred, and a great company of men) that coffin was found to

longitudinis ad mensuram corporis, adeo ut a parte capitis etiam cervical posset interponi; a parte vero pedum, mensura quatuor digitorum in sarcofago corpus excederet. Conditus est autem in ecclesia beati doctoris gentium, cuius edoctus monitis caelestia sperare didicerat.

CAP. XII

Ut episcopatum Occidentalium Saxonum pro Leutherio Haeddi, episcopatum Hrofensis ecclesiae pro Putta Cuichelm, et pro ipso Gefmund acceperit: et qui tunc Nordanhymbrorum fuerint episcopi.

Quartus Occidentalium Saxonum antistes Leutherius fuit. Siquidem primus Birinus, secundus Agilberctus, tertius exstitit Vini. Cumque mortuus esset Coinvalch, quo regnante idem Leutherius episcopus factus est, acceperunt subreguli regnum gentis, et divisum inter se tenuerunt annis circiter decem: ipsisque regnantibus defunctus est ille, et episcopatu functus est Haeddi pro eo: consecratus a Theodoro in civitate Lundonia. Cuius episcopatus tempore devictis atque amotis subregulis, Caedualla suscepit imperium: et cum duobus annis hoc tenuisset, tandem superni regni amore compunctus reliquit, eodem adhuc praesule ecclesiam gubernante; ac Roman abiens, ibi vitam finivit, ut in sequentibus latius dicendum est.

---

[1] 1 Tim. ii. 7.

be of a fit length for the quantity of the body, so much so that at the head there might also a pillow be laid between; while at the feet there was a quantity of four fingers' breadth beyond the body in the coffin. Moreover, he was buried in the church of the blessed teacher of the Gentiles,[1] by whose good lessons he being taught had learned to long for heavenly things.

CHAPTER XII

How in the room of Lothere Heddi took the bishopric of the West Saxons, in the room of Putta Cwichelm took the bishopric of the church of Rochester, and in the room of Cwichelm Gebmund became bishop: and who were bishops of Northumberland at that time [676].

THE fourth bishop of the West Saxons was Lothere. For the first was Birinus, the second Agilbert, the third Wini. And after the death of Cenwalh, in whose reign the said Lothere was made bishop, aldermen took the kingdom of the nation and divided it between them and so held it about 10 years: and in their reign the bishop died, and Heddi had charge of the bishopric in his place: being consecrated thereto by Theodore in the city of London. In the time of whose bishopric Cadwalla did overcome and put out the aldermen and took the government to himself: and when he had kept the same by the space of two years, at length, being pricked with the love of the kingdom on high, he left it, while the same prelate did yet govern the church; and going into Rome there ended his life, as must be told more at large hereafter.

Anno autem Dominicae incarnationis sexcentesimo septuagesimo sexto, cum Aedilred rex Merciorum, adducto maligno exercitu, Cantiam vastaret, et ecclesias ac monasteria sine respectu pietatis vel divini timoris foedaret, civitatem quoque Hrofi, in qua erat Putta episcopus, quamvis eo tempore absens, communi clade absumpsit. Quod ille ubi comperit, ecclesiam videlicet suam rebus ablatis omnibus depopulatam, divertit ad Sexuulfum Merciorum antistitem, et accepta ab eo possessione ecclesiae cuiusdam et agelli non grandis, ibidem in pace vitam finivit, nil omnino de restaurando episcopatu suo agens: quia sicut supra diximus, magis in ecclesiasticis quam in mundanis rebus erat industrius; sed in illa solum ecclesia Deo serviens, ubicumque rogabatur, ad docenda ecclesiae carmina divertens. Pro quo Theodorus in civitate Hrofi Cuichelmum consecravit episcopum. Sed illo post non multum temporis, prae inopia rerum, ab episcopatu decedente, atque ad alia loca secedente, Gebmundum pro eo substituit antistitem.

Anno Dominicae incarnationis sexcentesimo septuagesimo octavo, qui est annus imperii regis Ecgfridi octavus, apparuit mense Augusto stella quae dicitur cometa; et tribus mensibus permanens, matutinis horis oriebatur, excelsam radiantis flammae quasi columnam praeferens. Quo etiam anno, orta inter ipsum regem Ecgfridum et reverentissimum anti-

---

[1] Became later himself a monk and abbot of Bardney, A. S. Chron. 704.

Moreover, in the 676th year of the Lord's incarnation, when Ethelred[1] king of the Marchmen led into Kent a fell army, and spoiled the country and profaned the churches and monasteries without regard of pity or fear of God, he also ransacked with the same general ruin the city of Rochester wherein Putta was bishop, howbeit at that time he was not there. And when he heard hereof, namely, that his church was spoiled and all things rifled, he went away unto Sexwulf bishop of the Marchmen and received of him the possession of a certain church and piece of ground not large, and in that place ended his life in peace, not taking any care at all for the restoration of his bishopric (for, as we have above said, he was a man more zealous in ecclesiastical than in worldly matters), but serving God in that church[2] only, and going abroad wherever he was desired, for the teaching of the hymns of the church. In whose place did Theodore consecrate Cwichelm bishop of Rochester. But when he not long after for lack of things necessary departed from the bishopric and went his way elsewhere, Theodore appointed Gebmund bishop in his place.

The 678th year of the Lord's incarnation, which is the 8th year of the reign of king Egfrid, there appeared in the month of August a star which is called a comet; the which continued three months, rising in the morning hours and giving forth as it were an high pillar of glittering flame. In the which year also, through a dissension that rose between the selfsame king Egfrid and the most

[2] Hereford, but Bede says nothing of Putta's being bishop there.

stitem Vilfridum dissensione, pulsus est idem antistes a sede sui episcopatus, et duo in locum eius substituti episcopi, qui Nordanhymbrorum genti praeessent: Bosa videlicet, qui Derorum, et Eata, qui Berniciorum provinciam gubernaret: hic in civitate Eburaci, ille in Hagustaldensi, sive in Lindisfarnensi ecclesia cathedram habens episcopalem, ambo de monachorum collegio in episcopatus gradum adsciti. Cum quibus et Eadhaed in provinciam Lindisfarorum, quam nuperrime rex Ecgfrid, superato in bello et fugato Vulfhere, obtinuerat, ordinatur episcopus. Et hunc primum eadem provincia proprium accepit praesulem, secundum Ediluini, tertium Eadgarum, quartum Cyniberctum, quem in praesenti habet. Habebat enim ante Eadhaedum, antistitem Sexuulfum, qui etiam Merciorum et Mediterraneorum Anglorum simul episcopus fuit: unde et expulsus de Lindissi, in illarum provinciarum regimine permansit. Ordinati sunt autem Eadhaed, Bosa, et Eata Eboraci ab archiepiscopo Theodoro: qui etiam post tres abscessionis Vilfridi annos, horum numero duos addidit antistites, Tunberctum ad ecclesiam Hagustaldensem, remanente Eata ad Lindisfarnensem, et Trumuini ad provinciam Pictorum quae tunc temporis Anglorum erat imperio subiecta. Eadhaedum de Lindissi reversum, eo quod Aedilred provinciam recepisset, Hrypensi ecclesiae praefecit.

---

[1] Bede is evidently reluctant to go into the history of the division of Wilfrid's diocese and his appeal to Rome, cf. Bright, p. 282. Egfrid was irritated because Wilfrid encouraged his first wife to become a nun, and his second wife was Wilfrid's enemy because of his wealth and power. This

reverend bishop Wilfrid,[1] the said bishop was put out of the see of his bishopric and two bishops appointed in his place to be over the people of the Northumbrians: Bosa, namely, to govern the province of the Derans, and Eata the province of the Bernicians: which Bosa had his episcopal see in the city of York, and Eata in Hexham or else in the church of Lindisfarne, both men being taken from out of the cloister of monks and called to the degree of bishop. And with them also was Eadhed made bishop in the province of Lindsey which king Egfrid had very lately conquered of Wulfhere, whom he overcame in battle and put to flight. And the same province received this man as the first prelate they had of their own; the next was Ethelwin, the third Edgar, the fourth Cynibert, who is there at this present. For before Eadhed the province had Sexwulf for bishop, who was bishop also of the Marchmen and Middle English as well: whereby too being put out of Lindsey he remained in control of those other provinces. Now Eadhed, Bosa and Eata were ordained at York by Archbishop Theodore: who also three years after Wilfrid's departing thence, added two more to the number of these, namely, Tunbert at the church of Hexham, Eata remaining at Lindisfarne, and Trumwine for the province of the Redshanks,[2] which at that time was subject to the dominion of the English. Because that Ethelred had recovered the province of Lindsey, Eadhed came back from thence and was by Theodore set over the church of Ripon.

court quarrel concurred with Theodore's scheme of dividing the dioceses.

[2] North of the Forth.

CAP. XIII

Ut Vilfrid episcopus provinciam Australium Saxonum ad Christum converterit.

Pulsus est autem ab episcopatu suo Vilfrid, et multa diu loca pervagatus, Romam adiit, Brittaniam rediit; et si propter inimicitias memorati regis in patria sive parochia sua recipi non potuit, non tamen ab evangelizandi potuit ministerio cohiberi: siquidem divertens ad provinciam Australium Saxonum, quae post Cantuarios ad austrum et ad occidentem usque ad Occidentales Saxones pertingit, habens terram familiarum septem millium, et eo adhuc tempore paganis cultibus serviebat; huic verbum fidei et lavacrum salutis ministrabat. Erat autem rex gentis ipsius Aedilvalch, non multo ante baptizatus in provincia Merciorum praesente ac suggerente rege Vulfhere, a quo etiam egressus de fonte, loco filii susceptus est: in cuius signum adoptionis, duas illi provincias donavit, Vectam videlicet insulam, et Meanuarorum provinciam in gente Occidentalium Saxonum. Itaque episcopus, concedente, immo multum gaudente rege, primos provinciae duces ac milites sacrosancto fonte abluebat; verum presbyteri Eappa, et Padda, et Burghelm, et Oiddi, ceteram plebem, vel tunc vel tempore sequente baptizabant. Porro regina nomine Eabae in sua, id est, Huicciorum provincia, fuerat baptizata. Erat autem filia

---

[1] "As it is observed of nightingales, that they sing the sweetest, when farthest from their nests: so this Wilfride was most diligent in God's service, when at the greatest distance from his own home." Fuller, § 97.

[2] The name survives in East and West Meon and Meonstoke in Hants.

CHAPTER XIII

How bishop Wilfrid converted the province of the South Saxons to Christ [678–686].

Now when Wilfrid was put out of his bishopric, he wandered through many places a long time, and came to Rome, and returned into Britain; and if, because of the displeasure of the said king, he could not get into his own country or diocese again, yet he could not be kept from doing the office of preaching the gospel:[1] for he turned aside to the province of the South Saxons, which from Kent reached southward and westward as far as the West Saxons, containing 7000 hides of land, and was yet at that time in bondage to paynim worship, and to this province he ministered the word of faith and the laver of salvation. Now the king of the same people was Ethelwalch, who was baptized not long before in the province of the Marchmen, in the presence and at the exhortation of king Wulfhere, by whom also he was raised up for son on stepping out of the font: and in sign of that adoption Wulfhere gave him two provinces, that is to say, the Isle of Wight and the province of the Meanwaras[2] among the people of the West Saxons. By the permission, therefore, nay rather with the great rejoicing of the king, the bishop cleansed the chief lords and thanes of the province in the holy font; but the rest of the folk either at that time or soon after were baptized by the priests Eappa, Padda, Burghelm and Oiddi. Furthermore, the queen, named Eaba, had been baptized in her own country, that is to say, in the province of the Hwiccas. Now she was daughter of Eanfrid,

Eanfridi, fratris Aenheri, qui ambo cum suo populo Christiani fuere. Ceterum tota provincia Australium Saxonum divini nominis et fidei erat ignara.

Erat autem ibi monachus quidam de natione Scottorum, vocabulo Dicul, habens monasteriolum permodicum in loco qui vocatur Bosanhamm, silvis et mari circumdatum, et in eo fratres quinque sive sex, in humili et paupere vita Domino famulantes. Sed provincialium nullus eorum vel vitam aemulari, vel praedicationem curabat audire.

Evangelizans autem genti episcopus Vilfrid, non solum eam ab aerumna perpetuae damnationis, verum et a clade infanda temporalis interitus eripuit. Siquidem tribus annis ante adventum eius in provinciam, nulla illis locis pluvia ceciderat, unde et fames acerbissima plebem invadens impia nece prostravit. Denique ferunt quia saepe quadraginta simul aut quinquaginta homines inedia macerati procederent ad praecipitium aliquod sive ripam maris, et iunctis misere manibus, pariter omnes aut ruina perituri, aut fluctibus absorbendi deciderent. Verum ipso die, quo baptisma fidei gens suscepit illa, descendit pluvia serena sed copiosa, refloruit terra, rediit viridantibus arvis annus laetus et frugifer. Sicque abiecta prisca superstitione, exsufflata idolatri, cor omnium et caro omnium exultaverunt in Deum vivum: intelligentes, eum qui verus est Deus, et

[1] Bosham near Chichester.

Eanhere's brother, which were both Christian men, and all their people. But all the province of the South Saxons had not heard of the name of God nor of the faith.

Yet there was in that country a certain monk, a Scot born, named Dicul, which had a very little monastery in the place called Bosanhamm,[1] all compassed about with woods and the sea, and therein five or six brethren serving the Lord in humble and poor life. But none of the people of the province did give themselves either to follow their life or hear their preaching.

But when bishop Wilfrid came preaching the Gospel to the people, he not only delivered them from the misery of eternal damnation, but also from a horrible murrain of temporal death. For in three years before his coming to that province, no rain had fallen in those quarters, whereby too a very sore famine came upon the common people and overthrew them with pitiless destruction. In short, it is reported that ofttimes 40 or 50 men being famished for hunger would go together to some cliff or bank of the sea, and there joining hand in miserable sort would cast themselves all down together, either to be killed with the fall or drowned in the waves. But on the very day on which that people received the baptism of the faith, there fell a mild but plentiful rain, wherewith the earth flourished again, a joyful and plentiful year returned, and the fields were clothed with green. And thus, their old superstition being laid away and idolatry blown upon, the hearts of all and the bodies of all did rejoice in the living God: knowing that He which is the true God had by His heavenly grace enriched

interioribus se bonis et exterioribus caelesti gratia ditasse. Nam et antistes cum venisset in provinciam, tantamque ibi famis poenam videret, docuit eos piscando victum quaerere. Namque mare et flumina eorum piscibus abundabant; sed piscandi peritia genti nulla nisi ad anguillas tantum inerat. Collectis ergo undecumque retibus anguillaribus, homines antistitis miserunt in mare, et divina se iuvante gratia mox cepere pisces diversi generis trecentos: quibus trifariam divisis, centum pauperibus dederunt, centum his a quibus retia acceperant, centum in suos usus habebant. Quo beneficio multum antistes cor omnium in suum convertit amorem, et libentius eo praedicante caelestia sperare coeperunt, cuius ministerio temporalia bona sumpserunt.

Quo tempore rex Aedilualch donavit reverentissimo antistiti Vilfrido terram octoginta septem familiarum, ubi suos homines qui exules vagabantur, recipere posset, vocabulo Selaeseu, quod dicitur Latine Insula Vituli Marini. Est enim locus ille undique mari circumdatus praeter ab occidente, unde habet ingressum amplitudinis quasi iactus fundae: qualis locus a Latinis peninsula, a Graecis solet cherronesos vocari. Hunc ergo locum cum accepisset episcopus Vilfrid, fundavit ibi monasterium, ac regulari vita instituit, maxime ex his quos secum adduxerat fratribus: quod usque hodie successores eius tenere noscuntur. Nam ipse illis in partibus annos quinque, id est, usque ad mortem Ecgfridi regis, merito

[1] Selsey in Sussex.

them both with inward and outward benefits. For the bishop also when he had come into the country and saw so great a plague of famine there, taught them to seek their sustenance by fishing. For the sea and the rivers there about them had abundance of fish; but the people had no skill to fish save for eels only. Therefore they of the bishop's company gat whencesoever they might eel nets together and cast them into the sea, and by the help of grace divine soon took 300 fishes of divers kinds: the which they divided into three parts, and gave 100 to the poor folk, 100 to them of whom they had the nets, and 100 they kept for their own use. By the which benefit the bishop turned the hearts of all much to love him, and they began the more willingly to hope for heavenly things at his preaching, by whose succour they received temporal benefits.

And at this time did Ethelwalch give to the most reverend bishop Wilfrid 87 hides of land, where he might take in his company that were wandering in exile, in the place called Selaeseu,[1] the Latin for which meaneth Sea Calf Island. For that place is compassed of the sea round about, saving on the west, where it hath an entrance into it as broad as a man can cast a stone with a sling: which kind of place is wont in Latin to be called peninsula, in Greek chersonese. When then bishop Wilfrid had received this place, he founded a monastery there, and did bind to monastical life them that were therein, being for the most part of the brethren whom he had brought with him: which monastery his successors are known to keep unto this day. For until the death of king Egfrid, which was five years' space, Wilfrid did the office of a bishop both in word

omnibus honorabilis, officium episcopatus et verbo exercebat et opere. Et quoniam illi rex cum praefata loci possessione omnes, qui ibidem erant, facultates cum agris et hominibus donavit, omnes fide Christi institutos, unda baptismatis abluit; inter quos, servos et ancillas ducentos quinquaginta: quos omnes ut baptizando a servitute daemonica salvavit, etiam libertate donando humanae iugo servitutis absolvit.

CAP. XIV

Ut intercessione Osualdi regis pestifera mortalitas sit sublata.

In quo tunc monasterio nonnulla caelestis gratiae dona specialiter ostensa fuisse perhibentur; utpote ubi nuper expulsa diaboli tyrannide Christus iam regnare coeperat: e quibus unum quod mihi reverentissimus antistes Acca saepius referre, et a fidelissimis eiusdem monasterii fratribus sibi relatum asserere solebat, memoriae mandare commodum duximus. Eodem ferme tempore quo ipsa provincia nomen Christi susceperat, multas Brittaniae provincias mortalitas saeva corripiebat. Quae cum praefatum quoque monasterium, cui tunc regendo religiosissimus Christi sacerdos, vocabulo Eappa, praefuit, nutu divinae dispensationis attingeret; multique sive de his qui cum antistite illo venerant,

---

[1] The MSS. vary in the numbering of the following chapters. In some MSS. this chapter is omitted.

[2] Sussex.

and deed in those quarters, in great honour among all for his good deserving. And because the king with the foresaid possession of the place granted to him all the goods with the fields and the men that were therein, he instructed them all in the faith of Christ and cleansed them in the water of baptism; among the which there were bondmen and bond-women 250: whom all when by baptizing he did deliver from the bondage of the devil, by giving them their freedom he did also loose from the yoke of the bondage of man.

CHAPTER XIV[1]

How by the intercession of king Oswald a pestilent mortality was taken away.

And in this monastery at that time there were, it is related, some gifts of heavenly grace especially shewed; as in which place, the tyranny of the devil being lately driven out, Christ had now begun to reign: one of which things we have thought good to put in writing to be remembered, the which the most reverend bishop Acca was ofttimes wont to tell me, and affirmed that he had it reported to him of the brethren of the same monastery, men most worthy to be credited. About the same time that this province[2] had received the name of Christ, a sore mortality attacked many provinces of Britain, and when that this plague, by the pleasure of God's ordinance, touched also the foresaid monastery (which at that time the most devout priest of Christ, by name Eappa, did rule and govern), and that many, whether of them that had come thither with the bishop, or of those that had been lately called

sive de illis qui de eadem provincia Saxonum nuper ad fidem fuerant vocati, passim de hac vita raperentur; visum est fratribus triduanum ieiunium agere, et divinam suppliciter obsecrare clementiam, ut misericordiam sibi dignaretur impendere, et sive periclitantes hoc morbo a praesenti morte liberaret, seu raptos e mundo a perpetua animae damnatione servaret.

Erat tunc temporis in eodem monasterio puerulus quidam de natione Saxonum, nuper vocatus ad fidem, qui eadem tactus infirmitate, non pauco tempore recubans in lectulo iacebat. Cum ergo secunda memorati ieiunii ac supplicationum dies ageretur, contigit forte ipsum puerum hora ferme secunda diei, in loco in quo aeger iacebat, solum inveniri: cui divina dispositione subito beatissimi apostolorum principes dignati sunt apparere. Erat enim puer multum simplicis ac mansueti animi, sinceraque devotione sacramenta fidei quae susceperat servans. Salutantes ergo illum verbis piissimis apostoli dicebant: "Noli timere, fili, mortem pro qua sollicitis es: nos enim te hodierna die ad caelestia sumus regna perducturi. Sed primum exspectare habes donec missae celebrentur, ac viatico Dominici corporis ac sanguinis accepto, sic infirmitate simul et morte absolutus ad aeterna in caelis gaudia subleveris. Clama ergo ad te presbyterum Eappan, et dicito illi quia Dominus exaudivit preces vestras, et devotionem ac ieiunia propitius aspexit: neque aliquis de hoc monasterio, sive adiacentibus ei possessiunculis hac clade ultra

[1] About 8 p.m.

to the faith from the same province of the Saxons, were far and near taken from this life, it seemed good to the brethren to keep a fast of three days and humbly to beseech the mercy of God that He would vouchsafe to shew pity toward them, and either to deliver them from this perilous plague and present death, or when they were taken from the world to save their souls from eternal damnation.

There was at that time in the same monastery a certain little boy that was lately called to the faith, a Saxon born, which was taken with the same sickness and kept his bed upon his back no small time. When, therefore, the second day of the said fasting and praying was being observed, it happened that about the second hour[1] of the day this boy was found by himself alone in the place where he lay sick: and suddenly by the appointment of God there vouchsafed to appear unto him the most blessed chiefs of the apostles. For the boy was of very innocent and meek nature, and with sincere devotion kept the sacraments of faith which he had received. The apostles then saluted him with most gentle words, saying: "Fear not, son, the death for which thou art so pensive: for we are to bring thee this day to the heavenly realms. But first thou hast to tarry till the masses be said, and after thou hast received thy voyage-provision of the body and blood of the Lord, till (being so released of sickness as well as death) thou be lifted up to everlasting joys in heaven. Do thou therefore call for the priest Eappa unto thee, and tell him that the Lord hath heard your prayers and hath looked with favour upon your devotion and fastings: neither is anyone more to die of this plague from this monastery

moriturus est; sed omnes qui alicubi de vestris hac aegritudine laborant, resurrecturi a languore, pristina sunt sospitate recuperandi, praeter te solum qui hodierna es die liberandus a morte, et ad visionem Domini Christi cui fideliter servisti, perducendus in caelum: quod divina vobis misericordia per intercessionem religiosi ac Deo dilecti regis Osualdi, qui quondam genti Nordanhymbrorum et regni temporalis auctoritate et Christianae pietatis quae ad regnum perenne ducit devotione sublimiter praefuit, conferre dignata est. Hac etenim die idem rex ab infidelibus in bello corporaliter exstinctus, mox ad sempiterna animarum gaudia adsumptus in caelum et electorum est sociatus agminibus. Quaerant in suis codicibus in quibus defunctorum est adnotata depositio, et invenient illum hac, ut diximus, die raptum esse de saeculo. Celebrent ergo missas per cuncta monasterii oratoria huius, sive pro gratiarum actione exauditae suae deprecationis, sive etiam in memoriam praefati regis Osualdi, qui quondam ipsorum genti praeerat. Ideoque pro eis quasi pro suae gentis advenis supplex orabat ad Dominum: et cunctis convenientibus ad ecclesiam fratribus, communicent omnes sacrificiis caelestibus, et ita soluto ieiunio corpus quoque suis reficiant alimentis."

Quae cum omnia vocato ad se presbytero puer verba narrasset, interrogavit eum sollicitus quales essent habitu vel specie viri qui sibi apparuissent.

---

[1] Northumbrians. [2] Converts, Pl.

or from the possessions that adjoin the same; but all that belong to you anywhere and suffer from this sickness are to rise again from their weakness and be restored to their former health, save only thou, which this day art to be delivered from death and brought to heaven to the vision of the Lord Christ whom thou hast faithfully served: which thing the divine compassion hath vouchsafed to bestow upon you through the intercession of the godly and beloved of God king Oswald, which sometime did right nobly govern the people of the Northumbrians, both with the authority of the temporal kingdom and devoutness of Christian piety which leadeth to the everlasting kingdom. For on this day the same king, being bodily slain in battle of the infidels, was by and by taken up into heaven to the eternal joys of the soul and fellowship with the companies of the elect. Let them seek in their books that have the notes of the burial of the dead, and they shall find that he was taken from the world on this day, as we have said. Let them therefore say masses in all the chapels of this monastery, whether for giving of thanks that their prayer is heard, or also for the memory of the said king Oswald which sometime was over their nation.[1] And therefore did he make humble prayer to the Lord for them as if for strangers [2] of his own people; and when all the brethren are come together to the church, let them all be houseled, and so finishing their fast let them refresh also their bodies with their proper sustenance."

All the which words when the boy had declared to the priest being called unto him, the priest enquired of him diligently what manner of array

Respondit: "Praeclari omnino habitus et vultus erant, laetissimi ac pulcherrimi, quales nunquam ante videram, neque aliquos hominum tanti decoris ac venustatis esse posse credebam. Unus quidem attonsus erat ut clericus, alius barbam habebat prolixam: dicebantque quod unus eorum Petrus, alius vocaretur Paulus: et ipsi essent ministri Domini et Salvatoris nostri Jesu Christi, ad tuitionem nostri monasterii missi ab ipso de caelis." Credidit ergo verbis pueri presbyter, ac statim egressus requisivit in annali suo, et invenit eadem ipsa die Osualdum regem fuisse peremptum: vocatisque fratribus, parari prandium, missas fieri, atque omnes communicare more solito praecepit: simul et infirmanti puero de eodem sacrificio Dominicae oblationis particulam deferri mandavit.

Quibus ita gestis, non multo post, eadem ipsa die puer defunctus est, suaque morte probavit vera fuisse verba quae ab apostolis Christi audierat. Sed et hoc eius verbis testimonium perhibuit, quod nemo praeter ipsum tempore illo ex eodem est monasterio raptus de mundo. Ex qua nimirum visione multi qui haec audire potuerunt, ad exorandam in adversis divinam clementiam, et ad salutaria ieiuniorum remedia subeunda sunt mirabiliter accensi: et ex eo tempore non solum in eodem monasterio, sed et in plerisque locis aliis, coepit annuatim eiusdem regis ac militis Christi natalitius dies missarum celebratione venerari.

and likeness the men had which had appeared unto him. He answered: "They were altogether notable in their array and countenance, exceeding joyful and beautiful, such as I never had seen before nor did believe that any men could be of so great comeliness and beauty. The one was shaven like a clerk, while the other had a long beard: and they said the one of them was called Peter, the other Paul: and that they were the ministers of our Lord and Saviour Jesus Christ, sent from heaven itself for the defence of our monastery." Wherefore the priest believed the words of the boy, and went out straightway and sought in his book of chronicles, and found that king Oswald had been slain on that very day: and calling the brethren he commanded dinner to be provided, masses to be said, and that they should all communicate after the accustomed manner: and at the same time he willed a small portion of the same sacrifice of the Lord's oblation to be brought to the sick boy.

Which things being so done, not long after the boy died the very same day, and proved by his death that the words were true which he had heard of Christ's apostles. Moreover, too, this gave witness to his words, that at that time no one from the same monastery was taken out of the world except him only; by which vision without doubt many that might hear of these things were marvellously stirred to pray and obtain God's mercy in adversity, and to undergo the salutary medicine of fasting: and from that time, not in the same monastery only but in very many other places too, the birthday of the said king and champion of Christ began yearly to be kept holy with the saying of masses.

CAP. XV

Ut Caedualla rex Geuissorum, interfecto rege Aediluualch, provinciam illam saeva caede ac depopulatione attriverit.

INTEREA superveniens cum exercitu Caedualla, iuvenis strenuissimus de regio genere Geuissorum, cum exularet a patria sua, interfecit regem Aedilualch, ac provinciam illam saeva caede ac depopulatione attrivit; sed mox expulsus est a ducibus regis, Bercthuno et Andhuno, qui deinceps regnum provinciae tenuerunt: quorum prior postea ab eodem Caedualla, cum esset rex Geuissorum, occisus est, et provincia graviore servitio subacta. Sed et Ini qui post Caeduallan regnavit, simili provinciam illam adflictione plurimo annorum tempore mancipavit. Quare factum est ut toto illo tempore episcopum proprium habere nequiret; sed revocato domum Vilfrido primo suo antistite, ipsi episcopo Geuissorum, id est, Occidentalium Saxonum, qui essent in Venta civitate, subiacerent.

CAP. XVI

Ut Vecta insula Christianos incolas susceperit, cuius regii duo pueri statim post acceptum baptisma sint interempti.

POSTQUAM ergo Caedualla regno potitus est Geuissorum, cepit et insulam Vectam, quae eatenus erat

[1] Sussex. [2] A.S. ealdormen.

CHAPTER XV

How Cadwalla king of the Gewissas slew king Ethelwalch and wasted that province[1] *with cruel death and ruin* [688].

In the meantime Cadwalla, a young man of great might and power, of the royal blood of the Gewissas, being banished from his country, came suddenly with an host of men and slew king Ethelwalch, and wasted that province with cruel death and ruin; but he was soon driven out by the king's captains[2] Berthun and Andhun, which from that time did hold the dominion of the province: the former of which two was afterwards slain of the same Cadwalla, being then king of the Gewissas, and the province brought into more grievous bondage than it was before. Moreover, Ini who reigned after Cadwalla afflicted that province with like misery a great many years. Whereby it came to pass that all that time its people could have no bishop of their own; but, their first bishop Wilfrid being called home again,[3] as many as were in the city of Venta were subject to the bishop of the Gewissas,[4] that is, of the West Saxons.

CHAPTER XVI

How the Isle of Wight received Christian inhabitants, in which isle two boys of the king's blood were forthwith slain after receiving baptism [686].

When then Cadwalla had obtained the kingdom of the Gewissas, he took the Isle of Wight also, which

[3] To Northumbria, 686. [4] Heddi bishop of Winchester.

tota idolatriae dedita; ac stragica[1] caede omnes indigenas exterminare, ac suae provinciae homines pro his substituere contendit, voto se obligans, quamvis necdum regeneratus, ut ferunt, in Christo, quia, si cepisset insulam, quartam partem eius, simul et praedae, Domino daret. Quod ita solvit, ut hanc Vilfrido episcopo, qui tunc forte de gente sua superveniens aderat, utendam pro Domino offerret. Est autem mensura eiusdem insulae, iuxta aestimationem Anglorum, mille ducentarum familiarum: unde data est episcopo possessio terrae trecentarum familiarum. At ipse partem quam accepit, commendavit cuidam de clericis suis, cui nomen Bernuini, et erat filius sororis eius, dans illi presbyterum nomine Hiddila, qui omnibus qui salvari vellent, verbum ac lavacrum vitae ministraret.

Ubi silentio praetereundum non esse reor, quod in primitias eorum qui de eadem insula credendo salvati sunt, duo regii pueri fratres videlicet Arualdi regis insulae, speciali sunt Dei gratia coronati: siquidem imminentibus insulae hostibus, fuga lapsi sunt de insula, et in proximam Iutorum provinciam translati: ubi cum delati in locum qui vocatur Ad Lapidem, occulendos se a facie regis victoris credidissent, proditi sunt, atque occidi iussi. Quod cum audisset abbas quidam et presbyter, vocabulo Cyniberct, habens non longe ab inde monasterium in loco qui vocatur Hreutford, id est, Vadum harundinis, venit ad regem, qui tunc eisdem in partibus occultus

[1] For *tragica*, Pl.

---

[1] Stoneham near Southampton.
[2] Redbridge in Hants.

until that time had been wholly given up to the worshipping of idols; and he intended to do away with all the natives by fell slaughter and to put people of his own province in their place, binding himself by vow (though not yet regenerated in Christ, as it is said), that if he took the island, he would give unto the Lord the fourth part thereof and of the prey as well. Which thing he so performed, that, bishop Wilfrid happening to be there (coming suddenly from his own country), he offered the same unto him for the service of the Lord. Now the said isle contained, as the English do rate it, 1200 hides of land: whereof was given to the bishop the possession of 300 hides of land. But the bishop committed the portion he received to one of his clerks named Berwin, his sister's son, and gave him a priest, Hiddila by name, to minister the word and laver of life to all that would be saved.

And here I think it not to be passed over in silence, that for the first-fruits of them that of the same isle were saved through believing, two boys of the blood royal, being, that is, brothers of Arwald king of the island, were crowned with a special grace of God: for when the enemy were coming upon the island, they fled and escaped therefrom and were taken over to the next province of the Jutes: and there they gat to a place called At Stone,[1] and thought that they should be hidden from the face of the king that had the victory, but they were betrayed and commanded to be put to death. Which thing when a certain abbot and priest named Cynibert had heard of, whose monastery was not far from thence at a place called Hreutford,[2] that is to say, Reed's Ford, he came to the king, which then lying secretly in the

curabatur a vulneribus quae ei inflicta fuerant praelianti in insula Vecta: postulavitque ab eo, ut si necesse esset pueros interfici, prius eos liceret fidei Christianae sacramentis imbui. Concessit rex, et ipse instructos eos verbo veritatis, ac fonte Salvatoris ablutos, de ingressu regni aeterni certos reddidit. Moxque illi instante carnifice, mortem laeti subiere temporalem per quam se ad vitam animae perpetuam non dubitabant esse transituros. Hoc ergo ordine, postquam omnes Brittaniarum provinciae fidem Christi susceperant, suscepit et insula Vecta, in quam tamen ob aerumnam externae subiectionis, nemo gradum ministerii ac sedis episcopalis ante Danihelem, qui nunc Occidentalium Saxonum est episcopus, accepit.

Sita est autem haec insula contra medium Australium Saxonum et Geuissorum, interposito pelago latitudinis trium millium quod vocatur Soluente: in quo videlicet pelago bini aestus oceani qui circum Brittaniam ex infinito oceano septentrionali erumpunt, sibimet invicem quotidie compugnantes occurrunt, ultra ostium fluminis Homelea, quod per terras Iutorum, quae ad regionem Geuissorum pertinent, praefatum pelagus intrat; finitoque conflictu, in oceanum refusi, unde venerant, redeunt.

same parts was being healed of his wounds that he had taken fighting in the Isle of Wight; and desired of him that, if he must needs have the boys put to death, yet they might first be instructed in the mysteries of the Christian faith. The king granted his request, and the abbot catechizing them in the word of truth and cleansing them in the font of the Saviour, made them sure of entrance into the kingdom everlasting. And anon coming the executioner, they joyfully submitted to the temporal death, by the which they doubted not but they should pass to the eternal life of the soul. When then after this order all the provinces of the Britains had received the faith of Christ, the Isle of Wight received the same also, over which notwithstanding, because of the misery of foreign subjection, no man took the degree of the ministry and see of a bishopric before Daniel, who now is bishop of the West Saxons.

Now the situation of this island is over against the midst of the South Saxons and Gewissas, the sea which is called the Solent coming between, the breadth of three miles: in which sea to wit two tides of the ocean sea, that break out from the boundless north ocean about Britain, do daily meet and run together beyond the mouth of the river Homelea [1] (which runneth through the lands of the Jutes, that reach to the district of the Gewissas, and so entereth into the aforesaid sea); and when their striving together is ended they go back and flow again into the ocean from whence they came.

[1] The Hamble.

CAP. XVII

De synodo facta in campo Haethfelda, praesidente archiepiscopo Theodoro.

His temporibus audiens Theodorus fidem ecclesiae Constantinopoli per haeresim Eutychetis multum esse turbatam, et ecclesias Anglorum quibus praeerat ab huiusmodi labe immunes perdurare desiderans, collecto venerabilium sacerdotum doctorumque plurimorum coetu, cuius essent fidei singuli sedulus inquirebat, omniumque unanimem in fide catholica reperit consensum: et hunc synodalibus literis ad instructionem memoriamque sequentium commendare curavit, quarum videlicet literarum istud exordium est:

"In nomine Domini nostri Jesu Christi Salvatoris, imperantibus dominis piissimis nostris Ecgfrido rege Hymbronensium, anno decimo regni eius, sub die quintadecima Kalendas Octobres, indictione octava; et Aedilredo rege Mercinensium, anno sexto regni eius; et Alduulfo rege Estranglorum, anno decimo septimo regni eius; et Hlothario rege Cantuariorum, regni eius anno septimo: praesidente Theodoro, gratia Dei archiepiscopo Brittaniae insulae, et civitatis Doruuernis; una cum eo sedentibus ceteris episcopis Brittaniae insulae viris venerabilibus, praepositis sacrosanctis evangeliis, in loco qui Saxonico vocabulo Haethfelth nominatur, pariter tractantes, fidem rectam et orthodoxam exposuimus; sicut Dominus noster Jesus Christus incarnatus

[1] For the Monophysite and Monothelite heresies cf. Bright, p. 220.

CHAPTER XVII

Of the synod made in the plain of Heathfield, Theodore the archbishop being president [680].

At this time Theodore, having word that the faith of the Church at Constantinople was sore troubled through the heresy of Eutyches,[1] and wishing that the churches of the English over which he governed might continue clear from such a taint, gathered an assembly of reverend bishops and many doctors, and enquired diligently of each of them what faith they were of, and found one consent of them all in the catholic faith: which consent he procured to commit to a synodical letter for the instruction and remembrance of aftercomers, the beginning of which letter was this:

"In the name of our Lord Jesus Christ the Saviour, and in the reign of our most godly lords Egfrid king of the Northumbrians, the 10th year of his reign, on the 17th day of September, in the 8th indiction; and Ethelred king of the Marchmen, in the 6th year of his reign; and Aldwulf king of the East English, in the 17th year of his reign; and Lothere king of Kent, in the 7th year of his reign[2]: being there president Theodore by the grace of God archbishop of the isle of Britain, and of the city of Canterbury; and with him sitting the other bishops of the isle of Britain, reverend men, having the holy Gospels set before them, at a place called in the Saxon tongue Heathfield, in conference together we have set forth the right and orthodox faith; in such sort as our Lord Jesus Christ being incarnate delivered it to His

[2] Wessex is not mentioned. It was in a disturbed state.

tradidit discipulis suis, qui praesentialiter viderunt et audierunt sermones eius, atque sanctorum patrum tradidit symbolum, et generaliter omnes sancti et universales synodi, et omnis probabilium catholicae ecclesiae doctorum chorus. Hos itaque sequentes nos pie atque orthodoxe, iuxta divinitus inspiratam doctrinam eorum professi credimus consonanter, et confitemur secundum sanctos patres, proprie et veraciter Patrem et Filium et Spiritum Sanctum Trinitatem in unitate consubstantialem, et Unitatem in Trinitate, hoc est, unum Deum in tribus Subsistentiis vel Personis consubstantialibus, aequalis gloriae et honoris."

Et post multa huiusmodi quae ad rectae fidei confessionem pertinebant, haec quoque sancta synodus suis literis addit:

"Suscepimus sanctas et universales quinque synodos beatorum et Deo acceptabilium patrum; id est, qui in Nicaea congregati fuerunt trecentorum decem et octo, contra Arium impiissimum et eiusdem dogmata; et in Constantinopoli centum quinquaginta, contra vesaniam Macedonii et Eudoxii et eorum dogmata; et in Epheso primo ducentorum, contra nequissimum Nestorium et eiusdem dogmata; et in Chalcedone sexcentorum et triginta, contra Eutychen et Nestorium, et eorum dogmata; et iterum in Constantinopoli quinto congregati sunt concilio in tempore Iustiniani minoris, contra Theodorum, et Theodoreti et Ibae epistolas et eorum dogmata contra Cyrillum."

---

[1] *i.e.* Nicene fathers.

[2] *Substantia*, equivalent to *οὐσία*, is the substance which may not be divided: *subsis entiae* are the Persons which may not be confounded. The Greek *ὑπόστασις* is used in both senses in Greek theology; cf. Pl. II. 232.

disciples which saw Him in presence and heard His words, and as the creed of the holy fathers[1] hath delivered it, and generally as all holy and general councils and all the company of the authentic doctors of the catholic Church have delivered it. These therefore we following in godly and right believing manner, according to their doctrine inspired into them by God, do profess and believe agreeably to the same, and do confess with the holy fathers the Father, the Son and the Holy Ghost to be the Trinity in unity of one substance, and the Unity in Trinity, that is to say, one God in three consubstantial Subsistences[2] or Persons, of equal glory and honour."

And after many like things pertaining to the confession of the right faith, the holy synod did also add to their letter these things following:

"We have received the five holy and general synods of the blessed fathers acceptable to God; that is to say, of the 318 which were assembled at Nicaea[3] against the ungodly Arius and the doctrines of the same; and of the 150 at Constantinople[4] against the madness of Macedonius and Eudoxius and the doctrines of the same; and of the 200 at Ephesus[5] the first time against the most wicked Nestorius and the doctrines of the same; and of the 630 at Chalcedon[6] against Eutyches and Nestorius and their doctrines; and at Constantinople the second time[7] was assembled the fifth Council in the time of Justinian the younger against Theodore and the letters of Theodoret and Ibas[8] and their doctrines against Cyril.

[3] 325.
[4] 381, 382. Macedonius and Eudoxius were Arian bishops.
[5] 431. [6] 451. [7] 553.
[8] Supporters of Nestorius.

Et paulo post :

" Et synodum quae facta est in urbe Roma, in tempore Martini papae beatissimi, indictione octava, imperante Constantino piissimo anno nono, suscipimus. Et glorificamus Dominum nostrum Jesum, sicut isti glorificaverunt; nihil addentes vel subtrahentes: et anathematizamus corde et ore quos anathematizarunt; et quos susceperunt, suscipimus: glorificantes Deum Patrem sine initio, et Filium eius unigenitum ex Patre generatum ante saecula, et Spiritum Sanctum procedentem ex Patre et Filio inenarrabiliter, sicut praedicaverunt hi quos memoravimus supra, sancti apostoli, et prophetae, et doctores. Et nos omnes subscribimus, qui cum Theodoro archiepiscopo fidem catholicam exposuimus."

CAP. XVIII

De Iohanne cantatore sedis apostolicae, qui propter docendum Brittaniam venerit.

INTERERAT huic synodo, pariterque catholicae fidei decreta firmabat vir venerabilis Iohannes archicantator ecclesiae sancti apostoli Petri, et abbas monasterii beati Martini, qui nuper venerat a Roma per iussionem papae Agathonis, duce reverentissimo abbate Biscopo, cognomine Benedicto, cuius supra meminimus. Cum enim idem Benedictus construxisset monasterium Brittaniae, in honorem

[1] The first Lateran Council, 649.

[2] Constantinus IV or Constans II. This Council condemned Monothelitism.

And a little after:

"And we receive the synod [1] made at the city of Rome in the time of the most blessed pope Martin, in the eighth indiction, in the ninth year of the most godly emperor Constantine.[2] And we glorify our Lord Jesus in such sort as these men have glorified Him; adding or diminishing nothing: and we accurse with heart and mouth them whom they have accursed: and whom they have received we receive: glorifying God the Father without beginning, and His only begotten Son begotten of the Father before the worlds, and the Holy Ghost proceeding from the Father and the Son in unspeakable wise; according as these above mentioned holy apostles and prophets and doctors have proclaimed. And all we, that with Theodore the archbishop have set forth the catholic faith, do subscribe."

CHAPTER XVIII

Of John the Chanter of the see apostolic who came to Britain to teach.

At this synod there was present and likewise confirmed [3] the decrees of the catholic faith a venerable man, John, archchanter of the church of the holy apostle Peter, and abbot of the monastery of the blessed Martin, which was come of late from Rome by the commandment of pope Agatho, having for his guide the most reverend abbot Biscop, surnamed Benedict, of whom we have spoken before.[4] For when the said Benedict had built a monastery, in the honour of the most blessed chief of the apostles,

[3] As the pope's legate.

[4] Not in this history, but in Bede's *History of the Abbots.*

beatissimi apostolorum principis, iuxta ostium fluminis Viuri, venit Romam cum cooperatore ac socio eiusdem operis Ceolfrido, qui post ipsum eiusdem monasterii abbas fuit, quod et ante saepius facere consueverat, atque honorifice a beatae memoriae papa Agathone susceptus est: petiitque, et accepit ab eo in munimentum libertatis monasterii quod fecerat, epistolam privilegii ex auctoritate apostolica firmatam; iuxta quod Ecgfridum regem voluisse, ac licentiam dedisse noverat, quo concedente et possessionem terrae largiente, ipsum monasterium fecerat.

Accepit et praefatum Iohannem abbatem Brittaniam perducendum; quatenus in monasterio suo cursum canendi annuum, sicut ad sanctum Petrum Romae agebatur, edoceret: egitque abba Iohannes ut iussionem acceperat pontificis, et ordinem videlicet, ritumque canendi ac legendi viva voce praefati monasterii cantores edocendo, et ea quae totius anni circulus in celebratione dierum festorum poscebat, etiam literis mandando: quae hactenus in eodem monasterio servata, et a multis iam sunt circumquaque transcripta. Non solum autem idem Iohannes ipsius monasterii fratres docebat, verum de omnibus pene eiusdem provinciae monasteriis ad audiendum eum, qui cantandi erant periti, confluebant. Sed et ipsum per loca in quibus doceret, multi invitare curabant.

Ipse autem excepto cantandi vel legendi munere, et aliud in mandatis ab apostolico papa acceperat, ut cuius esset fidei Anglorum ecclesia, diligenter

---

[1] Northumbria.

by the mouth of the river Wear, he came to Rome, as he had often been wont to do before, with his fellow-worker and helper in the same work, Ceolfrid (who after Biscop was abbot of the same monastery), and was received honourably of pope Agatho of blessed memory; of whom he desired and obtained for the assurance of the liberty of the monastery that he had erected a letter of privilege confirmed by the authority apostolic; in such form as he knew the will and grant of king Egfrid to be, by whose leave and liberal gift of possession of land he had made the said monastery.

He obtained also to bring the foresaid abbot John to Britain; to the intent he might teach in his monastery the yearly course of singing as it was done in Saint Peter's at Rome: and the abbot John did, as he had commandment by the pope, that is to say, both teaching with his own voice the chanters of the said monastery the order and form of singing and reading, and also putting in writing those things that were required for the celebration of festival days for the whole compass of the year; which things have been hitherto kept in the same monastery, and by now have been copied out by many everywhere about. And the same John did not only teach the brethren of that monastery, but they that were skilful in song flocked together to hear him from almost all the monasteries of the same province.[1] Moreover, many were forward to entreat him, in such places where he might teach, to come to them himself.

Now beside this office of singing and reading, he had also received another charge in commandment from the pope apostolic, which was that he should diligently learn of what faith the English Church was,

edisceret, Romamque rediens referret. Nam et synodum beati papae Martini, centum quinque episcoporum consensu non multo ante Romae celebratam, contra eos maxime qui unam in Christo operationem et voluntatem praedicabant, secum veniens attulit; atque in praefato religiosissimi abbatis Benedicti monasterio transcribendam commodavit. Tales namque eo tempore fidem Constantinopolitanae ecclesiae multum conturbaverunt; sed Domino donante proditi iam tunc et victi sunt. Unde volens Agatho papa, sicut in aliis provinciis, ita etiam in Brittania qualis esset status ecclesiae, quam ab haereticorum contagiis castus, ediscere hoc negotium reverentissimo abbati Iohanni Brittaniam destinato iniunxit. Quamobrem collecta pro hoc in Brittania synodo quam diximus, inventa est in omnibus fides inviolata catholica: datumque illi exemplar eius Romam perferendum.

Verum ille patriam revertens, non multo postquam oceanum transiit, arreptus infirmitate, ac defunctus est: corpusque eius ab amicis propter amorem sancti Martini cuius monasterio praeerat, Turonis delatum, atque honorifice sepultum est. Nam et benigno ecclesiae illius hospitio, cum Brittaniam iret, exceptus est, rogatusque multum a fratribus, ut Romam revertens, illo itinere veniret, atque ad eam diverteret ecclesiam. Denique ibidem adiutores itineris et iniuncti operis accepit: qui etsi in itinere defunctus est, nihilominus exemplum catholicae fidei Anglorum

[1] The decision of the synod.
[2] Thirty years before.
[3] Monothelitism.

and bring word thereof at his return to Rome. For not long before he brought with him at his coming the synod [1] of the blessed pope Martin, which had been kept at Rome not long before,[2] of the consent of 105 bishops against them principally that preached one only working and will in Christ; [3] and gave it to be copied out in the foresaid monastery of the most devout abbot Benedict. For such men at that time sore troubled the faith of the church of Constantinople; but by the gift of the Lord they were at that very time espied out and vanquished. Wherefore Agatho the pope minding, as in other provinces, so also in Britain, to be informed what was the state of the Church, and how pure it was from the contagion of heretics, laid this business upon the most reverend abbot John, being now appointed to go to Britain. And therefore when the synod, which we have spoken of, was gathered together for this purpose in Britain, the catholic faith was in them all found uncorrupted: and a copy thereof was given him to carry to Rome.

But in his returning to his own country, not long after he passed the sea, he was taken with sickness and died: and his body, for the love of Saint Martin whose monastery he governed, was by his friends brought unto Tours and buried honourably. For as he went toward Britain he was both received with kindly entertainment in that church, and desired earnestly of the brethren that in returning to Rome he would come that way and lodge at that church. Finally, he took with him at that place certain to help him in his journey and the work he was charged with: and, although he died by the way, nevertheless the copy of the catholic faith of the English was

Romam perlatum est, atque ab apostolico papa omnibusque qui audiere vel legere, gratantissime susceptum.

CAP. XIX

Ut Edilthryd regina virgo perpetua permanserit, cuius nec corpus in monumento corrumpi potuerit.

ACCEPIT autem rex Ecgfrid coniugem nomine Aedilthrydam, filiam Anna regis Orientalium Anglorum, cuius saepius mentionem fecimus, viri bene religiosi, ac per omnia mente et opere egregii: quam et alter ante illum vir habuerat uxorem, princeps videlicet australium Guruiorum, vocabulo Tondberct. Sed illo post modicum temporis ex quo eam accepit, defuncto, data est regi praefato: cuius consortio cum duodecim annis uteretur, perpetua tamen mansit virginitatis integritate gloriosa: sicut mihimet sciscitanti, cum hoc an ita esset quibusdam venisset in dubium, beatae memoriae Vilfrid episcopus referebat, dicens se testem integritatis eius esse certissimum: adeo ut Ecgfridus promiserit se ei terras ac pecunias multas esse donaturum, si reginae posset persuadere eius uti connubio, quia sciebat illam nullum virorum plus illo diligere. Nec diffidendum est nostra etiam aetate fieri potuisse, quod aevo praecedente aliquoties factum fideles historiae narrant: donante uno eodemque Domino, qui se nobiscum usque in finem saeculi manere pollicetur. Nam etiam signum divini miraculi, quo eiusdem

---

[1] St. Etheldred or Audrey.
[2] Wilfrid.

brought to Rome, and most joyfully received of the pope apostolic and of all that heard or read the same.

CHAPTER XIX

How queen Ethelthryth[1] *continued a perpetual virgin, whose body could not either be putrefied in her tomb* [672–680].

Now King Egfrid took to wife Ethelthryth, as was her name, the daughter of Anna king of the East English, of whom we have often made mention, a man marvellous godly and in all points notable in thought and deed: which same woman had also been wedded to another man, that is to say, to the prince of the South Gyrwas, named Tondbert, before Egfrid wedded her. But Tondbert dying a little after he took her to wife, she was given to the foresaid king: with whom she lived twelve years and yet remained always a pure and glorious virgin: even as bishop Wilfrid of blessed memory did shew me, when I enquired of the matter, seeing that certain had come to doubt whether this was so, and he said that he could be a very sure witness of her virginity, for so much as king Egfrid promised to give him lands and much money if he could persuade the queen to use his company, because he knew that she loved no man in the world more than him.[2] And it is not to be mistrusted but that the same thing may be done in our time also, which hath been sometime done in a past age, as true histories do witness: by the grace of the one and the same Lord which promiseth that He abideth with us unto the end of the world. For beside, the divine miracle, whereby the buried

feminae sepulta caro corrumpi non potuit, indicio est quia a viri contactu incorrupta duraverit.

Quae multum diu regem postulans ut saeculi curas relinquere, atque in monasterio, tantum vero regi Christo servire permitteretur; ubi vix aliquando impetravit, intravit monasterium Aebbae abbatissae, quae erat amita regis Ecgfridi, positum in loco quem Coludi urbem nominant, accepto velamine sanctimonialis habitus a praefato antistite Vilfrido. Post annum vero ipsa facta est abbatissa in regione quae vocatur Elge; ubi constructo monasterio virginum Deo devotarum perplurium mater virgo, et exemplis vitae caelestis esse coepit et monitis. De qua ferunt, quia ex quo monasterium petiit, nunquam lineis, sed solum laneis vestimentis uti voluerit: raroque in calidis balneis, praeter imminentibus sollemniis maioribus, verbi gratia paschae, pentecostes, epiphaniae, lavari voluerit; et tunc novissima omnium, lotis prius suo suarumque ministrarum obsequio ceteris quae ibi essent famulis Christi. Raro praeter maiora sollemnia, vel arctiorem necessitatem, plus quam semel per diem manducavit: semper, si non infirmitas gravior prohibuisset, ex tempore matutinae synaxeos, usque ad ortum diei, in ecclesia precibus intenta perstiterit. Sunt etiam qui dicant quia per prophetiae spiritum, et pestilentiam qua ipsa esset moritura, praedixerit, et numerum quoque eorum, qui de suo monasterio hac essent de mundo rapiendi, palam cunctis praesentibus

---

[1] Coldingham in Berwickshire.

[2] Hence came Egfrid's enmity to Wilfrid.

[3] Ely.

[4] *Love's Labour's Lost*, V. ii. I have no shirt: I go woolward for penance.

[5] Washing of the feet, John xiii. 14.

[6] Matins.

flesh of the same woman could not be putrefied, doth well shew that she continued uncorrupted and untouched by any man.

And she long and earnestly besought the king that she might have leave to forsake the cares of the world, and in a monastery serve only Christ the true king; and when hardly did she sometime obtain leave, she entered into the monastery of abbess Ebba who was aunt to king Egfrid, and it standeth in the place they name the town of Coludi,[1] where she received the veil of a nun's habit from the aforesaid bishop Wilfrid.[2] But after a year she was herself made abbess in the country which is called Elge[3]; where having built a monastery she began to be a virgin mother of very many virgins dedicated to God, both in examples and lessons of heavenly life. And of her it is said, that from the time that she went to the monastery she would never wear linen but only woollen clothes[4]: and seldom wash herself in warm baths, save against solemn high feasts, namely Easter, Whitsuntide and Twelfth-tide; and then would she be last of all, and with her own hands and the hands of her servants first washed[5] the rest of Christ's handmaids that were there. Seldom except on high feasts or closer need did she eat more than once a day: always, unless a sorer sickness had let her, from the time of the morning assembling[6] until the rising of the day she would abide in the church, still continuing at her prayers. There are too that say that by the spirit of prophecy she did foretell both the pestilence whereof she should die herself, and also did openly in all their presence let them know the number of those that should be taken thereby from this world out of her monastery.

intimaverit. Rapta est autem ad Dominum in medio suorum, post annos septem ex quo abbatissae gradum susceperat: et aeque ut ipsa iusserat, non alibi quam in medio eorum, iuxta ordinem quo transierat, ligneo in locello sepulta.

Cui successit in ministerium abbatissae soror eius Sexburg, quam habuerat in coniugem Earconberct rex Cantuariorum. Et cum sedecim annis esset sepulta, placuit eidem abbatissae levari ossa eius, et in locello novo posita in ecclesiam transferri; iussitque quosdam e fratribus quaerere lapidem, de quo locellum in hoc facere possent: qui ascensa navi, ipsa enim regio Elge undique est aquis ac paludibus circumdata, neque lapides maiores habet, venerunt ad civitatulam quandam desolatam, non procul inde sitam, quae lingua Anglorum Grantacaestir vocatur: et mox invenerunt iuxta muros civitatis locellum de marmore albo pulcherrime factum, operculo quoque similis lapidis aptissime tectum. Unde intelligentes a Domino suum iter esse prosperatum, gratias agentes retulerunt ad monasterium.

Cumque corpus sacrae virginis ac sponsae Christi aperto sepulcro esset prolatum in lucem, ita incorruptum inventum est, ac si eodem die fuisset defuncta, sive humo condita; sicut et praefatus antistes Vilfrid, et multi alii qui novere, testantur. Sed certiori notitia medicus Cynifrid, qui et morienti illi, et elevatae de tumulo adfuit: qui referre erat solitus, quod illa infirmata habuerit tumorem maximum sub

---

[1] Grantchester.

Now she was taken away to the Lord in the midst of her company seven years after she had taken the degree of abbess: and just as she herself had bidden, she was buried in a coffin of wood in none other place than in the midst of them, in such order as she had departed.

After whom succeeded in the office of abbess her sister Sexburg, whom Earconbert king of Kent had had to wife. And when Ethelthryth had lain buried sixteen years, it seemed good to the same abbess to have her bones taken up and put in a new coffin and be carried over into the church; and she bade certain of the brethren to seek a stone whereof they might make a coffin for this purpose; and they taking ship (for this same country of Elge is roundabout compassed with waters and fens nor hath stones of larger size), came to a certain little city left uninhabited, the which was not far from thence and in the English tongue is called Grantacaestir [1]: and by and by they found by the walls of the town a coffin of white marble, very fairly made, and covered also very trim with a lid of like stone. Whereby understanding that the Lord had prospered their journey, they gave Him thanks and came back with it to the monastery.

And when the grave was opened and the body of the holy virgin and spouse of Christ brought forth into the light, it was found so clean from corruption as if she had died or been put in the ground the same day; even as both the aforesaid bishop Wilfrid and many other that knew it, bear witness. But Cynifrid, a physician, which was present with her both when she was dying and when she was raised out of the tomb, was wont of more certain knowledge to tell, that when she lay sick she had a great swelling

maxilla. "Iusseruntque me," inquit, "incidere tumorem illum, ut efflueret noxius humor qui inerat: quod cum facerem, videbatur illa per biduum aliquanto levius habere; ita ut multi putarent, quia sanari posset a languore. Tertia autem die prioribus adgravata doloribus, et rapta confestim de mundo, dolorem omnem ac mortem perpetua salute ac vita mutavit. Cumque post tot annos elevanda essent ossa de sepulcro, et extento desuper papilione, omnis congregatio, hinc fratrum, inde sororum psallens circumstaret, ipsa autem abbatissa intus cum paucis ossa elatura et dilutura intrasset, repente audivimus abbatissam intus voce clara proclamare: 'Sit gloria nomini Domini.' Nec multo post clamaverunt me intus, reserato ostio papilionis: vidique elevatum de tumulo, et positum in lectulo corpus sacrae Deo virginis quasi dormientis simile. Sed et discooperto vultus indumento, monstraverunt mihi etiam vulnus incisurae quod feceram, curatum; ita ut mirum in modum pro aperto et hiante vulnere cum quo sepulta erat, tenuissima tunc cicatricis vestigia parerent." Sed et linteamina omnia quibus involutum erat corpus, integra apparuerunt, et ita nova, ut ipso die viderentur castis eius membris esse circumdata. Ferunt autem quia cum praefato tumore ac dolore maxillae sive colli premeretur, multum delectata sit hoc genere infirmitatis, ac solita dicere: "Scio certissime, quia merito in collo pondus languoris

under her cheek-bone. "And they bade me," quoth he, "to lance that swelling, that the ill humour that was within might issue out: which when I did, for the space of two days she seemed to be somewhat better at ease; so that many thought that she might be cured of her grief. But the third day her former pains were made more grievous, and straightway was she taken out of the world, and changed all pain and death with health and life everlasting. And when after so many years her bones should be raised out of the tomb, they spread a tent over the same, and all the company of the brethren on the one side, and sisters on the other, stood about singing, while the abbess herself with a few had gone in to take up and wash the bones, and suddenly we heard the abbess within cry out with a loud voice: 'Glory be to the name of the Lord.' And anon after they called me in, opening the entrance of the tent: and I saw the body of the holy virgin of God raised up out of the tomb and lying on a bed like one that were asleep. Moreover, they did also open the covering of her face and shewed me too the wound of the cut which I had made, cured; so that in marvellous wise in the place of the open and gaping wound wherewith she was buried, there appeared then but slightest traces of the scar." Beside this too all the linen clothes wherein the body was wound appeared whole, and so new that they seemed to have been put about her chaste limbs that very day. And the report is that, when she was grieved with the foresaid swelling and pain of her cheek-bone and neck, she took great joy in this kind of sickness and was wont to say: "I know most certainly that I worthily do bear the burden of pain in my neck, on the which I remember,

porto, in quo iuvenculam me memini supervacua monilium pondera portare: et credo quod ideo me superna pietas dolore colli voluit gravari, ut sic absolvar reatu supervacuae levitatis; dum mihi nunc pro auro et margaritis, de collo rubor tumoris, ardorque promineat." Contigit autem tactu indumentorum eorumdem, et daemonia ab obsessis effugata corporibus, et infirmitates alias aliquoties esse curatas. Sed et loculum in quo primo sepulta est, nonnullis oculos dolentibus saluti fuisse perhibent; qui cum suum caput eidem loculo apponentes orassent, mox doloris sive caliginis incommodum ab oculis amoverent. Laverunt igitur virgines corpus, et novis indutum vestibus intulerunt in ecclesiam, atque in eo quod adlatum erat sarcophago posuerunt, ubi usque hodie in magna veneratione habetur. Mirum vero in modum ita aptum corpori virginis sarcophagum inventum est, ac si ei specialiter praeparatum fuisset: et locus quoque capitis seorsum fabrefactus, ad mensuram capitis illius aptissime figuratus apparuit.

Est autem Elge in provincia Orientalium Anglorum regio familiarum circiter sexcentarum, in similitudinem insulae, vel paludibus, ut diximus, circumdata, vel aquis: unde et a copia anguillarum quae in iisdem paludibus capiuntur, nomen accepit; ubi monasterium habere desideravit memorata Christi famula, quoniam de provincia eorumdem Orientalium Anglorum ipsa, ut praefati sumus, carnis originem duxerat.

that when I was a girl, I did bear the superfluous burdens of necklaces: and I believe that the heavenly pity hath therefore willed me to be grieved with the pain in my neck, that so I may be acquitted from the guilt of superfluous vanity; whereas now instead of gold and pearls, the redness and burning of the swelling breaketh out of my neck." It happened, moreover, that by the touching of the same clothes both evil spirits were driven out of bodies that were possessed, and other diseases healed sometimes. Moreover, it is said that the coffin in which she was first buried did heal some that suffered in their eyes; which, when they set their heads to the same coffin and had prayed, by and by had the grief of their sore or dimness taken away from their eyes. The virgins therefore washed the body, and after putting thereon new clothes carried it into the church, and laid it in that coffin which had been brought, where it is kept unto this day and had in great reverence. Now the coffin was found fitted in so marvellous manner for the virgin's body, as if it had been of purpose made ready for her: and the place also of the head was made by itself severally, and seemed to be fashioned as just as could be for the bigness of her head.

Now the country of Ely is in the province of the East English, and containeth about 600 hides of land, and is compassed, as we said, like an island round about with either fens or water: wherefore too it hath had its name from the great store of eels which are plentifully taken in the same fens; in which isle the said handmaid of Christ desired to have a monastery, because, as we said before, she herself after the flesh was born of the province of the same East English.

CAP. XX

Hymnus de illa.

VIDETUR opportunum huic Historiae etiam hymnum virginitatis inserere, quem ante annos plurimos in laudem ac praeconium eiusdem reginae ac sponsae Christi, et ideo veraciter reginae, quia sponsae Christi, elegiaco metro composuimus; et imitari morem sacrae scripturae, cuius historiae carmina plurima indita, et haec metro ac versibus constat esse composita.

" Alma Deus Trinitas, quae saecula cuncta gubernas,
  Adnue iam coeptis, alma Deus Trinitas.
Bella Maro resonet, nos pacis dona canamus:
  Munera nos Christi, bella Maro resonet.
Carmina casta mihi, foedae non raptus Helenae:
  Luxus erit lubricis, carmina casta mihi.
Dona superna loquar, miserae non praelia Trojae;
  Terra quibus gaudet, dona superna loquar.
En Deus altus adit venerandae virginis alvum
  Liberet ut homines, en Deus altus adit.
Femina virgo parit mundi devota parentem,
  Porta Maria Dei, femina virgo parit.
Gaudet amica cohors, de virgine matre tonantis:
  Virginitate micans gaudet amica cohors.

---

[1] These verses with the recurrence of the beginning of the first line at the end of each couplet are called *echoing* or *serpentine*. They are also alphabetic.

CHAPTER XX

An Hymn concerning her.

It seemeth convenient to put also in this History an hymn of virginity, which many years past we made in the elegiac metre [1] in praise and laudation of the same queen and spouse of Christ, and therefore verily a queen, for that she is the spouse of Christ; and herein to follow the custom of Holy Scripture, in the history whereof many songs are put in among, which were, as is well known, made in metre and verse.

"O God, O gracious Trinity, in Whom all rule doth always stand,
O gracious God, the One in Three, aid Thou the theme we take in hand.
Of arms let Virgil's verse indite, sing we the pleasant fruits of peace:
Aeneas' wars let Virgil write, Christ's gifts to sing let us not cease.
My verse is chaste, it is not made to tell of sinful Helen's stelth:
My verse is chaste, such wanton trade write they that live in wanton wealth.
Of heavenly gifts to speak I long, not of the fights of piteous Troy;
Of heavenly gifts shall be my song, the which the earth doth now enjoy.
Behold, high God comes from above, pure womb of Virgin to possess:
Behold, high God comes for men's love, by freeing them from sin to bless.
A maiden mother bears a child, the parent of the world to be;
Born is a son of maiden mild, Mary the gate of God we see.
In her delight the blessed band, the mother maid of Him whose voice
Doth hold the thunder in command, in her the virgins bright rejoice.

Huius honor genuit casto de germine plures,
  Virgineos flores huius honor genuit.
Ignibus usta feris virgo non cessat Agatha,
  Eulalia et perfert ignibus usta feris.
Casta feras superat mentis pro culmine Tecla,
  Euphemia sacra casta feras superat.
Laeta ridet gladios ferro robustior Agnes,
  Caecilia infestos laeta ridet gladios,
Multus in orbe viget per sobria corda triumphus,
  Sobrietatis amor multus in orbe viget.
Nostra quoque egregia iam tempora virgo beavit:
  Aedilthryda nitet nostra quoque egregia.
Orta patre eximio, regali et stemmate clara:
  Nobilior Domino est, orta patre eximio.
Percipit inde decus reginae, et sceptra sub astris,
  Plus super astra manens, percipit inde decus.
Quid petis, alma, virum, sponso iam dedita summo?
  Sponsus adest Christus, quid petis, alma, virum?
Regis ut aetherei matrem iam credo sequaris:
  Tu quoque sis mater regis ut aetherei.
Sponsa dicata Deo bis sex regnaverat annis,
  Inque monasterio est sponsa dicata Deo.

---

[1] Sicilian martyr in the persecution of Decius.
[2] Spanish martyr in Diocletian's persecution.
[3] Honoured in the Greek Church as the first female martyr.
[4] Suffered in Bithynia in the tenth persecution.
[5] Early Roman martyr.
[6] Roman martyr and patroness of music.

Her worthiness hath made more spring of this chaste virgin stock and bough:
Her worthiness doth ever bring more virgin flowers to bud and blow.
The cruel flames, that virgin pure, when burned, shrank Agatha [1] not to bide,
The flames Eulalia [2] did endure, when she was in the furnace tried.
Before the beasts with gaping jaws pure Tecla's [3] courage did not fail,
Nor found Euphemia's [4] soul more cause before the savage beasts to quail.
The deadly sword with laughing look Agnes,[5] more strong than steel, surveyed,
Of deadly sword Cecilia [6] took great joy that she was undismayed.
The wide world through there flourisheth great triumphing of sober hearts;
The wide world through this nourisheth great love of chaste and sober parts.
So too our days with one are blest, a noble maid to call our own;
Our Ethelthryth now manifest with like bright glorious renown.
Of royal birth and line she came, her father famed for worth and might:
Of royal birth, yet now her fame is made more noble in God's sight.
Of him she had the sovereignty a queen on earth below to reign:
Of Him she hath the majesty on high in glory to remain.
Why seekst thou, gracious maid, a man, thou that art vowed to Christ above?
What other husband seekst thou then? Christ is thy only Spouse and Love.
I think that thou as she mayst do, the mother of the heavenly King;
Mayst be like her a mother too, and to thyself like glory bring.
This spouse of God, when she had passed twelve years in worldly pomp and pride,
She, spouse of God, made joyful haste in monastery to abide.

Tota sacrata polo celsis ubi floruit actis,
  Reddidit atque animam tota sacrata polo.
Virginis alma caro est tumulata bis octo Novembres,
  Nec putet in tumulo virginis alma caro.
Christe, tui est operis, quia vestis et ipsa sepulcro
  Inviolata nitet: Christe, tui est operis.
Ydros et ater abit sacrae pro vestis honore,
  Morbi diffugiunt, ydros et ater abit.
Zelus in hoste furit quondam qui vicerat Evam:
  Virgo triumphat ovans, zelus in hoste furit.
Aspice nupta Deo, quae sit tibi gloria terris:
  Quae maneat caelis, aspice nupta Deo.
Munera laeta capis festivis fulgida taedis,
  Ecce venit sponsus, munera laeta capis.
Et nova dulcisono modularis carmina plectro:
  Sponsa hymno exultas et nova dulcisono.
Nullus ab Altithroni comitatu segregat agni,
  Quam affectu tulerat nullus ab Altithroni."

[1] Her day is 17 Oct., *i.e.* A.D. xvi kal. Novembres.

Where she to heaven wholly bent flourished in deeds of virtue high:
From whence her soul to heaven went, to which she wholly did apply.
This virgin's body pure in ground had lain the space of sixteen year,[1]
Yet was that body sweet and sound as when it first was laid on bier.
O Christ, this was thine own work true: the very clothes about the corse,
O Christ, were whole and fair and new: for time on them had lost his force.
Away the serpent black[2] doth hie, the holy raiment honouring:
Away with him diseases fly, that to the devilish serpent cling.
The furious fiend that erst beguiled our mother Eve maliciously,
This fiend so fell a virgin mild doth put to flight ingloriously.
Lo, bride of God, see and behold what honour on the earth is thine:
O bride of God, a thousandfold awaits thee now in bliss divine.
The joyful gift thou dost possess, and torches light thee to thy home:
The joyful gift that grows no less, lo, Christ is now thy bridegroom come.
To Him on harp melodiously thou soundest sweet and tuneful strain,
To Him with psalm and harmony, new and sweet spouse, in glad refrain.
The Lamb that sits enthroned above shall have thee in His company,[3]
For from the Lamb's own bond of love none ever had dissevered thee."

[2] *Ydros* properly means water-snake, but is used for the serpent of Gen. iii. Black is the colour of fiends.

[3] Cf. Rev. xiv. 4.

CAP. XXI

Ut Theodorus episcopus inter Ecgfridum et Aedilredum reges pacem fecerit.

ANNO regni Ecgfridi nono, conserto gravi praelio inter ipsum et Aedilredum regem Merciorum iuxta fluvium Treanta, occisus est Aelfuini frater regis Ecgfridi, iuvenis circiter decem et octo annorum utrique provinciae multum amabilis. Nam et sororem eius quae dicebatur Osthryd, rex Aedilred habebat uxorem. Cumque materies belli acrioris et inimicitiae longioris inter reges populosque feroces videretur exorta, Theodorus Deo dilectus antistes divino functus auxilio, salutifera exhortatione coeptum tanti periculi funditus exstinguit incendium: adeo ut pacatis alterutrum regibus ac populis, nullius anima hominis pro interfecto regis fratre, sed debita solummodo multa pecuniae regi ultori daretur. Cuius foedera pacis multo exinde tempore inter eosdem reges eorumque regna durarunt.

CAP. XXII

Ut vincula cuiusdam captivi, cum pro eo missae cantarentur, soluta sint.

IN praefato autem praelio quo occisus est rex Aelfuini, memorabile quoddam factum esse constat, quod nequaquam silentio praetereundum arbitror, sed multorum saluti, si referatur, fore proficuum.

[1] The wergeld, the price at which each man was valued.

CHAPTER XXI

How the bishop Theodore made peace between the kings Egfrid and Ethelred [679].

The ninth year of the reign of Egfrid a sore battle was fought between him and Ethelred king of the Marchmen by the river of Trent, in which was slain Elfwine king Egfrid's brother, a young man of about 18 years of age and well beloved of both the countries. For his sister too, named Osthryth, was wife unto king Ethelred. And whereas there seemed to be arisen an occasion of sharper war and longer enmity between the high-minded kings and peoples, Theodore the bishop beloved of God, making use of divine help did by his wholesome exhortation utterly quench the fire of so great a peril begun: in such sort that the kings and people being pacified on both sides, the life of no man perished for the death of the king's brother, but only a due amercement of money [1] was given to the king that was the avenger. The bonds of which peace did a long time after endure between the same kings and their dominions.

CHAPTER XXII

How the fetters of a certain prisoner were loosed when masses were sung for him.

Now in the foresaid battle in which was slain king [2] Elfwine, a certain notable thing, as is well known, happened, which I think in no ways ought to be passed by in silence, but the telling thereof will profit the salvation of many. There was among

[2] Jointly with Egfrid.

Occisus est ibi inter alios de militia eius iuvenis, vocabulo Imma, qui cum die illo et nocte sequenti inter cadavera occisorum similis mortuo iaceret, tandem recepto spiritu revixit, ac residens sua vulnera, prout potuit, ipse alligavit: dein modicum requietus levavit se, et coepit abire sicubi amicos qui sui curam agerent, posset invenire. Quod dum faceret, inventus est, et captus a viris hostilis exercitus, et ad dominum ipsorum, comitem videlicet Aedilredi regis, adductus: a quo interrogatus quis esset, timuit se militem fuisse confiteri; rusticum se potius et pauperem, atque uxoreo vinculo conligatum fuisse respondit; et propter victum militibus adferendum in expeditionem se cum suis similibus venisse testatus est. At ille suscipiens eum, curam vulneribus egit; et ubi sanescere coepit, noctu eum ne aufugeret, vinciri praecepit. Nec tamen vinciri potuit: nam mox ut abiere qui vinxerant, eadem eius sunt vincula soluta.

Habebat enim germanum fratrem cui nomen erat Tunna, presbyterum et abbatem monasterii in civitate quae hactenus ab eius nomine Tunnacaestir cognominatur: qui cum eum in pugna peremptum audiret, venit quaerere si forte corpus eius invenire posset, inventumque alium illi per omnia simillimum, putavit ipsum esse: quem ad monasterium suum deferens, honorifice sepelivit, et pro absolutione animae eius saepius missas facere curavit. Quarum celebratione factum est quod dixi, ut nullus eum

[1] A.S. *gesith*. [2] Not identified. Towcester is not likely.

other a young thane of the king left for dead, called Imma, which after lying that day and the night following among the bodies of the slain men, like as he had been dead, at last recovered breath and came to life again, and sitting up bound his wounds himself as well as he could: after, resting himself a little, he arose up and began to go his way, seeking where he might find friends to take care of him. But as he so did, he was found and taken of men of the enemies' army, and brought unto their lord, to wit a retainer [1] of king Ethelred's: of whom being demanded what he was, he feared to confess that he had been a soldier; answering rather that he was a poor countryman and one that was bound with the tie of marriage; and testified that he had come to the campaign with them that were his like to bring victuals to the soldiers. Whereupon the retainer treated him well and had care for his wounds; and when he began to wax whole, he commanded him to be kept in bonds lest he should scape away by night. But yet he could not be held in bonds: for as soon as they that had bound him were gone, his same bonds were loosed.

For he had a brother german whose name was Tunna, a priest and abbot of a monastery in the city which of his name is called unto this day Tunnacaestir [2]: who, when he heard that his brother was slain in the battle, came to seek if he might haply find his body, where he, finding another that was in all points very like him, and thinking it to be him indeed, brought him to his monastery and buried him honourably, and did often times cause masses to be said for the absolution of his soul. By the celebration of which masses that which I said came

posset vincire, quin continuo solveretur. Interea comes qui eum tenebat, mirari, et interrogare coepit quare ligari non posset, an forte literas solutorias de qualibus fabulae ferunt, apud se haberet, propter quas ligari non posset. At ille respondit, nihil se talium artium nosse; "sed habeo fratrem," inquit, "presbyterum in mea provincia, et scio quia ille me interfectum putans, pro me missas crebras facit: et si nunc in alia vita essem, ibi anima mea per intercessiones eius solveretur a poenis." Dumque aliquanto tempore apud comitem teneretur, animadverterunt qui eum diligentius considerabant, ex vultu et habitu et sermonibus eius, quia non erat de paupere vulgo, ut dixerat, sed de nobilibus. Tunc secreto advocans eum comes, interrogavit eum intentius unde esset, promittens se nihil ei mali facturum pro eo, si simpliciter sibi quis fuisset, proderet. Quod dum ille faceret, ministrum se regis fuisse manifestans, respondit: "Et ego per singula tua responsa cognoveram quia rusticus non eras, et nunc dignus quidem es morte, quia omnes fratres et cognati mei in illa sunt pugna interempti; nec te tamen occidam, ne fidem mei promissi praevaricer."

Ut ergo convaluit, vendidit eum Lundoniam Freso cuidam; sed nec ab illo cum illuc duceretur ullatenus potuit alligari. Verum cum alia atque alia vinculorum ei genera hostes imponerent; cumque vidisset qui

[1] Charms written down and worn as amulets: Pl.
[2] Northumbria.

to pass, that no man could bind him, but that he was straightway loosed. In the meantime the retainer that kept him began to wonder and to enquire of him what the cause was that he could not be bound, and whether he chanced to have about him spells for loosing,[1] such as men talk of, that by the virtue of them he could not be bound. But he answered that he had no cunning in such arts; "but I have a brother," quoth he, "a priest in my country,[2] and I know that he thinks I am slain and doth often say masses for me: and if I were now in another life, my soul would there be loosed from pains through his intercessions." And while he was kept a certain space in the retainer's house, they that marked him more diligently, saw by his countenance, behaviour and talk that he was not of common poor sort of people, as he had said, but of good degree. Then the retainer calling him secretly did examine him more straitly of whence he was, promising that he would do him no harm therefor, if he would plainly show what he was. Which thing when he did and declared him to have been a thane of the king, the retainer answered: "And indeed I knew by thy several answers that thou wert no countryman, and thou art well worthy to die now, for that all my brethren and kinsmen were slain in that battle; but yet I will not put thee to death, that I prove not false to my promised word."

When therefore he was full cured, he sold him to a certain Frisian to go to London; but neither was he able to be bound by any means of the Frisian as he was led thither. But when his enemies did lay on him many and sundry kinds of fetters, and when he that had bought him had seen that he could be

emerat, vinculis eum non potuisse cohiberi, donavit ei facultatem sese redimendi si posset. A tertia autem hora quando missae fieri solebant, saepissime vincula solvebantur. At ille dato iureiurando ut rediret vel pecuniam illi pro se mitteret, venit Cantiam ad regem Hlotheri, qui erat filius sororis Aedilthrydae reginae de qua supra dictum est, quia et ipse quondam eiusdem reginae minister fuerat: petiitque et accepit ab eo pretium suae redemptionis, ac suo domino pro se, ut promiserat, misit.

Qui post haec patriam reversus atque ad suum fratrem perveniens, replicavit ex ordine cuncta quae sibi adversa, quaeve in adversis solatia provenissent: cognovitque referente illo, illis maxime temporibus sua fuisse vincula soluta quibus pro se missarum fuerant celebrata sollemnia. Sed et alia quae periclitanti ei commoda contigissent et prospera, per intercessionem fraternam et oblationem hostiae salutaris caelitus sibi fuisse donata intellexit. Multique haec a praefato viro audientes accensi sunt in fide ac devotione pietatis ad orandum, vel ad eleemosynas faciendas, vel ad offerendas Domino victimas sacrae oblationis, pro ereptione suorum qui de saeculo migraverant: intellexerunt enim quia sacrificium salutare ad redemptionem valeret et animae et corporis sempiternam.

Hanc mihi historiam etiam quidam eorum, qui ab ipso viro in quo facta est audiere, narrarunt: unde eam quia liquido comperi, indubitanter Historiae nostrae Ecclesiasticae inserendam credidi.

---

[1] Sexburg, p. 107.

holden in no bonds, he gave him his leave to ransom himself, if he were able. Now after the third hour when masses were wont to be said, his fetters were most often loosed. Whereupon he upon his oath to come again or send his ransom to the Frisian, came to Kent to king Lothere (who was son to the sister [1] of queen Ethelthryth of whom we have spoken before), for that he had himself too been sometime thane to the same queen: and sued to the king and obtained the price of his ransom, and sent it in place of himself to his owner, as he had promised.

And after this he returned to his own country, and coming to his brother unfolded in order all the adversities that had befallen him, and what comforts he had had in his adversities: and by what his brother told him he knew that his fetters had been loosed at those times specially at which the solemnities of the masses had been celebrated for him. Moreover, he understood that the other helps and succours that had happened to him in his danger had been given of the heavenly grace through his brother's intercession and offering of the wholesome host. And many on hearing these things from the foresaid man were kindled in faith and godly devoutness unto prayer, or to giving of alms, or to offering to the Lord hosts of the holy oblation, for the delivery of their friends that were departed this world: for they understood that the wholesome sacrifice was effectual to the everlasting ransoming both of soul and body.

This history was told me also of certain of them that heard it of the very man in whom it was done: and therefore having ascertained it clearly, I doubted no whit to put it into our Ecclesiastical History.

CAP. XXIII

De vita, et obitu Hildae abbatissae.

ANNO post hunc sequente, hoc est, anno Dominicae incarnationis sexcentesimo octogesimo, religiosissima Christi famula Hild, abbatissa monasterii quod dicitur Streaneshalch, ut supra retulimus, post multa quae fecit in terris opera caelestia, ad percipienda praemia vitae caelestis de terris ablata transivit die quinta decima Kalendarum Decembrium, cum esset annorum sexaginta sex: quibus aequa portione divisis, triginta tres primos in saeculari habitu nobilissime conversata complevit, et totidem sequentes nobilius in monachica vita Domino consecravit. Nam et nobilis natu erat, hoc est, filia nepotis Eduini regis, vocabulo Hererici: cum quo etiam rege, ad praedicationem beatae memoriae Paulini, primi Nordanhymbrorum episcopi, fidem et sacramenta Christi suscepit, atque haec usquedum ad eius visionem pervenire meruit, intemerata servavit.

Quae cum relicto habitu saeculari illi soli servire decrevisset, secessit ad provinciam Orientalium Anglorum: erat namque propinqua regis illius, desiderans exinde, si quo modo posset, derelicta patria et omnibus quaecumque habuerat, in Galliam pervenire, atque in monasterio Cale peregrinam pro Domino vitam ducere, quo facilius perpetuam in caelis patriam posset mereri. Nam et in eodem monasterio soror ipsius Heresuid, mater Alduulfi

---

[1] III. 25. [2] II. 9.
[3] Ethelhere, successor to Anna and husband of Hereswith.
[4] III. 8.

CHAPTER XXIII

Of the life and death of abbess Hild [614–680].

The year following after this, that is, in the 680th year of the Lord's incarnation, the most devout handmaid of Christ, Hild, abbess of the monastery that is called Whitby (as we before mentioned),[1] after many heavenly deeds that she did upon earth was taken away from the earth and passed away to receive the rewards of the life of heaven, the 17th day of November, when she was threescore and six years of age: the which number of years being divided in equal parts, she lived the first 33 full years in secular condition with most worthy life and conversation, and as many after did she dedicate more worthily to the Lord in monastical life. For she was come too of noble birth, that is to say, was daughter of king Edwin's nephew named Hereric: with which king also at the preaching of Paulinus of blessed memory,[2] the first bishop of the Northumbrians, she received the faith and sacraments of Christ, and did sincerely keep the same, until she deserved to attain to the sight of the Lord.

And when she had determined to forsake the secular condition and serve Him only, she departed to the province of the East English: for she was allied to the king there,[3] and from thence she desired, if by any means she might, to forsake her country and all that ever she had, and go into France, and lead a life abroad in the monastery of Cale [4] for the Lord's sake, that she might the more easily deserve an everlasting country in heaven: for in the same monastery too her sister Hereswith, mother to

regis Orientalium Anglorum, regularibus subdita disciplinis, ipso tempore coronam exspectabat aeternam: cuius aemulata exemplum, et ipsa proposito peregrinandi annum totum in praefata provincia retenta est: deinde ab Aidano episcopo in patriam revocata, accepit locum unius familiae ad septentrionalem plagam Viuri fluminis, ubi aeque anno uno monachicam cum perpaucis sociis vitam agebat.

Post haec facta est abbatissa in monasterio quod vocatur Herutcu; quod videlicet monasterium factum erat non multo ante a religiosa Christi famula Heiu, quae prima feminarum fertur in provincia Nordanhymbrorum propositum vestemque sanctimonialis habitus, consecrante Aidano episcopo, suscepisse. Sed illa post non multum tempus facti monasterii, secessit ad civitatem Calcariam quae a gente Anglorum Kaelcacaestir appellatur, ibique sibi mansionem instituit. Praelata autem regimini monasterii illius famula Christi Hild, mox hoc regulari vita per omnia, prout a doctis viris discere poterat, ordinare curabat: nam et episcopus Aidan, et quique noverant eam religiosi, pro insita ei sapientia et amore divini famulatus, sedulo eam visitare, obnixe amare, diligenter erudire solebant.

Cum ergo aliquot annos huic monasterio, regularis vitae institutioni multum intenta praeesset, contigit eam suscipere etiam construendum sive ordinandum monasterium in loco qui vocatur Streaneshalch, quod

[1] Tadcaster probably.

Aldwulf king of the East English, was at that very time subject to the rules of religious life, and was looking for the crown everlasting: whose example she followed, and was by her vow of sojourning abroad herself kept a whole year in the said province: after which, being called home again to her own country by bishop Aidan, she received a place of one hide of land on the north coast of the river Wear, in which she lived likewise by the space of one year a monastical life with a very small company.

After this she was made abbess in the monastery called Hartlepool; which indeed had been made a monastery not long before of the devout handmaid of Christ, Heiu, which is said to have been the first woman in the province of Northumberland that took the vow and dress of a nun's habit, being consecrated by bishop Aidan. But not long after the making of the monastery she departed thence to the city of Calcaria, which is called of the English race Kaelcacaestir,[1] and there she appointed to abide. Now Hild the handmaid of Christ being chosen to rule the monastery of Hartlepool did straight procure to dispose the same in all points with the rule of monastical life, in such wise as she could be instructed of learned men: for both bishop Aidan and as many religious persons as knew her, for the wisdom and love of godly service that was in her, were wont continually to visit, steadfastly to love, and diligently to instruct her.

For some years then she governed the monastery and was straitly given to forward monastical life and order, and meantime it was her chance to take in hand also the building and disposing of a monastery in the place which is called Whitby, which business

opus sibi iniunctum non segniter implevit. Nam eisdem quibus prius monasterium, etiam hoc disciplinis vitae regularis instituit: et quidem multam inibi quoque iustitiae, pietatis, et castimoniae, ceterarumque virtutum, sed maxime pacis et caritatis custodiam docuit: ita ut in exemplum primitivae ecclesiae nullus ibi dives, nullus esset egens, omnibus essent omnia communia, cum nihil cuiusquam esse videretur proprium. Tantae autem erat ipsa prudentiae, ut non solum mediocres quique in necessitatibus suis, sed etiam reges ac principes nonnunquam ab ea quaererent consilium, et invenirent. Tantum lectioni divinarum Scripturarum suos vacare subditos, tantum operibus iustitiae se exercere faciebat, ut facillime viderentur ibidem qui ecclesiasticum gradum, hoc est, altaris officium apte subirent, plurimi posse reperiri.

Denique quinque ex eodem monasterio postea episcopos vidimus, et hos omnes singularis meriti ac sanctitatis viros, quorum haec sunt nomina, Bosa, Aetla, Oftfor, Iohannes, et Vilfrid. De primo supra diximus, quod Eboraci fuerit consecratus antistes: de secundo breviter intimandum, quod in episcopatum Dorciccaestrae fuerit ordinatus: de ultimis infra dicendum est, quod eorum primus Hagustaldensis, secundus Eboracensis ecclesiae sit ordinatus episcopus. De medio nunc dicamus, quia cum in utroque Hildae abbatissae monasterio lectioni et observationi Scripturarum operam dedisset, tandem

[1] Agilbert, III. 7, is the last bishop of Dorchester named. Aetla's name does not appear in any of the lists of bishops, and this makes it doubtful to what province Dorchester in his time belonged; cf. Bright, 320.

being brought upon her she finished in no slothful manner. For she furnished this monastery also with the same rules of monastical life with which she had disposed the earlier one: and truly she did there teach also singularly to keep righteousness, godliness, chastity and all other virtues, but specially peace and charity: in such wise that after the example of the primitive Church there was therein none rich, none poor, and all things were common to all, seeing that nothing seemed peculiar to anyone. She was, moreover, of such wisdom that not only all mean persons in their times of need, but also kings and princes did sometime seek and find counsel of her. The men under her governance she made to bestow their time so well in the reading of the Holy Scriptures, and so busily in the exercise of the works of righteousness, that right easily it appeared that very many could there be found to take upon them fitly the rank of ecclesiastic, that is to say, the service of the altar.

In short, we have since seen five from the same monastery, afterwards bishops, and all these men of singular worth and holiness, whose names are: Bosa, Aetla, Oftfor, John and Wilfrid. Of the first we have said before, that he was consecrated bishop of York: of the second we must briefly state that he was ordained to the bishopric of Dorchester:[1] of the last two we must speak afterward, that the first of them was ordained bishop of Hexham, the second,[2] bishop of the church of York: of the middlemost let us now say that, after he had in both the monasteries of abbess Hild diligently applied to the reading and study of the Scriptures, at last desiring more

[2] Wilfrid II or junior.

perfectiora desiderans, venit Cantiam ad archiepiscopum beatae recordationis Theodorum: ubi postquam aliquandiu lectionibus sacris vacavit, etiam Romam adire curavit, quod eo tempore magnae virtutis aestimabatur: et inde cum rediens Brittaniam adiisset, divertit ad provinciam Huicciorum cui tunc rex Osric praefuit; ibique verbum fidei praedicans, simul et exemplum vivendi sese videntibus atque audientibus exhibens, multo tempore mansit. Quo tempore antistes provinciae illius, vocabulo Bosel, tanta erat corporis infirmitate depressus, ut officium episcopatus per se implere non posset: propter quod omnium iudicio praefatus vir in episcopatum pro eo electus, ac iubente Aedilredo rege, per Vilfridum beatae memoriae antistitem qui tunc temporis Mediterraneorum Anglorum episcopatum gerebat, ordinatus est: pro eo quod archiepiscopus Theodorus iam defunctus erat, et necdum alius pro eo ordinatus episcopus. In quam videlicet provinciam paulo ante, hoc est, ante praefatum virum Dei Boselum, vir strenuissimus et doctissimus, atque excellentis ingenii, vocabulo Tatfrid, de eiusdem abbatissae monasterio electus est antistes: sed priusquam ordinari posset, morte immatura praereptus est.

Non solum ergo praefata Christi ancilla et abbatissa Hild quam omnes qui noverant ob insigne pietatis et gratiae matrem vocare consueverant, in suo monasterio vitae exemplo praesentibus exstitit: sed etiam plurimis longe manentibus, ad quos felix industriae ac virtutis eius rumor pervenit, occasionem

[1] Hild was on the side of the Scots, III. 25.
[2] Bishop of Leicester 692–705.
[3] He died 690.

perfectness [1] he came to Kent to archbishop Theodore of blessed memory: where after spending some time in sacred studies he found also the means to go to Rome, which at that time was accounted a thing of great merit: and from thence returning home, when he had reached Britain, he went away unto the province of the Hwiccas, over which king Osric reigned then; and there he remained a long time preaching the word of faith and likewise giving an example of life to them that saw and heard him. At which time the bishop of that province, named Bosel, was so grieved with sickness of body that he could not of himself fulfil the office of the bishopric: for which thing's sake by all men's judgment the foresaid man was chosen bishop in his place, and at the commandment of king Ethelred was ordained by the hands of bishop Wilfrid of blessed memory, who at that time held the bishopric of the Middle English: [2] for that archbishop Theodore was now dead [3] and none other as yet ordained bishop for him. And over this province of the Hwiccas a little before, that is to wit, before the said man of God, Bosel, one Tatfrid, a man of very stout heart and well learned and of excellent wit, was chosen bishop out of the monastery of the same abbess: but he was taken and died before his time, ere that he might be ordained.

The foresaid handmaid of Christ and abbess, Hild, whom all that knew her were wont to call mother to mark her grace and godliness, did not only in her own monastery stand forth as an example of life to them that were with her: but also to very many that were far off, to whom the happy report of her diligence and goodness came, she ministered

salutis et correctionis ministravit. Oportebat namque impleri somnium quod mater eius Bregusuid in infantia eius vidit: quae cum vir eius Hereric exularet sub rege Brettonum Cerdice, ubi et veneno periit, vidit per somnium, quasi subito sublatum eum quaesierit cum omni diligentia, nullumque eius uspiam vestigium apparuerit. Verum cum sollertissime illum quaesisset, extemplo se reperire sub veste sua monile pretiosissimum: quod dum attentius consideraret, tanti fulgore luminis refulgere videbatur, ut omnes Brittaniae fines illius gratia splendoris impleret. Quod nimirum somnium veraciter in filia eius de qua loquimur, expletum est: cuius vita non sibi solummodo, sed multis bene vivere volentibus exempla operum lucis praebuit.

Verum illa cum multis annis huic monasterio praeesset placuit pio Provisori salutis nostrae, sanctam eius animam longa etiam infirmitate carnis examinari, ut iuxta exemplum apostoli, virtus eius in infirmitate perficeretur. Percussa etenim febribus, acri coepit ardore fatigari; et per sex continuos annos eadem molestia laborare non cessabat: in quo toto tempore nunquam ipsa vel Conditori suo gratias agere, vel commissum sibi gregem et publice et privatim docere praetermittebat. Nam suo praedocta exemplo, monebat omnes, et in salute accepta corporis Domino obtemperanter serviendum, et in adversis rerum sive infirmitatibus membrorum fideliter Domino esse gratias semper agendas. Septimo

[1] 2 Cor. xii. 9.

occasion of salvation and amendment. For it was meet that the dream should be fulfilled, which, when Hild was an infant, was seen of her mother Breguswid: who, when her husband Heriric was an outlaw under Cerdic king of the Britons (where also he died of poison), saw in a dream, as it were, that he was suddenly taken away and sought for of her with all diligence, and no token of him anywhere did appear. But when she had sought very busily for him, she found suddenly a very precious necklace under her garment: which as she did well mark and consider, it seemed to glisten with brightness of so great a light that it filled all the borders of Britain with the grace of its clearness. The which dream without doubt was truly brought to fulfilment in her daughter of whom we speak: whose life, not only to herself but to many that would live well, did give examples of the works of light.

But when she was many years over this monastery, it pleased the merciful Worker of our salvation, that her holy soul should also be tried with long weakness of the flesh, that after the example of the apostle her goodness should be made perfect in weakness.[1] For she was stricken with fevers and began to be vexed with the sore heat thereof; and for six years continuously she ceased not to suffer of the same trouble: in all which time she did never let pass either to give thanks to her Creator herself, or to teach openly and privately the flock committed to her charge. For taught beforehand by her own example she warned them all, both that they should serve the Lord duly when He giveth bodily health, and should faithfully give thanks to the Lord in worldly adversities or sicknesses of the

ergo suae infirmitatis anno, converso ad interanea dolore, ad diem pervenit ultimum, et circa galli cantum, percepto viatico sacrosanctae communionis, cum accersitis ancillis Christi quae erant in eodem monasterio, de servanda eas invicem, immo cum omnibus pace evangelica admoneret; inter verba exhortationis laeta mortem vidit, immo, ut verbis Domini loquar, de morte transivit ad vitam.

Qua videlicet nocte Dominus omnipotens obitum ipsius in alio longius posito monasterio quod ipsa eodem anno construxerat et appellatur Hacanos, manifesta visione revelare dignatus est. Erat in ipso monasterio quaedam sanctimonialis femina, nomine Begu, quae triginta et amplius annos dedicata Domino virginitate, in monachica conversatione serviebat. Haec tunc in dormitorio sororum pausans, audivit subito in aere notum campanae sonum, quo ad orationes excitari vel convocari solebant, cum quis eorum de saeculo fuisset evocatus: apertisque, ut sibi videbatur, oculis aspexit, detecto domus culmine, fusam desuper lucem omnia replevisse: cui videlicet luci dum sollicita intenderet, vidit animam praefatae Dei famulae in ipsa luce comitantibus ac ducentibus angelis ad caelum ferri. Cumque somno excussa videret ceteras pausantes circa se sorores, intellexit vel in somnio vel in visione mentis ostensum sibi esse quod viderat. Statimque exsurgens nimio timore perterrita cucurrit ad vir-

[1] Near Whitby.

limbs. In the seventh year then of her sickness, the pain turning toward the inward parts, she came to her last day, and about the crowing of the cock, after she had received the voyage-provision of holy housel, she called unto her the handmaids of Christ, that were in the same monastery, and as she counselled them to keep the peace of the Gospel amongst themselves, yea rather with all men; in the midst of her words of exhortation she gladly beheld her death, yea rather, to speak with the Lord's words, she passed from death unto life.

In which night indeed the almighty Lord vouchsafed to reveal her death by a clear vision in another monastery that was a good way off, called Hackness,[1] the which she had herself built the same year. There was in that same monastery a certain nun named Begu which had been dedicated to the Lord in virginity for thirty years and more, and served Him in monastical conversation. This nun taking her rest at that time in the sisters' dortoir heard suddenly in the air the known sound of the bell, wherewith they were wont to be awaked or called together, whenas any of them had been called out of the world: and opening her eyes (as she thought), she saw the roof of the house uncovered and all filled with light poured from above: and as she earnestly marked this light, she saw the soul of the foresaid handmaid of God in that very light carried toward heaven, accompanied and led by angels. And as she started up out of her sleep and saw the other sisters taking their rest about her, she understood that that which she had seen was shewn her either in a dream or in a vision of the mind. And straightway she rose up for overmuch fear that she

ginem quae tunc monasterio abbatissae vice praefuit, cui nomen erat Frigyd, fletuque ac lacrymis multum perfusa, ac suspiria longa trahens nuntiavit, matrem illarum omnium Hild abbatissam iam migrasse de saeculo, et se aspectante cum luce immensa ducibus angelis ad aeternae limina lucis et supernorum consortia civium ascendisse. Quod cum illa audisset, suscitavit cunctas sorores, et in ecclesiam convocatas, orationibus ac psalmis pro anima matris operam dare monuit. Quod cum residuo noctis tempore diligenter agerent, venerunt primo diluculo fratres qui eius obitum nuntiarent, a loco ubi defuncta est. At illae respondentes dixerunt, se prius eadem cognovisse: et cum exponerent per ordinem quomodo haec vel quando didicissent, inventum est, eadem hora transitum eius illis ostensum esse per visionem, qua illam referebant exisse de mundo. Pulchraque rerum concordia procuratum est divinitus, ut cum illi exitum eius de hac vita viderent, tunc isti introitum eius in perpetuam animarum vitam cognoscerent. Distant autem inter se monasteria haec tredecim ferme millibus passuum.

Ferunt autem quod eadem nocte, in ipso quoque monasterio ubi praefata Dei famula obiit, cuidam virginum Deo devotarum quae illam immenso amore diligebat, obitus illius in visione apparuerit, quae animam eius cum angelis ad caelum ire conspexerit, atque hoc ipsa qua factum est hora, his quae secum

had and ran to the virgin which was then over the monastery in the abbess' stead, whose name was Frigyth, and bathed with the tears of her much weeping, and drawing long sighs, told her that the mother of them all, abbess Hild, was now departed this world, and had with a marvellous great light, which she saw, and in the company of angels, ascended up to the gates of everlasting light and fellowship of the citizens on high. Which when Frigyth had heard, she roused all the sisters and calling them to church counselled them to be occupied in prayers and psalms for the soul of their mother. And as they diligently did this the rest of the night, at the break of the day there came brethren from the place where Hild died to bring word of her departing. Whereupon the sisters answering said that the same was known of them before: and declaring in order how and when they had learned this, it was found that her passing was shewn them by the vision at the same hour she had passed out of the world according to the report. And with a goodly agreement of events it was by the work of God so disposed, that when the one saw her departing from this life, at that time did the other know her entering into the everlasting life of souls. Moreover, these monasteries are distant asunder almost 13 miles.

It is further reported that in the very monastery also where the foresaid handmaid of God died, one of the virgins vowed to God, that loved her with an exceeding great love, had her passing shewed unto her the same night by a vision, for she saw Hild's soul go to heaven with angels, and this, the very same hour it was done, she declared plainly to those

erant famulis Christi manifeste narraverit, easque ad orandum pro anima eius, etiam priusquam cetera congregatio eius obitum cognovisset, excitaverit. Quod ita fuisse factum mox congregationi mane facto innotuit. Erat enim haec ipsa hora cum aliis nonnullis Christi ancillis in extremis monasterii locis seorsum posita, ubi nuper venientes ad conversationem [1] feminae solebant probari, donec regulariter institutae in societatem congregationis susciperentur.

CAP. XXIV

Quod in monasterio eius fuerit frater, cui donum canendi sit divinitus concessum.

In huius monasterio abbatissae fuit frater quidam divina gratia specialiter insignis, quia carmina religioni et pietati apta facere solebat; ita ut quicquid ex divinis literis per interpretes disceret, hoc ipse post pusillum verbis poeticis maxima suavitate et compunctione compositis, in sua, id est, Anglorum lingua proferret. Cuius carminibus multorum saepe animi ad contemptum saeculi, et appetitum sunt vitae caelestis accensi. Et quidem et alii post illum in gente Anglorum religiosa poemata facere tentabant;

[1] Should perhaps be *conversionem*, Pl.

---

[1] The sisters were sent for by the abbess, as stated earlier.
[2] And so professed nuns.

handmaids of Christ that were with her, and called them up to pray for Hild's soul, even before the rest of the company knew of her death.[1] Which thing to have been so was by and by made known to the company when morning came. For this nun at that very hour was with some other handmaids of Christ laid apart in the outmost places of the monastery, where the women newly coming to religious life were wont to be under probation, until they were instructed in the rule and order and were received into the fellowship of the community.[2]

CHAPTER XXIV

How that in her monastery there was a brother to whom the gift of singing was divinely given.

In the monastery of this abbess there was a certain brother made notable by a grace of God specially given, for that he was wont to make songs fit for religion and godliness;[3] insomuch that, whatsoever of the divine writings he learned by them that expounded them, he set it forth after a little time with poetical language, put together with very great sweetness and pricking of the heart, in his own, that is to say, the English tongue. With whose songs the minds of many men were oft inflamed to the contempt of the world and desire of the heavenly life. And indeed other too among the English people after him assayed to make religious

[3] The story and the name of Caedmon are known to us only from Bede. A considerable body of verse has come down under his name, but modern criticism does not hold it all to be the work of one author.

sed nullus eum aequiparare potuit. Namque ipse non ab hominibus, neque per hominem institutus canendi artem didicit; sed divinitus adiutus gratis canendi donum accepit. Unde nihil unquam frivoli et supervacui poematis facere potuit; sed ea tantummodo quae ad religionem pertinent, religiosam eius linguam decebant. Siquidem in habitu saeculari usque ad tempora provectioris aetatis constitutus nil carminum aliquando didicerat. Unde nonnunquam in convivio, cum esset laetitiae causa decretum ut omnes per ordinem cantare deberent, ille ubi adpropinquare sibi citharam cernebat, surgebat a media coena et egressus ad suam domum repedabat.

Quod dum tempore quodam faceret, et relicta domo convivii egressus esset ad stabula iumentorum quorum ei custodia nocte illa erat delegata, ibique hora competenti membra dedisset sopori, adstitit ei quidam per somnium, eumque salutans, ac suo appellans nomine: "Caedmon," inquit, "canta mihi aliquid." At ille respondens, "Nescio," inquit, "cantare; nam et ideo de convivio egressus huc secessi, quia cantare non poteram." Rursum ille qui cum eo loquebatur, "Attamen," ait, "mihi cantare habes," "Quid," inquit, "debeo cantare?" At ille, "Canta," inquit, "principium creaturarum." Quo accepto responso, statim ipse coepit cantare in laudem Dei Conditoris versus, quos nunquam audierat, quorum iste est sensus; "Nunc laudare debemus auctorem regni caelestis, potentiam Creatoris, et consilium illius, facta Patris gloriae; quomodo ille, cum sit aeternus Deus, omnium miraculorum

---

[1] Cf. Gal. i. 1.

[2] Beer-drinking, in King Alfred's translation.

poems; but no man could match his cunning. For he himself learned the art of singing without being taught of men nor of men's help;[1] but he received the gift of singing freely by the aid of God. And therefore he could never make any fond or vain poem, but only such as belong to religion befitted his religious mouth. For as long time as he was settled in secular life, until he was well stricken in age, he had at no time learned any songs. And so it was that sometimes at the table,[2] when the company was set to be merry and had agreed that each man should sing in his course, he, when he saw the harp to be coming near him, would rise up at midst of supper and going out get him back to his own house.

And as he did so on a certain time, and leaving the house of feasting had gone out to the stable of the beasts which had been appointed him to look to that night, and there at the fitting hour had bestowed his limbs to rest, there stood by him a certain man in a dream and bade him God speed, and calling him by his name said to him: "Caedmon, sing me something!" Whereupon he answering said: "I know not how to sing; for that too is the matter why I came out from the table to this place apart, because I could not sing." "But yet," quoth he again that spake with him, "thou hast to sing to me." "What," quoth he, "should I sing?" Whereupon the other said: "Sing the beginning of the creatures!" At which answer he began forthwith to sing in praise of God the Creator verses which he had never heard before, of which the sense is this: "Now ought we to praise the Maker of the heavenly kingdom, the power of the Creator and His counsel, the acts of the Father of glory; how He, being God eternal,

auctor exstitit; qui primo filiis hominum caelum pro culmine tecti, dehinc terram custos humani generis omnipotens creavit." Hic est sensus, non autem ordo ipse verborum quae dormiens ille canebat: neque enim possunt carmina, quamvis optime composita, ex alia in aliam linguam ad verbum sine detrimento sui decoris ac dignitatis transferri. Exsurgens autem a somno, cuncta quae dormiens cantaverat memoriter retinuit, et eis mox plura in eundem modum verba Deo digni carminis adiunxit.

Veniensque mane ad villicum qui sibi praeerat, quid doni percepisset indicavit, atque ad abbatissam perductus, iussus est, multis doctioribus viris praesentibus, indicare somnium et dicere carmen, ut universorum iudicio quid vel unde esset quod referebat, probaretur. Visumque est omnibus, caelestem ei a Domino concessam esse gratiam. Exponebantque illi quendam sacrae historiae sive doctrinae sermonem, praecipientes eum, si posset, hunc in modulationem carminis transferre. At ille suscepto negotio abiit, et mane rediens, optimo carmine quod iubebatur, compositum reddidit. Unde mox abbatissa amplexata gratiam Dei in viro, saecularem illum habitum relinquere, et monachicum suscipere propositum docuit, susceptumque in monasterium cum omnibus suis fratrum cohorti adsociavit, iussitque illum seriem sacrae historiae doceri. At ipse cuncta

[1] Of this hymn there are two versions in Saxon, Pl. ii. 251.

was the author of all miracles; Which first created unto the children of men heaven for the top of their dwelling-place, and thereafter the almighty Keeper of mankind created the earth."[1] This is the sense but not the selfsame order of the words which he sang in his sleep: for songs, be they never so well made, cannot be turned of one tongue into another, word for word, without loss to their grace and worthiness. Now on rising from slumber he remembered still all the things that he had sung in his sleep, and did by and by join thereto in the same measure more words of the song worthy of God.

And coming on the morrow to the town reeve under whom he was, he shewed unto him what gift he had received; and being brought to the abbess, he was commanded in the presence of many learned men to tell his dream and rehearse the song, that it might by the judgment of them all be tried what or whence the thing was which he reported. And it seemed to them all, that a heavenly grace was granted him of the Lord. And they recited unto him the process of a holy story or lesson, bidding him, if he could, to turn the same into metre and verse. Whereupon he undertaking so to do went his way, and on the morrow came again and brought the same which they had required of him, made in very good verse. Wherefore by and by the abbess embracing the grace of God in the man, instructed him to forsake the secular habit and take upon him the monastical vow, and when he had so done she placed him in the company of the brethren with all them that were with her, and gave commandment for him to be instructed in the regular course of holy history. But he by thinking again with

quae audiendo discere poterat, rememorando secum et quasi mundum animal ruminando, in carmen dulcissimum convertebat; suaviusque resonando, doctores suos vicissim auditores sui faciebat. Canebat autem de creatione mundi, et origine humani generis, et tota Genesis historia, de egressu Israel ex Aegypto et ingressu in terram repromissionis, de aliis plurimis sacrae Scripturae historiis, de incarnatione Dominica, passione, resurrectione, et ascensione in caelum, de Spiritus Sancti adventu, et apostolorum doctrina. Item de terrore futuri iudicii, et horrore poenae gehennalis, ac dulcedine regni caelestis multa carmina faciebat; sed et alia perplura de beneficiis et iudiciis divinis, in quibus cunctis homines ab amore scelerum abstrahere, ad dilectionem vero et sollertiam bonae actionis excitare curabat. Erat enim vir multum religiosus, et regularibus disciplinis humiliter subditus; adversum vero illos qui aliter facere volebant, zelo magni fervoris accensus: unde et pulchro vitam suam fine conclusit.

Nam propinquante hora sui decessus, quatuordecim diebus, praeveniente corporea infirmitate, pressus est; adeo tamen moderate, ut et loqui toto eo tempore posset et ingredi. Erat autem in proximo casa, in qua infirmiores et qui prope morituri esse videbantur, induci solebant. Rogavit ergo ministrum suum vespere incumbente, nocte qua de saeculo erat exiturus, ut in ea sibi locum quiescendi

himself upon all that he could hear and learn, and chewing thereon as a clean beast cheweth the cud, would turn it into very sweet song; and by melodiously singing the same again would make his teachers to become in their turn his hearers. Now he sang of the creation of the world, and beginnings of mankind, and all the story of Genesis, of the going of Israel out of Egypt, and their entering in the land of promise, and of very many other histories of Holy Scripture, of the incarnation of the Lord, of His passion, resurrection and ascension into heaven, of the coming of the Holy Ghost, and the teaching of the apostles. Also he would make many songs of the dread of judgment to come, of the terror of the pains of hell, and of the sweetness of the kingdom of heaven; moreover, many other songs of the divine benefits and judgments, in all which his endeavour was to pull men away from the love of wickedness and stir them up to the love and readiness to do well. For he was a man very devout and humbly obedient to the discipline of the rules; but very zealous and fervently inflamed against them that would do otherwise: wherefore too he closed his life with a goodly end.

For when the hour of his departing was at hand, he was taken before with bodily sickness which was heavy upon him fourteen days; and yet so temperately, that he might all that time both speak and walk. Now there was thereby a building wherein they that were sick, and such as seemed near to die, were wont to be brought. He desired, therefore, him that served him, at the falling of evening on the night that he was to depart from the world, to provide him a place to rest in that building: and

praepararet: qui miratus cur hoc rogaret, qui nequaquam adhuc moriturus esse videbatur, fecit tamen quod dixerat. Cumque ibidem positi vicissim aliqua gaudente animo, una cum eis qui ibidem ante inerant, loquerentur ac iocarentur, et iam mediae noctis tempus esset transcensum, interrogavit, sit eucharistiam intus haberent. Respondebant, " Quid opus est eucharistia? neque enim mori adhuc habes qui tam hilariter nobiscum velut sospes loqueris." Rursus ille: " Et tamen," ait, " afferte mihi eucharistiam." Qua accepta in manu, interrogavit, si omnes placidum erga se animum, et sine querela controversiae ac rancoris haberent. Respondebant omnes, placidissimam se mentem ad illum, et ab omni ira remotam habere: eumque vicissim rogabant, placidam erga ipsos mentem habere. Qui confestim respondit: " Placidam ego mentem, filioli, erga omnes Dei famulos gero." Sicque se caelesti muniens viatico, vitae alterius ingressui paravit; et interrogavit, quam prope esset hora qua fratres ad dicendas Domino laudes nocturnas excitari deberent. Respondebant, " Non longe est." At ille: " Bene, ergo exspectemus horam illam." Et signans se signo sanctae crucis, reclinavit caput ad cervical, modicumque obdormiens, ita cum silentio vitam finivit. Sicque factum est ut quomodo simplici ac pura mente tranquillaque devotione Domino servierat, ita etiam tranquilla morte mundum relinquens ad eius visionem veniret, illaque lingua quae tot

the other marvelling why he desired this, when he seemed nothing likely to die yet, nevertheless did as he was bid. And when they were laid in the same place, and were having some merry talking and sporting among themselves and them that were there before, and the season of midnight was now passed, he asked whether they had the sacrament there within. They answered: "What need is there of the sacrament, for your time is not come to die yet, that art so merrily talking with us as a man in good health." "And yet," quoth he again, "do ye bring me hither the sacrament." Which when he had taken in his hand, he asked them, whether they were all of a quiet mind toward him, and without complaint of quarrel and bitterness. They answered all that they were very peaceably disposed toward him and were far from all wrath: and they asked him in their turn to have a quiet mind toward them. And he forthwith answered: "I do bear, my dear children, a quiet mind toward all God's servants." And so arming himself with the heavenly voyage-provision he made him ready to enter into the other life; and asked how nigh the hour was at which the brethren should be roused to say their night lauds to the Lord. "It is not far off," answered they. "Well then," quoth he thereat, "let us tarry for that hour." And signing himself with the sign of the holy cross, he laid his head on the bolster, and falling a little in slumber so ended his life in silence. And thus was it brought about that, even as he had served the Lord with a simple and pure mind and peaceful devoutness, so likewise leaving the world with a peaceful death he might come to His sight, and that tongue, which had

salutaria verba in laudem conditoris composuerat, ultima quoque verba in laudem ipsius, signando sese, et spiritum suum in manus eius commendando clauderet: qui etiam praescius sui obitus exstitisse, ex his quae narravimus, videtur.

CAP. XXV

Qualis visio cuidam viro Dei apparuerit, priusquam monasterium Coludanae urbis esset incendio consumptum.

His temporibus monasterium virginum quod Coludi Urbem cognominant, cuius et supra meminimus, per culpam incuriae flammis absumptum est. Quod tamen a malitia inhabitantium in eo, et praecipue illorum qui maiores esse videbantur contigisse, omnes qui novere facillime potuerunt advertere. Sed non defuit puniendis admonitio divinae pietatis qua correcti, per ieiunia, fletus et preces iram a se, instar Ninivitarum, iusti Iudicis averterent.

Erat namque in eodem monasterio vir de genere Scottorum, Adamnanus vocabulo, ducens vitam in continentia et orationibus multum Deo devotam, ita ut nihil unquam cibi vel potus, excepta die Dominica et quinta sabbati perciperet; saepe autem noctes integras pervigil in oratione transigeret. Quae quidem illi districtio vitae arctioris, primo ex

[1] Not the abbot of Iona, V. 15.

framed so many wholesome words in the praise of the Creator, might also close up its last words in His praise, by the signing of himself and commending his spirit into His hands; and by these things that we have told it appeareth also that he had known beforehand of his departing.

CHAPTER XXV

What manner of vision appeared to a certain man of God, before that the monastery of the town of Coludi was consumed with fire.

About this time the monastery of virgins which they call Coldingham, of which too we have made mention above, was through fault of negligence destroyed with fire. Which thing notwithstanding happened by reason of the wickedness of them that dwelt therein, and especially of them which seemed to be the elders thereof, as all that knew it could very easily see. But there lacked not to them that should be punished the warning of God's pitifulness, whereby they might be amended, and, like the Ninevites, turn away the wrath of the just Judge from them by fastings, weeping and prayers.

For in the same monastery there was a man of Scottish race, named Adamnan,[1] leading a very devout life unto God in continence and prayer; in such sort that he did never take food nor drink, save only on the Sunday and the fifth day after the Sabbath; and farther oftentimes passed whole nights watching in prayer. And this straitness of hard life had fallen to him at the first of necessity to

necessitate emendandae suae pravitatis obvenerat, sed procedente tempore necessitatem in consuetudinem verterat.

Siquidem in adolescentia sua sceleris aliquid commiserat, quod commissum, ubi ad cor suum rediit, gravissime exhorruit, et se pro illo puniendum a districto Iudice timebat. Accedens ergo ad sacerdotem a quo sibi sperabat iter salutis posse demonstrari, confessus est reatum suum, petiitque ut consilium sibi daret quo posset fugere a ventura ira. Qui audito eius commisso dixit: " Grande vulnus grandioris curam medelae desiderat: et ideo ieiuniis, psalmis et orationibus, quantum vales, insiste, quo praeoccupando faciem Domini in confessione propitium eum invenire merearis." At ille quem nimius reae conscientiae tenebat dolor, et internis peccatorum vinculis quibus gravabatur, ocius desiderabat absolvi: " Adolescentior sum," inquit, " aetate, et vegetus corpore: quidquid mihi imposueris agendum, dummodo salvus fiam in die Domini, totum facile feram, etiamsi totam noctem stando in precibus peragere, si integram septimanam iubeas abstinendo transigere." Qui dixit: " Multum est ut tota septimana absque alimento corporis perdures; sed biduanum vel triduanum sat est observare ieiunium. Hoc facito, donec post modicum tempus rediens ad te, quid facere debeas, et quamdiu poenitentiae insistere, tibi plenius ostendam." Quibus dictis, et descripta illi mensura poenitendi, abiit sacerdos,

correct his evil living, but in process of time he had turned the necessity into a custom.

For whereas in his youth he had committed some grievous offence, and when the thought of this that he had done came back to his heart, he trembled thereat exceedingly and feared the punishment of the sharp Judge upon him for the same. Resorting, therefore, to a priest and hoping of him to be able to learn a way of salvation for himself, he confessed his sin and desired him to give him counsel whereby he might flee from the wrath to come. And the priest, when he had heard his offence, said: "A great wound requireth a greater cure and medicine: and therefore give thyself to fastings, psalms and prayers, as much as thou art able, to the end that first coming before the face of the Lord in confession thou mayest deserve to find Him merciful unto thee." But he for the passing grief of the guilty conscience that held him, and desiring to be sooner assoiled too of the inward bonds of the sins wherewith he was laden, said: "I am yet young of age and strong of body: whatsoever ye put upon me to do, so that I may be saved in the day of the Lord, I will easily bear it all, even if ye bid me to stand the whole night and spend it in prayers, if ye bid me pass over the whole week in abstinence." "It is much," quoth the priest, "to endure the whole week without sustenance of the body; but it sufficeth to keep fast two or three days at once. This do thou, until I come again to thee after a short time, and shew thee more fully what thou must do and how long thou must continue in penance." After which words the priest appointed the measure of his penance and went his way, and through a

et ingruente causa subita, secessit Hiberniam unde originem duxerat, neque ultra ad eum iuxta suum condictum rediit. At ipse memor praecepti eius simul et promissi sui, totum se lacrymis poenitentiae, vigiliis sanctis, et continentiae mancipavit; ita ut quinta solum sabbati et Dominica, sicut praedixi, reficeret, ceteris septimanae diebus ieiunus permaneret. Cumque sacerdotem suum Hiberniam secessisse ibique defunctum esse audisset, semper ex eo tempore iuxta condictum eius memoratum, continentiae modum observabat; et quod causa divini timoris semel ob reatum compunctus coeperat, iam causa divini amoris delectatus praemiis indefessus agebat.

Quod dum multo tempore sedulus exsequeretur, contigit eum die quadam de monasterio illo longius egressum, comitante secum uno de fratribus, peracto itinere redire: qui cum monasterio propinquarent et aedificia illius sublimiter erecta aspicerent, solutus est in lacrymis vir Dei, et tristitiam cordis vultu indice prodebat. Quod intuens comes, quare faceret inquisivit. At ille: "Cuncta," inquit, "haec quae cernis aedificia publica vel privata, in proximo est ut ignis absumens in cinerem convertat." Quod ille audiens, mox ut intraverunt monasterium, matri congregationis, vocabulo Aebbae, curavit indicare. At illa merito turbata de tali praesagio vocavit ad

sudden occasion that befell he passed into Ireland, where he was born, and came not to him again as he had agreed to do. Yet the young man, remembering both his commandment and his own promise as well, gave himself wholly to tears of repentance, holy watchings and continence; in such wise that, as I said before, he took sustenance only on the fifth day after the Sabbath and on Sunday, and continually fasted all the other days of the week. And when he had heard that his ghostly father was gone into Ireland and had died there, ever after from that time he kept this measure of restraint that was agreed on, as hath been said; and the thing which he had once begun for compunction of his sin because of the fear of God, this he now did without weariness from delight for the reward that followed because of the love of God.

And as he now long time continued diligently the same, it chanced that on a certain day he went out of that monastery a good way, having with him one of the brethren in his company, and when their journey was finished they were returning home: and as they drew near to the monastery and beheld the goodly high buildings of the same, the man of God burst out into tears and by his face betrayed the heaviness of his heart. Which thing, when his fellow saw, he asked him why he did so. Whereat he said: "All these buildings that thou seest, both common and private, shall shortly be turned to ashes by devouring fire." Which the other hearing, as soon as they came into the monastery, found the means to tell the mother of the convent, named Ebba. Whereat she being troubled at such a foretelling, as good cause was, called the man unto

se virum, et diligentius ab eo rem, vel unde hoc ipse nosset, inquirebat. Qui ait: "Nuper occupatus noctu vigiliis et psalmis, vidi adstantem mihi subito quendam incogniti vultus: cuius praesentia cum essem exterritus, dixit mihi ne timerem; et quasi familiari me voce alloquens, "Bene facis," inquit, "qui tempore isto nocturno quietis non somno indulgere, sed vigiliis et orationibus insistere maluisti." At ego, "Novi," inquam, "multum mihi esse necesse vigiliis salutaribus insistere, et pro meis erratibus sedulo Dominum deprecari." Qui adiciens, "Verum," inquit, "dicis, quia et tibi et multis opus est peccata sua bonis operibus redimere, et cum cessant a laboribus rerum temporalium, tunc pro appetitu aeternorum bonorum liberius laborare; sed hoc tamen paucissimi faciunt. Siquidem modo totum hoc monasterium ex ordine perlustrans singulorum casas ac lectos inspexi, et neminem ex omnibus praeter te erga sanitatem animae suae occupatum reperi: sed omnes prorsus et viri et feminae aut somno torpent inerti, aut ad peccata vigilant. Nam et domunculae quae ad orandum vel legendum factae erant, nunc in commessationum, potationum, fabulationum, et ceterarum sunt inlecebrarum cubilia conversae; virgines quoque Deo dictae, contempta reverentia suae professionis, quotiescumque vacant, texendis subtilioribus indumentis operam dant quibus aut seipsas ad vicem sponsarum in periculum sui status adornent, aut externorum sibi virorum amicitiam comparent. Unde merito loco huic et habi-

her and enquired the matter of him diligently, and how he himself knew the same. And he said: "Of late being busied at night in watching and saying of psalms, I suddenly saw one standing by me of an unknown favour: at whose presence when I was sore afraid, he bade me not to fear; and in familiar wise he spake to me and said: "Thou doest well, in that this night-time of rest thou hast preferred not to give thyself to sleep but to be occupied in watching and praying." Whereat I say: "I know myself to have great need to continue in wholesome watching, and to make diligent intercession to the Lord for my misdeeds." "Thou sayest true," quoth he further, "that both thou and many have need to redeem their sins with good works, and at such time as they have rest from worldly pains and business, to labour the more freely for the desire of everlasting blessings; but yet very few do so. For right now have I walked through all this monastery in order and looked in every hut and bed, and of them all, saving thee, have I not found one occupied with the health of his own soul: but all in short, both men and women, either sunk in sluggish sleep or watching unto sin. For the little houses too that were made to pray or read in are now turned into chambers of eating, drinking, talking and all other enticements; the virgins also vowed unto God, despising the regard due to their profession, as often as they have leisure, do busy themselves in weaving fine garments wherewith they may set themselves forth like brides to the danger of their estate, or else to get themselves the love of strange men abroad. Wherefore is there worthily prepared from heaven for this place and

tatoribus eius gravis de caelo vindicta flammis saevientibus praeparata est." Dixit autem abbatissa: "Et quare non citius hoc compertum mihi revelare voluisti?" Qui respondit: "Timui propter reverentiam tuam, ne forte nimium conturbareris; et tamen hanc consolationem habeas, quod in diebus tuis haec plaga non superveniet." Qua divulgata visione aliquantulum loci accolae paucis diebus timere, et seipsos intermissis facinoribus castigare coeperunt. Verum post obitum ipsius abbatissae redierunt ad pristinas sordes, immo sceleratora fecerunt. Et cum dicerent, "Pax et securitas," extemplo praefatae ultionis sunt poena multati.

Quae mihi cuncta sic esse facta reverentissimus meus compresbyter Aedgils referebat, qui tunc in illo monasterio degebat. Postea autem discedentibus inde ob desolationem plurimis incolarum, in nostro monasterio plurimo tempore conversatus ibidemque defunctus est. Haec ideo nostrae Historiae inserenda credidimus, ut admoneremus lectorem operum Domini, quam terribilis in consiliis super filios hominum; ne forte nos tempore aliquo carnis inlecebris servientes minusque Dei iudicium formidantes, repentina eius ira corripiat, et vel temporalibus damnis iuste saeviens affligat, vel ad perpetuam perditionem districtius examinans tollat.

them that dwell therein a grievous vengeance by the fury of flames." Then quoth the abbess: "And why would ye not sooner discover this to me, when ye knew it?" And he answered: "I feared so to do for respect of you, lest ye should maybe overmuch troubled therewith; and nevertheless have ye this comfort, that this visitation shall not fall in your days." And when this vision was spread abroad and known, the inhabitants of the place began somewhat to fear for a few days and to leave their naughty ways and amend themselves. But after the death [1] of this same abbess they returned to their former filthiness, yea they did commit more villainy. And saying, "Peace and safety," [2] they were suddenly stricken with the punishment of the foresaid vengeance.

All which things to have been so done, the most reverend Aedgils, my fellow-priest who lived then in that monastery reported unto me. And afterward (for that many dwellers there went thence because of the ruin) he lived a long time in our monastery and there died. These things have I thought good to be put in our History, to the end that we might give the reader warning of the works of the Lord, how terrible He is in His counsels over the children of men; that when perchance at any time we serve the allurements of the flesh and have little fear of the judgment of God, His sudden wrath take hold of us and either in His righteous fury crush us with temporal losses, or else trying us more hardly take us away to everlasting perdition.

[1] Ebba, St. Ebbe, the abbess, was alive in 681.
[2] 1 Thess. v. 3.

CAP. XXVI

De morte Ecgfridi et Hlotheri regum.

ANNO Dominicae incarnationis sexcentesimo octogesimo quarto, Ecgfrid rex Nordanhymbrorum misso Hiberniam cum exercitu duce Bercto, vastavit misere gentem innoxiam et nationi Anglorum semper amicissimam; ita ut ne ecclesiis quidem aut monasteriis manus parceret hostilis. At insulani, et quantum valuere armis arma repellebant, et invocantes divinae auxilium pietatis, caelitus se vindicari continuis diu imprecationibus postulabant. Et quamvis maledici regnum Dei possidere non possint, creditum est tamen quod hi qui merito impietatis suae maledicebantur, ocius Domino vindice poenas sui reatus luerent. Siquidem anno post hunc proximo idem rex, cum temere exercitum ad vastandam Pictorum provinciam duxisset, multum prohibentibus amicis et maxime beatae memoriae Cudbercto qui nuper fuerat ordinatus episcopus, introductus est, simulantibus fugam hostibus, in angustias inaccessorum montium, et cum maxima parte copiarum quas secum adduxerat exstinctus anno aetatis sua quadragesimo, regni autem quinto decimo, die tertiadecima kalendarum Iuniarum. Et quidem, ut dixi, prohibuerunt amici ne hoc bellum iniret: sed quoniam anno praecedente noluerat audire reverentissimum patrem Ecgberctum, ne Scottiam nil se

---

[1] Bertred, V. 24. [2] Cf. p. 220.

[3] Battle of Nechtansmere, Dunnichen near Forfar.

[4] Meaning Ireland, as always in Bede.

CHAPTER XXVI

Of the death of the kings Egfrid and Lothere.

IN the 684th year of the Lord's incarnation, Egfrid king of Northumberland sent Bert [1] his captain-general with an host of men into Ireland, and miserably spoiled the harmless people, which had ever been great friends to the English nation; insomuch that the hand of the enemy spared not even the churches or monasteries. Yet the men of the isle, as they were able, did both withstand force with force, and calling on the aid of God's mercy did long with continual cursings [2] make supplication to be revenged from heaven. And although such as curse cannot possess the kingdom of heaven, yet it was believed that they, which for their unmercifulness were worthily accursed, did shortly after suffer the punishments of their offence by the vengeance of the Lord. For the next year after this, the same king, against the earnest withholding of his friends and specially of Cuthbert of blessed memory, who of late had been ordained bishop, did rashly go forth with an army to waste the province of the Redshanks, who, making as though they fled, brought him into the straits of the mountains where was no passage,[3] and there with the most part of his host that he had brought with him, he was slain, the 40th years of his age and the 15th years of his reign, on the 20th day of May. And indeed (as I said) his friends did withhold him from beginning this war: but as the year before he had refused to give ear to the most reverend father Egbert warning him not to set upon Scotland [4] that did him no harm,

laedentem impugnaret, datum est illi ex poena peccati illius, ne nunc eos qui ipsum ab interitu revocare cupiebant, audiret.

Ex quo tempore spes coepit et virtus regni Anglorum "fluere, ac retro sublapsa referri." Nam et Picti terram possessionis suae quam tenuerunt Angli; et Scotti qui erant in Brittania; Brettonum quoque pars nonnulla, libertatem receperunt, quam et hactenus habent per annos circiter quadraginta sex; ubi inter plurimos gentis Anglorum vel interemptos gladio. vel servitio addictos, vel de terra Pictorum fuga lapsos, etiam reverentissimus vir Dei Trumuini qui in eos episcopatum acceperat, recessit cum suis qui erant in monasterio Aebbercurnig, posito quidem in regione Anglorum, sed in vicinia freti quod Anglorum terras Pictorumque disterminat; eosque ubicumque poterat, amicis per monasteria commendans, ipse in saepedicto famulorum famularumque Dei monasterio quod vocatur Streanaeshalch, locum mansionis elegit; ibique cum paucis suorum in monachica districtione vitam non sibi solummodo, sed et multis utilem plurimo annorum tempore duxit: ubi etiam defunctus, in ecclesia beati Petri apostoli, iuxta honorem et vita et gradu eius condignum conditus est. Praeerat quidem tunc eidem monasterio regia virgo Aelbfled una cum matre Eanflede quarum supra fecimus mentionem. Sed adveniente illuc episcopo, maximum regendi auxilium

---

[1] Verg. *Aen.* II. 169. [2] III. 24.

it was given him for a punishment of that sin, that he would not now hearken unto them that were desirous to call him back from his own destruction.

And after this time the hope and prowess of the dominion of the English began "to ebb and slide away backwards."[1] For the Redshanks recovered the land which once belonged to them, which the English did hold; and so did the Scots that were in Britain; also some part of the Britons got again their freedom, which also they hitherto have yet these 46 years or thereabout; where among very many of the Englishmen that were either slain with the sword, or made bondmen, or escaped from the land of the Redshanks by fleeing, also the most reverend man of God Trumwine, which had been bishop over them there, withdrew with his company that were in the monastery of Abercorn, the which standeth in the English region but nigh unto the strait that divideth the lands of the English and the Redshanks; and commending his fellows to his friends abroad in divers monasteries where he best might, himself chose his abiding-place in the oft-mentioned monastery of God's servants and handmaids, which is called Whitby; and there with a few of his company for a long time of years he led his life in monastical strictness, not only profitably to himself but to many beside: where also he died and was buried in the church of the blessed apostle Peter, with the honour convenient to his life and rank. There was at that time over the same monastery a virgin of the king's blood, Elfled, along with her mother Eanfled, of whom we have before made mention.[2] But when the bishop came thither, the teacher devoted to God found thereby very great help in

simul et suae vitae solatium devota Deo doctrix invenit. Successit autem Ecgfrido in regnum Aldfrid, vir in Scripturis doctissimus, qui frater eius et filius Osuiu regis esse dicebatur: destructumque regni statum, quamvis intra fines angustiores, nobiliter recuperavit.

Quo videlicet anno qui est ab incarnatione Dominica sexcentesimus octogesimus quintus, Hlotheri Cantuariorum rex, cum post Ecgberctum fratrem suum qui novem annis regnaverat, ipse duodecim annis regnasset, mortuus erat octavo idus Februarias. Vulneratus namque est in pugna Australium Saxonum, quos contra eum Edric filius Ecgbercti adgregarat, et inter medendum defunctus. Ac post eum idem Edric anno uno ac dimidio regnavit: quo defuncto regnum illud per aliquod temporis spatium reges dubii vel externi disperdiderunt; donec legitimus rex Victred, id est, filius Ecgbercti, confortatus in regno, religione simul et industria gentem suam ab extranea invasione liberaret.

CAP. XXVII

Ut vir Domini Cudberct sit episcopus factus: utque in monachica adhuc vita positus vixerit vel docuerit.

Ipso etiam anno quo finem vitae accepit rex Ecgfrid episcopum, ut diximus, fecerat ordinari Lindisfarnensium ecclesiae virum sanctum et venerabilem Cudberctum qui in insula permodica quae

---

[1] Not legitimate. [2] Owing to the invasions of Cadwalla.

her governance as well as also comfort to her own life. Now after Egfrid there succeeded him in the kingdom Aldfrid, a man very well learned in the Scriptures, who was said to be Egfrid's brother[1] and son to king Oswy: and he did nobly recover the ruined estate of the kingdom, though the bounds thereof were now more narrow.

And in the same year, which is the 685th of the Lord's incarnation, died Lothere king of Kent the 6th day of February, when he had himself reigned 12 years after his brother Egbert, who had reigned 9 years. For he was wounded in the battle of the South Saxons whom Edric the son of Egbert had gathered against him, and while he was yet in curing he died. And after him the said Edric reigned one year and a half: and after his death that kingdom was for some space of time brought to ruin[2] through kings of uncertain right or not of the royal kin; until the lawful king Wictred, that is to say, the son of Egbert, was established on the throne, and by religion as well as by diligence delivered his people from foreign assault.

CHAPTER XXVII

How Cuthbert, the man of the Lord, was made bishop: and how he lived and taught while he was yet in monastical life.

In the very year also in which king Egfrid ended his life, he had caused, as we have said,[3] Cuthbort, an holy and reverend man, to be ordained bishop of the church of Lindisfarne, who had led a solitary

[3] In Bede's life of the saint.

appellatur Farne, et ab eadem ecclesia novem ferme millibus passuum in oceano procul abest, vitam solitariam per annos plures in magna corporis et mentis continentia duxerat. Qui quidem a prima aetate pueritiae, studio religiosae vitae semper ardebat; sed ab ineunte adolescentia monachicum et nomen adsumpsit et habitum. Intravit autem primo monasterium Mailros, quod in ripa Tuidi fluminis positum, tunc abbas Eata, vir omnium mansuetissimus ac simplicissimus regebat: qui postea episcopus Hagustaldensis, sive Lindisfarnensis ecclesiae factus est, ut supra memoravimus: cui tempore illo praepositus Boisil magnarum virtutum et prophetici spiritus sacerdos fuit. Huius discipulatui Cudberct humiliter subditus, et scientiam ab eo Scripturarum et bonorum operum sumpsit exempla.

Qui postquam migravit ad Dominum, Cudberct eidem monasterio factus praepositus, plures et auctoritate magistri, et exemplo suae actionis regularem instituebat ad vitam. Nec solum ipsi monasterio regularis vitae monita simul et exempla praebebat, sed et vulgus circumpositum longe lateque a vita stultae consuetudinis ad caelestium gaudiorum convertere curabat amorem. Nam et multi fidem quam habebant iniquis profanabant operibus: et aliqui etiam tempore mortalitatis neglectis fidei sacramentis quibus erant imbuti, ad erratica idolatriae medicamina concurrebant; quasi missam a Deo conditore plagam, per incantationes, vel fylac-

[1] III. 26. [2] *I.e.* prior.

life many years in great continence of body and mind, in the very small isle called Farne, which lieth distant from the said church almost nine miles, a good way in the main ocean sea. And from the first beginning indeed of his boyhood he was always fervently desirous of religious life; but from the time he began to come to man's estate he took both the name and habit of a monk. Now he entered first into the monastery of Melrose, which standeth on the bank of the river Tweed, and was at that time governed of abbot Eata, the meekest and most sincere of men: who afterward was made bishop of the church of Hexham and Lindisfarne, as we have fore said:[1] and over this monastery at that time Boisil was provost,[2] a priest of great virtues and of a prophetical spirit. Cuthbert had been his humble scholar, and learned of him both the knowledge of the Scriptures and examples of good works.

And after this man was gone to the Lord, Cuthbert was made provost of the same monastery; and both by the authority of his master and example of his own doing, he instructed and brought many unto the life of regular discipline. Neither did he only give unto the monastery admonishments as well as examples of life according to the rule, but also laboured to turn the common people far and near thereabout from the foolish custom of their way of life to the love of the joys of heaven. For many folk too did defile the faith that they had with unrighteous works: and some also in the time of the mortal sickness, setting at naught the mysteries of the faith in which they had been instructed, ran to the erroneous medicines of idolatry; as though they had power by charms or amulets or any other

teria, vel alia quaelibet daemoniacae artis arcana cohibere valerent. Ad utrorumque ergo corrigendum errorem crebro ipse de monasterio egressus, aliquoties equo sedens, sed saepius pedes incedens, circumpositas veniebat ad villas, et viam veritatis praedicabat errantibus; quod ipsum etiam Boisil suo tempore facere consueverat. Erat quippe moris eo tempore populis Anglorum, ut veniente in villam clerico vel presbytero, cuncti ad eius imperium verbum audituri confluerent; libenter ea quae dicerentur, audirent; libentius ea quae audire et intelligere poterant, operando sequerentur. Porro Cudbercto tanta erat dicendi peritia, tantus amor persuadendi quae coeperat, tale vultus angelici lumen, ut nullus praesentium latebras ei sui cordis celare praesumeret; omnes palam quae gesserant, confitendo proferrent, quia nimirum haec eadem illum latere nullo modo putabant; et confessa dignis, ut imperabat, poenitentiae fructibus abstergerent. Solebat autem ea maxime loca peragrare, illis praedicare in viculis, qui in arduis asperisque montibus procul positi, aliis horrori erant ad visendum, et paupertate pariter ac rusticitate sua doctorum arcebant accessum. Quos tamen ille pio libenter mancipatus labori tanta doctrinae sollertis excolebat industria, ut de monasterio egressus saepe ebdomade integra, aliquando duabus vel tribus, non-

secret art of the devil to stay the visitation sent from God the Creator. To amend, therefore, the going astray of both sorts of people, Cuthbert would ofttimes himself go out of the monastery, sometime on horseback but more times on foot, and coming to the townships lying thereabout would preach the way of truth to them that were going astray; which very thing also Boisil had been wont to do in his time. For it was the manner of the people of England at that time, that when one of the clergy or a priest came to a township, they would all at his calling flock together to hear the word; and willingly hearken to such things as should be said; and more willingly follow in works those things that they could hear and understand. Further, Cuthbert had such skill in utterance, such a love of persuading in what he had begun, such a light upon his face like the countenance of an angel, that none that was present durst presume to hide the secrets of his heart from him; that all did openly declare in confession the things they had done, for that without doubt they thought that these same could in no wise be hid from him; and at his bidding wiped away the things they had confessed by worthy fruits of repentance. Moreover, he was wont to resort most commonly unto those places and preach in those hamlets lying afar off in steep and craggy hills, which other men had dread to visit, and which from their poverty as well as uplandish rudeness teachers shunned to approach. And yet he did so gladly give himself to godly travail, and laboured so diligently in careful teaching of them, that he would go out of the monastery and ofttimes not come home again in an whole week, sometimes not in two or three,

nunquam etiam mense pleno domum non rediret; sed demoratus in montanis, plebem rusticam verbo praedicationis simul et opere virtutis ad caelestia vocaret.

Cum ergo venerabilis Domini famulus multos in Mailronensi monasterio degens annos, magnis virtutum signis efulgeret, transtulit eum reverentissimus abbas ipsius Eata ad insulam Lindisfarnensium, ut ibi quoque fratribus custodiam disciplinae regularis et auctoritate praepositi intimaret, et propria actione praemonstraret. Nam et ipsum locum tunc idem reverentissimus pater abbatis iure regebat. Siquidem a temporibus ibidem antiquis et episcopus cum clero, et abbas solebat manere cum monachis; qui tamen et ipsi ad curam episcopi familiariter pertinerent. Quia nimirum Aidan qui primus eius loci episcopus fuit, cum monachis illuc et ipse monachus adveniens, monachicam in eo conversationem instituit: quomodo et prius beatus pater Augustinus in Cantia fecisse noscitur, scribente ei reverentissimo papa Gregorio, quod et supra posuimus. "Sed quia tua fraternitas," inquit, "monasterii regulis erudita, seorsum fieri non debet a clericis suis; in ecclesia Anglorum, quae nuper auctore Deo ad fidem perducta est, hanc debet conversationem instituere, quae initio nascentis ecclesiae fuit patribus nostris;

---

[1] 664.

at times not even in a full month; but tarrying in the hilly parts, he would call the poor folk of the country to heavenly things with the word of preaching as well as work of virtuous example.

When, therefore, the reverend servant of the Lord, living many years in the monastery of Melrose, made his light to shine by mighty signs of power, the most reverend abbot of the same, Eata, removed him over to the isle of Lindisfarne,[1] that he might there also make known to the brethren the keeping of the discipline of the rule, both with the authority of a provost and also set forth the same by his own doing.[2] For the same most reverend father did at that time govern that very place as abbot thereof. Forasmuch as of old time in that same place both the bishop was wont to abide together with his clergy and the abbot with the monks; though the monks themselves also did notwithstanding belong to the household and cure of the bishop. For Aidan, which was the first bishop of that place, came thither with monks, being also a monk himself, and did there place and begin monastical life: even as too before the blessed father Augustine is known to have done in Kent, at what time as the most reverend pope Gregory, as also we have declared before, wrote unto him on this wise: "But forasmuch as, dear brother, it is not meet for you that are instructed in monastical rules to dwell several from your clergy; you ought in the Church of England, which is of late by the work of God brought unto the faith, to establish this manner of life which our fathers used in the beginning of the Church at its

[2] He had to face much opposition. Bright, p. 274.

in quibus nullus eorum ex his quae possidebant aliquid suum esse dicebat, sed erant illis omnia communia."

CAP. XXVIII

Ut idem in vita anachoretica et fontem de arente terra orando produxerit, et segetem de labore manuum ultra tempus serendi acceperit.

Exin Cudberct crescentibus meritis religiosae intentionis, ad anachoreticae quoque contemplationis, quae diximus, silentia secreta pervenit. Verum quia de vita illius et virtutibus ante annos plures sufficienter et versibus heroicis, et simplici oratione conscripsimus, hoc tantum in praesenti commemorare satis sit, quod aditurus insulam protestatus est fratribus, dicens: "Si mihi divina gratia in loco illo donaverit, ut de opere manuum mearum vivere queam, libens ibi morabor; sin alias, ad vos citissime Deo volente revertar." Erat autem locus et aquae prorsus et frugis et arboris inops, sed et spirituum malignorum frequentia humanae habitationi minus accommodus: sed ad votum viri Dei habitabilis per omnia factus est, siquidem ad adventum eius spiritus recessere maligni. Cum autem ipse sibi ibidem expulsis hostibus mansionem angustam circumvallante aggere, et domos in ea necessarias, iuvante fratrum manu, id est, oratorium, et habitaculum commune construxisset, iussit fratres in

[1] P. 119.

[2] Most of the rest of this book is taken from Bede's *Life of St. Cuthbert.*

first rising: among whom none of them did call anything his own of the things that they possessed, but all things were common among them."[1]

CHAPTER XXVIII

How the same living an anchoret's life did both by praying bring forth water out of a stone ground, and received a crop from the labour of his hands out of sowing time.

After this Cuthbert increasing in the merit of religious devotion came also to the secret silence of an anchoret's life of contemplation, as we have told.[2] But because many years past we have sufficiently written of his life and mighty works both in heroical verse and in plain prose, let it suffice at this present only to rehearse thus much, that when he was at the point to go to the island he did declare to the brethren and say: "If the grace of God do grant me in that place, that I may live by the work of mine own hands, I will gladly abide there; but if not, I will, God willing, very shortly return to you again." Now the place was quite destitute both of water and grain and wood, and, moreover, less meet for any man to dwell in because of the evil spirits that haunted there: yet at the prayer of the man of God it was made in all ways fit to dwell in, forasmuch as at his coming the evil spirits went their way. Now when, after the enemy had been driven out, he had made himself a narrow place of abode compassed about with a bank, and with the helping hand of the brethren had builded necessary houses in the same, that is to say, a chapel and a common dwelling-place, he commanded the brethren to make

eiusdem habitaculi pavimento foveam facere: erat autem tellus durissima et saxosa, cui nulla omnino spes venae fontanae videretur inesse. Quod dum facerent, ad fidem et preces famuli Dei, alio die aqua plena inventa est, quae usque ad hanc diem sufficientem cunctis illo advenientibus gratiae suae caelestis copiam ministrat. Sed et ferramenta sibi ruralia cum frumento adferri rogavit, quod dum praeparata terra tempore congruo seminaret, nil omnino, non dico spicarum, sed ne herbae quidem ex eo germinare usque ad aestatis tempora contigit. Unde visitantibus se ex more fratribus, hordeum iussit adferri, si forte vel natura soli illius, vel voluntas esset superni largitoris, ut illius frugis ibi potius seges oriretur. Quod dum sibi adlatum, ultra omne tempus serendi, ultra omnem spem fructificandi, eodem in agro sereret, mox copiosa seges exorta desideratam proprii laboris viro Dei refectionem praebebat.

Cum ergo multis ibidem annis Deo solitarius serviret (tanta autem erat altitudo aggeris quo mansio eius erat vallata, ut caelum tantum ex ea, cuius introitum sitiebat, aspicere posset), contigit ut congregata synodo non parva sub praesentia regis Ecgfridi iuxta fluvium Alne, in loco qui dicitur Adtuifyrdi, quod significat, "ad duplex vadum," cui beatae memoriae Theodorus archiepiscopus praesidebat, uno animo omniumque consensu ad episco-

[1] Twyford in Northumberland.

a pit in the floor of the same dwelling-place: yet was the earth very hard and stony, wherein there seemed to be no hope in the world of a vein of spring water. And when they did this, at the faithful prayers of the servant of God the pit was found the next day full of water, which unto this day doth furnish sufficient abundance of its heavenly grace to all that come thither. Beside this too he desired to have iron tools for tilling brought him and wheat withal, but when, after he had made ready ground before, he sowed it in due season, it so happened that up to the time of summer there grew thereof, I do not say no ears, but not so much as any blade at all. Wherefore when the brethren came to visit him, as their manner was, he willed barley to be brought him, to see if haply either the nature of that soil or the good pleasure of the high Giver were that a crop of that grain would grow any better there. And when this was brought him and he sowed it in the same field, out of all season of sowing and out of all hope of having fruit again, there arose anon a plentiful crop, and gave to the man of God the wished-for refreshing of his own labour.

When, therefore, he there served God solitarily many years (now the bank wherewith his abode was fenced about was so high that he could see nothing else out of it but the heaven which he thirsted to enter into), it happened that there was a great synod assembled in the presence of king Egfrid by the river Alne, at a place called Adtuifyrdi[1] (which signifies as much as at the double ford), in which archbishop Theodore of blessed memory was president, and there with one mind and consent of them

patum ecclesiae Lindisfarnensis eligeretur. Qui cum multis legatariis ac literis ad se praemissis, nequaquam suo monasterio posset erui; tandem rex ipse praefatus, una cum sanctissimo antistite Trumuine, nec non et aliis religiosis ac potentibus viris insulam navigavit. Conveniunt et de ipsa insula Lindisfarnensi in hoc ipsum multi de fratribus, genuflectunt omnes, adiurant per Dominum, lacrimas fundunt, obsecrant; donec ipsum quoque lacrimis plenum dulcibus extrahunt latebris, atque ad synodum pertrahunt. Quo dum perveniret, quamvis multum renitens, unanima cunctorum voluntate superatur, atque ad suscipiendum episcopatus officium collum submittere compellitur: eo maxime victus sermone, quod famulus Domini Boisil, cum ei mente prophetica cuncta quae eum essent superventura patefaceret, antistitem quoque eum futurum esse praedixerat. Nec tamen statim ordinatio decreta, sed peracta hieme quae imminebat, in ipsa solemnitate paschali completa est Eboraci sub praesentia praefati regis Ecgfridi, convenientibus ad consecrationem eius septem episcopis, in quibus beatae memoriae Theodorus primatum tenebat. Electus est autem primo in episcopatum Hagustaldensis ecclesiae pro Tunbercto qui ab episcopatu fuerat depositus: sed quoniam ipse plus Lindisfarnensi ecclesiae in qua conversatus fuerat dilexit praefici; placuit ut Eata reverso ad sedem ecclesiae Hagu-

[1] The reason is not known, but cf. IV. 6 for Wynfrid's deposition.

all Cuthbert was chosen to be bishop of the church of Lindisfarne. And when he could in no wise be drawn out of his hermitage for all the messengers and letters that were sent him, at last the foresaid king himself, having the most holy bishop Trumwine with him, and also other religious persons and men of authority, did pass over into the island. Many too of the brethren of the isle of Lindisfarne itself came with them for this very purpose, all which on their knees earnestly desired him for the Lord's sake, and with weeping tears besought him; until they made his own eyes full of tears and gat him out of his sweet retreat and brought him to the synod. And when he came thither, though much against his will, he was overcome by the one assent and will of all the rest, and was made to submit his neck to bear the yoke and office of a bishop: being forced thereto most of all by the word of Boisil the servant of the Lord, who, when with the prophetical spirit which he had he did declare all the things that should befall Cuthbert, had also foretold that he should be bishop. And yet his ordination was not appointed to be straightway, but after the winter had passed, which was then at hand, it was finished at York in the solemnization of the feast of Easter itself in the presence of the foresaid king Egfrid, and there came to his consecration seven bishops, among whom Theodore of blessed memory held the chief place. Now Cuthbert was first chosen to be bishop of the church of Hexham in Tunbert's place, who had been deposed from his bishopric:[1] but inasmuch as he himself rather desired to be set over Lindisfarne church in which he had sometime lived, it seemed good that Eata should return to the

staldensis cui regendae primo fuerat ordinatus, Cudberct ecclesiae Lindisfarnensis gubernacula susciperet.

Qui susceptum episcopatus gradum ad imitationem beatorum apostolorum virtutum ornabat operibus. Commissam namque sibi plebem et orationibus protegebat adsiduis, et admonitionibus saluberrimis ad caelestia vocabat. Et, quod maxime doctores iuvare solet, ea quae agenda docebat, ipse prius agendo praemonstrabat. Erat quippe ante omnia divinae caritatis igne fervidus, patientiae virtute modestus, orationum devotioni sollertissime intentus, affabilis omnibus qui ad se consolationis gratia veniebant; hoc ipsum quoque orationis loco ducens, si infirmis fratribus opem suae exhortationis tribueret; sciens quia qui dixit, "Diliges Dominum Deum tuum"; dixit et, "Diliges proximum." Erat abstinentiae castigatione insignis, erat gratia conpunctionis semper ad caelestia suspensus. Denique cum sacrificium Deo victimae salutaris offerret, non elevata in altum voce, sed profusis ex imo pectore lacrymis, Domino suo vota commendabat.

Duobus autem annis in episcopatu peractis repetiit insulam ac monasterium suum, divino admonitus oraculo, quia dies sibi mortis vel vitae magis illius quae sola vita dicenda est iam adpropiaret introitus: sicut ipse quoque tempore eodem nonnullis, sed verbis obscurioribus, quae tamen postmodum mani-

---

[1] Mark xii. 30, 31.

see of Hexham church, to the governance of which he had first been ordained, and Cuthbert should take the charge of Lindisfarne church.

And when Cuthbert had taken upon him the degree of bishop, he did adorn the same with works of power, following the example of the blessed apostles. For he did defend the people committed unto him with continual prayers, and call them to heavenly things with most wholesome exhortations. And (the thing which most of all is wont to help teachers) he first in his own doing gave example of the things which he taught should be done. For he was above all things kindled with the fire of divine love, forbearing by the virtue of patience, most diligently given to devotion of praying, courteous to all that came to him for comfort; for he took this same for a kind of prayer too, if he should minister the help of his exhortation to weak brethren; knowing that He that said:[1] "Thou shalt love the Lord thy God"; said also, "Thou shalt love thy neighbour." He was also notable for his abstinence and straight living, and was ever lifted up to heavenly things by the grace of contrition. Finally, when he offered the host of wholesome sacrifice to God, he commended his prayers to his Lord, not with a voice lifted up on high, but with tears poured out from the bottom of his heart.

Now when he had passed two years in his bishopric, he went again to his isle and hermitage, being warned by a divine message that the day of his death was now at hand, or rather the entrance into that life which only should be called life: as he did himself also at the same time open unto some after his wonted simple manner, but in words of veiled

feste intelligerentur, solita sibi simplicitate pandebat; quibusdam autem hoc idem etiam manifeste revelabat.

CAP. XXIX

Ut idem iam episcopus obitum suum proxime futurum Hereberecto anachoretae praedixerit.

Erat enim presbyter vitae venerabilis, nomine Hereberct, iamdudum viro Dei spiritalis amicitiae foedere copulatus; qui in insula stagni illius pergrandis de quo Deruuentionis fluvii primordia erumpunt, vitam ducens solitariam, annis singulis eum visitare et monita ab eo perpetuae salutis audire solebat. Hic cum audiret eum ad civitatem Lugubaliam devenisse, venit ex more, cupiens salutaribus eius exhortationibus ad superna desideria magis magisque accendi. Qui dum sese alterutrum caelestis vitae poculis debriarent, dixit inter alia antistes "Memento, frater Hereberct, ut modo quidquid opus habes, me interroges, mecumque loquaris: postquam enim ab invicem digressi fuerimus, non ultra nos in hoc saeculo carnis obtutibus invicem aspiciemus. Certus sum namque quod tempus meae resolutionis instat, et velox est depositio tabernaculi mei." Qui haec audiens provolutus est eius vestigiis, et fusis cum gemitu lacrimis, "Obsecro," inquit, "per Dominum, ne me deseras, sed tui memor sis

[1] St. Herbert's Island, Derwentwater.
[2] 2 Peter i. 14.

meaning, yet such as afterwards should be plainly understood; to certain men, however, he did discover this same thing even plainly.

CHAPTER XXIX

How the same being now bishop did foretell his death to be very nigh at hand to Herbert an anchoret.

For there was a priest worthy of veneration in his life, by name Herbert, which had a long time been coupled to the man of God in the bond of spiritual friendship; and he living a solitary life in the island [1] of that great wide lake from which break forth the beginnings of the river Derwent, was wont to visit Cuthbert every year and hear the lessons of eternal salvation at his mouth. And when this priest heard that Cuthbert was come to the city of Carlisle, he came after his accustomed manner, desiring to be inflamed more and more to longing for the things above by his wholesome exhortations. And as they did inebriate one another with the cups of the life of heaven, among other things the bishop said: "Remember, brother Herbert, that whatever ye have to ask of me and speak of with me, you do it now: for after we depart the one from the other, we shall not see one another with the eyes of the flesh any more in this world. For I know well that the time of my release is at hand, and the laying away of my tabernacle [2] shall be very shortly." And when Herbert heard this he fell down at his feet, and with sighs and pouring tears, "I beseech you," quoth he, "for the Lord's sake, forsake me not, but remember your most

fidissimi sodalis, rogesque supernam pietatem, ut cui simul in terris servivimus, ad eius videndam gratiam simul transeamus ad caelos. Nosti enim quia ad tui oris imperium semper vivere studui, et quicquid ignorantia vel fragilitate deliqui, aeque ad tuae voluntatis examen mox emendare curavi." Incubuit precibus antistes, statimque edoctus in spiritu impetrasse se quod petebat a Domino: "Surge," inquit, "frater mi, et noli plorare, sed gaudio gaude quia quod rogavimus, superna nobis clementia donavit."

Cuius promissi et prophetiae veritatem sequens rerum astruxit eventus, quia et digredientes ab invicem non se ultra corporaliter viderunt, sed uno eodemque die, hoc est, tertiadecima Kalendarum Aprilium, egredientes e corpore spiritus eorum mox beata invicem visione coniuncti sunt, atque angelico ministerio pariter ad regnum caeleste translati. Sed Hereberct diutina prius infirmitate decoquitur; illa, ut credibile est, dispensatione Dominicae pietatis, ut si quid minus haberet meriti a beato Cuthbercto, suppleret hoc castigans longae aegritudinis dolor: quatenus aequatus gratia suo intercessori, sicut uno eodemque tempore cum eo de corpore egredi, ita etiam una atque indissimili sede perpetuae beatitudinis meruisset recipi.

Obiit autem pater reverentissimus in insula Farne, multum deprecatus fratres ut ibi quoque sepeliretur,

faithful companion, and make intercession to the mercy above, that we may pass unto heaven together to behold His grace, Whom we have on earth served together. For you know that I have ever laboured to live after the bidding of your lips, and whatsoever I have failed in through ignorance or frailty I did likewise soon make endeavour to amend after the judgment of your good pleasure." To his prayers the bishop did incline himself, and straightway being certified in spirit that he had obtained the thing that he sought of the Lord: "Arise," quoth he, "my brother, and weep not, but rejoice with joy that the mercy from above hath granted unto us that we have asked."

The truth of which promise and prophecy was well made sure in that which befell after, for after departing asunder they saw not one another bodily any more, but on one selfsame day, which was the 20th of March, their spirits went out of their bodies and were shortly joined together in blessed vision of one another, and carried both to the kingdom of heaven by the service of angels. But Herbert was first tried in the fire of long sickness; that by such dispensation of the kindness of the Lord, as it is to be believed, any want of merit as he had in comparison of blessed Cuthbert might be filled up in the pain of long chastening sickness: so that being equal in grace with his predecessor that made prayer for him, even as he had deserved to depart out of the body at the selfsame time with him, so also he should be found worthy to be received into the selfsame and like seat of unending bliss.

Now the most reverend father died in the isle of Farne, and besought the brethren earnestly, that he

ubi non parvo tempore pro Domino militarat. Attamen tandem eorum precibus victus assensum dedit, ut ad insulam Lindisfarnensium relatus, in ecclesia deponeretur. Quod dum factum esset, episcopatum ecclesiae illius anno uno servabat venerabilis antistes Vilfrid, donec eligeretur qui pro Cudbercto antistes ordinari deberet.

Ordinatus est autem post haec Eadberct, vir scientia divinarum Scripturarum simul et praeceptorum caelestium observantia, ac maxime eleemosynarum operatione insignis; ita ut iuxta legem, omnibus annis decimam non solum quadrupedum, verum etiam frugum omnium atque pomorum necnon et vestimentorum partem pauperibus daret.

CAP. XXX

Ut corpus illius post undecim annos sepulturae sit corruptionis immune repertum : nec multo post successor episcopatus eius de mundo transierit.

Volens autem latius demonstrare divina dispensatio, quanta in gloria vir Domini Cudberct post mortem viveret, cuius ante mortem vita sublimis crebris etiam miraculorum patebat indiciis, transactis sepulturae eius annis undecim, immisit in animo fratrum ut tollerent ossa illius, quae more mortuorum consumpto iam et in pulverem redacto corpore reliquo, sicca invenienda putabant: atque in novo recondita loculo, in eodem quidem loco, sed supra pavimentum dignae venerationis gratia locarent.

might also be buried there where he had no small time been in warfare for the Lord. But yet at last overcome with their request he was content that he might be brought to Lindisfarne isle and laid in the church there. And when this had been done, the venerable bishop Wilfrid kept the bishopric of that church one year, until choice was made of him who should be ordained bishop for Cuthbert.

Now after this Eadbert was ordained, a notable man in the knowledge of the Holy Scriptures as well as in the due keeping of heavenly precepts, and most of all in the doing of alms; insomuch that according to the Law he gave every year to poor folk the tenth not only of his cattle, but also of all grain and fruit and part of his apparel too.

CHAPTER XXX

How the body of Cuthbert, after eleven years' burial, was found free of corruption: and how not long after the successor of that bishopric passed from the world.

Now the dispensation of God willing to shew more largely abroad in how great glory Cuthbert the man of the Lord lived after his death (whose high godly life before his death was manifested by many signs and miracles), did put it into the minds of the brethren eleven years past after his burial to take up his bones, thinking to find them all dry, the rest of the body being now consumed and brought to dust, as dead bodies commonly are: and so intending to put them in a new coffin and lay them in the same place, but above the pavement for the more rever-

Quod dum sibi placuisse Eadbercto antistiti suo referrent, adnuit consilio eorum, iussitque ut die depositionis eius hoc facere meminissent. Fecerunt autem ita: et aperientes sepulcrum, invenerunt corpus totum quasi adhuc viveret integrum, et flexilibus artuum compagibus multo dormienti quam mortuo similius: set et vestimenta omnia quibus indutum erat, non solum intemerata, verum etiam prisca novitate et claritudine miranda parebant. Quod ubi videre fratres, nimio mox timore perculsi, festinaverunt referre antistiti quae invenerant, qui tum forte in remotiore ab ecclesia loco refluis undique pelagi fluctibus cincto, solitarius manebat. In hoc etenim semper quadragesimae tempus agere, in hoc quadraginta ante Dominicum natale dies in magna continentiae, orationis et lacrymarum devotione transigere solebat: in quo etiam venerabilis praedecessor eius Cudberct priusquam insulam Farne peteret, aliquandiu secretus Domino militabat.

Adtulerunt autem ei et partem indumentorum quae corpus sanctum ambierant, quae cum ille et munera gratanter acciperet et miracula libenter audiret, nam et ipsa indumenta quasi patris adhuc corpori circumdata miro deosculabatur affectu, "Nova," inquit, "indumenta corpori pro his quae tulistis, circumdate, et sic reponite in arca quam parastis. Scio autem certissime quia non diu vacuus remanebit locus ille, qui tanta miraculi caelestis gratia sacratus est; et quam beatus est cui in eo facultatem quiescendi Dominus totius beatitudinis

ence due thereunto. Which intent of theirs they did declare to Eadbert their bishop, who agreed to their purpose, and bade them remember to do it on the day of his burying. And so they did: and opening the tomb they found the body all whole as if it were still alive, and the joints of the limbs supple, much liker a sleeping body than a dead; moreover, the clothes that were about him appeared not only without blemish, but also marvellous fresh and bright as when they were first made. Which when the brethren saw, they were stricken straight with exceeding fear, and in haste went to tell the bishop what they had found; who as it happened was that time solitary in a place at a distance from the church, being closed about with the waves of the sea at the flowing of the tide. For there was he wont always to keep the time of Lent, and there the forty days before the Lord's nativity in great devotion of abstinence, prayer and tears: in which place also his venerable predecessor Cuthbert, before that he went to the isle of Farne, did sometimes do warfare for the Lord apart.

Moreover, they brought him also a part of the clothes that were about the holy body, and these for presents he both thankfully received and gladly heard of the miracles; for he also kissed with a great affection those same clothes as if they were yet about the father's body and, "Put ye on," quoth he, "new clothes about the body for these that ye have brought me, and so lay it again in the chest ye have provided. And I know most certainly that that place shall not remain long empty, which is hallowed by such a grace of heavenly miracle; and how happy is he unto whom the Lord, the author

auctor atque largitor praestare dignabitur." Haec et huiusmodi plura ubi multis cum lacrymis et magna compunctione antistes lingua etiam tremente complevit, fecerunt fratres ut iusserat, et involutum novo amictu corpus novaque in theca reconditum, supra pavimentum sanctuarii posuerunt.

Nec mora, Deo dilectus antistes Eadberct morbo correptus est acerbo, ac per dies crescente multumque ingravescente ardore languoris, non multo post, id est, pridie Nonas Maias etiam ipse migravit ad Dominum: cuius corpus in sepulcro benedicti patris Cudbercti ponentes, adposuerunt desuper arcam in qua incorrupta eiusdem patris membra locaverant: in quo etiam loco signa sanitatum aliquoties facta, meritis amborum testimonium ferunt, e quibus aliqua in libro vitae illius olim memoriae mandavimus. Sed et in hac Historia quaedam quae nos nuper audisse contigit, superadicere commodum duximus.

CAP. XXXI

Ut quidam ad tumbam eius sit a paralysi sanatus.

Erat in eodem monasterio frater quidam, nomine Badudegn, tempore non pauco hospitum ministerio deserviens, qui nunc usque superest, testimonium habens ab universis fratribus cunctisque supervenientibus hospitibus, quod vir esset multae pietatis ac religionis, iniunctoque sibi officio supernae tantum mercedis gratia subditus. Hic cum quadam die

and giver of all bliss, will vouchsafe to give leave to rest in that place." These and many like things when the bishop had ended with many tears and great sorrow of heart and trembling tongue, the brethren did as he had bidden, and wound the body in a new garment and put it in a new coffin, and so laid it above the pavement of the sanctuary.

And shortly after the bishop Eadbert, beloved of God, was taken with a grievous disease, and the burning of the sickness daily increasing and waxing greatly, he also not long after, that is, on the sixth day of May, passed to the Lord; and his body was laid in the grave of the blessed father Cuthbert, with the coffin over him in which they had put the uncorrupted body of the said father: in which place too signs sometimes done in healing the sick do bear witness to the merits of them both, of which miracles we have formerly put some in memory in the book of his life. Yet we have thought it convenient to add thereto in this History also certain which we happen to have heard of late.

CHAPTER XXXI

How a certain man was cured of the palsy at his tomb.

THERE was in the same monastery a certain brother named Badudegn, whose office was of long time to serve the guests, and who is alive yet to this day; a man of whose much godliness and religion all the brethren and guests that resort thither do bear witness, and that he doth obediently do the office put upon him only for the reward that cometh from above. This man on a certain day, when he had

lenas sive saga quibus in hospitale utebatur, in mari lavasset, rediens domum repentina medio itinere molestia tactus est, ita ut corruens in terram et aliquandiu pronus iacens, vix tandem resurgeret; resurgens autem sensit dimidiam corporis sui partem a capite usque ad pedes paralysis languore depressam: et maximo cum labore baculo innitens domum pervenit. Crescebat morbus paulatim, et nocte superveniente gravior effectus est, ita ut die redeunte vix ipse per se exsurgere aut incedere valeret. Quo affectus incommodo, concepit utillimum mente consilium, ut ad ecclesiam quoquo modo posset perveniens, intraret ad tumbam reverentissimi patris Cudbercti, ibique genibus flexis supplex supernam pietatem rogaret, ut vel ab huiuscemodi languore, si hoc sibi utile esset, liberaretur; vel si se tali molestia diutius castigari divina providente gratia oporteret, patienter dolorem ac placida mente sustineret inlatum. Fecit igitur ut animo disposuerat, et imbecilles artus baculo sustentans intravit ecclesiam; ac prosternens se ad corpus viri Dei, pia intentione per eius auxilium Dominum sibi propitium fieri precabatur: atque inter preces velut in soporem solutus sensit, ut ipse postea referre erat solitus, quasi magnam latamque manum caput sibi in parte qua dolebat, tetigisse, eodemque tactu totam illam quae languore pressa fuerat corporis sui partem, paulatim fugiente dolore, ac sanitate subsequente, ad pedes usque pertransisse. Quo

washed in the sea the mantles or cloaks that he used in the guest chamber, coming home again was in the midway taken with a sudden distress, in such wise that he fell down on the ground and lay flat for a space, and could scant at last get up again; but upon getting up he felt the half part of his body from the head to the feet to be stricken with a palsy: and so with much toil he came home leaning on a staff. The disease increased little by little, and when night came was waxen so grievous, that the next day he was scant able to rise or go by himself. And being brought into this trouble he conceived in his mind a very profitable thought, which was to get him to the church howsoever he might, and entering to go to the tomb of the most reverend father Cuthbert, and there upon his knees humbly to beseech the goodness on high, that either he might be delivered from a sickness of this sort, if so it were profitable for him; or else, if it behoved him to be longer chastened with such distress by the gracious provision of God, that he might patiently and with a quiet mind bear the pain put upon him. He did therefore as he had devised in his thought, and staying his feeble limbs with a staff went into the church; and falling prostrate at the corse of the man of God, he prayed with godly earnestness that through his help the Lord would become merciful unto him: and as he was at his prayers, falling as it were into a deep sleep, he felt (as he himself was afterwards wont to tell) like as a great broad hand had touched his head in that place where the grief was, and with that same touching passed along all that part of his body, which had been sore vexed with sickness, down to his feet, and by little and little the pain passed away and health followed

facto, mox evigilans sanissimus surrexit, ac pro sua sanitate Domino gratias denuo referens, quid erga se actum esset fratribus indicavit: cunctisque congaudentibus ad ministerium quod solicitus exhibere solebat, quasi flagello probante castigatior rediit.

Sed et indumenta, quibus Deo dicatum corpus Cudbercti, vel vivum antea, vel postea defunctum vestierant, etiam ipsa a gratia curandi non vacarunt, sicut in volumine vitae et virtutum eius quisque legerit inveniet.

CAP. XXXII

Ut alter ad reliquias eius nuper fuerit ab oculi languore curatus.

Nec silentio praetereundum quod ante triennium per reliquias eius factum, nuper mihi per ipsum in quo factum est fratrem innotuit. Est autem factum in monasterio quod iuxta amnem Dacore constructum ab eo cognomen accepit, cui tunc vir religiosus Suidberct abbatis iure praefuit. Erat in eo quidam adolescens cui tumor deformis palpebram oculi foedaverat; qui cum per dies crescens oculo interitum minaretur, curabant medici hunc adpositis pigmentorum fomentis emollire, nec valebant. Quidam abscindendum esse dicebant; alii hoc fieri metu maioris periculi vetabant. Cumque tempore non pauco frater praefatus tali incommodo laboraret, neque imminens oculo exitium humana manus curare

[1] Near Penrith.

thereon. Which done, he shortly awoke and rose up perfectly whole, and giving thanks anew to the Lord for his health, came and shewed the brethren what had been done unto him; and at the rejoicing of all men he returned to the office that he was wont diligently to perform, being now as it were made better by the trial of the scourge.

Moreover, the clothes also wherewith the body of Cuthbert, dedicated to God, was clad, either before in his lifetime or after, when he was dead, did not themselves lack the grace of healing, as whoso will read shall find in the book of his life and mighty works.

CHAPTER XXXII

How a second man was of late healed of an affliction of the eye at Cuthbert's relics.

Nor is that to be passed over unspoken of, which three years past was done through his relics, as was lately made known to me by the very brother on whom it was done. Now it was done in the monastery which is built by the river Dacre[1] and thereof hath his name, in which at that time Swidbert, a devout man, was head as abbot. In that monastery there was a certain young man that had a foul unhandsome swelling in the lid of his eye; the which daily growing bigger, and being like to put him in danger of the loss of his eye, the physicians tried to assuage by laying salves and plasters thereto, but could do no good. Some would have it to be cut off; other said no, for fear of a further danger. And when the foresaid brother continued in such sad case no small time and could get no help at man's hand against the peril of the loss of his eye, but rather it daily in-

valeret, quin per dies augesceret, contigit eum subito divinae pietatis gratia per sanctissimi patris Cudbercti reliquias sanari. Nam quando fratres sui corpus ipsius post multos sepulturae annos incorruptum reperierunt, tulerunt partem de capillis quam more reliquiarum rogantibus amicis dare, vel ostendere in signum miraculi possent.

Harum particulam reliquiarum eo tempore habebat penes se quidam de presbyteris eiusdem monasterii, nomine Thruidred, qui nunc ipsius monasterii abbas est. Qui cum die quadam ingressus ecclesiam aperuisset thecam reliquiarum, ut portionem earum roganti amico praestaret, contigit et ipsum adolescentem cui oculus languebat, in eadem ecclesia tunc adesse. Cumque presbyter portionem quantam voluit, amico dedisset, residuum dedit adolescenti, ut suo in loco reponeret. At ille salubri instinctu admonitus, cum accepisset capillos sancti capitis, adposuit palpebrae languenti, et aliquandiu tumorem illum infestum horum adpositione comprimere ac mollire curabat. Quo facto, reliquias, ut iussus erat, sua in theca recondidit. credens suum oculum capillis viri Dei quibus adtactus erat ocius esse sanandum. Neque eum sua fides fefellit. Erat enim, ut referre erat solitus, tunc hora circiter secunda diei. Sed cum alia, quaeque dies illa exigebat, cogitaret et faceret, imminente hora ipsius diei sexta, repente contingens oculum, ita sanum cum palpebra invenit, ac si nil unquam in eo deformitatis ac tumoris apparuisset.

creased, it was his chance through the grace of God's goodness to be healed suddenly by the relics of the most holy father Cuthbert. For when his brethren found his body not corrupted after it had lain many years buried, they took a part of the hair, which in manner of relics they might give to friends that asked of them, or shew for a sign of the miracle.

A little part of these relics were at that time in the keeping of one of the priests of the same monastery, Thrwidred by name, who now is abbot of that same house. Which man on a certain day went to the church, and after he had opened the shrine of the relics to give a part thereof to a friend who asked for it, it chanced the young man whose eye was afflicted was then present in the church. And when the priest had given his friend such part thereof as he would, he gave the rest to the young man to lay up again in his place. Whereupon he by a good motion that came to his mind, as soon as he had received the hairs of the holy head, put them to his sore eyelid, and held them there a space, endeavouring to keep down and assuage that noisome swelling. And that done he laid the relics up again in the shrine, as he had been bidden, believing that his eye should shortly be healed by the hair of the man of God, wherewith he had been touched. And his faith deceived him not. For it was at that time, as he was wont to tell, about the second hour of the day. But as he thought upon his business and went about other things, as that day required, towards the sixth hour of that very day he happened suddenly to touch his eye, the which he found, with the eyelid and all, as whole as if there had never been seen any blemish and swelling therein.

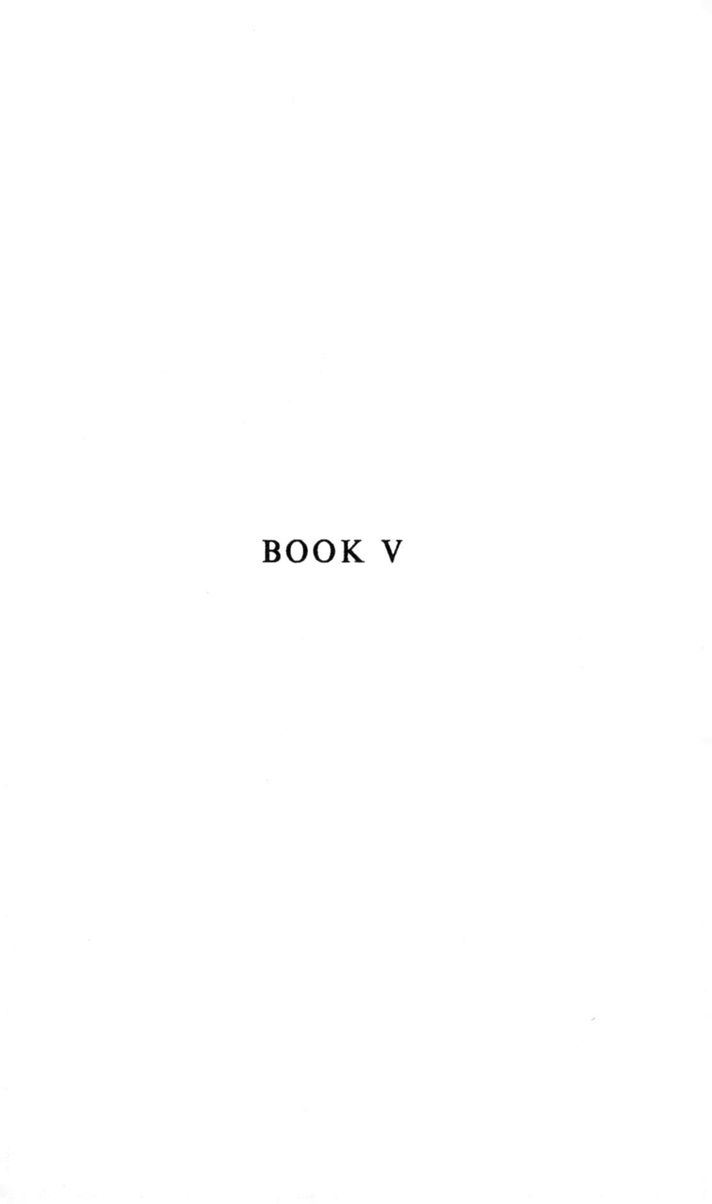

BOOK V

HISTORIAE ECCLESIASTICAE GENTIS ANGLORUM

LIBER QUINTUS

CAP. I

Ut Oidilvald successor Cudbercti in anachoretica vita, laborantibus in mari fratribus, tempestatem orando sedaverit.

SUCCESSIT autem viro Domini Cudbercto, in exercenda vita solitaria quam in insula Farne ante episcopatus sui tempora gerebat, vir venerabilis Oidilualdd, qui multis annis in monasterio quod dicitur Inhrypum acceptum presbyteratus officium condignis gradu ipse consecrabat actibus. Cuius ut meritum vel vita qualis fuerit, certius clarescat, unum eius narro miraculum quod mihi unus e fratribus propter quos et in quibus patratum est, ipse narravit, videlicet Gudfrid, venerabilis Christi famulus et presbyter, qui etiam postea fratribus eiusdem ecclesiae Lindisfarnensis in qua educatus est, abbatis iure praefuit.

"Veni," inquit, "cum duobus fratribus aliis ad insulam Farne, loqui desiderans cum reverentissimo patre Oidilualdo: cumque allocutione eius refecti et benedictione petita domum rediremus, ecce subito, positis nobis in medio mari, interrupta est

THE FIFTH BOOK OF THE ECCLESIASTICAL HISTORY OF THE ENGLISH NATION

CHAPTER I

How Ethelwald, Cuthbert's successor, living a hermit's life, allayed by prayer a storm for his brethren in peril at sea.

Now Ethelwald, a venerable man, which many years in the monastery called Ripon sanctified the office of priesthood taken upon him by behaviour of himself worthy of his degree, succeeded Cuthbert in practice of that loneful life which he passed in Farne Island before the time he was made bishop. Whose worthiness and the manner of his life, that all men may more surely perceive, I declare one miracle wrought by him, which one of the brethren, for whom and among whom it was wrought, himself declared to me: to wit, Guthfrid, a venerable servant and priest of Christ, who also afterward, as abbot, was over the same church of Lindisfarne where he was brought up.

"I came," said he, "with two other brethren, to Farne Island desiring to speak with the most reverend father Ethelwald; and when we had talked with him to our comfort and besought his blessing, and were now on our way homeward, behold suddenly, as we were in the midst of the sea, the calm in which we

serenitas qua vehebamur, et tanta ingruit tamque fera tempestatis hiems, ut neque velo neque remigio quicquam proficere, neque aliud quam mortem sperare valeremus. Cumque diu multum cum vento pelagoque frustra certantes tandem post terga respiceremus, si forte vel ipsam de qua egressi eramus insulam aliquo conamine repetere possemus, invenimus nos undiqueversum pari tempestate praeclusos, nullamque spem nobis in nobis restare salutis. Ubi autem longius visum levavimus, vidimus in ipsa insula Farne, egressum de latibulis suis amantissimum Deo patrem Oidilualdum iter nostrum inspicere. Audito etenim fragore procellarum ac ferventis oceani, exierat videre quid nobis accideret: cumque nos in labore ac desperatione positos cerneret, flectebat genua sua ad patrem Domini nostri Iesu Christi pro nostra vita et salute precaturus. Et cum orationem compleret, simul tumida aequora placavit; adeo ut cessante per omnia saevitia tempestatis, secundi nos venti ad terram usque per plana maris terga comitarentur. Cumque evadentes ad terram, naviculam quoque nostram ab undis exportaremus, mox eadem quae nostri gratia modicum siluerat tempestas rediit, et toto illo die multum furere non cessavit; ut palam daretur intelligi, quia modica illa quae provenerat intercapedo quietis ad viri Dei preces nostrae evasionis gratia caelitus donata est."

Mansit autem idem vir Dei in insula Farne duodecim annis ibidemque defunctus: sed in insula Lindisfarnensi iuxta praefatorum corpora episco-

sailed was broken, and so great a tempest and terrible storm came upon us that neither with sail nor oar could we prevail, nor look for anything else than death. And when we, striving long with the wind and sea to no effect, looked back at the length, if perchance by any means we might return again to the island from which we had come, we found ourselves on every side shut off with like tempest, and no hope remaining of escape in ourselves. And when we raised our eyes to look afar off, we saw on the selfsame island of Farne, the father Ethelwald, most dear to God, come out of his retreat and look upon our voyage. For, as soon as he heard the blustering of the storm and rage of the ocean, he had come forth to see what was happening to us; and when he saw us labouring hard and in desperate case, he fell upon his knees to pray to the Father of our Lord Jesus Christ for our life and safety. And as he ended his prayer he therewith appeased the swelling waters; in such sort, that, the violence of the storm altogether ceasing, we had fair winds with us till we came to land over the face of the sea that was now smooth. And when we were on ground and were carrying our boat too out of reach of the waves, straightways the same storm, which for our sakes had been a little while allayed, began again and ceased not all that day to rage furiously; to the end that it might clearly be given us to understand that that little interval of calm which had happened was given from heaven in answer to the prayers of the man of God, to obtain our deliverance."

Now the said man of God continued in Farne Island 12 years, and there died: but he was buried in Lindisfarne Island near to the bodies of the fore-

porum, in ecclesia beati apostoli Petri sepultus est. Gesta vero sunt haec temporibus Aldfridi regis, qui post fratrem suum Ecgfridum genti Nordanhymbrorum decem et novem annis praefuit.

CAP. II

Ut episcopus Iohannes mutum et scabiosum benedicendo curaverit.

Cuius regni principio defuncto Eata episcopo, Iohannes, vir sanctus, Hagustaldensis ecclesiae praesulatum suscepit: de quo plura virtutum miracula qui eum familiariter noverunt dicere solent, et maxime vir reverentissimus ac veracissimus Bercthun, diaconus quondam eius, nunc autem abbas monasterii quod vocatur Inderauuda, id est, In Silva Derorum: e quibus aliqua memoriae tradere commodum duximus.

Est mansio quaedam secretior, nemore raro et vallo circumdata, non longe ab Hagustaldensi ecclesia, id est, unius ferme milliarii et dimidii spatio interfluente Tino amne separata, habens clymeterium [1] sancti Michaelis archangeli, in qua vir Dei saepius ubi opportunitas adridebat temporis, et maxime in quadragesima, manere cum paucis, atque orationibus ac lectioni quietus operam dare consueverat. Cumque tempore quodam, incipiente quadragesima, ibidem mansurus adveniret, iussit suis quaerere pauperem aliquem maiore infirmitate vel inopia gravatum, quem secum habere illis diebus ad facien-

[1] For *coemeterium*, Pl.

---

[1] Beverley.

mentioned bishops in the church of the blessed apostle Peter. These things were of a truth done in the days of King Aldfrid, who ruled over the Northumbrian people after his brother Egfrid 19 years.

CHAPTER II

How bishop John cured a dumb and scabby man with blessing of him.

AND in the beginning of this king his reign, when bishop Eata was dead, John a holy man took the prelacy of Hexham church upon him: of whom his near acquaintance are wont to report many mighty miracles, and specially amongst other Berthun, sometime his deacon, but now abbot of the monastery called Inderauuda,[1] that is to say, In the Wood of the Deirans, a man of great reverence and credit for his truth: of some of which miracles we have thought good to bear record.

There was a certain dwelling-place withdrawn apart, compassed about with a scant wood and a dyke, not far from Hexham church (that is to say, not past a mile and a half, but divided with the river Tyne which runneth between them both), having an oratory and church [2] of St. Michael the archangel, where the man of God had ofttime been used to sojourn with a few companions, as occasion and time served, and give himself in peace to prayer and study, but specially in Lent. And when at a certain time (Lent being at hand) he came thither to abide, he commanded those that were about him to seek some poor man labouring under some grievous impotence

[2] According to the A.S. version, Pl.

dam eleemosynam possent: sic enim semper facere solebat.

Erat autem in villa non longe posita quidam adolescens mutus, episcopo notus, nam saepius ante illum percipiendae eleemosynae gratia venire consueverat, qui ne unum quidem sermonem unquam profari poterat; sed et scabiem tantam ac furfures habebat in capite, ut nil unquam capillorum ei in superiore parte capitis nasci valeret, tantum in circuitu horridi crines stare videbantur. Hunc ergo adduci praecipit episcopus, et ei in conseptis eiusdem mansionis parvum tugurium fieri in quo manens quotidianam ab eis stipem acciperet. Cumque una quadragesimae esset impleta septimana, sequente Dominica iussit ad se intrare pauperem, ingresso eo linguam proferre ex ore ac sibi ostendere iussit; et adprehendens eum de mento, signum sanctae crucis linguae eius impressit, quam signatam revocare in os, et loqui illum praecepit: " Dicito," inquiens, " aliquod verbum, dicito Gae," quod est, lingua Anglorum, verbum adfirmandi et consentiendi, id est, etiam. Dixit ille statim, soluto vinculo linguae, quod iussus erat. Addidit episcopus nomina literarum: " Dicito A "; dixit ille A. " Dicito B "; dixit ille et hoc. Cumque singula literarum nomina dicente episcopo responderet, addidit et syllabas ac verba dicenda illi proponere. Et cum in omnibus consequenter responderet, praecepit eum sententias longiores dicere, et fecit: neque ultra cessavit tota die illa et nocte sequente, quantum vigilare potuit,

or beggary, whom they might have with them for those days to deal alms unto.

Now there was in a township not far off a certain young man that was dumb, well known of the bishop (for he used to come before him oftentimes to receive his alms), the which was never able to speak so much as one word; besides, too, he had so much scab and scurf in his head, that in the crown of the head there could not a hair take root, only rough hairs were seen to be standing around it. This man then the bishop commanded to be brought thither, and a small hut made for him within the precincts of the said dwelling-place, where he might abide and receive of them his daily alms. And when one week of Lent was past, the next Sunday the bishop willed the poor man to come in to him, and when he was come he bid him put out his tongue and shew it unto him; and taking him by the chin he made a sign of the holy cross upon his tongue, and when he had so signed and blessed it, he commanded him to pluck it in again and speak, saying: "Speak me some word, say *Gae*" (which in the English tongue is a word of affirmation and consent, in such signification as *Yea*). Incontinent the strings of his tongue were loosed, and he said that which he had been commanded to say. The bishop added the names of letters: "Say A"; he said it. "Say B"; he said this too. And when after the bishop he recited the name of each of the letters, the bishop went on to put unto him syllables and words for him to pronounce. And when in all points he answered orderly, he commanded him to speak sentences of length, and so he did: nor further did he cease all that day and night following, so long as he could keep awake (as they make report that

ut ferunt qui praesentes fuere, loqui aliquid, et arcana suae cogitationis ac voluntatis, quod nunquam antea potuit, aliis ostendere; in similitudinem illius diu claudi qui curatus ab apostolis Petro et Iohanne, exsiliens stetit et ambulabat; et intravit cum illis in templum ambulans, et exsiliens, et laudans Dominum; gaudens nimirum uti officio pedum, quo tanto erat tempore destitutus. Cuius sanitati congaudens episcopus praecepit medico etiam sanandae scabredini capitis eius curam adhibere.

Fecit ut iusserat, et iuvante benedictione ac precibus antistitis nata est cum sanitate cutis venusta species capillorum, factusque est iuvenis limpidus vultu et loquela promptus, capillis pulcherrime crispis, qui ante fuerat deformis, pauper, et mutus. Sicque de percepta laetatus sospitate, offerente etiam ei episcopo ut in sua familia manendi locum acciperet, magis domum reversus est.

CAP. III

Ut puellam languentem orando sanaverit.

Narravit idem Berethun et aliud de praefato antistite miraculum. Quia cum reverentissimus vir Vilfrid post longum exilium in episcopatum esset Hagustaldensis ecclesiae receptus, et idem Iohannes, defuncto Bosa viro multae sanctitatis et humilitatis, episcopus pro eo Eboraci substitutus, venerit ipse

were present) to speak something and declare his secret thoughts and purposes to other, the which before that day he could never utter; in like manner as that long-lamed lazar, who restored by the apostles Peter and John,[1] stood up leaping, and walked; and entered into the temple with them, walking and leaping and praising the Lord; rejoicing surely that he could now go upon his feet, the which benefit he had lacked so long time before. And rejoicing in his healing the bishop commanded the physician to give heed also to cure the scurfiness of his head.

He did as he was bid, and by help of the bishop's blessing and prayers the man's skin was made whole, and the hairs of his head grew to be sightly to the eyes, so that he, that had before been evil-favoured, poor and dumb, was now made a young man of clear countenance and his tongue expedite to speak, his hair curled and most fair to see. And so rejoicing for the possession of health, notwithstanding the bishop also offered him opportunity to remain in his household, he would rather return home.

CHAPTER III

How he healed a sick maiden by prayer.

THE same Berthun told me another miracle of the said bishop. That, when the most reverend man Wilfrid after long banishment was recovered again to the bishopric of the church of Hexham, and the same John (after the death of Bosa, a man of much holiness and humility) was translated to York in his

[1] Acts iii. 8.

tempore quodam ad monasterium virginum in loco qui vocatur Vetadun, cui tunc Heriburg abbatissa praefuit. " *Ubi cum venissemus,*" *inquit*, " et magno universorum gaudio suscepti essemus, indicavit nobis abbatissa, quod quaedam de numero virginum quae erat filia ipsius carnalis gravissimo languore teneretur: quia phlebotomata est nuper in brachio, et cum esset in studio, tacta est infirmitate repentini doloris, quo mox increscente magis gravatum est brachium illud vulneratum, ac versum in tumorem, adeo ut vix duabus manibus circumplecti posset, ipsaque iacens in lecto prae nimietate doloris iam moritura videretur. Rogavit ergo episcopum abbatissa ut intraret ad eam, ac benedicere illam dignaretur, quia crederet eam ad benedictionem vel tactum illius mox melius habituram. Interrogans autem ille quando phlebotomata esset puella, et ut cognovit quia in luna quarta, dixit: ' Multum insipienter et indocte fecistis in luna quarta phlebotomando. Memini enim beatae memoriae Theodorum archiepiscopum dicere, quia periculosa sit satis illius temporis phlebotomia, quando et lumen lunae, et rheuma oceani in cremento est. Et quid ego possum puellae, si moritura est, facere? ' At illa instantius obsecrans pro filia quam oppido diligebat, nam et abbatissam eam pro se facere disposuerat, tandem obtinuit ut ad languentem intraret. Intravit ergo me secum adsumpto ad virginem quae iacebat

---

[1] Watton, between Driffield and Beverley.

[2] The A.S. version means " during the blood-letting."

room, he came on a certain time to a nunnery in the place called Wetadun,[1] over which Heriburg was then abbess. "And when we were come there," said he, "and had been entertained with great joyfulness of all, the abbess told us that one of the number of the virgins, which was her own daughter in the flesh, lay pining of a grievous malady; because she was let blood of late in her arm, and while it was being looked to,[2] she was stricken with a sudden affliction of pain, which growing upon her more and more, the arm that was wounded waxed very sore, and passed to be so swollen that a man could scarce clip it with both his hands, and she lying in bed for the great intolerable pain seemed to be at the point to die. The abbess therefore besought the bishop to go in to see her and vouchsafe to bless her, because she believed that, if he did either bless or touch her, she should straightway begin to amend. And he asking when the maiden had been let blood, and understanding it was done at the fourth day of the moon, said: 'Ye have done very unskilfully and indiscreetly to let her blood at the fourth of the moon. For I remember archbishop Theodore of blessed memory said that letting of blood was very dangerous at that time, when both the light of the moon and the tide of the ocean are coming to the full. And what can I do for the maid if she is at death's door?' But she besought him very instantly for her daughter, which she loved tenderly (for it was her purpose to make her abbess in her stead), and at length obtained so much of him as to go in and see the sick maiden. He therefore went in and took me with him to the virgin, which lay, as I have said, in great anguish of pain, and with her arm growing so

multo, ut dixi, dolore constricta, et brachio in tantum grossescente, ut nihil prorsus in cubito flexionis haberet: et adstans dixit orationem super illam, ac benedicens egressus est. Cumque post haec hora competente consederemus ad mensam, adveniens quidam clamavit me foras, et ait: 'Postulat Quoenburg,' hoc enim erat nomen virginis, 'ut ocius regrediaris ad eam.' Quod dum facerem, reperi illam ingrediens vultu hilariorem, et velut sospiti similem. Et dum adsiderem illi, dixit: 'Vis petamus bibere?' At ego; 'Volo,' inquam, 'et multum delector, si potes.' Cumque oblato poculo biberemus ambo, coepit mihi dicere quia 'ex quo episcopus oratione pro me, et benedictione completa egressus est, statim melius habere incipio; etsi necdum vires pristinas recepi, dolor tamen omnis et de brachio ubi ardentior inerat, et de toto meo corpore, velut ipso episcopo foras eum exportante, funditus ablatus est, tametsi tumor adhuc brachii manere videretur.' Abeuntibus autem nobis inde, continuo fugatum dolorem membrorum fuga quoque tumoris horrendi secuta est; et erepta morti ac doloribus virgo, laudes Domino Salvatori una cum ceteris qui ibi erant, servis illius referebat."

great that it could not once bow at the elbow: and standing there he said a prayer over her and blessed her, and went out. And when after this at the fitting hour we were sitting at table, one came and called me out and said: 'Cwenburg,' for that was the maid's name, 'desireth you to come again to her as soon as you can.' Which when I did, upon entering I found her more cheerful of countenance and like as it were to one in sound health. And as I sat by her she said: 'Shall we call for some drink?' 'Marry!' quoth I thereat, 'with a good will, and I am right glad if you should drink.' And when the cup was brought and we both drank, she began to declare unto me that, 'since the bishop ended praying for me and blessed me and went out, forthwith I begin to amend; and albeit I have not yet recovered my former strength, yet all the pain is utterly gone both out of my arm (where it was more fervent) and out of all my body, the bishop as it were carrying it out of doors with him, though yet the swelling seemed scant all allayed in my arm.' Farther, as we were departing thence, incontinently the horrible swelling fled [1] after the pain which had been put to flight from her limbs; and the maiden delivered from death and pain returned praise to the Lord and Saviour with the rest of them that were there waiting upon her."

[1] For this personifying of sickness cf. III. 12 and Luke iv. 39.

CAP. IV

Ut coniugem comitis infirmam aqua benedicta curaverit.

Aliud quoque non multum huic dissimile miraculum de praefato antistite narravit idem abbas, dicens: "Villa erat comitis cuiusdam qui vocabatur Puch, non longe a monasterio nostro, id est, duum ferme millium spatio separata: cuius coniux quadraginta ferme diebus erat acerbissimo languore detenta, ita ut tribus septimanis non posset de cubiculo in quo iacebat foras efferri. Contigit autem eo tempore virum Dei illo ad dedicandam ecclesiam ab eodem comite vocari. Cumque dedicata esset ecclesia, rogavit comes eum ad prandendum in domum suam ingredi. Renuit episcopus, dicens se ad monasterium quod proxime erat, debere reverti. At ille obnixius precibus instans, vovit etiam se eleemosynas pauperibus daturum, dummodo ille dignaretur eo die domum suam ingrediens ieiunium solvere. Rogavi et ego una cum illo, promittens etiam me eleemosynas in alimoniam inopum dare, dum ille domum comitis pransurus ac benedictionem daturus intraret. Cumque hoc tarde ac difficulter impetraremus, intravimus ad reficiendum. Miserat autem episcopus mulieri quae infirma iacebat de aqua benedicta quam in dedicationem ecclesiae consecraverat, per unum de his qui mecum venerant fratribus, praecipiens ut gustandam illi daret, et ubicumque maximum ei dolorem inesse didicisset, de ipsa eam aqua lavaret.

---

[1] Thane according to the A.S. version.
[2] South Burton, now Bishop Burton.

CHAPTER IV

How he healed a thane's[1] wife that was sick, with holy water.

Of the foresaid bishop the same abbot told another miracle not much unlike this, saying: "A certain thane called Puch had his manor[2] not far from our monastery, that is to say, about the space of 2 miles away: whose lady had languished with such a grievous malady for well-nigh 40 days, that in 3 weeks' space she was not able to be carried out of her chamber where she lay. Now it fortuned the man of God at that time to be called thither by the said thane to dedicate a church. And when the church had been dedicated, the thane invited him home to his house to dinner. The bishop refused, saying that of duty he must return to the monastery which was nigh at hand. But the other most instantly entreating him, promised also that he would give alms to the poor if only the bishop would vouchsafe to go home to his house that day and break his fast. I too asked him in like manner as the thane did, promising that I would give alms also to relieve the poor, if he would go to dinner to the thane's house and give him his blessing. And when we obtained so much of him with long entreaty, we entered in to take our repast. Now the bishop had sent to the woman which was lying sick, by one of these brethren which had come with me, some of the holy water which he had hallowed for the dedication of the church, commanding him to give it her to drink, and to wash her with the same water, in whatsoever part he should learn her pain to be most vehement. Which being done,

Quod ut factum est, surrexit statim mulier sana, et non solum se infirmitate longa carere, sed et perditas dudum vires recepisse sentiens, obtulit poculum episcopo ac nobis: coeptumque ministerium nobis omnibus propinandi usque ad prandium completum non omisit; imitata socrum beati Petri, quae cum febrium fuisset ardoribus fatigata, ad tactum manus Dominicae surrexit, et sanitate simul ac virtute recepta, ministrabat eis."

CAP. V

Ut item puerum comitis orando a morte revocaverit.

Alio item tempore vocatus ad dedicandam ecclesiam comitis vocabulo Addi, cum postulatum complesset ministerium, rogatus est ab eodem comite intrare ad unum de pueris eius qui acerrima aegritudine premebatur, ita ut deficiente penitus omni membrorum officio, iamiamque moriturus esse videretur; cui etiam loculus iam tunc erat praeparatus in quo defunctus condi deberet. Addidit autem vir etiam lacrimas precibus, diligenter obsecrans ut intraret oraturus pro illo, quia multum necessaria sibi esset vita ipsius; crederet vero quia si ille ei manum imponere atque eum benedicere voluisset, statim melius haberet. Intravit ergo illo episcopus, et vidit eum moestis omnibus iam morti proximum, positumque loculum iuxta eum in quo sepeliendus poni deberet; dixitque orationem ac benedixit eum,

---

[1] Luke iv. 39.
[2] North Burton, now Cherry Burton.

incontinent the woman rose out of her bed whole and sound, and perceiving that she was not only rid of her long malady but had also recovered her strength now so long lost, she offered the cup to the bishop and to us: and did not fail to serve us all with drink, as she had begun, all the dinner-time; following blessed Peter's mother-in-law,[1] who, after being wasted with hot burning fever, rose up at the touch of the Lord's hand, and her health as well as strength being recovered, ministered unto them."

CHAPTER V

How by his prayers he likewise recovered a thane's servant from death.

The bishop, being called another time likewise to dedicate the church [2] of a thane called Addi, was invited, after the duty desired had been fulfilled, by the same thane to go in to one of his servants which was vexed with a very sore sickness, so that, losing utterly all the use of his limbs, he seemed to be already at the point of death; and the coffin also where he should be laid after his death had by that time been made ready. Furthermore, the thane also entreated with weeping tears, earnestly desiring that he would go in to pray for the servant, because his life was very necessary to him; and he verily believed that if the bishop would lay his hand upon him and bless him, he should straightway begin to amend. The bishop therefore went in thither and saw him ready (to the distress of all) to yield up the ghost, and the coffin hard by him in which he should be placed for burial; and he made his prayer and

et egrediens dixit solito consolantium sermone: "Bene convalescas, et cito." Cumque post haec sederent ad mensam, misit puer ad dominum suum, rogans sibi poculum vini mittere, quia sitiret. Gavisus ille multum quia bibere posset, misit ei calicem vini benedictum ab episcopo; quem ut bibit, surrexit continuo, et veterno infirmitatis discusso, induit se ipse vestimentis suis; et egressus inde intravit, ac salutavit episcopum et convivas, dicens, quia ipse quoque delectaretur manducare et bibere cum eis. Iusserunt eum sedere secum ad epulas, multum gaudentes de sospitate illius. Residebat, vescebatur, bibebat, laetabatur, quasi unus e convivis agebat; et multis post haec annis vivens, in eadem quam acceperat salute permansit. Hoc autem miraculum memoratus abbas non se praesente factum, sed ab his qui praesentes fuere, sibi perhibet esse relatum.

CAP. VI

Ut clericum suum cadendo contritum, aeque orando ac benedicendo a morte revocaverit.

Neque hoc praetereundum silentio, quod famulus Christi Herebald in seipso ab eo factum solet narrare miraculum, qui tunc quidem in clero illius conversatus, nunc monasterio quod est iuxta ostium Tini fluminis abbatis iure praeest. "Vitam," inquit, "illius, quantum hominibus aestimare fas est, quod

blessed him, and going out said those comfortable words men use to the sick: " May you have good and quick recovery!" And after this as they sat at table, the servant sent to his master, desiring to have a cup of wine sent him, for he was thirsty. The thane being glad with all his heart that he could drink, sent him a cup of wine which the bishop had blessed; and as soon as he had drunk of it, he rose straightways out of bed, and shaking off the sluggishness of his sickness he put on his clothes of himself; and coming out of his chamber went in and saluted the bishop and the guests, saying that he also had a good appetite to eat and drink with them. They commanded him to sit with them at the feast, and rejoiced much that he was so well recovered. He sat down, he ate, he drank, he made merry and behaved himself as one of the guests; and living many years after continued in the same state of health which he had gained. Now the foresaid abbot says that this miracle was not done in his presence, but he had it by relation of them that were present.

CHAPTER VI

How by his prayer and blessing he called back from death one of his clerks when bruised with a fall.

NEITHER should this miracle be passed over in silence, which Herebald, Christ's servant, is wont to report to have been done by the bishop upon himself, who at that time was one of his clergy but is now over the monastery that bordereth upon the mouth of the Tyne, as abbot. " So far forth," said he, " as it is lawful for man to judge, I found his way of life

praesens optime cognovi, per omnia episcopo dignam esse comperi. Sed et cuius meriti apud internum testem habitus sit, et in multis aliis, et in meipso maxime expertus sum: quippe quem ab ipso, ut ita dicam, mortis limite revocans, ad viam vitae sua oratione ac benedictione reduxit. Nam cum primaevo adolescentiae tempore in clero illius degerem legendi quidem canendique studiis traditus, sed non adhuc animum perfecte a iuvenilibus cohibens inlecebris, contigit die quadam nos iter agentes cum illo devenisse in viam planam et amplam aptamque cursui equorum: coeperuntque iuvenes qui cum ipso erant, maxime laici, postulare episcopum ut cursu maiore equos suos invicem probare liceret. At ille primo negavit, otiosum dicens esse quod desiderabant; sed ad ultimum multorum unanima intentione devictus; 'Facite,' inquit, 'si vultis, ita tamen ut Herebald ab illo se certamine funditus abstineat.' Porro ipse diligentius obsecrans, ut et mihi certandi cum illis copia daretur, fidebam namque equo quem mihi ipse optimum donaverat, nequaquam impetrare potui.

"At cum saepius huc atque illuc spectante me et episcopo, concitatis in cursum equis reverterentur; et ipse lascivo superatus animo non me potui cohibere, sed, prohibente licet illo, ludentibus me miscui, et simul cursu equi contendere coepi. Quod dum agerem, audivi illum post tergum mihi cum gemitu dicentem: 'O quam magnum vae facis mihi sic

in all ways worthy of a bishop, and of that I am right well assured, because I was conversant with him. But touching his worthiness in the sight of Him that judgeth men's hearts I have had experience both in many other and specially in myself, as a man whom he in a manner called back from the very gate of death to the way of life by his prayer and benediction. For when in the days of my lusty youth I lived among his clergy and was set to school to learn both to read and sing, but did not yet fully restrain my fantasy from youthful enticements, it fortuned one day, that as we journeyed with him, we came into a goodly plain way which was a trim place to course our horses in; and the young men that were in his company, especially of the lay sort, began to desire the bishop to give them leave to gallop and make trial of their horses one against the other. But at first he told them nay, saying it was a fond thing they wished for; but at the last, not being able to withstand the earnest request of all that number, he said: 'Do if you will, marry so that yet Herebald utterly refrain from that race.' Then did I right earnestly entreat him to let me have leave to race with them, for I trusted well the excellency of my horse which the bishop had given me, but could not prevail at all.

"But as many times they fetched their horses to and fro at full speed before the eyes of the bishop and me, I too overcome with wantonness of spirit could not stay myself, but, for all his withholding, I joyned myself to their pastime, and began to race with them at the full speed of my horse. And as I did so, I heard him behind my back with a deep sigh saying: 'O what grievous woe workest thou to me in riding

equitando!' Et ego audiens, nihilominus coeptis insta vetitis. Nec mora, dum fervens equus quoddam itineris concavum valentiore impetu transiliret, lapsus decidi, et mox velut emoriens sensum penitus motumque omnem perdidi. Erat namque illo in loco lapis terrae aequalis obtectus cespite tenui, neque ullus alter in tota illa campi planitie lapis inveniri poterat; casuque evenit, vel potius divina provisione, ad puniendam inobedientiae meae culpam, ut hunc capite ac manu quam capiti ruens subposueram, tangerem, atque infracto pollice capitis quoque iunctura solveretur; et ego, ut dixi, simillimus mortuo fierem. Et quia moveri non poteram, tetenderunt ibidem papilionem in qua iacerem. Erat autem hora diei circiter septima, a qua ad vesperum usque quietus, et quasi mortuus permanens tunc paululum revivisco, ferorque domum a sociis, ac tacitus tota nocte perduro. Vomebam autem sanguinem, eo quod et interanea essent ruendo convulsa. At episcopus gravissime de casu et interitu meo dolebat, eo quod me speciali diligeret affectu: nec voluit nocte illa iuxta morem cum clericis suis manere, verum solus in oratione persistens noctem ducebat pervigilem, pro mea ut reor sospitate supernae pietati supplicans. Et mane primo ingressus ad me, ac dicta super me oratione, vocavit me nomine meo, et quasi de somno gravi excitatum interrogavit si nossem quis esset qui loqueretur ad

after this sort!' And I hearing these words, notwithstanding, went on in the course he had forbidden. And behold, even as my fiery horse leapt with a mighty bound over a hollow place that was in the way, down fell I to the ground, and, as one ready to die, by and by utterly lost my senses and was no wise able to move. For in that place there lay a stone close to the ground, covered with a little green turf, and not one other could be found in all that level ground; and it fortuned by chance, or rather by the providence of God to punish my fault of disobedience, that I pitched upon this stone with my head and hand, which in the fall I had put under my head, and so broke my thumb and also cracked my skull; and, as I said, was most like one that was dead. And because I could not be moved, they stretched forth a tent for me to lie in upon the place. Now it was about the 7th hour of the day,[1] and from that hour until evening I tarried there still and as it had been dead, and then I began to come to myself again and was carried home of my fellows, and lay speechless all night. Moreover, I cast up blood because my inner parts had been sore shaken with the fall. But the bishop, for the singular affection he bare to me, was marvellous sorry for my misfortune and deadly wound; and would not that night after his accustomed manner tarry with his clergy, but continuing alone in watch all that night, as I may well conjecture, besought the goodness that is above for my preservation. And coming in to me early in the morning, he said a prayer over me and called me by my name, and when I waked as it were out of a great slumber, he asked me, if I knew who it was that spoke to me.

[1] One hour past midday.

me. At ego aperiens oculos, aio, 'Etiam: tu es antistes meus amatus.' 'Potes,' inquit, 'vivere?' Et ego; 'Possum,' inquam, 'per orationes vestras, si voluerit Dominus.'

"Qui imponens capiti meo manum, cum verbis benedictionis, rediit ad orandum: et post pusillum me revisens invenit sedentem et iam loqui valentem: coepitque me interrogare, divino, ut mox patuit, admonitus instinctu, an me esse baptizatum absque scrupulo nossem: cui ego, absque ulla me hoc dubietate scire respondi, quia salutari fonte in remissionem peccatorum essem ablutus; et nomen presbyteri a quo me baptizatum noveram, dixi. At ille: 'Si ab hoc,' inquit, 'sacerdote baptizatus es, non es perfecte baptizatus: novi namque eum, et quia cum esset presbyter ordinatus, nullatenus propter ingenii tarditatem potuit catechizandi vel baptizandi ministerium discere, propter quod et ipse illum ab huius praesumptione ministerii quod regulariter implere nequibat, omnimodis cessare praecepi.' Quibus dictis, eadem hora me catechizare ipse curavit; factumque est ut exsufflante illo in faciem meam, confestim me melius habere sentirem. Vocavit autem medicum, et dissolutam mihi emicranii iuncturam componere atque alligare iussit. Tantumque mox accepta eius benedictione convalui, ut in crastinum ascendens equum, cum ipso iter in alium locum facerem: nec multo post plene curatus, vitali etiam unda perfusus sum."

Mansit autem in episcopatu annos triginta tres, et sic caelestia regna conscendens sepultus est in

---

[1] Pope Zacharias, 746, took the opposite view to this, Pl. II. 277.

Whereupon I opening my eyes, said: 'Yea; thou art my dear bishop.' 'Can you live?' said he. And I said: 'I can by your prayers, if the Lord will.'

"And he laying his hand upon my head and repeating the words of benediction, returned again to his prayers: and coming to see me again a little while after, he found me sitting up and now able to speak; and moved, as was soon plain, with divine inspiration, he began to ask me whether I knew for certain that I had been baptized: to which I answered that this I knew without any doubt, that I had been cleansed in the health-giving font in remission of sins; and I named the priest by whom I knew that I had been baptized. But he said: 'If you were christened of this priest, you are not well christened[1]: for I know him, and that having been ordained priest, he could not for his dull-headed wit in any wise learn nor to instruct nor to baptize: and for that cause too I myself charged him not to presume to this ministry which he could not do according to rule, but wholly to desist therefrom.' And when he had so said, he set himself the same hour to instruct me; and it came to pass, that as he blew in my face,[2] immediately I felt myself to be better. Further, he called the surgeon, and commanded him to set my cracked skull and bind it up. And by and by after receiving his blessing I was so well recovered, that the next day I mounted to my horse and journeyed with him to another place; and not long after, being fully healed, I was also bathed in the water of life."

Now John continued in the bishopric 33 years, and so ascending to the heavenly realms was buried in

[2] A custom at baptism to exorcise evil spirits. Bright, p. 306.

porticu sancti Petri, in monasterio suo, quod dicitur " In Silva Derorum," anno ab incarnatione Dominica septingentesimo vicesimo primo Nam cum prae maiore senectute minus episcopatui administrando sufficeret, ordinato in episcopatum Eboracensis ecclesiae Vilfrido presbytero suo, secessit ad monasterium praefatum, ibique vitam in Deo digna conversatione complevit.

CAP. VII

Ut Caedualla, rex Occidentalium Saxonum, baptizandus Romam venerit: sed et successor eius Ini eadem beatorum apostolorum limina devotus adierit.

Anno autem regni Aldfridi tertio, Caedualla rex Occidentalium Saxonum, cum genti suae duobus annis strenuissime praeesset, relicto imperio propter Dominum regnumque perpetuum, venit Romam, hoc sibi gloriae singularis desiderans adipisci, ut ad limina beatorum apostolorum fonte baptismatis ablueretur, in quo solo didicerat generi humano patere vitae caelestis introitum: simul etiam sperans quia mox baptizatus, carne solutus ad aeterna gaudia iam mundus transiret: quod utrumque ut mente disposuerat, Domino iuvante completum est. Etenim illo perveniens, pontificatum agente Sergio, baptizatus est die sancto sabbati paschalis, anno ab incarnatione Domini sexcentesimo octuagesimo nono: et in albis adhuc positus, languore correptus, duodecimo kalendarum Maiarum die solutus a carne, et beatorum est regno sociatus in caelis. Cui etiam tempore

---

[1] Wilfrid II, or the younger.

the side chapel of St. Peter, in his own monastery named Derewood, in the 721st year of the Lord's incarnation. For when he was not able for increasing old age to govern his bishopric he ordained Wilfrid,[1] his priest, bishop of the church of York, and departed to the said monastery, and there ended his life in holy conversation.

CHAPTER VII

How Cadwalla king of the West Saxons came to Rome to be baptized: moreover, how his successor Ini of devotion went to the churches of the blessed Apostles.

The third year of king Aldfrid's reign, Cadwalla king of the West Saxons, after keeping the sovereignty over his nation very stoutly for two years, for the Lord's sake and the hope of the everlasting kingdom forsook his power and came to Rome, desiring to obtain the singular renown to be cleansed in the font of baptism at the churches of the blessed apostles, by the which alone he had learned the entry to the heavenly life is opened to mankind: withal too he had hope that by and by being baptized he should be released from the body, and being now cleansed should pass to eternal joys: the which both by the Lord's help were fulfilled as he had in his mind determined. For coming to Rome, when Sergius was pope, he was baptized on the holy Saturday before Easter, in the 689th year after the Lord's incarnation; and wearing still his white robes he fell sick and was released from the body the 20th day of April, and made partaker of the kingdom of the blessed in the heavens. Whom the said pope had

baptismatis papa memoratus Petri nomen imposuerat, ut beatissimo apostolorum principi, ad cuius sacratissimum corpus a finibus terrae pio ductus amore venerat, etiam nominis ipsius consortio iungeretur: qui in eius quoque ecclesia sepultus est: et iubente pontifice epitaphium in eius monumento scriptum, in quo et memoria devotionis ipsius fixa per saecula maneret, et legentes quoque vel audientes exemplum facti, ad studium religionis accenderet. Scriptum est ergo hoc modo:

" Culmen, opes, subolem, pollentia regna, triumphos,
Exuvias, proceres, moenia, castra, lares;
Quaeque patrum virtus, et quae congesserat ipse
Caedual armipotens, liquit amore Dei,
Ut Petrum, sedemque Petri rex cerneret hospes,
Cuius fonte meras sumeret almus aquas.
Splendificumque iubar radianti carperet haustu,
Ex quo vivificus fulgor ubique fluit.
Percipiensque alacer redivivae praemia vitae,
Barbaricam rabiem, nomen et inde suum
Conversus convertit ovans: Petrumque vocari
Sergius antistes iussit, ut ipse pater
Fonte renascentis, quem Christi gratia purgans
Protinus albatum vexit in arce poli.
Mira fides regis! clementia maxima Christi,
Cuius consilium nullus adire potest!
Sospes enim veniens supremo ex orbe Brittani,
Per varias gentes, per freta, perque vias,

also at his baptism named Peter, that by communion of name he might be united to the most blessed chief of the apostles, to whose most holy body his godly love had brought him to come from the ends of the earth; and in his church too he was buried: and at the pope's commandment an epitaph was written upon his tomb, that the memory of his devoutness thereupon engraved might continue throughout all ages, and the readers and hearers also might be stirred to religious zeal by the example of that he had done. The epitaph was written after this sort:

"All high estate and wealth and rule, all hope of race to come,
All triumphs, spoil and captive chiefs, walled cities, camp and home;
All that his fathers' might or he had hoarded for their pride,
The warrior prince Cadwalla set for love of God aside,
That Peter he a pilgrim king might see and Peter's place,
And in his font the waters pure might take of saving grace;
And drink the dazzling radiance of that bright shining beam
Which spreadeth through the world its light in one life-giving stream.
And in his eagerness of heart a life renewed to claim,
His former barbarous rage he changed, he changed his former name,
And triumph in the change he gat: pope Sergius gave command
That Peter he be called, and took as godfather his hand,
When from the font new-born he rose, and straight in robes of white
He whom Christ's grace had cleansed, above was borne to heavenly height.
O wondrous was that princely faith! and yet more wondrous far
Christ's mercy, unapproachable to all Whose judgments are.
From Britain's furthest clime to Rome he was in safety brought
Through divers nations, over seas, by roads with peril fraught.

Urbem Romuleam vidit, templumque verendum
  Aspexit, Petri mystica dona gerens.
Candidus inter oves Christi sociabilis ibit:
  Corpore nam tumulum, mente superna tenet.
Commutasse magis sceptrorum insignia credas,
  Quem regnum Christi promeruisse vides.

"Hic depositus est Caedual, qui et Petrus, rex Saxonum, sub die duodecimo kalendarum Maiarum, indictione secunda; qui vixit annos plus minus triginta, imperante domno Iustiniano piissimo Augusto, anno eius consulatus quarto, pontificante apostolico viro domno Sergio papa anno secundo."

Abeunte autem Romam Caedualla, successit in regnum Ini de stirpe regia; qui cum triginta et septem annis imperium tenuisset gentis illius, et ipse relicto regno ac iuvenioribus commendato, ad limina beatorum apostolorum Gregorio pontificatum tenente profectus est, cupiens in vicinia sanctorum locorum ad tempus peregrinari in terris, quo familiarius a sanctis recipi mereretur in caelis: quod his temporibus plures de gente Anglorum, nobiles, ignobiles, laici, clerici, viri ac feminae certatim facere consuerunt.

Of Romulus the city saw, and Peter's reverend fane
He gazed upon, and mystic gifts he bare his aid to gain.
To feed amongst the flock of Christ, to him, white sheep, is given;
His body lies within the tomb; his soul is passed to heaven.
Well may we think that he which thus willed from his realm to range,
For earthly throne Christ's kingdom won and lost naught by exchange.

"Here was buried Cadwal, also named Peter, king of the Saxons, on the 20th of April, in the second indiction; who lived 30 years or thereabouts, when our lord Justinian the most religious Augustus was emperor, in the 4th year of his consulship, in the second year that the apostolic lord Sergius was pope."

Now as Cadwalla was taking his journey to Rome, Ini, one of the king's blood, succeeded unto the crown; who after he had reigned 37 years over that nation, himself likewise gave over his kingdom and committed the governance of it to younger men, and set out to the churches of the blessed apostles, at the time that Gregory was pope, having a desire to wander like a pilgrim upon earth for a while in the neighbourhood of the holy places, that he might deserve to be received more willingly of the saints in heaven: the which practice in these days many Englishmen, both of the nobility and commons, spiritual and temporal, men and women, were wont to use with much emulation.

CAP. VIII

Ut Theodoro defuncto archiepiscopatus gradum Berctuald susceperit: et inter plurimos quos ordinavit, etiam Tobiam virum doctissimum Hrofensi ecclesiae fecerit antistitem.

Anno autem post hunc quo Caedualla Romae defunctus est proximo, id est, sexcentesimo nonagesimo incarnationis Dominicae, Theodorus beatae memoriae archiepiscopus senex et plenus dierum, id est, annorum octoginta octo, defunctus est; quem se numerum annorum fuisse habiturum, ipse iamdudum somnii revelatione edoctus suis praedicere solebat. Mansit autem in episcopatu annis viginti duobus, sepultusque est in ecclesia sancti Petri, in qua omnium episcoporum Doruvernensium sunt corpora deposita: de quo una cum consortibus eiusdem sui gradus recte ac veraciter dici potest, quia "corpora ipsorum in pace sepulta sunt, et nomen eorum vivet in generationes et generationes." Ut enim breviter dicam, tantum profectus spiritalis tempore praesulatus illius Anglorum ecclesiae, quantum nunquam antea potuere, ceperunt. Cuius personam, vitam, aetatem, et obitum, epitaphium quoque monumenti ipsius versibus heroicis triginta et quatuor palam ac lucide cunctis illo advenientibus pandit; quorum primi sunt hi:

"Hic sacer in tumba pausat cum corpore praesul,
Quem nunc Theodorum lingua Pelasga vocat.

CHAPTER VIII

How after the death of Theodore, Bertwald took the degree of archbishop upon him; and amongst many other ordained by him he made too Tobias, a man very well learned, bishop of the church of Rochester.

Now the year after this in which Cadwalla died at Rome, that is to say in the 690th of the Lord's incarnation, archbishop Theodore of blessed memory died, being an old man and full of days, to wit fourscore and eight years; the which number of years that he should live was long before signified unto him by revelation, as he was wont to make report to his friends. Now he continued in his bishopric 22 years, and was buried in St. Peter's church, where the bodies of all the bishops of Canterbury were laid: of whom along with his fellows equal in degree it may rightly and truly be said, that "their bodies are buried in peace and their name shall live from generation to generation.[1]" For that I may use few words, the English churches, for the time he was prelate, received so much increase in spiritual matters as they could never before. As touching his personage, his life, his age and death, the epitaph also written upon his sepulchre in four-and-thirty heroical verses[2] doth manifestly and clearly set them out to all that have access thither: of the which these are the first:

"A holy prelate resteth here his body in the grave,
To whom the name of Theodore the Greek tongue newly gave.

[1] Cf. Ecclus. xliv. 14. [2] Cf. p. 51.

Princeps pontificum, felix, summusque sacerdos
Limpida discipulis dogmata disseruit."

Ultimi autem hi:

"Namque diem nonamdecimam September habebat,
Cum carnis claustra spiritus egreditur.
Alma novae scandens felix consortia vitae,
Civibus angelicis iunctus in arce poli."

Successit autem Theodoro in episcopatu Berctuald, qui erat abbas in monasterio quod iuxta ostium aquilonale fluminis Genladae positum Racuulfe nuncupatur: vir et ipse scientia Scripturarum imbutus, sed et ecclesiasticis simul ac monasterialibus disciplinis summe instructus, tametsi praedecessori suo minime comparandus: qui electus est quidem in episcopatum anno Dominicae incarnationis sexcentesimo nonagesimo secundo, die primo mensis Iulii, regnantibus in Cantia Victredo et Suaebhardo; ordinatus autem anno sequente tertio die kalendarum Iuliarum Dominica a Goduine metropolitano episcopo Galliarum: et sedit in sede sua pridie kalendarum Septembrium Dominica; qui inter multos quos ordinavit antistites, etiam Gebmundo Hrofensis ecclesiae praesule defuncto Tobiam pro illo consecravit, virum Latina, Graeca et Saxonica lingua atque eruditione multipliciter instructum.

---

[1] Reculver in Kent.
[2] Joint kings apparently.
[3] Archbishop of Lyons 693–713: the delay of three years in Bertwald's consecration is not explained.

A sovereign pontiff, prosperous, and priest of high degree,
To his disciples doctrine clear he taught as all can see."

But the last are these:

"For when September's moon had put full nineteen days away,
His spirit quits the prison-house of this our mortal clay.
New life where grace abounds to share he taketh blissful flight,
And joins the angel citizens above the starry height."

Now Bertwald succeeded Theodore in the bishopric, who was abbot in a monastry called Raculf,[1] which lieth hard by the north entry of the river Yenlade: a man who was too himself well travailed in the knowledge of the Scriptures and moreover fully instructed in ecclesiastical as well as monastical discipline, yet nothing to be compared to his predecessor: who was chosen indeed to be bishop in the 692nd year after the Lord's incarnation, the first day of the month July, when Witred and Swebhard were kings [2] of Kent; but he was ordained the next year after upon a Sunday, being then the 29th of June, by Godwin,[3] metropolitan bishop of France: and took his seat upon his throne the 31st day of August, being Sunday; who amongst many whom he ordained to be bishops, after Gebmund prelate of the church of Rochester was dead, also consecrated Tobias in his place, a man instructed in the Latin, Greek and Saxon tongues and of much learning beside in many ways.

CAP. IX

Ut Ecgberct vir sanctus ad praedicandum in Germaniam venire voluerit, nec valuerit: porro Victberct advenerit quidem; sed quia nec ipse aliquid profecisset, rursum in Hiberniam, unde venerat, redierit.

Eo tempore venerabilis et cum omni honorificentia nominandus famulus Christi et sacerdos Ecgberct, quem in Hibernia insula peregrinam ducere vitam pro adipiscenda in caelis patria retulimus, proposuit animo pluribus prodesse; id est, inito opere apostolico, verbum Dei aliquibus earum quae nondum audierant gentibus evangelizando committere: quarum in Germania plurimas noverat esse nationes, a quibus Angli vel Saxones qui nunc Brittaniam incolunt, genus et originem duxisse noscuntur; unde hactenus a vicina gente Brettonum corrupte Garmani nuncupantur. Sunt autem Fresones, Rugini, Danai, Hunni, Antiqui Saxones, Boructuari: sunt alii perplures eisdem in partibus populi paganis adhuc ritibus servientes, ad quos venire praefatus Christi miles circumnavigata Brittania disposuit, si quos forte ex illis ereptos Satanae ad Christum transferre valeret; vel si hoc fieri non posset, Romam venire ad videnda atque adoranda beatorum apostolorum ac martyrum Christi limina cogitavit.

Sed ne aliquid horum perficeret, superna illi oracula simul et opera restiterunt. Siquidem electis

---

[1] Or bishop, Pl. II. 285.
[2] Rugii, Tac. *Germ.* 43. The name remains in the Island of Rügen.
[3] The Bructeri in Westphalia.

CHAPTER IX

How Egbert, a holy man, would gladly have come to Germany to preach, and could not: further, how Witbert went thither in deed, but because he had not either done any good, returned back to Ireland, from whence he had come.

At that time the venerable servant of Christ and priest [1] Egbert, of me to be named with all honourable mention, who (as we said before) lived like a pilgrim in the isle of Ireland to obtain a country in the heavens, purposed with himself to profit many, that is to say, to take upon him the work of an apostle, and by preaching of the Gospel to bring the word of God to some of those nations which had not yet heard it: and many such countries he knew to be in Germany, of whom the English or Saxons, which now inhabit Britain, are well known to have had beginning and offspring; whereby it is that to this day they are corruptly called Garmans by the Britons that are their neighbours. Such now are the Frisons, Rugins,[2] Danes, Huns, Old Saxons, and Boructuars:[3] there are very many other nations in the same parts, observing yet the rites of paynims, to whom the foresaid soldier of Christ purposed to go after he had sailed round about Britain, if haply he might be able to deliver any of them from Satan and trade them toward Christ; or if this could not come to pass, he thought to come to Rome to see and to worship the churches of the blessed apostles and martyrs of Christ.

But messages from above and the working of God suffered him not to achieve any of these enterprises.

sociis strenuissimis et ad praedicandum verbum idoneis, utpote actione simul et eruditione praeclaris, praeparatisque omnibus quae navigantibus esse necessaria videbantur, venit die quadam mane primo ad eum unus de fratribus, discipulus quondam in Brittania, et minister Deo dilecti sacerdotis Boisili, cum esset idem Boisil praepositus monasterii Mailrosensis sub abbate Eata, ut supra narravimus, referens ei visionem quae sibi eadem nocte apparuisset: "Cum expletis," inquiens, "hymnis matutinalibus in lectulo membra posuissem, ac levis mihi somnus obrepsisset, apparuit magister quondam meus et nutritor amantissimus Boisil, interrogavitque me, an eum cognoscere possem. Aio, 'Etiam: tu es enim Boisil.' At ille: 'Ad hoc,' inquit, 'veni, ut responsum Domini Salvatoris Ecgbercto adferam, quod te tamen referente oportet ad illum venire. Dic ergo illi quia non valet iter quod proposuit, implere: Dei enim voluntatis est ut ad Columbae monasteria magis pergat docenda.'" Erat autem Columba primus doctor fidei Christianae transmontanis Pictis ad aquilonem, primusque fundator monasterii quod in Hii insula multis diu Scottorum Pictorumque populis venerabile mansit. Qui videlicet Columba nunc a nonnullis composito a cella et Columba nomine Columcelli vocatur. Audiens autem verba visionis Ecgberct, praecepit fratri qui retulerat ne cuiquam haec alteri referret, ne forte inlusoria esset visio.

---

[1] Cf. III. 4.

For when he had chosen stout men to accompany him and such as were meet to preach the word, as being notable for their good gesture and knowledge, and had made ready all things that seemed necessary for their voyage, there came to him one day early in the morning one of the brethren, that had been sometime in Britain scholar and servant of Boisil the priest beloved of God, at what time the said Boisil was provost of the monastery of Melrose under Eata their abbot (as we have signified before), and shewed him a vision that had, he said, appeared unto him that night: "When," quoth he, "the hymns of matins were done, I laid me down upon my bed, and falling in a little slumbering sleep, Boisil, that was sometime my master and bringer-up in love, appeared to me and asked me, whether I could know him. 'Yea,' quoth I, 'for thou art Boisil.' Then said he, 'For this am I come, to bring to Egbert the Lord and Saviour's answer, which nevertheless must come to him by thy report. Tell him, therefore, that he is not able to perform the journey he hath purposed: for it is God's will he go rather and instruct Columba's monasteries.'" Now Columba was the first teacher of the Christian faith to the Redshanks dwelling beyond the mountains northward, and the first founder of the monastery in the island of Hy, which was had in great reverence a long time of the Scots and of the Redshanks.[1] And this Columba to wit is now called of some Columcille, by composition of the words *cell* and *Columba.* Now Egbert, hearing the words said in the vision, gave the brother which had reported them charge, that he should reveal them to no man else, lest peradventure it might prove to be a

Ipse autem tacitus rem considerans, veram esse timebat: nec tamen a praeparando itinere, quo ad gentes docendas iret, cessare volebat.

At post dies paucos rursum venit ad eum praefatus frater, dicens quia et ea nocte sibi post expletos matutinos Boisil per visum apparuerit, dicens: "Quare tam negligenter ac tepide dixisti Ecgbercto quae tibi dicenda praecepi? At nunc vade, et dic illi quia, velit nolit, debet ad monasteria Columbae venire, quia aratra eorum non recte incedunt: oportet autem eum ad rectum haec tramitem revocare." Qui haec audiens denuo praecepit fratri, ne haec cui patefaceret. Ipse vero tametsi certus est factus de visione, nihilominus tentavit iter dispositum cum fratribus memoratis incipere. Cumque iam navi imposuissent quae tanti itineris necessitas poscebat, atque opportunos aliquot dies ventos exspectarent, facta est nocte quadam tam saeva tempestas, quae perditis nonnulla ex parte his quae in navi erant rebus, ipsam in littus iacentem inter undas relinqueret: salvata sunt tamen omnia quae erant Ecgbercti, et sociorum eius. Tum ipse quasi propheticum illud dicens quia, "propter me est tempestas haec," subtraxit se illi profectioni et remanere domi passus est.

At vero unus de sociis eius, vocabulo Victberct, cum esset et ipse contemptu mundi ac doctrinae scientia insignis (nam multos annos in Hibernia peregrinus anachoreticam in magna perfectione vitam egerat), ascendit navem, et Fresiam perveniens

---

[1] Jonah i. 12.

fantastical vision. But he himself, considering the matter secretly with himself, feared it was indeed true; but notwithstanding, he would not cease to make provision for the journey which he purposed to take for the teaching of those nations.

But a few days after, the foresaid brother came to him again saying that that night too, after matins was done, Boisil appeared unto him in a vision, and said: "Why didst thou speak to Egbert so negligently and coldly the things I charged thee to say? Yet go now and tell him that whether he will or no, he shall go to Columba's monasteries, because their ploughs go not straight; but he must bring them back to the straight way." And Egbert hearing this, charged the brother anew to reveal it to no man. Yet, albeit he was so certified of the vision, for all that, he none the less assayed to go forward on the journey he had purposed with the brethren before mentioned. And when they had now laid aboard all that should be requisite in such a long voyage, and tarried some days for a good wind, there arose one night such a vehement tempest that, good part of the merchandise in the ship being lost, she was left in the midst of the waves lying upon the shore: notwithstanding, all Egbert's goods were saved and his companions'. Then he, saying as it were the sentence of the prophet,[1] that "this tempest happeneth for my sake," withdrew himself from that setting forth and was content to stay at home.

But one of his fellows named Witbert, being a man notable for contempt of the world and knowledge of learning (for he had passed many years an anchoret's life in much perfection as a pilgrim in Ireland), took ship and arriving in Frisland preached

duobus annis continuis genti illi ac regi eius Rathbedo verbum salutis praedicabat, neque aliquem tanti laboris fructum apud barbaros invenit auditores. Tunc reversus ad dilectae locum peregrinationis, solito in silentio vacare Domino coepit; et quoniam externis prodesse ad fidem non poterat, suis amplius ex virtutum exemplis prodesse curabat.

CAP. X

Ut Vilbrord in Fresia praedicans multos ad Christum converterit; et ut socii eius Heuualdi sint martyrium passi.

Ut autem vidit vir Domini Ecgberct, quia nec ipse ad praedicandum gentibus venire permittebatur, retentus ob aliam sanctae ecclesiae utilitatem de qua oraculo fuerat praemonitus; nec Victberct illas deveniens in partes quicquam proficiebat: tentavit adhuc in opus verbi mittere viros sanctos et industrios, in quibus eximius Vilbrord presbyteri gradu et merito praefulgebat. Qui cum illo advenissent, erant autem numero duodecim, divertentes ad Pippinum ducem Francorum, gratanter ab illo suscepti sunt: et quia nuper citeriorem Fresiam, expulso inde Rathbedo rege, ceperat, illo eos ad praedicandum misit; ipse quoque imperiali auctoritate iuvans, ne quis praedi-

[1] Of Northumbria, born 657 and brought up at Ripon. After 12 years in Ireland he went on his mission to the Continent, 690.

[2] Then mayor of the palace and real ruler of the Franks.

the word of salvation two years in succession to that nation and Rathbod their king, but found no fruit of all his great labour amongst his barbarous hearers. Returning then to the place of his beloved pilgrimage, he began to give himself to the Lord in his wonted silence; and because he could do no good in converting foreigners to the faith, he studied how he might better profit his own countrymen by virtuous example of life.

CHAPTER X

How Wilbrord[1] preaching in Frisland converted many to Christ; and how the two Hewalds his companions suffered martyrdom.

Now when the man of the Lord, Egbert, perceived that neither was he suffered himself to go to preach to the heathen, but was stayed for some other commodity of the holy Church, whereof he had warning by an oracle of God; neither did Witbert coming into those parts profit anything: he assayed yet to send for the setting forth of the word holy men willing to take pains, amongst whom the excellent Wilbrord was chief for his merit and degree of priest. And they after their arrival thither, being in number 12, turned aside to Pippin[2] duke of the Franks, and were friendly entertained of him; and because he had lately taken hither[3] Frisland and driven out thence their king Rathbod,[4] he sent them thither to preach; aiding them also with his own princely authority, that no man should

[3] Nearest to the Franks.

[4] Rathbod had consented to be baptized, but withdrew from the font on being told that his ancestors were in hell.

cantibus quicquam molestiae inferret; multisque eos qui fidem suscipere vellent beneficiis adtollens: unde factum est, opitulante gratia divina, ut multos in brevi ab idolatria ad fidem converterent Christi.

Horum secuti exempla duo quidam presbyteri de natione Anglorum, qui in Hibernia multo tempore pro aeterna patria exulaverant, venerunt ad provinciam Antiquorum Saxonum, si forte aliquos ibidem praedicando Christo adquirere possent. Erant autem unius ambo, sicut devotionis, sic etiam vocabuli: nam uterque eorum appellabatur Heuuald; ea autem distinctione, ut pro diversa capillorum specie unus Niger Heuuald, alter Albus Heuuald diceretur: quorum uterque pietate religionis imbutus, sed Niger Heuuald magis sacrarum literarum erat scientia institutus. Qui venientes in provinciam, intraverunt hospitium cuiusdam villici, petieruntque ab eo, ut transmitterentur ad satrapam qui super eum erat, eo quod haberent aliquid legationis et causae utilis, quod deberent ad illum perferre. Non enim habent regem iidem Antiqui Saxones, sed satrapas plurimos suae genti praepositos, qui ingruente belli articulo mittunt aequaliter sortes, et quemcumque sors ostenderit, hunc tempore belli ducem omnes sequuntur, huic obtemperant; peracto autem bello, rursum aequalis potentiae omnes fiunt satrapae. Suscepit ergo eos villicus, et promittens se mittere eos ad satrapam qui super se erat, ut petebant, aliquot diebus secum retinuit.

Qui cum cogniti essent a barbaris quod essent

[1] According to the A.S. version.

bring any hindrance to their preaching, and bountifully rewarding such as should be ready to receive the faith; whereby it came to pass by the assistance of God's grace, that in short time they converted many from idolatry to the faith of Christ.

After the example of these men two other priests of the English nation, which had lived in banishment a long time in Ireland for hope of the eternal country, came to the province of the Old Saxons, if haply by their preaching they might there win some to Christ. Now as they both had like devotion, so had they both one name: for either of them was called Hewald; yet with this difference, that, because of the diverse colour of their hair, one was named Black Hewald, the other White Hewald; and both of them were filled with love to religion, but Black Hewald was better instructed in the knowledge of Scripture. And coming into the province they entered the guest-house of a certain reeve,[1] and desired of him that they might be conducted to the alderman [1] which was over him, for that they had an embassy and matter of importance which they must needs declare unto him. For the said Old Saxons have no king, but many aldermen set over their country, who, as often as there is occasion of war toward, do cast lots equally, and upon whomsoever the lot shall fall, him they all follow as their captain, as long as the war endures, and him they obey; but when the war is done, all the aldermen are equal in power again. The reeve therefore entertained them, and promising to send them to the alderman who was over him, according to their request, stayed them some days in his house.

And when they were known of the barbarous

alterius religionis (nam et psalmis semper atque orationibus vacabant, et quotidie sacrificium Deo victimae salutaris offerebant, habentes secum vascula sacra et tabulam altaris vice dedicatam) suspecti sunt habiti, quia si pervenirent ad satrapam et loquerentur cum illo, averterent illum a diis suis et ad novam Christianae fidei religionem transferrent, sicque paulatim omnis eorum provincia veterem cogeretur nova mutare culturam. Itaque rapuerunt eos subito, et interemerunt: Album quidem Heuualdum veloci occisione gladii, Nigellum autem longo suppliciorum cruciatu et horrenda membrorum omnium discerptione: quos interemptos in Rheno proiecerunt. Quod cum satrapa ille quem videre volebant audisset, iratus est valde quod ad se venire volentes peregrini non permitterentur: et mittens occidit vicanos illos omnes, vicumque incendio consumpsit. Passi sunt autem praefati sacerdotes et famuli Christi, quinto nonarum Octobrium die.

Nec martyrio eorum caelestia defuere miracula. Nam cum perempta eorum corpora amni, ut diximus, a paganis essent iniecta, contigit ut haec contra impetum fluvii decurrentis, per quadraginta fere millia passuum, ad ea usque loca ubi illorum erant socii, transferrentur. Sed et radius lucis permaximus atque ad caelum usque altus omni nocte supra locum fulgebat illum ubicumque ea pervenisse contingeret, et hoc etiam paganis qui eos occiderant intuentibus. Sed et unus ex eis in visione nocturna apparuit cuidam de sociis suis, cui nomen erat Tilmon, viro illustri, et

people to be of another religion (for they continued always in prayer and singing of psalms, and offered daily to God the sacrifice of the saving victim, having with them sacred vessels and a table hallowed instead of an altar), they had them in suspicion that, if they came to the alderman and talked with him, they would turn him from their gods and bring him over to the new religion of Christ's faith, and so by little and little the whole country should be enforced to change their old worship for the new one. Wherefore they seized them suddenly and put them to death: White Hewald they slew swiftly with the sword, but Black Hewald with long and cruel torture and horrible dismembering of all parts of his body; and after they had murdered them, cast them into the Rhine. But when the alderman, whom they desired to see, had learned of this, he was very angry that strangers repairing to him should not have free passage; and he sent and slew all those villagers and burned the village with fire. Now the aforesaid priests and servants of Christ suffered on the third day of October.

Nor did their martyrdom lack the testimony of miracles from heaven. For when their dead bodies had been cast of the paynims, as we have said, into the river, it so fortuned that they were carried against the main running stream about 40 miles as far as that place where their companions were. Moreover, a very great beam of light reaching up to heaven shined every night over the place wheresoever it fortuned they came to, and this too in the sight of the paynims who had killed them. Moreover, one of them appeared by vision in the night to one of their companions, whose name was Tilmon,

ad saeculum quoque nobili, qui de milite factus fuerat monachus; indicans quod eo loci corpora eorum posset invenire, ubi lucem de caelo terris radiasse conspiceret. Quod ita completum est. Inventa namque eorum corpora iuxta honorem martyribus condignum recondita sunt, et dies passionis vel inventionis eorum congrua illis in locis veneratione celebratur. Denique gloriosissimus dux Francorum Pippin, ubi haec comperit, misit et adducta ad se eorum corpora condidit cum multa gloria in ecclesia Coloniae civitatis, iuxta Rhenum. Fertur autem quia in loco in quo occisi sunt fons ebullierit, qui in eodem loco usque hodie copiosa fluenti sui dona profundat.

CAP. XI

Ut viri venerabiles Suidberct in Brittania, Vilbrord Romae sint in Fresiam ordinati episcopi.

Primis sane temporibus adventus eorum in Fresiam mox ut comperit Vilbrod datam sibi a principe licentiam ibidem praedicandi, acceleravit venire Romam, cuius sedi apostolicae tunc Sergius papa praeerat, ut cum eius licentia et benedictione desideratum evangelizandi gentibus opus iniret: simul et reliquias beatorum apostolorum ac martyrum Christi ab eo se sperans accipere, ut dum in gente cui praedicaret destructis idolis ecclesias institueret, haberet in

[1] According to the A.S. version.
[2] Church of St. Cunibert.

a man of great renown and also noble, as the world judgeth, who from a thane[1] was become a monk; shewing that he might find their bodies in that place where he should see a beam of light shine from heaven to earth. The which so came to pass. For their bodies being found were buried with the honour worthy for martyrs, and the day of their suffering or rather of the finding of their bodies is solemnly kept in those parts with fitting reverence. Finally, when Pippin the most glorious duke of the Franks had understanding of these things, he sent and had their bodies brought to him, and buried very honourably in the church of the city of Cologne[2] by the Rhine. Besides, it is commonly said, that in the place where they were killed there gushed forth a fountain, which to this day in the same place poureth forth the benefits of its plentiful stream.

CHAPTER XI

How the venerable men, Swidbert in Britain, Wilbrord at Rome, were ordained bishops over Frisland.

At their first arrival indeed to Frisland, as soon as Wilbrord understood that he had licence of the prince to preach in the same, he hastened to go to Rome where Sergius at that time was over the see apostolic, that with his licence and benediction he might set upon the work of preaching the Gospel to the heathen, which he had long desired: hoping withal to receive of him too relics of the blessed apostles and martyrs of Christ, to the end that, when in the nation to which he preached he should erect churches, after the idols were destroyed, he

promptu reliquias sanctorum quas ibi introduceret; quibusque ibidem depositis, consequenter in eorum honorem quorum essent illae, singula quaeque loca dedicaret. Sed et alia perplura quae tanti operis negotium quaerebat, vel ibi discere, vel inde accipere cupiebat. In quibus omnibus cum sui voti compos esset effectus, ad praedicandum rediit.

Quo tempore fratres qui erant in Fresia verbi ministerio mancipati, elegerunt ex suo numero virum modestum moribus et mansuetum corde Suidberctum qui eis ordinaretur antistes, quem Brittaniam destinatum ad petitionem eorum ordinavit reverentissimus Vilfrid episcopus, qui tunc forte patria pulsus in Merciorum regionibus exulabat. Non enim eo tempore habebat episcopum Cantia, defuncto quidem Theodoro, sed necdum Berctualdo successore eius, qui trans mare ordinandus ierat, ad sedem episcopatus sui reverso.

Qui videlicet Suidberct accepto episcopatu, de Brittania regressus, non multo post ad gentem Boructuarorum secessit, ac multos eorum praedicando ad viam veritatis perduxit. Sed expugnatis non longo post tempore Boructuaris a gente Antiquorum Saxonum, dispersi sunt quolibet hi qui verbum receperant; ipse antistes cum quibusdam Pippinum petiit, qui interpellante Bliththrydae coniuge sua, dedit ei locum mansionis in insula quadam Rheni, quae lingua eorum vocatur "In littore": in qua ipse, constructo monasterio quod hactenus haeredes

[1] Commonly named Plectrude.
[2] Now Kaiserswerth.

might have in readiness saints' relics to put in them; and when these relics had been laid in the same, he might dedicate each several place accordingly in honour of them whose relics they were. Moreover, divers other things also he desired either to learn there or to receive from thence, requisite for the business of so great a work. In all which requests, when his desire was accomplished, he returned back to preach.

And at that time his brethren which were in Frisland, being bent to the ministry of the word, chose out of their company a man sober in outward behaviour and humble of heart, called Swidbert, to be ordained their bishop, whom being sent for that purpose into Britain, the most reverend bishop Wilfrid (living then it chanced as a banished man out of his country in the coasts of the Marchmen) did ordain at their request. For at that time Kent had never a bishop, Theodore being dead, while Bertwald, his successor, who had gone over the sea to be ordained, was not yet returned to the see of his bishopric.

The said Swidbert returning out of Britain, after he was made bishop, departed within a short time to the people of the Boructuars, and led many of them to the way of truth with his preaching. But shortly after, when the Boructuars were subdued by the people of the Old Saxons, they that had received the word were dispersed, some into this corner, some into that; the bishop himself with certain other went to Pippin, which, at the earnest suit of his lady Blithryd,[1] gave him a mansion-place in an island of the Rhine, which in their tongue is called "On the shore": [2] where he building a monastery,

eius possident, aliquandiu continentissimam gessit vitam, ibique diem clausit ultimum.

Postquam vero per annos aliquot in Fresia qui advenerant docuerunt, misit Pippin, favente omnium consensu, virum venerabilem Vilbrordum Romam, cuius adhuc pontificatum Sergius habebat, postulans ut eidem Fresonum genti archiepiscopus ordinaretur. Quod ita ut petierat impletum est anno ab incarnatione Domini sexcentesimo nonagesimo sexto. Ordinatus est autem in ecclesia sanctae martyris Ceciliae, die natalis eius, imposito sibi a papa memorato nomine Clementis: ac mox remissus ad sedem episcopatus sui, id est, post dies quatuordecim, ex quo in urbem venerat.

Donavit autem ei Pippin locum cathedrae episcopalis in castello suo inlustri, quod antiquo gentium illarum verbo Viltaburg, id est, Oppidum Viltorum, lingua autem Gallica Traiectum vocatur; in quo aedificata ecclesia, reverentissimus pontifex longe lateque verbum fidei praedicans, multosque ab errore revocans, plures per illas regiones ecclesias, sed et monasteria nonnulla construxit. Nam non multo post alios quoque illis in regionibus ipse constituit antistites ex eorum numero fratrum qui vel secum, vel post se illo ad praedicandum venerant; ex quibus aliquanti iam dormierunt in Domino. Ipse autem Vilbrord, cognomento Clemens, adhuc superest longa iam venerabilis aetate, utpote tricesimum et sextum in episcopatu habens annum, et post multiplices

[1] 713. [2] A second visit.

which his successors possess at this present, lived for some time a very austere life there, and there ended his days.[1]

Now after they that had come to Frisland and had taught there for some years, Pippin, with the common consent of all, sent the venerable man Wilbrord to Rome,[2] where Sergius was yet pope, desiring that he might be ordained archbishop of the said people of the Frisons. Which was so fulfilled, according to his request, in the 696th year since the incarnation of the Lord. Moreover, he was ordained in the church of the holy martyr Cecilia, upon her day, and the name Clement was given to him of the said pope: and by and by he was sent back to the see of his bishopric, to wit 14 days after his coming to Rome.

Moreover, Pippin assigned him a place for his episcopal seat in his famous castle, called by an ancient name of those countries Wiltaburg, as you would say Town of the Wilts, but in the French tongue it is called Trajectum;[3] and when a church had been built there, the most reverend prelate preaching the word of faith far and wide called back many from error, and erected many churches throughout those parts, and, moreover, some monasteries. For within short time after, he himself made other bishops also in those parts, out of the number of those brethren who had come thither to preach either with him or after him; of the which company not a few are now fallen asleep in the Lord. But Wilbrord himself, called otherwise Clement, liveth yet[4] venerable for the length of his days, seeing it is now the 36th year of his bishopric, and after the

[3] Utrecht. The church is St. Saviour's. [4] 731.

militiae caelestis agones ad praemia remunerationis supernae tota mente suspirans.

CAP. XII

Ut quidam in provincia Nordanhymbrorum a mortuis resurgens, multa et tremenda et desideranda quae viderat narraverit.

His temporibus miraculum memorabile et antiquorum simile in Brittania factum est. Namque ad excitationem viventium de morte animae quidam aliquandiu mortuus ad vitam resurrexit corporis, et multa memoratu digna quae viderat, narravit; e quibus hic aliqua breviter perstringenda esse putavi. Erat ergo paterfamilias in regione Nordanhymbrorum quae vocatur Incuneningum, religiosam cum domo sua gerens vitam: qui infirmitate corporis tactus, et hac crescente per dies ad extrema perductus, primo tempore noctis defunctus est; sed diluculo reviviscens ac repente residens, omnes qui corpori flentes assederant, timore immenso perculsos in fugam convertit: uxor tantum quae amplius amabat, quamvis multum tremens et pavida, remansit: quam ille consolatus, " Noli," inquit, " timere, quia iam vere resurrexi a morte qua tenebar, et apud homines sum iterum vivere permissus; non tamen ea mihi qua ante consueram conversatione, sed multum dissimili ex hoc tempore vivendum est." Statimque

---

[1] Some time before the death of King Aldfrid, 705.

[2] As, for instance, in the Apocryphal Acts of Thomas and the Apocalypse of Peter, which are as early as the second century A.D., Pl.

manifold strivings of his heavenly warfare he panteth with all his heart for the rewards of the recompense on high.

CHAPTER XII

How a certain man in the province of Northumberland rising from the dead told many things both terrible and worthy to be desired that he had seen.

At this time [1] was wrought in Britain a miracle worthy of remembrance and not unlike the miracles of times past.[2] For to stir up living men from the death of the soul, a certain man, stark dead for a time, rose again to bodily life, and told many notable things that he had seen; of the which I have thought it good to touch on certain briefly here. There was then in the coast of Northumberland, called Incuneningum,[3] a householder living a godly life with his family; and he fell sick and (the disease growing daily more and more upon him) was brought to extremity, and in the beginning of the night died; but in the dawning of the day reviving again and sitting up suddenly he caused all that had remained weeping about the corse to run away, as men wonderfully amazed with fear: only his wife which loved him more (although she trembled and quaked) tarried behind; and he comforting her, said: "Be not afraid, for I am now risen in very deed from the death that had dominion over me, and am permitted to live among men again; yet not after the manner I was wont before, but henceforth my conversation must be far unlike that other."

[3] Cunninghame, just over the Scotch border, or Chester-le-Street.

surgens abiit ad villulae oratorium, et usque ad diem in oratione persistens, mox omnem quam possederat substantiam in tres divisit portiones, e quibus unam coniugi, alteram filiis tradidit, tertiam sibi ipse retentans, statim pauperibus distribuit. Nec multo post saeculi curis absolutus ad monasterium Mailros, quod Tuidi fluminis circumflexu maxima ex parte clauditur, pervenit; acceptaque tonsura, locum secretae mansionis quam praeviderat abbas, intravit: et ibi usque ad diem mortis in tanta mentis et corporis contritione duravit, ut multa illum, quae alios laterent, vel horrenda vel desideranda vidisse, etiamsi lingua sileret, vita loqueretur.

Narrabat autem hoc modo quod viderat: "Lucidus," inquiens, "aspectu, et clarus erat indumento qui me ducebat. Incedebamus autem tacentes, ut videbatur mihi, contra ortum solis solstitialem; cumque ambularemus, devenimus ad vallem multae latitudinis ac profunditatis, infinitae autem longitudinis; quae ad laevam nobis sita, unum latus flammis ferventibus nimium terribile, alterum furenti grandine ac frigore nivium omnia perflante atque verrente non minus intolerabile praeferebat. Utrumque autem erat animabus hominum plenum, quae vicissim hinc inde videbantur quasi tempestatis impetu iactari. Cum enim vim fervoris immensi tolerare non possent, prosiliebant miserae in medium frigoris infesti: et cum neque ibi quippiam requiei invenire

[1] Towards the north-east quarter.

And forthwith rising he went away to the church of the little township, and continuing there in prayer till it was day, he by and by divided all the goods that he had into three parts, of the which he gave one to his wife, another to his sons, and the third part he reserved to himself, and made distribution of it straightways among the poor. And not long after, despatched of all worldly cares, he went to the monastery of Melrose, the which is almost closed in with a creek of the river Tweed; where being shoren in, he went into a place of abode apart, which the abbot had provided: and continued there until his dying day in such contrition of mind and mortification of body, that even if his tongue did not report, yet his life bare witness, that he had seen many things either terrible or comfortable, which were hidden from other.

Now what he had seen he used to tell after this sort: "He that was my guide had a shining countenance and bright apparel. Now, as it seemed to me, we went on in silence over against the rising of the summer sun;[1] and as we walked, we came to a great broad and deep valley, so long that no man could measure it; and this lay on the left hand as we went, and shewed one side exceeding terrible with flaming fire, the other no less unendurable with vehement hail and chilly snow beating and drifting into every corner. And both places were full of men's souls which appeared to be cast interchangeably, now hither, now thither, as it were with a violent tempest. For when they could no longer bear the insufferable might of the heat, they leaped pitifully to the midst of the deadly cold; and when they could find no rest there either, again

valerent, resiliebant rursus urendae in medium flammarum inextinguibilium. Cumque hac infelici vicissitudine longe lateque, prout aspicere poteram, sine ulla quietis intercapedine innumerabilis spirituum deformium multitudo torqueretur, cogitare coepi quod hic fortasse esset infernus, de cuius tormentis intolerabilibus narrare saepius audivi. Respondit cogitationi meae ductor qui me praecedebat: 'Non hoc,' inquiens, 'suspiceris; non enim hic infernus est ille quem putas.'

"At cum me hoc spectaculo tam horrendo perterritum paulatim in ulteriora produceret, vidi subito ante nos obscurari incipere loca, et tenebris omnia repleri. Quas cum intraremus, in tantum paulisper condensatae sunt, ut nihil praeter ipsas aspicerem, excepta dumtaxat specie et veste eius qui me ducebat. Et cum progrederemur 'sola sub nocte per umbras,' ecce subito apparent ante nos crebri flammarum tetrarum globi, ascendentes quasi de puteo magno, rursumque decidentes in eumdem. Quo cum perductus essem, repente ductor meus disparuit, ac me solum in medio tenebrarum et horridae visionis reliquit. At cum iidem globi ignium sine intermissione modo alta peterent, modo ima baratri repeterent, cerno omnia quae ascendebant fastigia flammarum plena esse spiritibus hominum, qui instar favillarum cum fumo ascendentium nunc ad sublimiora proiicerentur, nunc retractis ignium vaporibus relaberentur in profunda. Sed et foetor incomparabilis cum eisdem vaporibus ebulliens omnia illa tenebrarum loca replebat. Et cum diutius ibi pavi-

[1] Verg. *Aen.* vi. 268. [2] gusts.

[3] For *dungeon* in sense of profundity. Dr. Johnson was called "a dungeon of wit."

they leaped back into the midst of the unquenchable flames to be burned. And as an infinite number of evil-favoured spirits were tormented without ceasing with this unhappy interchange far and wide as I could see, I began to think that this peradventure might be hell, of whose intolerable torments I have heard men oftentimes tell. The guide who was in front made answer to this thought of mine: 'No, think not so! for this is not hell as thou dost suppose.'

"But when he brought me on further by little and little, being sorely affrighted with so terrible a sight, I saw the places before us suddenly lose their light and every corner full of darkness. And as we entered into it, within a little space it became so thick that I saw nothing but the darkness, saving only the bright glow and coat of him which did guide me. And as we went forward 'through the shadows beneath the solitary night,'[1] behold, suddenly there appeared before us many round flaws[2] of grisly flames, ascending as it were out of a great pit and falling down again into the same. And when I had been brought thither, suddenly my conductor vanished away, and left me alone in the midst of the darkness and horrible sight. But as the said flaws of fire without cessation would now fly up into the element, now fall back again into the deep dungel,[3] I saw the tops of every flaw that ascended, full of men's spirits, which in manner of sparkles mounting up with the smoke were sometimes thrown a-high, sometimes, when the fumes of the fire were gone, fell back into the depths below. Moreover, an insufferable stench breaking out with the same fumes filled all the dark places about. And as I tarried there somewhat long in fear, not

dus consisterem, utpote incertus quid agerem, quo verterem gressum, qui me finis maneret: audio subitum post terga sonitum immanissimi fletus ac miserrimi, simul et cachinnum crepitantem quasi vulgi indocti captis hostibus insultantis. Ut autem sonitus idem clarior redditus ad me usque pervenit, considero turbam malignorum spirituum, quae quinque animas hominum moerentes eiulantesque, ipsa multum exultans et cachinnans, medias illas trahebat in tenebras: e quibus videlicet hominibus, ut dignoscere potui, quidam erat adtonsus ut clericus, quidam laicus, quaedam femina. Trahentes autem eos maligni spiritus descenderunt in medium baratri illius ardentis; factumque est ut cum longius subeuntibus eis fletum hominum et risum daemoniorum clare discernere nequirem, sonum tamen adhuc promiscuum in auribus haberem. Interea ascenderunt quidam spirituum obscurorum de abysso illa flammivoma, et adcurrentes circumdederunt me, atque oculis flammantibus et de ore ac naribus ignem putidum efflantes angebant; forcipibus quoque igneis quos tenebant in manibus, minitabantur me comprehendere, nec tamen me ullatenus contingere, tametsi terrere praesumebant. Qui cum undiqueversum hostibus et caecitate tenebrarum conclusus huc illucque oculos circumferrem, si forte alicunde quid auxilii quo salvarer, adveniret, apparuit retro via qua veneram quasi fulgor stellae micantis[1] inter tenebras, qui paulatim crescens et ad me ocius festinans ubi adpropinquavit dispersi sunt et aufu-

[1] For *meantis*, Pl.

---

[1] Fuller and fuller. Cf. brimming over.

knowing what I should do, nor whither I should turn my steps, nor what end awaited me: suddenly I heard behind my back the sound of most dreadful and pitiful crying, and withal too a clatter of laughing, as it had been of the rude common folk insulting over their enemies brought in thraldom. Now when the same sound made brimmer and brimmer [1] came fully up to me, I was aware of a crowd of evil sprites which did hale five human souls lamenting and wailing into the midst of that darkness, the evil sprites meantime laughing and triumphing; and of these said beings, as well I could discern, one was a shoren clerk, one a lay man and one a woman. And the evil sprites hailing them went down into the midst of that burning pit; and it came to pass that as they sank farther I could not make distinction between the crying of the men and the laughing of the devils, yet for all that had still a confused noise in my ears. In the mean season there came up from that gulf that vented flame certain dark sprites, and running up they compassed me about and with the glare of their eyes, and the foul-smelling fire they breathed both from mouth and nostrils, went to stifling me; they threatened also to seize me with the fiery tongs in their hands, but yet they durst in no wise touch me, though they adventured to fray me. And when I was compassed on every side with foes and blinding darkness, and turned my eyes this way and that, if haply there might come from somewhere a help to save me, there appeared behind me, by the way I had come, the glimpsing of a star shining in the midst of the darkness, which waxing gradually and coming apace to me, as soon as it was drawn nigh, dispersed and put to flight all

gerunt omnes qui me forcipibus rapere quaerebant spiritus infesti.

"Ille autem qui adveniens eos fugavit, erat ipse qui me ante ducebat: qui mox conversus ad dexterum iter, quasi contra ortum solis brumalem me ducere coepit. Nec mora, exemptum tenebris in auras me serenae lucis eduxit: cumque me in luce aperta duceret, vidi ante nos murum permaximum, cuius neque longitudini hinc vel inde, neque altitudini ullus esse terminus videretur. Coepi autem mirari quare ad murum accederemus, cum in eo nullam ianuam vel fenestram, vel ascensum alicubi conspicerem. Cum ergo pervenissemus ad murum, statim nescio quo ordine fuimus in summitate eius. Et ecce ibi campus erat latissimus ac laetissimus, tantaque fragrantia vernantium flosculorum plenus, ut omnem mox foetorem tenebrosae fornacis, qui me pervaserat, effugaret admirandi huius suavitas odoris. Tanta autem lux cuncta ea loca perfuderat, ut omni splendore diei, sive solis meridiani radiis videretur esse praeclarior. Erantque in hoc campo innumera hominum albatorum conventicula, sedesque plurimae agminum laetantium. Cumque inter choros felicium incolarum medios me duceret, cogitare coepi quod hoc fortasse esset regnum caelorum, de quo praedicari saepius audivi. Respondit ille cogitatui meo: 'Non,' inquiens, 'non hoc est regnum caelorum quod autumas.'

"Cumque procedentes transissemus et has beatorum mansiones spirituum, aspicio ante nos multo maiorem luminis gratiam quam prius; in qua etiam

[1] South-east.

those hateful sprites which did seek to seize me with their tongs.

"Now he that came and chased them away was he who before was my guide: who turning by and by to the right-hand way began to lead me as it were over against the rising of the winter sun.[1] And with a trice he brought me out of darkness into air where was clear light; and as he led me in the open light, I saw before us a very great wall, which was so long this way and that and so high that it seemed to have no end. Now I began to marvel why we went to the wall, when I saw therein nowhere door or loophole or entrance up. When then we had come to the wall, I cannot tell by what means, we were straightway upon the top. And behold there was there a very broad and pleasant field, so full of the fragrance of fresh flourishing flowers, that by and by the marvellous sweetness of their scent drove away all the stench of the dark furnace, which had gone through and through me. Moreover, so goodly a light had bathed every place, that it seemed more fair than all the brightness of the day or the beams of the sun at midday. And there were in this field innumerable gatherings of men in white, and many bands seated there rejoicing. And as he led me through the midst of the companies of the blessed inhabitants, I began to think with myself that perchance this was the kingdom of heaven of the which I have heard men oftentimes preach. To this my thought he answered, saying: 'Nay, this is not the kingdom of heaven as thou dost imagine.'

"And when we went forward and had passed these resting places of blessed spirits also, I saw a far fairer light before us than the other was; wherein

vocem cantantium dulcissimam audivi; set et odoris fragrantia miri tanta de loco effundebatur, ut is quem antea degustans quasi maximum rebar, iam permodicus mihi odor videretur: sicut etiam lux illa campi florentis eximia, in comparatione eius quae nunc apparuit lucis, tenuissima prorsus videbatur, et parva. In cuius amoenitatem loci cum nos intraturos sperarem, repente ductor substitit; nec mora, gressum retorquens, ipsa me qua venimus via reduxit.

"Cumque reversi perveniremus ad mansiones illas laetas spirituum candidatorum, dixit mihi: 'Scis quae sint ista omnia quae vidisti?' Respondi ego, 'Non.' Et ait: 'Vallis illa quam aspexisti flammis ferventibus et frigoribus horrenda rigidis, ipse est locus in quo examinandae et castigandae sunt animae illorum, qui differentes confiteri et emendare scelera quae fecerunt,[1] in ipso tandem mortis articulo ad poenitentiam confugiunt, et sic de corpore exeunt: qui tamen quia confessionem et poenitentiam vel in morte habuerunt, omnes in die iudicii ad regnum caelorum perveniunt. Multos autem preces viventium et eleemosynae et ieiunia et maxime celebratio missarum, ut etiam ante diem iudicii liberentur, adiuvant. Porro puteus ille flammivomus ac putidus quem vidisti, ipsum est os gehennae, in quo quicumque semel inciderit nunquam inde liberabitur in aevum. Locus vero iste florifer, in quo pulcherrimam hanc iuventutem iocundari ac fulgere conspicis, ipse

[1] For *fecerant*, Pl.

---

[1] Purgatory.

too I heard a sweet melodious noise of musicians; besides that such a perfume of marvellous fragrant savour was shed from the spot, that the other that I smelled before, and regarded as the best that could be, seemed now to me a savour of little worth: in like manner too as that excellent light of the flowering field, in comparison with the light which now appeared, seemed quite poor and faint. Into the which delightsome place as I hoped well we should go, suddenly my conductor stood still; and quickly turning back brought me again the selfsame way we came.

"And in our return when we came to those glad dwelling-places of the spirits in white, he said to me: 'Do you know what all this is that you have seen?' I answered: 'No.' And he said: 'That valley which you saw horrible with hot flaming fire and biting cold is the very place where those souls remaineth to be examined and tried,[1] which, putting off confession and amendment of the crimes they did commit, have recourse at length to repentance in the very instant of death, and so depart out of the body; and yet, because they have made confession and repented even in death, they come all to the kingdom of heaven at the day of judgment. Moreover, the prayers, almsgiving, fasting and especially the celebration of masses of those that yet liveth help to deliver many even before the day of judgment. Further, that stinking pit that vented flame, which thou didst see, is the very mouth of hell, into the which whosoever once falleth, he shall never be delivered thence for all time. Yonder field indeed full of flowers, where thou seest this fair company of youth all joyful and bright, is the very

est in quo recipiuntur animae eorum qui in bonis quidem operibus de corpore exeunt; non tamen sunt tantae perfectionis, ut in regnum caelorum statim mereantur introduci: qui tamen omnes in die iudicii ad visionem Christi et gaudia regni caelestis intrabunt. Nam quicumque in omni verbo et opere et cogitatione perfecti sunt, mox de corpore egressi ad regnum caeleste perveniunt: ad cuius vicina pertinet locus ille, ubi sonum cantilenae dulcis cum odore suavitatis ac splendore lucis audisti. Tu autem quia nunc ad corpus reverti et rursum inter homines vivere debes, si actus tuos curiosius discutere, et mores sermonesque tuos in rectitudine ac simplicitate servare studueris, accipies et ipse post mortem locum mansionis inter haec quae cernis agmina laetabunda spirituum beatorum. Namque ego cum ad tempus abscessissem a te, ad hoc feci ut quid de te fieri deberet agnoscerem.' Haec mihi cum dixisset, multum detestatus sum reverti ad corpus, delectatus nimirum suavitate ac decore loci illius quem intuebar, simul et consortio eorum quos in illo videbam. Nec tamen aliquid ductorem meum rogare audebam: sed inter haec nescio quo ordine repente me inter homines vivere cerno."

Haec et alia quae viderat idem vir Domini, non omnibus passim desidiosis ac vitae suae incuriosis referre volebat; sed illis solummodo, qui vel tormentorum metu perterriti, vel spe gaudiorum peren-

same place where their souls are received, which depart out of the body in the doing of good works; yet are not of such perfection that they deserve to be brought straightways to the kingdom of heaven: but for all that, in the day of judgment they shall all have access to the sight of Christ and the joys of the heavenly kingdom. For all they which are perfect in all their words and works and thoughts come straight to the heavenly kingdom, as soon as they depart from the body; and next adjoining is that place where thou heardest the sound of melodious singing with the fragrant savour and shining light. Now for thyself, because thou must needs return to the body and live amongst men again, if thou wilt study diligently to examine thy doings, and keep thy way of living and speaking in uprightness and sincerity, thou too shalt receive after death a place of abode amongst these joyful companies of blessed spirits that thou seest. For when I had gone away for a time and left thee, it was for no other cause but to learn what should become of thee.' When he had so spoken to me, I loathed much to return to the body, being without doubt ravished with the sweetness and comeliness of that place which I did behold, and withal their society which I did see therein. Yet notwithstanding I durst not be so bold as to ask any question of my guide; but in the midst of these meditations I perceived that, by what means I cannot tell, I was suddenly alive amongst men."

These things and other that he had seen the said man of God would not report at random to any slothful folks and men that had no regard for their own life; but to such only as, either dismayed with fear of torments or ravished with hope of eternal

nium delectati, profectum pietatis ex eius verbis haurire volebant. Denique in vicinia cellae illius habitabat quidam monachus, nomine Haemgils, presbyteratus etiam, quem bonis actibus adaequabat, gradu praeeminens, qui adhuc superest, et in Hibernia insula solitarius ultimam vitae aetatem pane cibario et frigida aqua sustentat. Hic saepius ad eundem virum ingrediens, audivit ab eo repetita interrogatione, quae et qualia essent quae exutus corpore videret: per cuius relationem, ad nostram quoque agnitionem pervenere quae de his pauca perstrinximus. Narrabat autem visiones suas etiam regi Aldfrido viro undecumque doctissimo; et tam libenter, tamque studiose ab illo auditus est, ut eius rogatu monasterio supra memorato inditus, ac monachica sit tonsura coronatus, atque ad eum audiendum saepissime, cum illas in partes devenisset, accederet. Cui videlicet monasterio tempore illo religiosae ac modestae vitae abbas et presbyter Ediluald praeerat, qui nunc episcopalem Lindisfarnensis ecclesiae cathedram condignis gradu actibus servat.

Accepit autem in eodem monasterio locum mansionis secretiorem, ubi liberius continuis in orationibus famulatui sui Conditoris vacaret. Et quia locus ipse super ripam fluminis erat situs, solebat hoc creber ob magnum castigandi corporis affectum ingredi, ac saepius in eo supermeantibus undis immergi; sicque ibidem quamdiu sustinere posse videbatur, psalmis vel precibus insistere, fixusque manere ascendente

joy, would gladly suck increase of godliness out of his words. To be short, in the neighbourhood of his cell dwelt a monk called Hemgils, also admitted to the priesthood which he honoured with his good works, being eminent in his degree, who remaineth yet alive, and in the isle of Ireland leading a solitary life supporteth his last days with coarse bread and cold water. This monk resorting to the said man oftentimes understood by many questions put to him, what things he saw after he was separated from the body, and of what likeness they were; and by his reporting, the few things thereof we have touched upon have come to our knowledge. Moreover, he told his visions also to king Aldfrid,[1] a man most learned in all ways; who heard him with such comfort and attention, that at his desire he was placed in the aforementioned monastery and crowned with the tonsure of a monk, and the king very often went to hear him when he had come to those parts. Over the which monastery at that time Ethelwald, priest, of godly and sober life, was abbot, but now he holdeth the episcopal seat of the church of Lindisfarne with conduct worthy of his degree.

Now this man took in the same monastery a more separate place of abode, that there with more freedom he might devote himself to the service of his Creator in continual prayer. And because the place was situated right above the river bank, he was wont many times to step in and plunge himself oftentimes beneath the flowing waters, for the great desire that he had to chastise his body; and so used to continue there singing of psalms or praying, as long as he seemed able to abide it, standing still

[1] Of Northumbria.

aqua fluminis usque ad lumbos, aliquando usque ad collum; atque inde egrediens ad terram nunquam ipsa vestimenta uda atque algida deponere curabat, donec ex suo corpore calefierent et siccarentur. Cumque tempore hiemali defluentibus circa eum semifractarum crustis glacierum, quas et ipse aliquando contriverat quo haberet locum standi sive immergendi in fluvio, dicerent qui videbant: "Mirum, frater Drycthelme," hoc enim erat viro nomen, "quod tantam frigoris asperitatem ulla ratione tolerare praevales." Respondebat ille simpliciter, erat namque homo simplicis ingenii ac moderatae naturae: "Frigidiora ego vidi." Et cum dicerent: "Mirum quod tam austeram tenere continentiam velis." Respondebat: "Austeriora ego vidi." Sicque usque ad diem suae vocationis infatigabili caelestium bonorum desiderio corpus senile inter quotidiana ieiunia domabat, multisque et verbo et conversatione saluti fuit.

CAP. XIII

Ut e contra alter ad mortem veniens, oblatum sibi a daemonibus codicem suorum viderit peccatorum.

At contra, fuit quidam in provincia Merciorum cuius visiones ac verba, non autem et conversatio, plurimis, sed non sibimetipsi profuit. Fuit autem temporibus Coenredi qui post Aedilredum regnavit, vir in laico habitu atque officio militari positus; sed quantum pro industria exteriori regi placens, tantum

---

[1] 704–709.

[2] King's thane according to the A.S. version.

while the water of the river mounted up to his hips, and now and then to his neck; and when he came out to land he never sought to change his wet and cold garments, but tarried until they were warmed and dried by the heat of his body. And in the winter season, when half broken pieces of ice dropped down all about him, which too he had sometimes broken himself, to have space of standing or plunging in the river, divers men seeing him, said: "It is a strange case, brother Drythelm," for so the man was called, "that you can possibly suffer such bitter cold." He answered simply, for he was but a man of simple nature and sober-spirited: "I have seen greater cold." And when they said: "It is marvel that you will live so continent and austere a life," he answered: "I have seen more austerity." And so until the day of his being called hence, for the unwearied desire he had of heavenly felicity, he would subdue his aged body with daily fastings, and by his words and conversation brought salvation to many.

CHAPTER XIII

How another contrariwise, coming to die, saw a book having all his sins written, brought unto him by devils.

But contrariwise there was a man in the province of the Marchmen whose visions and words (yet not likewise his manner of life) did profit very many, but not himself. Now there was in the time of Cenred,[1] which reigned after Ethelred, a man that was a layman and set to be in office as a thane;[2] but as much as he was in favour with the king for

pro interna suimet negligentia displicens. Admonebat ergo illum sedulo ut confiteretur, et emendaret ac relinqueret scelera sua, priusquam subito mortis superventu tempus omne poenitendi et emendandi perderet. Verum ille, frequenter licet admonitus, spernebat verba salutis, seseque tempore sequente poenitentiam acturum esse promittebat. Haec inter tactus infirmitate, decidit in lectum, atque acri coepit dolore torqueri. Ad quem ingressus rex, diligebat enim eum multum, hortabatur ut vel tunc antequam moreretur, poenitentiam ageret commissorum. At ille respondit, non se tunc velle confiteri peccata sua, sed cum ab infirmitate resurgeret; ne exprobrarent sibi sodales, quod timore mortis faceret ea quae sospes facere noluerat; fortiter quidem, ut sibi videbatur, locutus, sed miserabiliter, ut post patuit, daemonica fraude seductus.

Cumque morbo ingravescente denuo ad eum visitandum ac docendum rex intraret, clamabat statim miserabili voce: "Quid vis modo? Quid huc venisti? Non enim mihi aliquid utilitatis aut salutis potes ultra conferre." At ille: "Noli," inquit, "ita loqui, vide ut sanum sapias." "Non," inquit, "insanio, sed pessimam mihi scientiam certus prae oculis habeo." "Et quid," inquit, "hoc est?" "Paulo ante," inquit, "intraverunt domum hanc duo pulcherrimi iuvenes, et resederunt circa me,

his diligence in outward business, so much was he in displeasure with him for his neglect of the inward man. Therefore the king charged him constantly to make confession, and amend, and forsake his heinous offences, before he should lose by the sudden prevention of death all time of repentance and amendment. But he, albeit ofttimes warned, set naught by the words of salvation, and promised that he would do penance afterward. In the mean season, being visited with sickness he took to his bed and began to be sore vexed with vehement pain. And the king coming to him (for he loved him tenderly) exhorted him that even then he would do penance for his naughty life, before he died. But he answered, that he would not then confess his sins, but would do so when he was recovered of his sickness; lest his fellows should lay it to his charge that he did for fear of death that which in his health he had not vouchsafed to do; wherein he spake (to his own liking) stoutly, but as it appeared after, he was miserably led astray by the craft of the devil.

And when, as the distemper grew upon him, the king again came in to visit him and give him good counsel, he cried out incontinent with a lamentable voice, saying: "What will you have now? Why have you come hither? For you cannot profit me or any longer do me any good." Whereupon the king said: "Say not so, see ye play the wise man's part." "Nay," quoth he, "I am not mad, but before mine eyes full surely I have knowledge of my ruin." "And what is this?" said the king. "A little while since," quoth he, "two most beautiful young men came into this house and sat down

unus ad caput, et unus ad pedes; protulitque unus libellum perpulchrum, sed vehementer modicum, ac mihi ad legendum dedit, in quo omnia quae unquam bona feceram, intuens scripta reperi, et haec erant nimium pauca et modica. Receperunt codicem, neque aliquid mihi dicebant. Tum subito supervenit exercitus malignorum et horridorum vultu spirituum, domumque hanc et exterius obsedit, et intus maxima ex parte residens implevit. Tunc ille qui et obscuritate tenebrosae faciei et primatu sedis maior esse videbatur eorum, proferens codicem horrendae visionis, et magnitudinis enormis, et ponderis pene importabilis, iussit uni ex satellitibus suis mihi ad legendum deferre. Quem cum legissem, inveni omnia scelera, non solum quae opere vel verbo, sed etiam quae tenuissima cogitatione peccavi, manifestissime in eo tetricis esse descripta literis. Dicebatque ad illos qui mihi adsederant viros albatos et praeclaros: 'Quid hic sedetis, scientes certissime quia noster est iste?' Responderunt: 'Verum dicitis: accipite, et in cumulum damnationis vestrae ducite.' Quo dicto, statim disparuerunt: surgentesque duo nequissimi spiritus, habentes in manibus vomeres, percusserunt me, unus in capite, et alius in pede; qui videlicet modo cum magno tormento irrepunt in interiora corporis mei, moxque ut ad se invicem perveniunt, moriar, et paratis ad rapiendum me daemonibus, in inferni claustra pertrahar."

Sic loquebatur miser desperans, et non multo post defunctus poenitentiam quam ad breve tempus cum

about me, one at my head and one at my feet; and one of them took out a goodly fair book but quite little in size, and gave it me to read, in the which, when I looked, I found all the good deeds that ever I had done written down, and they were exceeding few in number and little in effect. They took the book of me again and said nothing to me. Then suddenly there came a legion of evil, ill-favoured sprites, and both besieged this house outside, and sitting down replenished it almost all within. Then he who by the darkness and gloominess of his face, and highest seat, appeared to be the chief of them, taking out a book terrible to men's sight, unmeasurable for greatness and well-nigh unsupportable for weight, commanded one of his guards to bring it to me to read. And having read it I found all the heinous offences that I have committed, not only in word and deed but also in my lightest thought, written down most plainly therein in grisly letters. And he said to those fair men in white that were seated by me: 'Why sit you here, knowing most certainly that this fellow is ours?' They made answer: 'True it is: take him and lead him away to fill up the measure of your condemnation.' And so saying, forthwith they vanished away: and two most wicked sprites having ploughshares in their hands rose up and struck me, the one in the head, the other in the foot; the which strokes now with great anguish creep into the inward parts of my body, and as soon as they meet together I shall die, and the devils being ready to snatch me away, I shall be dragged to the dungels of hell."

So spake the miserable man in desperation, and not long after died, and now in thraldom unto ever-

fructu veniae facere supersedit, in aeternum sine fructu poenis subditus facit. De quo constat quia, sicut beatus papa Gregorius de quibusdam scribit, non pro se ista cui non profuere, sed pro aliis viderit, qui eius interitum cognoscentes, differre tempus poenitentiae, dum vacat, timerent, ne improviso mortis articulo praeventi impoenitentes perirent. Quod autem codices diversos per bonos sive malos spiritus sibi vidit offerri, ob id superna dispensatione factum est, ut meminerimus facta et cogitationes nostras non in ventum diffluere, sed ad examen summi Iudicis cuncta servari; et sive per amicos angelos in fine nobis ostendenda, sive per hostes. Quod vero prius candidum codicem protulerunt angeli, deinde atrum daemones; illi perparvum, isti enormem: animadvertendum est quod in prima aetate bona aliqua fecit, quae tamen universa prave agendo iuvenis obnubilavit. Qui si e contrario errores pueritiae corrigere in adolescentia, ac bene faciendo a Dei oculis abscondere curasset, posset eorum numero sociari, de quibus ait Psalmus: "Beati quorum remissae sunt iniquitates, et quorum tecta sunt peccata." Hanc historiam, sicut a venerabili antistite Pecthelmo didici, simpliciter ob salutem legentium sive audientium narrandam esse putavi.

---

[1] Ps. xxxii. 1.
[2] Bishop of Whitern in Galloway.

lasting punishment he doth (but all in vain) that penance which he forbore to do for a short space with the gain of pardon. Of whom it is evident that (as the blessed pope Gregory writeth of certain) he had not those visions for his own sake whom they availed nothing, but for the sake of other men which knowing his end might be afeared to put off the time of their repentance, while they have opportunity, lest by sudden prevention of the moment of death they die impenitent. Moreover, that he saw divers books brought to him by good and evil sprites, it was done by disposing from on high, to put us in remembrance that our doings and thoughts have not been scattered to the wind, but that all things are reserved for the examination of the supreme Judge; and at the end must needs be shewed to us either by friendly or enemy angels. Concerning, however, that first of all the angels brought forth a white book, and the devils afterward their black ledger; the angels a very little one, the other an immeasurable great one: it is to be noted that in his childhood he did some good deeds, yet, notwithstanding, he covered them all with a cloud by his lewd demeanour in youth. But if contrariwise he had endeavoured in youth to amend the errors of boyhood and with well-doing hidden them from God's eyes, he might have been brought to their society, of whom the Psalm saith [1]: "Blessed are they whose iniquities are forgiven and whose sins are covered." This history I have thought good to set forth simply, as it was declared unto me of the venerable prelate Pecthelm,[2] for the salvation of them that read or hear it.[3]

[3] If read aloud in the refectory of a convent, Pl.

CAP. XIV

Ut item alius moriturus deputatum sibi apud inferos locum poenarum viderit.

Novi autem ipse fratrem quem utinam non nossem, cuius etiam nomen si hoc aliquid prodesset dicere possem, positum in monasterio nobili, sed ipsum ignobiliter viventem. Corripiebatur quidem sedulo a fratribus ac maioribus loci, atque ad castigatiorem vitam converti ammonebatur. Et quamvis eos audire noluisset, tolerabatur tamen ab eis longanimiter, ob necessitatem operum ipsius exteriorum: erat enim fabrili arte singularis. Serviebat autem multum ebrietati et ceteris vitae remissioris inlecebris; magisque in officina sua die noctuque residere, quam ad psallendum atque orandum in ecclesia audiendumque cum fratribus verbum vitae, concurrere consuerat. Unde accidit illi, quod solent dicere quidam, quia qui non vult ecclesiae ianuam sponte humiliatus ingredi, necesse habet in ianuam inferni non sponte damnatus introduci. Percussus enim languore atque ad extrema perductus vocavit fratres, et multum moerens ac damnato similis coepit narrare, quia videret inferos apertos et Sathanan demersum in profundis tartari, Caiphanque cum ceteris qui occiderunt Dominum, iuxta eum flammis ultricibus contraditum: "In quorum vicinia," inquit, "heu misero mihi locum despicio aeternae per-

CHAPTER XIV

How another in like manner at the point of death saw a place of punishment appointed for him in hell.

FURTHERMORE, I myself knew a brother (whom would God I had never known!) placed in a famous monastery, yet himself infamous for his way of life, whose name I could tell if it were worth the telling. He was indeed constantly rebuked of his brethren and the head officers of the monastery, and warned to change to a more amended way of life. And albeit he had refused to hear them, yet did they tolerate him with long-suffering for his service in outward things which were necessary for them; for he was a singular good carpenter. But he was much given to drunkenness and all other enticements of dissolute life; and accustomed rather to sit in his shop day and night than to come to church to sing and pray and hear the word of life with the brethren. By which occasion it happened to him, as some are wont to say, that he that will not humble himself and come of his own accord within the church door, shall have to be brought under condemnation against his will to the door of hell. For being stricken with sickness and brought to extremity he called the brethren, and with much lamentation, like a man condemned already, began to declare unto them, that he saw hell opened and Satan drowned in the depths of the dungel, and Caiaphas with the whole rabblement that put Christ to death cast in the avenging flames hard by him: "And next to them, O miserable man that I am," said he, "I see a place of everlasting perdition prepared for

ditionis esse praeparatum." Audientes haec fratres, coeperunt diligenter exhortari, ut vel tunc positus adhuc in corpore poenitentiam faceret. Respondebat ille desperans: "Non est mihi modo tempus vitam mutandi, cum ipse viderim iudicium meum iam esse completum."

Talia dicens, sine viatico salutis obiit, et corpus eius in ultimis est monasterii locis humatum, neque aliquis pro eo vel missas facere, vel psalmos cantare, vel saltem orare praesumebat. O quam grandi distantia divisit Deus inter lucem et tenebras! Beatus protomartyr Stephanus passurus mortem pro veritate, vidit caelos apertos, vidit gloriam Dei, et Jesum stantem a dextris Dei; et ubi erat futurus ipse post mortem, ibi oculos mentis ante mortem, quo laetior occumberet, misit. At contra, faber iste tenebrosae mentis et actionis, imminente morte, vidit aperta tartara, vidit damnationem diaboli et sequacium eius; vidit etiam suum infelix inter tales carcerem, quo miserabilius ipse desperata salute periret, sed viventibus qui haec cognovissent, causam salutis sua perditione relinqueret. Factum est hoc nuper in provincia Berniciorum; ac longe lateque diffamatum, multos ad agendam et non differendam scelerum suorum poenitudinem provocavit. Quod utinam exhinc etiam nostrarum lectione literarum fiat.

me." The brethren hearing these words began to exhort him earnestly that even then he should repent while still in the body. He answered in despair: "There is no time now for me to change my life, since I have seen that my judgment is passed already."

With these words he died without having received the voyage-provision of salvation, and his body was interred in the remotest part of the monastery, and no one durst say masses or sing psalms or even pray for him. Oh! how far asunder hath God separated light and darkness! The blessed first martyr Stephen ready to suffer death for the truth saw the heavens open,[1] saw the glory of God and Jesus standing on the right hand of God; and to the end he might more joyfully die, fixed the eyes of his mind before death there where he was to be after death. But contrariwise this carpenter, whose mind and doings were in darkness, at the hour of his death saw hell open, saw the damnation of the devil and them that follow him; the unhappy man saw too his own prison among such company, to the intent he should himself die the more miserably in despair of his salvation, yet by his own damnation might leave occasion of salvation to the living which had heard these things. This chanced of late in the country of the Bernicians and was by common talk blasted far and wide, and stirred up many to do penance for their heinous acts and not to make delay. And may it be that hereafter it work also in such as shall read our present history.

[1] Acts vii. 56.

CAP. XV

Ut plurimae Scottorum ecclesiae, instante Adamnano, catholicum pascha susceperint; utque idem librum de locis sanctis scripserit.

Quo tempore plurima pars Scottorum in Hibernia, et non nulla etiam de Brettonibus in Brittania rationabile et ecclesiasticum paschalis observantiae tempus Domino donante suscepit. Siquidem Adamnan presbyter et abbas monachorum qui erant in insula Hii, cum legationis gratia missus a sua gente, venisset ad Aldfridum regem Anglorum, et aliquandiu in ea provincia moratus, videret ritus ecclesiae canonicos; sed et a pluribus qui erant eruditiores esset sollerter admonitus, ne contra universalem ecclesiae morem, vel in observantia paschali, vel in aliis quibusque decretis cum suis paucissimis, et in extremo mundi angulo positis vivere praesumeret, mutatus mente est; ita ut ea quae viderat et audierat in ecclesiis Anglorum, suae suorumque consuetudini libentissime praeferret. Erat enim vir bonus et sapiens, et scientia Scripturarum nobilissime instructus.

Qui cum domum rediisset, curavit suos qui erant in Hii, quive eidem erant subditi monasterio, ad eum quem cognoverat, quemque ipse toto ex corde susceperat, veritatis callem perducere, nec valuit. Navigavit Hiberniam, et praedicans eis, ac modesta

---

[1] North Ireland.

[2] Outside Wales, Pl.

[3] The biographer of St. Columba, and 9th abbot of Iona.

[4] Such as Ceolfrid. At this time Bede, then 14, may have seen Adamnan.

CHAPTER XV

How a great many churches of the Scots by the instant preaching of Adamnan did adopt the catholic Easter; and how the same wrote a book of the holy places.

At that time a great part of the Scots in Ireland,[1] and some also of the Britons in Britain,[2] adopted by the gift of the Lord the true and ecclesiastical time of keeping Easter. For whenas Adamnan[3] priest and abbot of the monks who were in the isle Hy, being sent upon an embassy from his own nation to Aldfrid king of the English, and tarrying a certain time in that country, saw the canonical rites of the Church; and besides was earnestly admonished by many who were more learned,[4] that he should not presume to live contrary to the universal custom of the Church, nor in keeping Easter, nor in other decrees, whatsoever they were, with his countrymen who were very few in number and dwelt in the furthermost corner of the world, he changed his mind; so much so that what he had seen and heard in the churches of England he most gladly preferred before the custom which he and his countrymen had followed. For he was a virtuous and wise man, and eminently learned in the knowledge of Scripture.

And after his return home he endeavoured to bring his own people that were in Hy, or that were subject to the said monastery,[5] unto that way of truth which he had learned and which he had adopted himself with his whole heart, but could not bring it to pass. He sailed to Ireland, and preaching there

[5] For federation cf. p. 343.

exhortatione declarans legitimum paschae tempus, plurimos eorum, et pene omnes qui ab Hiensium dominio erant liberi, ab errore avito correctos ad unitatem reduxit catholicam, ac legitimum paschae tempus observare perdocuit. Qui cum celebrato in Hibernia canonico pascha, ad suam insulam revertisset, suoque monasterio catholicam temporis paschalis observantiam instantissime praedicaret, nec tamen perficere quod conabatur posset, contigit eum ante expletum anni circulum migrasse de saeculo. Divina utique gratia disponente, ut vir unitatis ac pacis studiosissimus ante ad vitam raperetur aeternam, quam redeunte tempore paschali, graviorem cum eis qui eum ad veritatem sequi nolebant cogeretur habere discordiam.

Scripsit idem vir de locis sanctis librum legentibus multis utillimum; cuius auctor erat docendo ac dictando Galliarum episcopus Arcuulfus, qui locorum gratia sanctorum venerat Hierosolymam, et lustrata omni terra repromissionis, Damascum quoque, Constantinopolim, Alexandriam, multas maris insulas adierat; patriamque navigio revertens, vi tempestatis in occidentalia Brittaniae littora delatus est: ac post multa, ad memoratum Christi famulum Adamnanum perveniens, ubi doctus in Scripturis sanctorumque locorum gnarus esse compertus est, libentissime est ab illo susceptus, libentius auditus; adeo ut quaeque ille se in locis sanctis memoratu digna vidisse testabatur, cuncta mox iste literis

[1] 703 or 704.

[2] Bede himself wrote a book *De Locis Sanctis*.

and shewing them with gentle exhortation the lawful time of Easter, he brought back many of them, and almost all which were not under the dominion of the men of Hy, to catholic unity after amendment of their error of old time, and taught them to keep the lawful time of Easter. And when he had celebrated the canonical Easter in Ireland, he returned to his island and was instant in preaching to his own monastery the catholic keeping of Easter time, and yet not being able to accomplish his purpose, it fortuned that before the year was fully gone about he departed from the world.[1] It was specially by the appointment of divine grace that a man so desirous of unity and peace should be taken hence to eternal life, before Easter time came again, when he would have been forced to more grievous variance with them that would not follow him to the truth.

The same man wrote a book of the holy places,[2] very profitable to many readers; his authority for the which he had in the lectures and expositions of Arculf, a bishop in France, who to see the holy places had gone to Jerusalem, and when he had wandered over all the Land of Promise, he had come also to Damascus, Constantinople, Alexandria and many isles of the sea; and coming home by sea was driven by a mighty tempest to the west coasts of Britain; and after suffering many things he reached the aforesaid servant of Christ, Adamnan, and was there found to be learned in the Scriptures and acquainted with the holy places, and was most readily entertained and readily harkened to; insomuch that whatever things worthy of remembrance Arculf testified he had seen in the holy places, all these Adamnan by and by procured to be put in

mandare curaverit. Fecitque opus, ut dixi, multum utile, et maxime illis qui longius ab eis locis in quibus patriarchae et apostoli erant, secreti, ea tantum de his quae lectione didicerint, norunt. Porrexit autem librum hunc Adamnan Aldfrido regi, ac per eius est largitionem etiam minoribus ad legendum contraditus. Scriptor quoque ipse multis ab eo muneribus donatus, patriam remissus est. De cuius scriptis aliqua decerpere, ac nostrae huic Historiae inserere commodum fore legentibus reor.

CAP. XVI

Quae in eodem libro de loco Dominicae nativitatis, passionis, et resurrectionis commemoravit.

Scripsit ergo de loco Dominicae nativitatis in hunc modum:

"Bethleem, civitas David, in dorso sita est angusto ex omni parte vallibus circumdato, ab occidente in orientem mille passibus longa, humili sine turribus muro per extrema plani verticis instructo; in cuius orientali angulo quasi quoddam naturale semiantrum est, cuius exterior pars nativitatis Dominicae fuisse dicitur locus; interior Praesepe Domini nominatur. Haec spelunca tota interius pretioso marmore tecta, supra locum ubi Dominus natus specialius traditur, sanctae Mariae grandem gestat ecclesiam."

writing. And he made a book, as I have said, very profitable to many and most of all to those which being far removed from those places where the patriarchs and apostles were, know nothing of them but what they have learned with reading. Furthermore, Adamnan presented this book to king Aldfrid, and by his liberality it was handed on to inferior persons to read. The writer too himself was rewarded by the king with many goodly gifts and sent to his country again. Out of whose writings I think it will be profitable to our readers to gather some things and place them in this our History.

CHAPTER XVI

What things he mentioned in the same book touching the place of the nativity, passion and resurrection of our Lord.

Of the place then of the Lord's nativity he wrote in this sort:

"Bethlehem the city of David, situated in a narrow ridge compassed with valleys of every side, is a mile in length from the west to the east, having a low wall without towers built along the edge of the flat top; in the east corner whereof there is as it were a half-cave framed of nature, the outer part of which is said to have been the place of the Lord's nativity; the inner is named the Lord's Manger. This cave within is all covered with costly marble, over the place where it is especially reported that the Lord was born, and beareth above the great church of holy Mary."

Scripsit item hoc modo de loco passionis ac resurrectionis illius:

"Ingressis a septemtrionali parte urbem Hierosolymam, primum de locis sanctis pro conditione platearum divertendum est ad ecclesiam Constantinianam, quae Martyrium appellatur. Hanc Constantinus imperator, eo quod ibi crux Domini ab Helena matre reperta sit, magnifico et regio cultu construxit. Dehinc ab occasu Golgothana videtur ecclesia, in qua etiam rupis apparet illa, quae quondam ipsam adfixo Domini corpore crucem pertulit, argenteam modo pergrandem sustinens crucem, pendente magna desuper aerea rota cum lampadibus. Infra ipsum vero locum Dominicae crucis, excisa in petra crypta est, in qua super altare pro defunctis honoratis sacrificium solet offerri, positis interim in platea corporibus. Huius quoque ad occasum ecclesiae, Anastasis, hoc est, resurrectionis Dominicae rotunda ecclesia, tribus cincta parietibus, duodecim columnis sustentatur, inter parietes singulos latum habens spatium viae, quae tria altaria in tribus locis parietis medii continet, hoc est, australi, aquilonali, et occidentali. Haec bis quaternas portas, id est, introitus per tres e regione parietes habet, e quibus quatuor ad vulturnum, et quatuor ad eurum spectant. Huius in medio monumentum Domini rotundum petra excisum est, cuius culmen intrinsecus stans homo manu contingere potest, ab oriente habens introitum, cui lapis ille magnus adpositus est; quod intrinsecus ferramentorum vestigia usque in praesens ostendit. Nam extrinsecus usque ad culminis summitatem totum marmore tectum est.

He wrote likewise of the place of His passion and resurrection after this sort:

"When ye have entered into the city of Jerusalem on the north side, ye must by order of the streets turn aside first of the holy places to the church of Constantine which is called the Martyrdom. This the emperor Constantine built with royal splendour and magnificence, because, it is said, the Lord's cross was found in that place by his mother Helena. Going from thence on the west ye shall see the church of Golgotha, where too is to be seen that rock which sometime bore the cross and the Lord's body nailed to the same, and beareth now a mighty cross of silver, with a great brazen wheel hanging over it carrying lamps. Beneath the very place indeed where the Lord's cross stands a vault hath been hewn out of the rock, in the which upon an altar the sacrifice is offered for honourable men that dieth, the corpses standing meantime in the street. To the west of this church also is the Anastasis, that is to say, the round church of the Lord's resurrection, environed with 3 walls and borne up with 12 pillars, having betwixt every wall a fair broad way, which hath 3 altars in three places of the mid wall, that is to say, south, north and west. This church hath 8 gates, that is to say, places of entrance through the three walls opposite, of the which 4 face to the south-east and 4 to the east. In the middle of this church the round monument of the Lord has been hewn out of the rock, to the top of which a man standing within may reach with his hand: it hath an entrance on the east side, against which is laid that great stone; until this day it sheweth the print of the iron tools within. For without up to the top of the roof it is all covered

Summum vero culmen auro ornatum, auream magnam gestat crucem. In huius ergo monumenti aquilonali parte sepulcrum Domini in eadem petra excisum, longitudinis septem pedum, trium mensura palmarum pavimento altius eminet; introitum habens a latere meridiano, ubi die noctuque duodecim lampades ardent, quatuor intra sepulcrum, octo supra in margine dextro. Lapis qui ad ostium monumenti positus erat, nunc fissus est; cuius pars minor quadratum altare, ante ostium nihilominus eiusdem monumenti stat; maior vero in orientali eiusdem ecclesiae loco quadrangulum aliud altare sub linteaminibus exstat. Color autem eiusdem monumenti et sepulcri albo et rubicundo permixtus esse videtur."

CAP. XVII

Quae item de loco ascensionis Dominicae, et sepulchris patriarcharum.

De loco quoque Dominicae ascensionis praefatus auctor hoc modo refert.

" Mons Olivarum altitudine monti Sion par est, sed latitudine et longitudine praestat, exceptis vitibus et olivis rarae ferax arboris, frumenti quoque et hordei fertilis. Neque enim brucosa, sed herbosa et florida soli illius est qualitas: in cuius summo vertice, ubi Dominus ad caelos ascendit, ecclesia rotunda grandis, ternas per circuitum cameratas habet porticus, desuper tectas. Interior namque domus propter Dominici corporis meatum camerari

---

[1] *brucosus* is not in the dictionaries: *brocia, bruscia* mean a thicket; cf. *brush.*

with marble. The top of the roof indeed is gilded with gold and beareth a great gold cross. In the north part of this monument then the Lord's tomb, hewn out of the same rock, and made 7 foot long, stands 3 palms above the floor; it hath its coming in on the south side, where day and night 12 lamps burn, 4 within the tomb and 8 above in the right side. The stone which was set at the mouth of the monument is now cloven; whereof the less portion notwithstanding standeth at the door of the same monument as an altar of hewn stone; but the greater portion standeth for another square altar on the east part of the same church and is covered with linen cloths. Now the colour of the said monument and tomb seemeth to be white and red decently mixed."

CHAPTER XVII

What also he mentioned touching the place of the Lord's ascension, and the tombs of the patriarchs.

The author above mentioned speaketh also in this wise touching the place of the Lord's ascension:

"Mount Olivet is as high as Mount Sion but excels it in breadth and length: there groweth few trees but vines and olives; wheat and barley too it bringeth forth in good store. For it is not scrubby [1] either, but the nature of the soil is good for grass and flowers: upon the topmost height thereof, where the Lord ascended to the heavens, standeth a great round church, having 3 porches round in a circuit, vaulted and covered over. For the inner house could not be vaulted and covered because of the

et tegi non potuit: altare ad orientem habens angusto culmine protectum, in cuius medio ultima Domini vestigia, caelo desuper patente ubi ascendit, visuntur. Quae cum quotidie a credentibus terra tollatur, nihilominus manet, eandemque adhuc speciem veluti impressis signata vestigiis servat. Haec circa aerea rota iacet, usque ad cervicem alta, ab occasu habens introitum, pendente desuper in trochleis magna lampade, tota die et nocte lucente. In occidentali eiusdem ecclesiae parte fenestrae octo, totidemque e regione lampades in funibus pendentes usque Hierosolymam per vitrum fulgent; quarum lux corda intuentium cum quadam alacritate et compunctione pavefacere dicitur. In die ascensionis Dominicae per annos singulos, missa peracta, validi flaminis procella desursum venire consuevit, et omnes qui in ecclesia adfuerint terrae prosternere."

De situ etiam Chebron et monumentis patrum ita scribit:

"Chebron quondam civitas et metropolis regni David, nunc ruinis tantum quid tunc fuerit ostendens. Uno ad orientem stadio speluncam duplicem in valle habet, ubi sepulchra patriarcharum quadrato muro circumdantur, capitibus versis ad aquilonem; et haec singula singulis tecta lapidibus instar basilicae dolatis; trium patriarcharum candidis, Adam obscurioris et vilioris operis, qui haud longe ab illis ad borealem, extremamque muri illius partem pausat.

passage of the Lord's body: it hath an altar toward the east covered with a narrow roof: in the middle are to be seen the last prints of the Lord's feet, the heaven above, where he ascended, being open. And although the earth be taken away daily of believers, none the less it remaineth and keepeth still the same figure as if marked with the prints of His feet. Round about this earth lieth a brazen wheel, as high as a man's neck, having an entrance upon the west, and a great lamp hanging above it in a pulley, which burneth all day and night. In the west side of the same church be 8 windows, and as many lamps hanging in cords opposite shine through the glass to Jerusalem; and their light is said to make the hearts of them that behold it sore afraid, together with a lively zeal and pricking of heart. At the day of the Lord's ascension every year, when mass is done, a great gale of wind hath been wont to come down and cast to the ground all them that have come in the church."

Of the situation also of Hebron and the monuments of the fathers there he writeth in this sort:

"Hebron, sometime the city and chiefest town in David's kingdom, sheweth now only by the ruins what it was in that day. It hath toward the east within a furlong the double cave in a valley, where the patriarchs' tombs are environed with a wall of hewn stones, their heads turned toward the north: and each of these tombs is covered with a single stone worked like the stones of a church; the tombs of the three patriarchs[1] are white, Adam's is more dark and of meaner work, and lieth not far from the other toward the north at the uttermost part of that

[1] Abraham, Isaac, Jacob.

Trium quoque feminarum viliores et minores memoriae cernuntur.

"Mamre collis mille passibus a monumentis his ad boream, herbosus valde et floridus, campestrem habens in vertice planitiem; in cuius aquilonali parte quercus Abrahae, duorum hominum altitudinis truncus, ecclesia circumdata est."

Haec de opusculis excerpta praefati scriptoris ad sensum quidem verborum illius, sed brevioribus strictisque comprehensa sermonibus, nostris ad utilitatem legentium Historiis indere placuit. Plura voluminis illius si qui scire delectat, vel in ipso illo volumine, vel in eo quod de illo dudum strictim excerpsimus, epitomate requirat.

CAP. XVIII

Ut Australes Saxones episcopos acceperint Eadberctum et Eollan, Occidentales Danihelem et Aldhelmum; et de scriptis eiusdem Aldhelmi.

Anno Dominicae incarnationis septingentesimo quinto, Aldfrid rex Nordanhymbrorum defunctus est anno regni sui vicesimo necdum impleto; cui succedens in imperium filius suus Osred, puer octo circiter annorum, regnavit annis undecim. Huius regni principio antistes Occidentalium Saxonum Haeddi caelestem migravit ad vitam. Bonus quippe erat vir ac iustus, et episcopalem vitam sive doctrinam magis insito sibi virtutum amore quam lectionibus

---

[1] Sarah, Rebecca, Leah.

wall. The memorials also of the three women[1] are meaner and smaller.

"Mamre is a hill, a mile away from these monuments to the north, full of grass and flowers, and in the top it hath a goodly level field; in the north part whereof Abraham's oak, a stump as high as two men can reach, is compassed about with a church."

I have thought it good for the benefit of readers to put in our History these things gathered from the works of the aforesaid author after the true meaning of his words, but more briefly, and more closely knit together. If any man be desirous to know more of that book, let him seek it either in the book itself or in that little abridgment which we drew out of him but late.[2]

CHAPTER XVIII

How the South Saxons received Eadbert and Eolla for their bishops, the West Saxons Daniel and Aldhelm for theirs; and of the writings of the same Aldhelm.

The 705th year of the Lord's incarnation Aldfrid king of Northumberland died, the 20th year of his reign not yet fully expired; after whom succeeded his son Osred, a child of about 8 years old, and reigned 11 years.[3] In the beginning of his reign Heddi, bishop of the West Saxons, departed to the heavenly life. For he was a good and just man, and directed his episcopal life and teaching more by the love of virtue grafted in him than by what

[2] *De Locis Sanctis*, not mentioned in Bede's own list of his works, ch. 24.

[3] Described as a vicious youth.

institutus exercebat. Denique reverentissimus antistes Pecthelm, de quo in sequentibus suo loco dicendum est, qui cum successore eius Aldhelmo multo tempore adhuc diaconus sive monachus fuit, referre est solitus, quod in loco quo defunctus est, ob meritum sanctitatis eius multa sanitatum sint patrata miracula, hominesque provinciae illius solitos ablatum inde pulverem propter languentes in aquam mittere, atque huius gustum sive aspersionem multis sanitatem aegrotis et hominibus et pecoribus conferre: propter quod frequenti ablatione pulveris sacri, fossa sit ibidem facta non minima.

Quo defuncto, episcopatus provinciae illius in duas parochias divisus est. Una data Daniheli, quam usque hodie regit; altera Aldhelmo cui annis quatuor strenuissime praefuit; ambo et in rebus ecclesiasticis, et in scientia Scripturarum sufficienter instructi. Denique Aldhelm, cum adhuc esset presbyter, et abbas monasterii quod "Maildufi urbem" nuncupant, scripsit, iubente synodo suae gentis, librum egregium adversus errorem Brettonum quo vel pascha non suo tempore celebrant, vel alia perplura ecclesiasticae castitati et paci contraria gerunt, multosque eorum qui Occidentalibus Saxonibus subditi erant Brettones, ad catholicam Dominici paschae celebrationem huius lectione perduxit. Scripsit et de virginitate librum eximium, quem in exemplum Sedulii geminato opere, et versibus hexametris, et prosa composuit. Scripsit et alia

---

[1] Winchester and Sherborne.

[2] The name, which comes in another form in Tennyson's *Voyage of Maeldune*, is Irish. For another instance of Irish influence in South Britain compare Dieul at Selsey, IV. 13. The modern name Malmesbury seems to be a compound of the Irish name and Aldhelm, Pl. II. 311.

he had learned of study. In brief, the most reverend prelate Pecthelm, of whom we must speak hereafter in his proper place, and who was a long time (being yet but a deacon and monk) with his successor Aldhelm, was wont to report that in the place where Heddi died, for the reward of his holiness, many miracles of healing were done, and that men of that province used commonly to carry away dust from thence and put it in water for such as were sick, and that the tasting and sprinkling of the same did bring cure to many sick, both men and beasts: by which occasion through often carrying away of the sacred dust a pit of no little size was made there.

And after his death the bishopric of that province was divided into two dioceses.[1] The one was given to Daniel, which he keepeth at this present; the other to Aldhelm, where he ruled the people very diligently for 4 years; they were both men well learned in ecclesiastical affairs and in the knowledge of Scripture. In brief, Aldhelm, when he was but priest and abbot of the monastery which is called "Maiduf's[2] town," wrote by commandment of the synod of his country a notable book against the error of the Britons, for not keeping Easter in his due time and doing many things beside contrary to the purity and peace of the Church, and by reading of the same he brought many Britons who had been made subject to the West Saxons to the catholic solemnization of the Lord's Easter. He wrote too an excellent book of virginity, which after the example of Sedulius[3] he made with double pains both in hexameter verse and prose. He wrote too

[3] Sedulius' *Carmen Paschale.*

nonnulla, utpote vir undecumque doctissimus: nam et sermone nitidus, et scripturarum, ut dixi, tam liberalium quam ecclesiasticarum erat eruditione mirandus. Quo defuncto, pontificatum pro eo suscepit Fortheri, qui usque hodie superest; vir et ipse in Scripturis sanctis multum eruditus.

Quibus episcopatum administrantibus statutum est synodali decreto, ut provincia Australium Saxonum, quae eatenus ad civitatis Ventanae, cui tunc Danihel praeerat, parochiam pertinebat, et ipsa sedem episcopalem ac proprium haberet episcopum: consecratusque est eis primus antistes Eadberct, qui erat abbas monasterii beatae memoriae Vilfridi episcopi, quod dicitur Selaeseu: quo defuncto, Eolla suscepit officium pontificatus. Ipso autem ante aliquot annos ex hac luce subtracto, episcopatus usque hodie cessavit.

CAP. XIX

Ut Coinred Merciorum, et Offa Orientalium Saxonum rex in monachico habitu Romae vitam finierint; et de vita vel obitu Vilfridi episcopi.

Anno autem imperii Osredi quarto, Coinred, qui regno Merciorum nobilissime tempore aliquanto praefuerat, nobilius multo regni sceptra reliquit. Nam venit Romam, ibique adtonsus, pontificatum

---

[1] Aldhelm was grandiloquent and fond of unusual and foreign words. Bright, p. 269.

some other books, being a man of great learning in all ways: for he was both choice [1] in his manner of writing, and for knowledge, as well in liberal literature as in divinity, to be had in admiration. And after his death Forthere was made bishop in his place, who is living to this day; a man too himself much conversant in Holy Scripture.

And when these [2] had governance of the bishopric it was determined by decree in the synod, that the province of the South Saxons, which to that day appertained to the diocese of Winchester, over which Daniel then was, should also have a see and bishop of their own: and Eadbert, abbot of the monastery of bishop Wilfrid of blessed memory, called Selsey, was consecrated their first bishop; and when he died Eolla took the office of bishop upon him. And when he some years past was taken away from this life, the bishopric was left vacant to this day.

CHAPTER XIX

How Cenred king of the Marchmen and Offa king of the East Saxons ended their lives at Rome in the monastical habit; and of the life and death of bishop Wilfrid.

Now the 4th year of Osred's reign, Cenred, which had kept the sovereignty of the Marchmen very honourably for some time,[3] did much more honourably forsake the throne of his kingdom. For when Constantine was pontiff,[4] he went to Rome,

[2] Might be Aldhelm and Forthere, or Aldhelm and Daniel, or Daniel and Forthere.

[3] About five years.

[4] 708–715.

habente Constantino, ac monachus factus, ad limina apostolorum, in precibus, ieiuniis et eleemosynis usque ad diem permansit ultimum; succedente in regnum Ceolredo filio Aedilredi, qui ante ipsum Coinredum idem regnum tenebat. Venit autem cum illo et filius Sigheri regis Orientalium Saxonum, cuius supra meminimus, vocabulo Offa, iuvenis amantissimae aetatis et venustatis, totaeque suae genti ad tenenda servandaque regni sceptra exoptatissimus. Qui pari ductus devotione mentis, reliquit uxorem, agros, cognatos et patriam propter Christum, et propter Evangelium, ut in hac vita centuplum acciperet, et in saeculo venturo vitam aeternam. Et ipse ergo ubi ad loca sancta Romam pervenerunt, adtonsus, et in monachico vitam habitu complens, ad visionem beatorum apostolorum in caelis diu desideratam pervenit.

Eodem sane anno quo hi Brittaniam reliquere antistes eximius Vilfrid, post quadraginta et quinque annos accepti episcopatus, diem clausit extremum in provincia quae vocatur Inundalum: corpusque eius loculo inditum, perlatum est in monasterium ipsius, quod dicitur Inhrypum, et iuxta honorem tanto pontifici congruum, in ecclesia beati apostoli Petri sepultum. De cuius statu vitae, ut ad priora repedantes, paucis quae sunt gesta, memoremus, cum esset puer bonae indolis, atque aetatem moribus transiens, ita se modeste et circumspecte in omnibus gereret, ut merito a maioribus quasi unus ex ipsis

[1] Died 716.
[2] It is not certain whether Offa was actually on the throne.
[3] Matt. xix. 29.

and there receiving the tonsure and being made monk continued at the churches of the apostles in praying, fasting and giving of alms until his dying day. He was succeeded in the throne by Ceolred,[1] Ethelred's son, which had the government of the same realm before Cenred. Moreover, there went with him also the son of Sighere king of the East Saxons (whom we mentioned before), called Offa, a young man in the flower of his age and of most pleasing beauty, and much desired of all his people to remain and bear rule amongst them.[2] But he, moved with like devoutness of mind, forsook his lady, his lands, his kinsfolk and country for Christ's sake and the Gospel's, that in this life he might receive an hundredfold, and in the world to come life everlasting.[3] And he therefore, when they came to the holy places at Rome, was shoren, and passing the rest of his life in the monastical habit came to the vision of the blessed apostles in heaven, as he had long desired before.

Right in the same year that these princes left Britain, the very eminent prelate Wilfrid, after he had been made bishop 45 years, brought his days to an end in the province that is called Oundle: and his body being put in a coffin was carried to his own monastery named Ripon, and with all honour worthy for so noble a bishop was buried in the church of the blessed apostle Peter. Of whose life and behaviour let us briefly make mention what things were done, returning as it were back again to that we have spoken of before. Being a boy of natural goodness and towardness in conduct beyond his years, he shewed such sobriety and prudence in all points that his elders did deservedly love, rever-

amaretur, veneraretur, amplecteretur, ubi quartum decimum aetatis contigit annum, monasticam saeculari vitam praetulit. Quod ubi patri suo narravit, iam enim mater obierat, libenter eius votis ac desideriis caelestibus adnuit, eumque coeptis insistere salutaribus iussit. Venit ergo ad insulam Lindisfarnensem, ibique monachorum famulatui se contradens, diligenter ea quae monasticae castitatis ac pietatis erant, et discere curabat et agere. Et quia acris erat ingenii, didicit citissime psalmos, et aliquot codices; necdum quidem adtonsus, verum eis quae tonsura maiores sunt virtutibus, humilitatis et obedientiae, non mediocriter insignitus: propter quod et a senioribus, et coaetaneis suis iusto colebatur affectu. In quo videlicet monasterio cum aliquot annos Deo serviret, animadvertit paulatim adolescens animi sagacis, minime perfectam esse virtutis viam quae tradebatur a Scottis, proposuitque animo venire Romam, et qui ad sedem apostolicam ritus ecclesiastici sive monasteriales servarentur, videre. Quod cum fratribus referret, laudaverunt eius propositum, eumque id quod mente disposuerat, perficere suadebant. At ille confestim veniens ad reginam Eanfledam, quia notus erat ei, eiusque consilio et suffragiis praefato fuerat monasterio sociatus, indicavit ei desiderium sibi inesse beatorum apostolorum limina visitandi: quae delectata bono adolescentis proposito, misit eum Cantiam ad regem

[1] 648.

ence and cherish him as one of themselves, and when he reached his 14th year,[1] he chose the monastical life rather than the life of the world. The which thing when he had communicated with his father (for his mother was already departed) he gladly condescended to his earnest desires inspired of heaven, and bade him persist in his wholesome purpose. He came therefore to the isle Lindisfarne, and there giving himself up to attending upon the monks he diligently set himself both to learn and practise all points of chastity and godliness required in monastical life. And because he had a goodly pregnant wit he learned very speedily the Psalms and some books beside; being not yet shoren in, but garnished in no common measure with those virtues of lowliness and obedience which far surmount the tonsure: for the which he was justly loved and esteemed both of the elders and of his equals in years. And serving God some years in that monastery he perceived by little and little (being a youth of wise judgment) that the way of virtue taught by the Scots was no way perfect, and he determined to come to Rome and see what ceremonies were observed at the apostolic see of secular priests and religious persons. The which purpose the brethren did well commend, when it was communicated to them, and persuaded him to go forward in what he had determined. Whereupon he came incontinent to queen Eanfled (for he was well known to her and by her counsel and commendation had been received into that monastery) and declared to her that he had longing to visit the churches of the blessed apostles; and she, much delighted with the young man's good purpose, sent him

Erconberctum, qui erat filius avunculi sui, postulans ut eum honorifice Romam transmitteret. Quo tempore ibi gradum archiepiscopi Honorius, unus ex discipulis beati papae Gregorii, vir in rebus ecclesiasticis sublimiter institutus, servabat. Ubi cum aliquandiu demoratus adolescens animi vivacis, diligenter his quae inspiciebat, discendis operam daret, supervenit illo alius adolescens, nomine Biscop, cognomento Benedictus, de nobilibus Anglorum, cupiens et ipse Romam venire: cuius supra meminimus.

Huius ergo comitatui rex sociavit Vilfridum, utque illum secum Romam perduceret, iussit. Qui cum Lugdunum pervenissent, Vilfrid a Dalfino civitatis episcopo ibi retentus est, Benedictus coeptum iter naviter Romam usque complevit. Delectabatur enim antistes prudentia verborum iuvenis, gratia venusti vultus, alacritate actionis, et constantia ac maturitate cogitationis: unde et omnia quae necesse habebat, abundanter ipsi cum sociis suis, quamdiu secum erant, donabat: et insuper offerebat, ut si vellet, partem Galliarum non minimam illi regendam committeret, ac filiam fratris sui virginem illi coniugem daret, eumque ipso loco adoptivi semper haberet. At ille gratias agens pietati quam erga eum, cum esset peregrinus, habere dignaretur, respondit propositum se magis alterius conversationis habere, atque ideo patria relicta Romam iter agere coepisse.

---

[1] Eadbald, brother of Eanfled's mother.
[2] Cf. Lives of the Abbots.
[3] 653.
[4] Annemundus was the archbishop of Lyons and Dalfinus was his brother.

to Kent to king Erconbert, which was her uncle's [1] son, requiring him to send him honourably to Rome. And at this time Honorius, one of the blessed pope Gregory's disciples, a man profoundly learned in ecclesiastical matters, held the degree of archbishop there. And whenas the young man, lacking not in lively spirit, was tarrying there a space, and employed his diligence to learn that which he overlooked, there repaired thither, as it fell, another young man whose name was Biscop, surnamed Benedict, an English noble, desirous too himself to go to Rome: of whom we have made mention before.[2]

The king joined Wilfrid to Benedict's company, with charge that he should bring him with him safe to Rome.[3] And when they were come to Lyons, Wilfrid was stayed there of Dalfinus, bishop of the city,[4] while Benedict hastened on to accomplish the journey he had begun to Rome. For the bishop was delighted with the young man's wise talk, the fair comeliness of his countenance, his readiness in action, and the steadiness and ripe compass of his thought; for which cause also he gave him and his company all things that were needful plentifully, as long as they continued there; and further offered, if he would, to entrust him with the government of a large part of France, and give him to wife a maid that was his brother's daughter, and look upon him always as his adopted son. But Wilfrid thanking him for the goodness that the bishop vouchsafed to shew unto him, being but a stranger, answered that he was fully determined upon another course of life, and therefore had forsaken his country and taken the journey to Rome.

Quibus auditis, antistes misit eum Romam, dato duce itineris, et cunctis simul quae necessitas poscebat itineris, largiter subministratis; obsecrans sedulo, ut cum patriam reverteretur, per se iter facere meminisset. Veniens vero Romam, et orationibus ac meditationi rerum ecclesiasticarum, ut animo proposuerat, quotidiana mancipatus instantia, pervenit ad amicitiam viri doctissimi ac sanctissimi, Bonifatii videlicet archidiaconi, qui etiam consiliarius erat apostolici papae; cuius magisterio quatuor Evangeliorum libros ex ordine didicit, computum paschae rationabilem, et alia multa quae in patria nequiverat ecclesiasticis disciplinis accommoda, eodem magistro tradente percepit; et cum menses aliquot ibi studiis occupatus felicibus exegisset, rediit ad Dalfinum in Galliam, et tres annos apud eum commoratus, attonsus est ab eo, et in tanto habitus amore, ut heredem sibi illum facere cogitasset. Sed ne hoc fieri posset, antistes crudeli morte praereptus est, et Vilfrid ad suae potius, hoc est, Anglorum gentis episcopatum reservatus. Namque Baldhild regina, missis militibus, episcopum iussit interfici; quem ad locum quidem quo decollandus erat, secutus est Vilfrid clericus illius, desiderans cum eo, tametsi ipso multum prohibente, pariter occumbere. Sed hunc ubi peregrinum atque oriundum de natione Anglorum cognovere carnifices, pepercere illi, neque eum trucidare cum suo voluere pontifice.

At ille Brittaniam veniens, coniunctus est amicitiis

[1] Said to have been an Anglo-Saxon slave who married Clovis II. She retired to the monastery of Chelles, p. 361, and was made a saint. The execution has been attributed to Ebroin, IV. 1.

The which when the bishop heard, he sent him to Rome with a guide to conduct him in the way, and provided withal good store of all things requisite for the journey; desiring him earnestly that at his return to his own country he would remember to take his house by the way. But Wilfrid coming to Rome and applying himself constantly day by day to prayer and the contemplation of ecclesiastical things, according to his first determination, fell acquainted with a very learned and holy man, to wit archdeacon Boniface, who was also counsellor to the apostolical pope; by whose instruction he learned orderly the four books of the Gospels and the true reckoning of Easter, and many other things profitable to the disciplines of the Church, which he could not attain unto in his own country, he understood by the lessons of the said teacher; and when he had passed some months there in the happy exercise of study, he returned to Dalfinus again in France, and tarrying with him 3 years he after took the tonsure of him, and was so entirely loved of him, that the bishop had come to think of making him his heir. But by cruel death he was snatched away, that this could not come to pass, and Wilfrid was reserved to be bishop rather in his own country, that is to say, England. For queen Baldhild [1] sent a power and commanded the bishop to be put to death; whom Wilfrid his clerk followed to the place where he was to be beheaded, desiring to die along with him, albeit the bishop did utterly forbid him. But when the executioners knew he was a stranger and an Englishman born, they spared him and would not put him to death with his bishop.

Whereupon coming to Britain he was brought to

Alchfridi regis, qui catholicas ecclesiae regulas sequi semper et amare didicerat. Unde et ille, quia catholicum eum esse comperit, mox donavit terram decem familiarum in loco qui dicitur Stanford, et non multo post monasterium triginta familiarum in loco qui vocatur Inrhypum; quem videlicet locum dederat pridem ad construendum inibi monasterium his qui Scottos sequebantur. Verum quia illi postmodum optione data maluerunt loco cedere, quam pascha catholicum ceterosque ritus canonicos iuxta Romanae et apostolicae ecclesiae consuetudinem recipere, dedit hoc illi, quem melioribus imbutum disciplinis ac moribus vidit.

Quo in tempore ad iussionem praefati regis presbyter ordinatus est in eodem monasterio ab Agilbercto episcopo Geuissorum, cuius supra meminimus, desiderante rege ut vir tantae eruditionis ac religionis sibi specialiter individuo comitatu sacerdos esset ac doctor. Quem non multo post detecta et eliminata, ut et supra docuimus, Scottorum secta, Galliam mittens, cum consilio atque consensu patris sui Osuiu, episcopum sibi rogavit ordinari, cum esset annorum circita triginta, eodem Agilbercto tunc episcopatum agente Parisiacae civitatis; cum quo et alii undecim episcopi ad dedicationem antistitis convenientes, multum honorifice ministerium impleverunt. Quo adhuc in transmarinis partibus demorante, consecratus est in episcopatum Eboraci,

[1] Of Deira.

[2] Stamford in Lincolnshire, or Stamford in Yorkshire on the Derwent.

be in friendship with king Alchfrid,[1] who had learned to follow always and love the catholic rules of the Church. And for that he perceived Wilfrid to be catholic, he granted him straightways land of 10 households in the place named Stanford,[2] and within a short time after the monastery, of 30 households, in the place called Ripon; which certes he a while before had given to them that followed the Scots to build a monastery there. But because afterwards they being put to choice had rather depart thence than receive the catholic Easter and the other canonical ceremonies after the manner of the Roman and apostolic Church, he gave it to him, whom he found instructed in better discipline and customs.

And at this time in the same monastery Wilfrid was ordained priest by Agilbert bishop of the Gewissas, of whom we have spoken before, by commandment of the aforesaid king, who was desirous that a man of such great learning and devotion should expressly be priest and teacher for him in his court continually. Whom not long after, when the Scots' sect was, as we have shewed before, disclosed and banished, he sent him to France, with the advice and consent of his father Oswy, and asked for him to be ordained his bishop at about the age of 30 years, the same Agilbert then having the bishopric of the city of Paris;[3] and with Agilbert 11 other bishops also assembled to consecrate him, and fulfilled their duty in that behalf very honourably. But while he yet tarried beyond the seas, Chad, a holy man (as it is above mentioned), was

[3] Agilbert was at Whitby in 664, III. 7, and could not have been bishop of Paris before 666. Bright, p. 190.

iubente rege Osuio, Ceadda vir sanctus, ut supra memoratum est, et tribus annis ecclesiam sublimiter regens, dehinc ad monasterii sui, quod est in Laestingaeu, curam secessit, accipiente Vilfrido episcopatum totius Nordanhymbrorum provinciae.

Qui deinde regnante Ecgfrido pulsus est episcopatu, et alii pro illo consecrati antistites, quorum supra meminimus; Romamque iturus, et coram apostolico papa causam dicturus, ubi navem conscendit, flante favonio pulsus est Fresiam, et honorifice susceptus a barbaris ac rege illorum Aldgilso, praedicabat eis Christum, et multa eorum millia verbo veritatis instituens, a peccatorum suorum sordibus fonte Salvatoris abluit; et quod postmodum Vilbrord reverentissimus Christi pontifex in magna devotione complevit, ipse primus ibi opus evangelicum coepit. Ibi ergo hiemem cum nova Dei plebe feliciter exigens, sic Romam veniendi iter repetiit; et ubi causa eius ventilata est praesente Agathone papa et pluribus episcopis, universorum iudicio absque crimine accusatus fuisse, et episcopatu esse dignus inventus est.

Quo in tempore idem papa Agatho cum synodum congregaret Romae centum viginti quinque episcoporum, adversus eos qui unam in Domino Salvatore voluntatem atque operationem dogmatizabant, vocari iussit et Vilfridum, atque inter episcopos considentem dicere fidem suam simul et provinciae sive insulae de qua venerat: cumque catholicus fide cum suis

---

[1] III. 28. [2] Cf. IV. 12. [3] Bosa and Eata.

[4] Eddi's Life says that Wilfrid intended to go to Frisia. In France Ebroin was his enemy.

[5] Monothelitism. Bright, p. 220.

at the commandment of king Oswy, consecrated bishop of York,[1] who ruled the church nobly for 3 years, and thereupon departed to the charge of his monastery in Lastingham, while Wilfrid took the bishopric of all the province of the Northumbrians.

And afterward in the reign of king Egfrid, he was deprived of his bishopric[2] and others[3] consecrated bishops in his place, of whom we made mention before; and when he had taken ship to go to Rome and plead his cause before the apostolic pope, he was driven by a strong west wind into Frisia;[4] and being honourably entertained by the barbarous people and their king Aldgils, he preached unto them Christ and instructed many thousands of them in the word of truth, cleansing them from the defilement of their sins in the Saviour's font; and he was the first to begin there the work of the Gospel, which the most reverend bishop of Christ, Wilbrord, finished afterward with great devotion. There then he passed the winter happily with the new people of God, and so he set forward again on his journey to Rome; and when his cause was debated to and fro in the presence of pope Agatho and many bishops, he was found in process by all their judgments to have been accused without guilt of offence, and to be worthy of his bishopric.

And at that time the same pope Agatho gathering a synod at Rome of 125 bishops, against them that affirmed the doctrine that there was but one will and operation in our Saviour Lord,[5] commanded Wilfrid also to be summoned, and sitting amongst the bishops to declare his faith and withal the faith of the province and island from whence he had come; and when he and his countrymen were found

esset inventus, placuit hoc inter cetera eiusdem synodi gestis inseri, scriptumque est hoc modo: "Vilfridus Deo amabilis episcopus Eboracae civitatis, apostolicam sedem de sua causa appellans, et ab hac potestate de certis incertisque rebus absolutus, et cum aliis centum viginti quinque episcopis in synodo in iudicii sede constitutus, et pro omni aquilonali parte Brittaniae et Hiberniae insulisque quae ab Anglorum et Brettonum necnon Scottorum et Pictorum gentibus incoluntur, veram et catholicam fidem confessus est, et cum subscriptione sua corroboravit."

Post haec reversus Brittaniam provinciam Australium Saxonum ab idolatriae ritibus ad Christi fidem convertit. Vectae quoque insulae verbi ministros destinavit: et secundo anno Aldfridi qui post Ecgfridum regnavit, sedem suam et episcopatum, ipso rege invitante, recepit. Sed post quinque annos denuo accusatus, ab eodem ipso rege et plurimis episcopis praesulatu pulsus est: veniensque Romam, cum praesentibus accusatoribus acciperet locum se defendendi, considentibus episcopis pluribus cum apostolico papa Iohanne, omnium iudicio probatum est accusatores eius non nulla in parte falsas contra eum machinasse calumnias: scriptumque a praefato papa regibus Anglorum Aedilredo et Aldfrido, ut eum in episcopatum suum, eo quod iniuste fuerit condemnatus, facerent recipi.

---

[1] He was imprisoned by Egfrid for nine months. On his release he went first to Mercia and then to Wessex, but was driven out of both.

to be catholic in faith, it pleased them to have this put in among the other acts of the said synod, and it was recorded in this sort: "Wilfrid beloved of God, the bishop of York city, appealing to the apostolic see for his cause, and being by that authority acquitted of things laid to his charge and not laid to his charge, and sitting in the seat of judgment with 125 other bishops in synod made confession of the true and catholic faith for all the north part of Britain and Ireland and the isles which are inhabited with the races of the English, Britons, Scots and Picts, and confirmed the same with his subscription."

After this, returning again to Britain,[1] he converted the province of the South Saxons from idolatrous ceremonies to the faith of Christ.[2] He also sent ministers of the word to the Isle of Wight; and the second year of Aldfrid who reigned after Egfrid, received his see and bishopric again at the invitation of the king himself.[3] But five years after he was accused afresh and deprived of his prelacy by the said king and a number of bishops: and coming to Rome and obtaining leave to defend himself before his accusers, the apostolical pope John and many bishops sitting in judgment, it was by the sentence of all concluded that his accusers had in part devised false charges against him; and the aforesaid pope wrote to the English kings Ethelred and Aldfrid, requiring them to see him restored to his bishopric, because he was unjustly condemned.

[2] IV. 13.

[3] By Theodore's intervention; but Wilfrid's see was smaller than before, for Cuthbert was bishop of Lindisfarne, and in 687 John became bishop of Hexham. Bright, p. 362.

Iuvit autem causam absolutionis eius lectio synodi beatae memoriae papae Agathonis, quae quondam ipso praesente in urbe, atque in eodem concilio inter episcopos residente, ut praediximus, acta est. Cum ergo causa exigente synodus eadem coram nobilibus et frequentia populi iubente apostolico papa diebus aliquot legeretur, ventum est ad locum ubi scriptum erat: "Vilfridus, Deo amabilis episcopus Eboracae civitatis, apostolicam sedem de sua causa appellans, et ab hac potestate de certis incertisque rebus absolutus," et cetera quae supra posuimus. Quod ubi lectum est, stupor adprehendit audientes; et silente lectore coeperunt alterutrum requirere quis esset ille Vilfridus episcopus. Tunc Bonifatius consiliarius apostolici papae, et alii perplures qui eum temporibus Agathonis papae ibi viderant, dicebant ipsum esse episcopum qui nuper Romam accusatus a suis atque ab apostolica sede iudicandus advenerit: "Qui iamdudum," inquiunt, "aeque accusatus huc adveniens, mox audita ac diiudicata causa et controversia utriusque partis, a beatae memoriae papa Agathone probatus est contra fas a suo episcopatu repulsus; et tanti apud eum habitus est, ut ipsum in concilio quod congregaret episcoporum, quasi virum incorruptae fidei et animi probi residere praeciperet." Quibus auditis, dicebant omnes una cum ipso pontifice, virum tantae auctoritatis qui per quadraginta prope annos episcopatu fungebatur,

Now his acquittal was much furthered by the reading of the decrees of the synod assembled by pope Agatho of blessed memory, which was held when Wilfrid was himself sometime present in the city and had his seat amongst the bishops in the said council, as we have said before. When, therefore, as the cause required, the decrees of the said synod were for some days read before the nobility and a great throng of people, by the bidding of the apostolical pope, they came to that place where it was written: "Wilfrid beloved of God, the bishop of York city, appealing to the apostolic see for his cause and being by that authority acquitted of things laid to his charge and not laid to his charge," and the rest as we said before. And when this was read, amazement seized the hearers; and the reader ceasing, they began to enquire each of other, who that bishop Wilfrid was. Then Boniface, counsellor to the apostolical pope, and many other which had seen him there in pope Agatho's time, said that he was the bishop which was accused of his own countrymen and came of late to Rome to be judged by the see apostolic: "Who," quoth they, "long since having come hither on like accusation, after the cause and controversy between the two parties had presently been heard and examined, was concluded by pope Agatho of blessed memory to have been wrongfully deprived of his bishopric; and was had in such estimation of the pope that he commanded him to sit in the council of bishops, that he was assembling, as a man of unblemished faith and upright mind." And this being heard, the pope himself and all that were present said that a man of such great authority, who for nearly 40 years was in the

nequaquam damnari debere, sed ad integrum culpis accusationum absolutum patriam cum honore reverti.

Qui cum Brittaniam remeans in Galliarum partes devenisset, tactus est infirmitate repentina, et ea crescente adeo pressus, ut neque equo vehi posset, sed manibus ministrorum portaretur in grabato. Sic delatus in Maeldum civitatem Galliae, quatuor diebus ac noctibus quasi mortuus iacebat, halitu tantum pertenui quia viveret demonstrans. Cumque ita sine cibo et potu, sine voce et auditu quatriduo perseveraret, quinta demum inlucescente die, quasi de gravi experrectus somno exsurgens resedit; apertisque oculis, vidit circa se choros psallentium simul et flentium fratrum; ac modicum suspirans interrogavit, ubi esset Acca presbyter; qui statim vocatus intravit, et videns eum melius habentem ac loqui iam valentem, flexis genibus gratias egit Deo cum omnibus qui aderant fratribus. Et cum parum consedissent, ac de supernis iudiciis trepidi, aliqua confabulari coepissent: iussit pontifex ceteros ad horam egredi, et ad Accan presbyterum ita loqui exorsus est: "Visio mihi modo tremenda apparuit, quam te audire ac silentio tegere volo, donec sciam quid de me fieri velit Deus. Adstitit enim mihi quidam candido praeclarus habitu, dicens se Michahelem esse archangelum: 'Et ob hoc,' inquit, 'missus sum ut te a morte revocem: donavit enim tibi

office of bishop, ought by no means to be condemned, but once again, being quitted from the faults laid to his charge, to return home with honour to his country.

And on his way back to Britain he was stricken with sudden sickness, when he had come to the coasts of France, and was so weakened, the disease growing more and more upon him, that he could not keep his horse, but was carried in a bed by strength of his servants. Being thus brought to the city of Meaux in France he lay 4 days and nights, as though he had been dead, only declaring by a very faint breathing that he was alive. And thus continuing four days without meat and drink, as speechless and past hearing, at length on the fifth day at daybreak he sat up in bed as a man awaked out of a deep sleep; and when his eyes were opened, he saw a company of his brethren about him singing and weeping; and setting a little sigh asked where Acca the priest was; who forthwith being called entered in, and seeing the bishop better amended and now able to speak, fell upon his knees, and gave thanks to God with all the brethren that were present. And when they had sat a little while together, and entered fearfully upon some talk of the heavenly judgments, the bishop commanded all the other to go out for an hour and began after this manner to the priest Acca: "There appeared unto me even now a terrible vision, the which I will have thee hear and keep secret until I know what it is God's pleasure shall become of me. For there stood by me a certain man notably clothed in white, saying that he was Michael the archangel: 'And for this purpose,' said he, 'am I sent to call thee back from death;

Dominus vitam per orationes ac lacrymas discipulorum ac fratrum tuorum, et per intercessionem beatae suae genitricis semperque virginis Mariae. Quapropter dico tibi, quia modo quidem ab infirmitate hac sanaberis; sed paratus esto, quia post quadriennium revertens, visitabo te; patriam vero perveniens, maximam possessionum tuarum quae tibi ablatae sunt portionem recipies, atque in pace tranquilla vitam terminabis.' " Convaluit igitur episcopus, cunctis gaudentibus ac Deo gratias agentibus, coeptoque itinere Brittaniam venit.

Lectis autem epistolis quas ab apostolico papa advexerat, Berctuald archiepiscopus, et Aedilred quondam rex, tunc autem abbas, libentissime faverunt: qui videlicet Aedilred accitum ad se Coinredum quem pro se regem fecerat, amicum episcopo fieri petiit, et impetravit. Sed Aldfrid Nordanhymbrorum rex eum suscipere contemsit, nec longo tempore superfuit: unde factum est ut regnante Osredo filio eius, mox synodo facta iuxta fluvium Nidd, post aliquantum utriusque partis conflictum, tandem cunctis faventibus, in praesulatum sit suae receptus ecclesiae. Sicque quatuor annis, id est, usque ad diem obitus sui, vitam duxit in pace. Defunctus est autem in monasterio suo quod habebat in provincia Undalum sub regimine Cudualdi abbatis; et ministerio fratrum perlatus in primum suum monasterium quod vocatur Inhrypum, positus est in ecclesia beati apostoli Petri, iuxta altare ad

for the Lord hath granted thee life for the prayers and lamentations of thy scholars and brethren, and for the intercession of His blessed and ever virgin mother Mary. Wherefore I say unto thee that now thou shalt be healed of this sickness; but yet be in a readiness, for after four years I will return again and visit thee; but when thou comest to thy country, the greater part of thy possessions which have been taken away thou shalt receive again and end thy life in tranquillity and peace.'" The bishop accordingly recovered, and all rejoiced and gave thanks to God, and setting forward he came to Britain.

Now when the letters which he had brought from the apostolic pope were read, Bertwald the archbishop and Ethelred, sometime king but then an abbot,[1] were very readily on his side: the which Ethelred sending for Cenred, whom he had made king in his place, to come and see him, requested him to be a friend to the bishop, and this he obtained. But Aldfrid king of the Northumbrians scorned to receive him, and not long after died: by which occasion it fell out in the reign of Osred his son, that in a synod held presently by the river Nidd, after some contention in both parts, he was at length received into the prelacy of his church[2] again with the approval of all. And so by the space of four years, to wit to his dying day, he lived in peace. Now he died in his monastery which he had in the province of Oundle under the government of abbot Cuthbald; and by the hands of the brethren he was carried to his first monastery called Ripon, and interred in the church of the blessed apostle Peter, hard by the altar

[1] Abbot of Bardney.
[2] Hexham not York, for John was translated to York.

austrum, ut et supra docuimus; et hoc de illo supra epitaphium scriptum:

"Vilfridus hic magnus requiescit corpore praesul,
Hanc Domino qui aulam ductus pietatis amore
Fecit, et eximio sacravit nomine Petri,
Cui claves caeli Christus dedit arbiter orbis;
Atque auro ac tyrio devotus vestiit ostro.
Quin etiam sublime crucis, radiante metallo,
Hic posuit traphaeum, necnon et quatuor auro
Scribi Evangelii praecepit in ordine libros;
Ac thecam e rutilo hic condignam condidit auro:
Paschalis qui etiam sollemnia tempora cursus
Catholici ad iustum correxit dogma canonis,
Quem statuere patres, dubioque errore remoto
Certa suae genti ostendit moderamina ritus:
Inque locis istis monachorum examina crebra
Colligit, ac monitis cavit quae regula patrum
Sedulus instituit: multisque domique forisque
Iactatus nimium per tempora longa periclis,
Quindecies ternos postquam egit episcopus annos,

toward the south side, as also we signified before; and above is this epitaph written concerning him:

"Wilfrid the noble prelate rests his body in this grave,
Who moved with godly love to Christ, his Lord, this temple gave,
Which men by Peter's hallowed name St. Peter's church shall call,
Whom Christ the keys of heaven gave, the Governor of all;
He decked it in his zeal with gold, and hung with purple o'er,
And likewise reared a shining cross, on high above the floor;
Here was his trophy set, and here in golden letters writ
He bade the four evangelists be shewn in order fit;
And of red gold he had for them a worthy casing made.
Of Easter's solemn festival the course he also laid,
According to the catholic rule, canonically right,
Fixed by the fathers once, and so he banished out of sight
Erroneous doubt by shewing clear the true way to his race:
A goodly company of monks he gathered in this place,
And holding fast the fathers' rule was zealous to provide
By warning words: at home, abroad, he was by perils tried,
Tossed beyond measure for long years, but after he had spent
Thrice fifteen years ordained to hold a bishop's government,

Transiit, et gaudens caelestia regna petivit.
Dona, Jesu, ut grex pastoris calle sequatur."

CAP. XX

Ut religioso abbati Hadriano Albinus, Vilfrido in episcopatum Acca successerit.

Anno post obitum praefati patris proximo, id est, quinto Osredi regis, reverentissimus pater Hadrianus abbas, cooperator in verbo Dei Theodori beatae memoriae episcopi, defunctus est, et in monasterio suo in ecclesia beatae Dei genitricis sepultus; qui est annus quadragesimus primus, ex quo a Vitaliano papa directus est cum Theodoro; ex quo autem Brittaniam venit, tricesimus nonus. Cuius doctrinae simul et Theodori inter alia testimonium perhibet, quod Albinus discipulus eius qui monasterio ipsius in regimine successit, in tantum studiis scripturarum institutus est, ut Graecam quidem linguam non parva ex parte, Latinam vero non minus quam Anglorum, quae sibi naturalis est, noverit.

Suscepit vero pro Vilfrido episcopatum Hagustaldensis ecclesiae Acca presbyter eius, vir et ipse strenuissimus, et coram Deo et hominibus magnificus; qui et ipsius ecclesiae suae quae in beati Andreae apostoli honorem consecrata est, aedificium multifario decore ac mirificis ampliavit operibus. Dedit namque operam, quod et hodie facit, ut adquisitis undecumque reliquiis beatorum apostolorum et martyrum Christi, in venerationem illorum

[1] From which he was expelled in 731. He was a close friend of Bede's.

He passed away, in heavenly realms to dwell with
joyful heart,
Grant, Christ, his flock in following their shepherd
find their part."

CHAPTER XX

How Albinus succeeded to the devout abbot Hadrian and Acca to Wilfrid in his bishopric.

THE next year after the death of the aforesaid father, that is in the fifth year of king Osred, the most reverend father Hadrian, abbot, fellow-labourer in the word of God to Theodore bishop of blessed memory, died and was interred in his own monastery in the church of the blessed mother of God, the 41st year after he was sent by pope Vitalian with Theodore; but the 39th after he came to Britain. Of whose learning as well as Theodore's amongst other things testimony saith, that Albinus his scholar, who had governance of his monastery after him, was so well instructed in the study of the Scriptures that he had knowledge in no small measure of the Greek tongue, but the Latin he knew as well as he did English, which was his natural language.

But in the room of Wilfrid, Acca his priest took the bishopric of the church of Hexham,[1] a man also himself of a most stout courage and noble for his acts both in the sight of God and man; who enlarged too the building of his own church, dedicated in the honour of the blessed apostle Andrew, and adorned it with divers comely and sightful works. For he made endeavour, as he doth also this day, to procure out of all places the relics of the blessed apostles and martyrs of Christ, to the end he might set altars for

poneret altaria, distinctis porticibus in hoc ipsum intra muros eiusdem ecclesiae, sed et historias passionis eorum, una cum ceteris ecclesiasticis voluminibus, summa industria congregans, amplissimam ibi ac nobilissimam bibliothecam fecit, necnon et vasa sancta et luminaria aliaque huiusmodi quae ad ornatum domus Dei pertinent, studiosissime paravit. Cantatorem quoque egregium, vocabulo Maban, qui a successoribus discipulorum beati papae Gregorii in Cantia fuerat cantandi sonos edoctus, ad se suosque instituendos accersiit, ac per annos duodecim tenuit: quatenus et quae illi non noverant carmina ecclesiastica doceret; et ea quae quondam cognita longo usu vel negligentia inveterare coeperunt huius doctrina priscum renovarentur in statum. Nam et ipse episcopus Acca cantator erat peritissimus, quomodo etiam in literis sanctis doctissimus, et in catholicae fidei confessione castissimus, in ecclesiasticae quoque institutionis regulis sollertissimus exstiterat; et usquedum praemia piae devotionis accipiat, existere non desistit: utpote qui a pueritia in clero sanctissimi ac Deo dilecti Bosa, Eboracensis episcopi, nutritus atque eruditus est; deinde ad Vilfridum episcopum spe melioris propositi adveniens, omnem in eius obsequio usque ad obitum illius explevit aetatem: cum quo etiam Romam veniens, multa illic quae in patria nequiverat ecclesiae sanctae institutis utilia didicit.

worship of them, apart by themselves in side chapels made for this very purpose within the walls of the same church; moreover, he gathered with all possible diligence the histories of their sufferings along with the other ecclesiastical writings, and made up there a very large and worthy library, and also zealously prepared holy vessels, lights and other things of this sort appertaining to the adornment of the house of God. Again, he sent for a cunning musician called Maban, which was taught by the successors of the scholars of the blessed pope Gregory in Kent, to instruct him and his clergy to tune and sing, and kept him 12 years: to the end that he might both teach them the songs of the Church which they could not yet sing, and restore to their old fashion the songs sometime known which by reason of long use or neglect began to be corrupted. For bishop Acca was himself too a very skilful musician as well as also well learned in Holy Scripture, most sound in the confession of the catholic faith, and beside had become very expert in the rules of ecclesiastical discipline; and so doth he not cease to be until he receive the rewards of his godly devotion: seeing that from a child he was brought up and instructed among the clergy of the most holy Bosa, beloved of God, bishop of York; and afterwards coming to bishop Wilfrid upon hope of better advantage he spent all his life in his service until Wilfrid's death; and going to Rome also with him he learned there many things profitable to the ordinances of the holy Church, which he had not been able to attain unto in his own country.

CAP. XXI

Ut Ceolfrid abbas regi Pictorum architectos ecclesiae, simul et epistolam de catholico pascha, vel de tonsura miserit.

Eo tempore Naiton rex Pictorum, qui septemtrionales Brittaniae plagas inhabitant, admonitus ecclesiasticarum frequenti meditatione scripturarum, abrenunciavit errori, quo eatenus in observatione paschae cum sua gente tenebatur, et se suosque omnes ad catholicum Dominicae resurrectionis tempus celebrandum perduxit. Quod ut facilius et maiore auctoritate perficeret, quaesivit auxilium de gente Anglorum, quos iamdudum ad exemplum sanctae Romanae et apostolicae ecclesiae suam religionem instituisse cognovit. Siquidem misit legatarios ad virum venerabilem Ceolfridum, abbatem monasterii beatorum apostolorum Petri et Pauli, quod est ad ostium Viuri amnis, et iuxta amnem Tinam, in loco qui vocatur In Gyruum, cui ipse post Benedictum, de quo supra diximus, gloriosissime praefuit; postulans ut exhortatorias sibi literas mitteret, quibus potentius confutare posset eos qui pascha non suo tempore observare praesumerent; simul et de tonsurae modo vel ratione qua clericos insigniri deceret: excepto quod etiam ipse in his non parva ex parte esset imbutus. Sed et architectos sibi mitti petiit, qui iuxta morem Romanorum ecclesiam de lapide in gente ipsius facerent, promittens hanc in honorem beati apostolorum principis

---

[1] Nechtan.

[2] Cf. the goldsmith in Maitland, *Dark Ages*, No. VI.

CHAPTER XXI

How abbot Ceolfrid sent to the king of the Redshanks builders to make him a church, and an epistle withal touching the catholic Easter and touching the tonsure.

At that time Naiton [1] king of the Redshanks which inhabit the north coasts of Britain, admonished by often study of the writings of the Church, abandoned the error which he and his country till then had held in the keeping of Easter, and brought himself and all his subjects to the observance of the catholic time of the Lord's resurrection. Which that he might bring to pass with less difficulty and more authority, he required aid of the English people, whom he knew to have framed their religion long since after the example of the holy Roman and apostolic Church. For he sent ambassadors to the venerable man, Ceolfrid, abbot of the monastery of the blessed apostles Peter and Paul, situated at the mouth of the river Wear and nigh to the river Tyne, in the place called Jarrow, where he ruled with great honour after Benedict, of whom we have spoken before; desiring to receive from him letters of exhortation by the which he might more forcibly confute such as presumed to keep Easter out of his due time; as also to know of the fashion and manner of tonsure by which the clergy should be marked: not reckoning that he was himself too in great measure informed upon these matters. Moreover, he desired to have master-craftsmen sent him [2] to build in his country a church of stone according to the Roman manner of building, promising that he would dedicate the same in the honour of the blessed

dedicandam; se quoque ipsum cum suis omnibus morem sanctae Romanae et apostolicae ecclesiae semper imitaturum, in quantum dumtaxat tam longe a Romanorum loquela et natione segregati hunc ediscere potuissent. Cuius religiosis votis ac precibus favens reverentissimus abba Ceolfrid, misit architectos quos petebatur, misit illi et literas scriptas in hunc modum:

"Domino excellentissimo et gloriosissimo regi Naitano, Ceolfrid abbas in Domino salutem.

"Catholicam sancti paschae observantiam, quam a nobis, rex Deo devote, religioso studio quaesisti, promptissime ac libentissime tuo desiderio, iuxta quod ab apostolica sede didicimus, patefacere satagimus. Scimus namque caelitus sanctae ecclesiae donatum, quotiens ipsi rerum domini discendae, docendae, custodiendae veritati operam impendunt. Nam et vere omnino dixit quidam saecularium scriptorum, quia felicissimo mundus statu ageretur, si vel reges philosopharentur, vel regnarent philosophi. Quod si de philosophia huius mundi vere intellegere, de statu huius mundi merito diligere potuit homo huius mundi; quanto magis civibus patriae caelestis in hoc mundo peregrinantibus optandum est et totis animi viribus supplicandum, ut quo plus in mundo quique valent, eo amplius eius qui super omnia est Iudicis mandatis auscultare contendant, atque ad

[1] But composed it seems by Bede, Pl.

chief of the apostles; that he would beside follow evermore with all his folk the custom of the holy Roman and apostolic Church, so far forth as they not knowing the Roman tongue and being far from that nation, might attain to the knowing thereof. And the most reverend abbot Ceolfrid, lending a ready ear to his devout desires and prayers, sent him the craftsmen as he required, and a letter indited as followeth:[1]

"To the most excellent and most glorious king Naitan, Ceolfrid abbot sendeth greeting in the Lord.

"The catholic observation of holy Easter, which you have with godly zeal, O king devoted to God, desired to know of us, we have most readily and willingly endeavoured to set forth, as you have sought, according as we have been taught of the see apostolic. For we know well that, as often as lords of the earth do themselves employ their study to learn, teach and to observe the truth, it is a gift bestowed from heaven upon the holy Church. For also one of the writers of this world in all truth said that the world could be governed most happily when either kings might embrace philosophy, or else philosophers might bear the sovereignty.[2] Now if a man of this world could have a true understanding of the philosophy of this world, and could make so worthy a choice concerning the state of this world, how much the more ought such as are citizens of the heavenly country, and but pilgrims in this world, to desire and pray with all their heart, that the more power any bear in the world, the more they apply themselves to hearken after the commands of that Judge who is over all things, and likewise instruct them also that are committed to

[2] Plato, *Republ.* 473 D.

haec observanda secum eos quoque qui sibi commissi sunt exemplis simul et auctoritate instituant?

"Tres sunt ergo regulae sacris inditae literis, quibus paschae celebrandi tempus nobis praefinitum, nulla prorsus humana licet auctoritate mutari; e quibus duae in Lege Mosi divinitus statutae, tertia in Evangelio per effectum Dominicae passionis et resurrectionis adiuncta est. Praecepit enim lex ut pascha primo mense anni, et tertia eiusdem mensis septimana, id est, a quintadecima die usque ad vicesimam primam fieri deberet: additum est per institutionem apostolicam ex Evangelio, ut in ipsa tertia septimana diem Dominicam exspectare, atque in ea temporis paschalis initium tenere debeamus. Quam videlicet regulam triformem quisquis rite custodierit, nunquam in adnotatione festi paschalis errabit. Verum si de his singulis enucleatius ac latius audire desideras, scriptum est in Exodo, ubi liberandus de Aegypto populus Israel primum pascha facere iubetur, quia 'dixerit Dominus ad Moysen et Aaron: Mensis iste vobis principium mensium primus erit in mensibus anni. Loquimini ad universum coetum filiorum Israel et dicite eis: "Decima die mensis huius tollat unusquisque agnum per familias et domos suas."' Et paulo post: 'Et servabitis eum usque ad quartamdecimam mensis huius; immolabitque eum universa multitudo filiorum Israel ad vesperam.' Quibus verbis manifestissime constat, quod ita in observatione paschali mentio fit diei

[1] Exodus xii. 1–3.

their charge, by their example and authority to keep the same along with themselves?

"There are then three rules given in Holy Scripture by the which the time of solemnizing Easter is appointed for us, which by no authority at all of man may be changed; of the which rules two are established of God in the Law of Moses, the third was joined in the Gospel by the means of the Lord's passion and resurrection. For the Law commanded that in the first month of the year, and in the third week of the same month, that is from the 15th day until the 21st, the Passover should be kept: it was added by the institution of the apostles out of the Gospel that in the selfsame third week we should tarry for the Sunday and in it keep the beginning of the time of Easter. This triple rule certes whosoever shall duly observe, he shall never miss in the count of the festival of Easter. But if it be your pleasure to have every particular point more pithily and largely declared, it is written in Exodus,[1] where the people of Israel are commanded to keep the first Passover, when they should be delivered out of Egypt, that 'the Lord said to Moses and Aaron: This month shall be unto you the beginning of months, it shall be the first in the months of the year. Speak ye unto all the congregation of the children of Israel and say unto them: "In the 10th day of this month let then every man take a lamb according to the house of their fathers."' And a little after: 'And ye shall keep it until the 14th day of the same month: and the whole assembly of the children of Israel shall kill it at the evening.' By the which words it is most plainly seen, that in the observation of the Passover the 14th day is

quartaedecimae, ut non tamen in ipsa die quartadecima pascha fieri praecipiatur; sed adveniente tandem vespera diei quartaedecimae, id est, quintadecima luna, quae initium tertiae septimanae faciat, in caeli faciem prodeunte, agnus immolari iubeatur: et quod ipsa sit nox quintaedecimae lunae, in qua percussis Aegyptiis Israel est a longa servitute redemptus. 'Septem,' inquit, 'diebus azyma comedetis.' Quibus item verbis tota tertia septimana eiusdem primi mensis decernitur sollemnis esse debere. Sed ne putaremus easdem septem dies a quartadecima usque ad vicesimam esse conputandas, continuo subiecit: 'In die primo non erit fermentum in domibus vestris. Quicumque comederit fermentum, peribit anima illa de Israel, a die primo usque ad diem septimum,' et cetera, usquedum ait: 'In eadem enim ipsa die educam exercitum vestrum de terra Aegypti.'

"Primum ergo diem azymorum appellat eum in quo exercitum eorum esset educturus de Aegypto. Constat autem quia non quartadecima die, in cuius vespera agnus est immolatus, et quae proprie pascha sive phase dicitur; sed quintadecima sunt educti ex Aegypto, sicut in libro Numerorum apertissime scribitur: 'Profecti igitur de Ramesse quintadecima die mensis primi, altera die phase filii Israel in manu excelsa.' Septem ergo dies azymorum, in quarum prima eductus est populus Domini ex

---

[1] Exodus xii. 15–17. [2] Numbers xxxiii. 3.

mentioned, yet it is not so mentioned that on that very 14th day it is commanded the Passover should be kept, but that, when at length the evening of the 14th day approacheth, that is, when the 15th moon, which making the beginning of the third week, cometh forth into the face of the heaven, the lamb is bidden to be killed: and it is plain that it is the selfsame night of the 15th day of the moon in which the Egyptians were smitten and Israel redeemed from their long slavery. 'Seven days,'[1] He saith, 'shall ye eat unleavened bread.' With which words likewise all the third week of the said first month it is decreed should be solemn. But that we should not think the same 7 days to be counted from the 14th to the 20th, He added straightways: 'The first day there shall be no leaven in your houses. Whosoever eateth leavened bread from the first day until the seventh, that soul shall be cut off from Israel,' and so forth, till He says: 'For in this selfsame day will I bring your army out of the land of Egypt.'

"He calleth then that the first day of unleavened bread in the which he was to bring their army out of Egypt. But it is manifest that they were not brought out the 14th day, in the evening whereof the lamb was slain, and which is properly called the Passover or Phase; but in the 15th day they were brought out of Egypt, as it is evidently written in the book of Numbers[2]: 'They departed therefore from Rameses in the 15th day of the first month; on the morrow after the Phase the children of Israel went out with an high hand.' Therefore the seven days of unleavened bread, in the first of which the people of the Lord was brought out of Egypt,

Aegypto, ab initio, ut diximus, tertiae septimanae, hoc est, a quintadecima die mensis primi, usque ad vicesimam primam eiusdem mensis diem completam computari oportet. Porro dies quartadecima extra hunc numerum separatim sub paschae titulo praenotatur, sicut Exodi sequentia patenter edocent; ubi cum dictum esset: 'In eadem enim ipsa die educam exercitum vestrum de terra Aegypti'; protinus adiunctum est: 'Et custodietis diem istum in generationes vestras ritu perpetuo. Primo mense, quartadecima die mensis, comedetis azyma usque ad diem vicesimam primam eiusdem mensis ad vesperam. Septem diebus fermentatum non invenietur in domibus vestris.' Quis enim non videat, a quartadecima usque ad vicesimam primam, non septem solummodo, sed octo potius esse dies, si et ipsa quartadecima annumeretur? Sin autem, ut diligentius explorata Scripturae veritas docet, a vespera diei quartaedecimae usque ad vesperam vicesimae primae computaverimus, videbimus profecto quod ita dies quartadecima vesperam suam in festi paschalis initium prorogat, ut non amplius tota sacra sollemnitas quam septem tantummodo noctes cum totidem diebus comprehendat; unde vera esse probatur nostra definitio,[1] qua tempus paschale primo mense anni et tertia eius hebdomada celebrandum esse diximus. Veraciter enim tertia agitur hebdomada, quod a vespera quartaedecimae diei incipit, et in vespera vicesimae primae completur.

"Postquam vero pascha nostrum immolatus est Christus, diemque nobis Dominicam, quae apud antiquos una vel prima sabbati, sive sabbatorum,

[1] for *diffinitio*, Pl.

must be counted, as I have said, from the beginning of the third week, that is, from the 15th day of the first month to the 21st day of the same month fully complete. Further, the 14th day is noted down separately outside this number under the name of the Passover, as that which followeth in Exodus doth evidently declare[1]; where, after it was said: 'For in this selfsame day will I bring your armies out of the land of Egypt'; it was added straightway: 'And ye shall observe this day in your generations by an ordinance for ever. In the first month, on the 14th day of the month, ye shall eat unleavened bread until the 21st day of the month at even. Seven days shall there be no leaven found in your homes.' For who cannot see, that from the 14th to the 21st be not only 7 days but rather 8, if the 14th be itself also reckoned in? But if we will count from the evening of the 14th day to the evening of the 21st (as the verity of Holy Scripture diligently searched out doth declare) we shall well perceive that the 14th day continueth its evening to the beginning of the Paschal feast in such manner that the whole sacred solemnity containeth only 7 nights with as many days; wherefore our decision is proved to be true, wherein we said that the time of Easter must be kept in the first month of the year and the third week of that month. For truly is it celebrated in the third week, because it beginneth from the evening of the 14th day, and is complete and ended in the evening of the 21st day.

"After, however, Christ our Passover was sacrificed,[2] and made the Sunday (called amongst the ancients one or the first day after the Sabbath)

[1] Exodus xii. 17–19. [2] 1 Cor. v. 7.

vocatur, gaudio suae resurrectionis fecit esse sollemnem; ita hanc apostolica traditio festis paschalibus inseruit, ut nil omnimodis de tempore paschae legalis praeoccupandum, nihil minuendum esse decerneret. Quin potius statuit ut exspectaretur iuxta praeceptum Legis idem primus anni mensis, exspectaretur quartadecima dies illius, exspectaretur vespera eiusdem. Et cum haec dies in sabbatum forte inciderit, tolleret unusquisque agnum per familias et domos suas, et immolaret eum ad vesperam, id est, praepararent omnes ecclesiae per orbem, quae unam catholicam faciunt, panem et vinum in mysterium carnis et sanguinis agni immaculati, qui abstulit peccata mundi: et praecedente congrua lectionum, orationum, caeremoniarum paschalium sollemnitate, offerrent haec Domino in spem futurae suae redemptionis. Ipsa est enim eadem nox in qua de Aegypto per sanguinem agni Israelitica plebs erepta est; ipsa in qua per resurrectionem Christi liberatus est a morte aeterna populus omnis Dei. Mane autem inlucescente die Dominica, primam paschalis festi diem celebrarent. Ipsa est enim dies in qua resurrectionis suae gloriam Dominus multifario piae revelationis gaudio discipulis patefecit. Ipsa prima dies azymorum, de qua multum distincte in Levitico scriptum est: 'Mense primo, quartadecima die mensis, ad vesperam, phase Domini est, et quintadecima die mensis huius sollemnitas azymorum

solemn for us for the joy of His resurrection, the tradition of the apostles hath so put this Sunday in the feast of Easter that they determined in no way at all to prevent the time of the Passover in the Law, nor to diminish it in aught. Nay rather did they ordain that the same first month of the year according to the precept of the Law should be tarried for, and the 14th day of that month and the evening of the same be tarried for. And when this day should chance to fall upon the Sabbath, every man should take a lamb according to their families and households and kill him at the evening, that is to say, all the churches throughout the world, which make one catholic Church, should prepare bread and wine for the mystery of the flesh and blood of the spotless Lamb Which took away the sins of the world; and after fitting solemnity of lessons, prayers and Easter ceremonies should offer the same to the Lord in hope of their redemption to come. For this is the selfsame night that the people of Israel were delivered out of Egypt by the blood of the lamb; and the selfsame night in which all the people of God were by Christ's resurrection set free from everlasting death. But at the dawn of the morning, being Sunday, they should celebrate the first day of the Easter festival. For that is the day wherein the Lord opened the glory of his resurrection to the disciples to their manifold joy at that merciful revelation. This is the first day of unleavened bread of which it is right clearly written in Leviticus:[1] 'In the first month, in the 14th day of the month at evening is the Lord's Phase, and on the 15th day of this month is the feast of un-

[1] Lev. xxiii. 5–7.

Domini est. Septem diebus azyma comedetis. Dies primus erit celeberrimus sanctusque.'

"Si ergo fieri posset ut semper in diem quintum decimum primi mensis, id est, in lunam quintamdecimam Dominica dies incurreret, uno semper eodemque tempore cum antiquo Dei populo, quanquam sacramentorum genere discreto, sicut una eademque fide pascha celebrare possemus. Quia vero dies septimanae non aequali cum luna tramite procurrit, decrevit apostolica traditio, quae per beatum Petrum Romae praedicata, per Marcum evangelistam et interpretem ipsius Alexandriae confirmata est, ut adveniente primo mense, adveniente in eo vespera diei quartaedecimae, exspectetur etiam dies Dominica, a quintadecima usque ad vicesimam primam diem eiusdem mensis. In quacumque enim harum inventa fuerit, merito in ea pascha celebrabitur: quia nimirum haec ad numerum pertinet illarum septem dierum, quibus azyma celebrari iubentur. Itaque fit ut nunquam pascha nostrum a septimana mensis primi tertia in utramvis partem declinet: sed vel totam eam, id est, omnes septem legalium azymorum dies, vel certe aliquos de illis teneat. Nam etsi saltem unum ex eis, hoc est, ipsum septimum adprehenderit, quem tam excellenter Scriptura commendat; 'Dies autem,' inquiens, 'septimus erit celebrior et sanctior, nullumque servile opus fiet in eo'; nullus arguere nos poterit, quod non recte Dominicum paschae diem, quem de Evangelio suscepimus, in ipsa quam Lex statuit tertia primi mensis hebdomada celebremus.

[1] Easter week.
[2] Lev. xxiii. 8.

leavened bread unto the Lord. Seven days ye must eat unleavened bread. In the first day ye shall have an holy convocation.'

"If therefore it were possible that the Sunday might always fall upon the 15th day of the first month, that is to say, upon the 15th day of the age of the moon, we might celebrate Easter always at one and the same time with the ancient people of God (albeit the inner meaning differeth in kind), as we do in one and the same faith. Because, however, the days of the week do not run equally with the course of the moon, the tradition of the apostles preached at Rome by blessed Peter, and confirmed by Mark the Evangelist his interpreter, at Alexandria, hath appointed that, when the first month is come, and the evening of the 14th day of the same, the Sunday also should be waited for from the 15th to the 21st day of the same month. For in whichsoever of those it shall be found, Easter shall be rightly kept in the same: because without doubt it appertaineth to the number of those 7 days in which the observance of unleavened bread is commanded to be kept. And so it cometh to pass that our Easter [1] never passeth the third week of the first month, nor over, nor under; but either it hath the whole week, that is to say, all the seven days of unleavened bread according to the Law, or at least some of them. For even if it compriseth but one of them, to wit that 7th day which the Scripture so highly commendeth; [2] 'In the 7th day shall be an holy convocation: ye shall do no servile work therein'; no man can reprove us, and say we keep not Easter Sunday (which we took of the Gospel) in the selfsame third week of the first month appointed by the Law, as we should do.

"Cuius observantiae catholica ratione patefacta, patet e contrario error inrationabilis eorum qui praefixos in Lege terminos, nulla cogente necessitate, vel anticipare, vel transcendere praesumunt. Namque sine ratione necessitatis alicuius anticipant illi tempus in Lege praescriptum, qui Dominicum paschae diem a quartadecima mensis primi usque ad vicesimam putant lunam esse servandum. Cum enim a vespera diei tertiaedecimae vigilias sanctae noctis celebrare incipiunt, claret quod illam in exordio sui paschae diem statuunt, cuius nullam omnino mentionem in decreto Legis inveniunt. Et cum vicesima prima die mensis pascha Dominicum celebrare refugiunt, patet profecto, quod illam per omnia diem a sua sollemnitate secernunt, quam Lex maiore prae ceteris festivitate memorabilem saepenumero commendat: sicque diem paschae ordine perverso, et aliquando in secunda hebdomada totam compleant, et nunquam in hebdomadae tertiae die septimo ponant; rursumque qui a sextadecima die mensis saepedicti usque ad vicesimam secundam pascha celebrandum magis autumant, non minore utique errore, tametsi altero latere, a recto veritatis tramite divertunt, et veluti naufragia Scyllae fugientes, in Charybdis voraginem submergendi decidunt. Nam cum a luna sextadecima primi mensis oriente, id est, a vespera diei quintaedecimae pascha incipiendum doceant; nimirum constat quia quartamdecimam diem mensis eiusdem, quam Lex primitus et

"Seeing the reason which the Catholics allege for the observance of which feast is plainly set before your eyes, contrariwise the unreasonable error of those which presume to prevent or pass, without any force of necessity, the limits appointed in the Law, is manifest. For they which think that Easter Sunday must be kept from the 14th moon of the first month to the 20th anticipate the time commanded in the Law without any necessary reason. For whereas they begin to celebrate the vigil of the holy night from the evening of the 13th day, it appeareth that they appoint that day in the beginning of their Easter, whereof they find no mention at all in the commandment of the Law. And whereas they refuse to keep the Lord's Easter on the 21st day of the month, it is surely plain that they exclude utterly from their solemnity that day which the Law oftentimes commendeth to be had in memory above all other with a greater festival: and thus they would fix their Easter day after a perverse order, bringing it to an end sometimes wholly in the second week, and never place it in the 7th day of the third week; and again, they which think Easter should rather be kept from the 16th day of the oft-named month to the 22nd day, rove from the straight path of truth in an error no way less, albeit on the other side, and as it were shunning shipwreck on Scylla fall to be drowned into the whirlpool of Charybdis. For whereas they teach that Easter must begin from the rising of the 16th moon of the first month, that is, from the evening of the 15th day, it is without doubt manifest that they utterly separate from their solemnity the 14th day of the same month, which the Law doth at the first and

praecipue commendat, a sua prorsus sollemnitate secludunt: ita ut quintaedecimae, in qua populus Dei ab Aegyptia servitute redemptus est, et in qua Dominus suo mundum sanguine a peccatorum tenebris liberavit, in qua etiam sepultus spem nobis post mortem beatae quietis tribuit, vix vesperam tangant.

"Iidemque poenam erroris sui in semetipsos recipientes, cum in vicesima secunda die mensis paschae diem statuunt Dominicum, legitimos utique terminos paschae aperta transgressione violant, utpote qui ab illius diei vespera pascha incipiunt, in qua hoc Lex consummari et perfici debere decrevit, illam in pascha diem adsignent primam, cuius in Lege mentio nulla usquam reperitur, id est, quartae primam septimanae. Qui utrique non solum in definitione et computo lunaris aetatis, sed et in mensis primi nonnunquam inventione falluntur. Quae disputatio maior est, quam epistola hac vel valeat comprehendi, vel debeat. Tantum hoc dicam, quod per aequinoctium vernale semper inerrabiliter possit inveniri, qui mensis iuxta computum lunae primus anni, qui esse debeat ultimus. Aequinoctium autem, iuxta sententiam omnium Orientalium, et maxime Aegyptiorum, qui prae ceteris doctoribus calculandi palmam tenent, duodecimo kalendarum Aprilium die provenire consuevit, ut etiam ipsi horo-

principally commend: so that they scarce touch on the evening of the 15th day, in the which the people of God were ransomed from the bondage of Egypt, and in which the Lord delivered the world from the darkness of sin by His blood, in the which also He being buried bestowed on us the hope of blessed rest after death.

"And the same men taking upon themselves the punishment of their error, when they place the Lord's day of Easter in the 22nd day of the month, do in any case openly transgress and break the bounds of Easter commanded by the Law, as being men which begin their Easter from the evening of that day (in which evening by the Law they ought clean to end and finish their Easter), and would appoint that day the first day of Easter, which in the Law is nowhere mentioned at all, to wit the first day of the 4th week. And both these sorts of men are deceived not only in fixing and reckoning the age of the moon but sometimes in finding out of the first month. The debating of which matter is longer than either can or ought to be comprised in this epistle. Only this will I say, that the time being once known when the nights are as long as the days, at the spring time of the year, it may infallibly be found, which ought to be the first month of the year after the account of the moon, and which ought to be the last. Now the time when the days and nights are equal after the opinion of all the Easterns, and especially of the Egyptians which bear the prize for computation before all other teachers, customably cometh on the 12th day before the first of April, as also we ourselves prove by inspection of the means of measuring

logica inspectione probamus. Quaecumque ergo luna ante aequinoctium plena est, quartadecima videlicet vel quintadecima existens, haec ad praecedentis anni novissimum pertinet mensem, ideoque paschae celebrando habilis non est. Quae vero post aequinoctium vel in ipso aequinoctio suum plenilunium habet, in hac absque ulla dubietate, quia primi mensis est, et antiquos pascha celebrare solitos, et nos ubi Dominica dies advenerit, celebrare debere noscendum est. Quod ita fieri oportere illa nimirum ratio cogit, quia in Genesi scriptum est, quod 'fecit Deus duo luminaria magna; luminare maius, ut praeesset diei; et luminare minus, ut praeesset nocti'[1]: vel, sicut alia dicit editio,[2] 'luminare maius in inchoationem diei; et luminare minus in inchoationem noctis.' Sicut ergo prius sol a medio procedens orientis aequinoctium vernale suo praefixit exortu; deinde luna, sole ad vesperam occidente, et ipsa plena a medio secuta est orientis: ita omnibus annis idem primus lunae mensis eodem necesse est ordine servari, ut non ante aequinoctium, sed vel ipso aequinoctii die, sicut in principio factum est, vel eo transcenso plenilunium habere debeat. At si uno saltem die plenilunium tempus aequinoctii praecesserit, non hanc primo mensi anni incipientis, sed ultimo potius praeteriti lunam esse adscribendam; et ideo festis paschalibus inhabilem memorata ratio probat.

---

[1] Gen. i. 16. [2] The old Latin.

time. Whatsoever moon, therefore, is at full before the day and night be of one length, being to wit 14 or 15 days old, that moon pertaineth to the last month the year before, and therefore is not meet for keeping Easter. But that moon which is at full after the day and night be of equal length or in the very point of that equality, in that doubtless (because it is the full moon of the first month) we must understand both that the ancients were wont to keep the Passover, and that we ought to keep Easter, when the Sunday cometh. And that it should be so, this reason without doubt enforceth, that in Genesis it is written that,[1] 'God made two great lights; the greater light to rule the day; and the lesser light to rule the night': or as another rendering hath,[2] 'the greater light to begin the day; and the lesser light to begin the night.' Therefore as first the sun coming forth from the midst of the east made by that his rising the equality of day and night in the spring; and after, the moon (the sun going down at evening) followed itself also at the full from the midst of the east; so every year the same first month of the moon must be observed after the same order, so that she should be at the full not before the day and night be of one length, but either on the very day of that equality, as was done in the beginning, or when it is past. But if the full moon go but one day before the day and night be of one length, the aforesaid reason proveth that this moon must be assigned not to the first month of the year beginning, but rather to the last month of the year that is past; and for that consideration is not meet for the celebration of the Paschal festival.

"Quod si mysticam quoque vos in his rationem audire delectat, primo mense anni, qui etiam mensis novorum dictus est, pascha facere iubemur; quia renovato ad amorem caelestium spiritu mentis nostrae sacramenta Dominicae resurrectionis et ereptionis nostrae celebrare debemus, tertia eiusdem mensis septimana facere praecipimur; quia ante Legem et sub Lege promissus, tertio tempore saeculi cum gratia venit ipse qui pascha nostrum immolaretur Christus: quia tertia post immolationem suae passionis die resurgens a mortuis, hanc Dominicam vocari, et in ea nos annuatim paschalia eiusdem resurrectionis voluit festa celebrare: quia nos quoque ita solum veraciter eius sollemnia celebramus, si per fidem spem et caritatem pascha, id est, transitum de hoc mundo ad Patrem, cum illo facere curamus. Post aequinoctium veris, plenilunium mensis praecipimur observare paschalis; ut videlicet primo sol longiorem nocte faciat diem, deinde luna plenum suae lucis orbem mundo praesentet; quia primo quidem sol iustitiae, in cuius pennis est sanitas, id est, Dominus Jesus, per resurrectionis suae triumphum cunctas mortis tenebras superavit: ac sic ascendens in caelos, misso desuper Spiritu, ecclesiam suam quae saepe lunae vocabulo designatur internae gratiae luce replevit. Quem videlicet ordi-

" Now if it like you to hear also the mystical reason hereof, in the first month of the year, which is also called the month of new growth, we are commanded to keep Easter; because being renewed in the spirit of our mind toward the love of heavenly things we ought to celebrate the mysteries of the Lord's resurrection and our deliverance, we are bidden to do so in the third week of the said month; because Christ Himself, being promised before the Law and under the Law, came with grace in the third age of the world to be our Passover sacrificed for us: because rising from the dead the third day after the sacrifice of His passion, He would have this day to be called the day of the Lord, and have us celebrate yearly on that day the Easter festival of His resurrection: because we also do in this manner only truly keep His solemn festival, if we endeavour to make along with Him the Passover (that is to say, our passage out of this world to the Father) by faith, hope and charity. After the equality of day and night in spring we are commanded to watch for the full moon of the paschal month; to the end that first the sun may make the day longer than the night, and afterward the moon may shew to the world the full orb of her light; because first indeed the sun of righteousness with healing in his wings,[1] that is to say, the Lord Jesus by the triumph of His resurrection hath overcome all the darkness of death; and so ascending to heaven hath replenished His Church, which is oft signified by the name of moon, with the light of inward grace by sending the Spirit from above. The which order of our salvation certes the prophet

[1] Malachi iv. 2.

nem nostrae salutis propheta contemplatus aiebat: Elevatus est sol, et luna stetit in ordine suo.'

"Qui ergo plenitudinem lunae paschalis ante aequinoctium provenire posse contenderit, talis in mysteriorum celebratione maximorum a sanctarum quidem Scripturarum doctrina discordat; concordat autem eis qui sine praeveniente gratia Christi se salvari posse confidunt: qui etsi vera lux tenebras mundi moriendo ac resurgendo nunquam vicisset, perfectam se habere posse iustitiam dogmatizare praesumunt. Itaque post aequinoctialem solis exortum, post plenilunium primi mensis hunc ex ordine subsequens, id est, post completam diem eiusdem mensis quartam decimam, quae cuncta ex Lege observanda accepimus, exspectamus adhuc monente Evangelio in ipsa hebdomada tertia tempus diei Dominicae, et sic demum votiva paschae nostri festa celebramus, ut indicemus nos non cum antiquis excussum Aegyptiae servitutis iugum venerari, sed redemptionem totius mundi, quae in antiqui Dei populi liberatione praefigurata, in Christi autem resurrectione completa est, devota fide ac dilectione colere, utque [1] resurrectionis etiam nostrae, quam eadem die Dominica futuram credimus, spe nos certissima gaudere signemus.

"Hic autem quem vobis sequendum monstramus, computus paschae, decennovenali circulo continetur; qui dudum quidem, hoc est, ipsis apostolorum temporibus, iam servari in ecclesia coepit, maxime

[1] *utque*, Pl.

beholding, said 'The sun was lifted up and the moon stood in her order.'[1]

"And he therefore that contendeth that the full Paschal moon may come before the equality of day and night, is at variance with the teaching of Holy Scripture in the celebration of the greatest mysteries; while he agreeth with them which trust they can be saved without the preventing grace of Christ:[2] which presume to teach that man might have perfect righteousness, though the true Light had never overcome the darkness of the world by dying and rising again. To conclude therefore, after the equinoctial rising of the sun, after the full moon of the first month orderly following the same, that is to say, after the 14th day of the said month is fully ended (the observation of all which we have received from the Law), we do yet in the selfsame third week (as the Gospel warneth) wait for the time of Sunday, and thus at length celebrate the consecrated festival of our Easter, to shew that we do not with the ancients honour the shaking off of the yoke of Egyptian bondage, but that with devout faith and love we honour the redemption of the whole world, prefigured in that deliverance of the ancient people of God, but fully ended in Christ's resurrection, and to the end we may signify that we rejoice in the assured hope of our resurrection also, which we believe shall be on the same Lord's day.

"This account of Easter which we shew you is to be followed, is comprised in the compass of 19 years, which long since, that is to say, right in the apostles' time, began already to be observed in the Church,

[1] Habakkuk iii. 11, according to the old Latin version, Pl.
[2] The Pelagians.

Romae et Aegypti, ut supra iam diximus. Sed per industriam Eusebii qui a beato martyre Pamphilo cognomen habet, distinctius in ordinem compositus est; ut quod eatenus per Alexandriae pontificem singulis annis per omnes ecclesias mandari consueverat, iam deinde congesta in ordinem serie lunae quartaedecimae facillime posset ab omnibus sciri. Cuius computum paschalis Theophilus Alexandriae praesul in centum annorum tempus Theodosio imperatori composuit. Item successor eius Cyrillus seriem nonaginta et quinque annorum in quinque decennovenalibus circulis comprehendit: post quem Dionysius Exiguus totidem alios ex ordine pari schemate subnexuit, qui ad nostra usque tempora pertingebant. Quibus termino adpropinquantibus, tanta hodie calculatorum exuberat copia, ut etiam in nostris per Brittaniam ecclesiis plures sint qui mandatis memoriae veteribus illis Aegyptiorum argumentis facillime possint in quotlibet spatia temporum paschales protendere circulos, etiamsi ad quingentos usque et triginta duos voluerint annos; quibus expletis, omnia quae ad solis et lunae, mensis et septimanae consequentiam spectant eodem quo prius ordine recurrunt. Ideo autem circulos eosdem temporum instantium vobis mittere supersedimus, quia de ratione tantum temporis paschalis instrui quaerentes, ipsos vobis circulos paschae catholicos abundare probastis.

"Verum his de pascha succincte, ut petistis, strictimque commemoratis, tonsuram quoque, de

specially at Rome and Egypt, as we have already said before. But by the industry of Eusebius, who of the blessed martyr Pamphilus hath his surname, it was more clearly set in order; so that what until then was wont every year to be sent through all the churches by the pontiff of Alexandria, might henceforth, now that the course of the 14th moon had been brought into order, be readily known of all. And this count of Easter Theophilus prelate of Alexandria made to serve for the time of 100 years at the request of the emperor Theodosius. Likewise Cyril his successor comprised a course of 95 years in 5 tables of 19 years; and after him Dionysius Exiguus added thereto as many other in like style and order, which reached even to our time. And these now approaching to their end, there is nowadays such store of reckoners, that even in our churches throughout Britain there be many which can by those old precepts of the Egyptians, which they have committed to memory, very readily carry on the Easter cycles unto as far extent of time as them liketh, even to the number of 532 years, if they will; which number of years being expired, all that appertaineth to the succession of sun and moon, month and week, returneth into the same order that it did before. For this reason, however, we have forborne to send you the said cycles of times to come, because demanding only to be instructed of the reason of the time of Easter you shewed that you had good store of those same catholic cycles of Easter.

" But having briefly and compendiously said thus much concerning Easter, as you requested, I exhort you to provide to have the tonsure also, which the

qua pariter vobis literas fieri voluistis, hortor ut ecclesiasticam et Christianae fidei congruam habere curetis. Et quidem scimus quia neque apostoli omnes uno eodemque sunt modo adtonsi, neque nunc ecclesia catholica sicut una fide spe et caritate in Deum consentit, ita etiam una atque indissimili totum per orbem tonsurae sibi forma congruit. Denique ut superiora, id est, patriarcharum tempora respiciamus, Job exemplar patientiae, dum ingruente tribulationum articulo caput totondit, probavit utique quia tempore felicitatis capillos nutrire consueverat. At Joseph, et ipse castitatis, humilitatis, pietatis ceterarumque virtutum executor ac doctor eximius, cum servitio absolvendus, attonsus esse legitur: patet profecto quia tempore servitutis, intonsis in carcere crinibus manere solebat. Ecce uterque vir Dei diversum ab altero vultus habitum foris praemonstrabat, quorum tamen intus conscientia in parili virtutum sibi gratia concordabat.

" Verum, etsi profiteri nobis liberum est, quia tonsurae discrimen non noceat, quibus pura in Deum fides, et caritas in proximum sincera est; maxime cum nunquam patribus catholicis sicut de paschae vel fidei diversitate conflictus, ita etiam de tonsurae differentia legatur aliqua fuisse controversia; inter omnes tamen quas vel in ecclesia, vel in universo hominum genere reperimus tonsuras, nullam magis sequendam nobis amplectendamque iure dixerim,

---

[1] Job i. 20. [2] Gen. xli. 14.

Church doth receive as agreeable to the Christian faith, whereof you likewise desired me to write to you. It is true we know that neither were the apostles shaven all after one and the same sort, nor now doth the catholic Church, though it agreeth in one faith, hope and charity towards God, likewise use one and the selfsame fashion of tonsure throughout the world. In short, that we may look back to the times before us, to wit the times of the patriarchs, Job a pattern of patience, by shaving his head [1] at the time his afflictions fell upon him, shewed at any rate that in time of prosperity he was accustomed to let his hair grow. But Joseph, himself too the truly excellent practiser and teacher of chastity, lowliness, godliness and all other virtues, is said to have been shorn when he was to be taken out of bondage [2]: whereby it is well manifest that in the time of his bondage he was wont to remain in prison with his hair unshorn. Lo, here two men of God, though their inward conscience did agree together in like grace of virtuous actions, yet shewed abroad a different fashion of countenance the one from the other.

"But though I may boldly say that the diversity of tonsure hurteth nothing them that have a pure faith in God and unfeigned charity toward their neighbour; especially seeing we do not read there hath been ever any controversy between the catholic fathers touching difference of tonsure, as there hath been strife touching the diversity of Easter, or in matters of faith; yet notwithstanding, amongst all kinds of tonsure which we find either in the Church or among mankind at large, I may rightly say that none is rather to be followed and embraced of us

ea quam in capite suo gestabat ille, cui se confitenti Dominus ait: 'Tu es Petrus, et super hanc petram aedificabo Ecclesiam meam, et portae inferni non praevalebunt adversus eam; et tibi dabo claves regni caelorum.' Nullam magis abominandam detestandamque merito cunctis fidelibus crediderim, ea quam habebat ille, cui gratiam sancti Spiritus comparare volenti dicit idem Petrus: 'Pecunia tua tecum sit in periditionem, quoniam donum Dei existimasti per pecuniam possideri: non est tibi pars neque sors in sermone hoc.' Neque vero ob id tantum in coronam adtondemur, quia Petrus ita attonsus est; sed quia Petrus in memoriam Dominicae passionis ita attonsus est, idcirco et nos qui per eandem passionem salvari desideramus, ipsius passionis signum cum illo in vertice, summa videlicet corporis nostri parte, gestamus. Sicut enim omnis ecclesia, quia per mortem sui vivificatoris ecclesia facta est, signum sanctae crucis eius in fronte portare consuevit, ut crebro vexilli huius munimine a malignorum spirituum defendatur incursibus; crebra huius admonitione doceatur, se quoque carnem suam cum vitiis et concupiscentiis crucifigere debere: ita etiam oportet eos, qui vel monachi votum, vel gradum clericatus habentes arctioribus se necesse habent pro Domino continentiae frenis astringere,[1] formam quoque coronae quam ipse in passione spineam por-

[1] The comma as in Pl.

---

[1] Matt. xvi. 18, 19.

[2] Acts viii. 20, 21.

[3] The coronal tonsure came into use late in the 5th century. Its more zealous wearers attributed the rival fashion to Simon Magus. Bright, p. 84.

than that which he wore on his head, to whom the Lord said, when he confessed Him to be Christ[1]: 'Thou art Peter, and upon this rock I will build my Church, and the gates of hell shall not prevail against it; and to thee I will give the keys of the kingdom of heaven.' None I may believe to be more abhorred and detested deservedly by all faithful men than that which he had to whom, when he would buy the grace of the Holy Spirit, the same Peter said[2]: 'Thy money perish with thee, because thou hast thought the gift of God may be purchased with money: thou hast no part or lot in this word.' And truly we do not shave ourselves in the shape of a crown only because Peter was so shaven[3]; but because Peter was so shaven in the remembrance of the Lord's passion, therefore we also desiring to be saved by the same passion, do bear with Him the sign of the selfsame passion upon the crown of our head, being the highest part of our body. For as all the Church, because it was made a Church by the death of Him that quickeneth it, is accustomed to bear the sign of His holy cross in the forehead, that by the frequent protection of this banner it may be defended from the assaults of evil spirits; and by the admonition of the same may be taught that it ought to crucify its flesh with all its sin and concupiscence: so also it behoveth them, which either being made by vow monks, or having degree among the clergy are required to bind themselves more straitly with the bridle of continency for the Lord's sake, to bear also each of them in their head by means of the tonsure the form of the crown, as He Himself carried upon His head at His passion a crown of thorns, to the intent He might bear the

tavit in capite, ut spinas ac tribulos peccatorum nostrorum portaret, id est, exportaret et auferret a nobis, suo quemque in capite per tonsuram praeferre, ut se etiam inrisiones et opprobria pro illo libenter ac promte omnia sufferre ipso etiam frontispicio doceant: ut coronam vitae aeternae, quam repromisit Deus diligentibus se, se semper exspectare, proque huius perceptione et adversa se mundi et prospera contemnere designent. Ceterum tonsuram eam quam magum ferunt habuisse Simonem, quis, rogo, fidelium non statim cum ipsa magia primo detestetur, et merito exsufflet adspectu? Quae in frontis quidem superficie coronae videtur speciem praeferre; sed ubi ad cervicem considerando perveneris, decurtatam eam quam te videre putabas invenies coronam; ut merito talem Simoniacis et non Christianis habitum convenire cognoscas: qui in praesenti quidem vita a deceptis hominibus putabantur digni perpetuae gloria coronae; sed in ea quae hanc sequitur vitam, non solum omni spe coronae privati, sed aeterna insuper sunt poena damnati.

"Neque vero me haec ita prosecutum aestimes, quasi eos qui hanc tonsuram habent, condemnatos iudicem, si fide et operibus unitati catholicae faverint: immo confidenter profiteor, plurimos ex eis sanctos ac Deo dignos exstitisse, ex quibus est Adamnan abbas et sacerdos Columbiensium egregius, qui cum legatus suae gentis ad Aldfridum regem missus,

thorns and thistles of our sins (that is to say, bear out and take away from us), and to the end too that they may shew, even by their open head itself, that they are ready and glad to suffer even mockery and all reproaches for His sake: that they may testify that they look ever for the crown of eternal life, which God hath promised to them that love Him, and that for the gain of this they despise both the buffets and the blessings of this world. For the rest, as touching that fashion of shaving which Simon the magician is said to have used, what believer, I ask, would not straight at the first sight thereof abhor and rightly cast it forth together with his magic? Which indeed seemeth to shew the likeness of a crown in the outermost part of the head, but when a man cometh near and beholdeth the hinder part, he shall find that which seemed to him to be a crown, to come very short thereof; so that we may rightly understand that such a fashion suiteth not Christians, but Simoniacs: who in this present life indeed were thought by persons misled to be worthy of the glory of an everlasting crown; but in the life which followeth are not only deprived of all hope of a crown, but (which is more) are condemned to eternal punishment.

"But I would not have you think either that I have gone so largely into this matter, as though I judge them condemned which use this manner of shaving, if they tender catholic unity in faith and deed: nay, I boldly affirm that many of them have been holy men and worthy of God, of the which Adamnan, abbot and notable priest of the followers of Columba, is one, to whom, when he was sent embassy for his own country to king Aldfrid and

nostrum quoque monasterium videre voluisset, miramque in moribus ac verbis prudentiam, humilitatem, religionem ostenderet, dixi illi inter alia conloquens: 'Obsecro, sancte frater, qui ad coronam te vitae quae terminum nesciat tendere credis, quid contrario tuae fidei habitu terminatam in capite coronae imaginem portas? et si beati consortium Petri quaeris, cur eius quem ille anathematizavit tonsurae imaginem imitaris? et non potius eius cum quo in aeternum beatus vivere cupis etiam nunc habitum te, quantum potes, diligere monstras?' Respondit ille: 'Scias pro certo, frater mi dilecte, quia etsi Simonis tonsuram ex consuetudine patria habeam, Simoniacam tamen perfidiam tota mente detestor ac respuo: beatissimi autem apostolorum principis, quantum mea parvitas sufficit, vestigia sequi desidero.' At ego: 'Credo,' inquam, 'vere quod ita sit; sed tamen indicio fit, quod ea quae apostoli Petri sunt, in abdito cordis amplectimini, si quae eius esse nostis etiam in facie tenetis. Namque prudentiam tuam facillime diiudicare reor, quod aptius multo sit, eius quem corde toto abhominaris, cuiusque horrendam faciem videre refugis, habitum vultus a tuo vultu Deo iam dicato separare; et e contra, eius quem apud Deum habere patronum quaeris, sicut facta vel monita cupis sequi, sic etiam morem habitus te imitari condeceat.'

"Haec tunc Adamnano dixi, qui quidem quantum

---

[1] Cf. Vol. I, p. 342.

having been desirous to see our monastery also, shewed in his behaviour and talk wonderful wisdom, lowliness and godliness, I said amongst other things in discourse[1]: 'I beseech you, holy brother, why do you, believing that you are on the way to a crown of life which knoweth no end, wear on your head the form of a crown which hath an end, of a fashion contrary to your faith? and if you seek the fellowship of the blessed Peter, why do you follow his form of shaving, whom Peter put under a curse? and do not rather shew even now that with all your might you love the fashion of him with whom you desire to live in bliss for ever?' 'Know you for a surety, my beloved brother,' answered he, 'that albeit I use the fashion of shaving that Simon did, after the custom of my country, yet with all my mind I abhor and reject the unbelief of Simon; and desire to follow, so far as my poor ability doth serve, the steps of the most blessed chief of the apostles.' Whereat I said: 'I believe it is so in very deed; but yet proof is given that you embrace in your secret heart the things that belong to the apostle Peter, if you keep that outwardly which you know to be his. For I think your wisdom do very easily judge it much more convenient to make division between your countenance (now dedicated to God) and the fashion of his countenance, whom you abhor with all your heart and whose abominable face you shun the sight of; and contrariwise that, as you desire to follow his steps and counsel, whom you look to have as advocate with God, so also it seemeth you to copy the outward fashion that he used.'

"This for that time I spoke to Adamnan, who

conspectis ecclesiarum nostrarum statutis profecisset probavit, cum reversus ad Scottiam multas postea gentis eiusdem turbas ad catholicam temporis paschalis observantiam sua praedicatione correxit: tametsi eos qui in Hii insula morabantur monachos, quibusque speciali rectoris iure praeerat, necdum ad viam statuti melioris reducere valebat. Tonsuram quoque, si tantum sibi auctoritatis subesset, emendare meminisset.

"Sed et tuam nunc prudentiam, rex, admoneo, ut ea quae unitati catholicae et apostolicae ecclesiae concinunt, una cum gente cui te Rex regum et Dominus dominorum praefecit, in omnibus servare contendas. Sic enim fit ut post acceptam temporalis regni potentiam ipse beatissimus apostolorum princeps caelestis quoque regni tibi tuisque cum ceteris electis libens pandat introitum. Gratia te Regis aeterni longiori tempore regnantem ad nostram omnium pacem custodiat incolumem, dilectissime in Christo fili."

Haec epistola cum praesente rege Naitono, multisque viris doctioribus, esset lecta, ac diligenter ab his qui intelligere poterant in linguam eius propriam interpretata, multum de eius exhortatione gavisus esse perhibetur; ita ut exsurgens de medio optimatum suorum consessu genua flecteret in terram, Deo gratias agens, quod tale munusculum de terra Anglorum mereretur accipere. "Et quidem et antea novi," inquit, "quia haec erat vera paschae celebratio, sed in tantum modo rationem huius tem-

after well shewed how much he had profited by seeing the ordinances of our churches, when after his return to Scotland he amended great number of the said country and brought them to the catholic observance of the time of Easter by his preaching: albeit he could not bring back those monks that lived in the island of Hy, over whom he had special right of governance, to the way of the better order. He would have thought also to redress the tonsure, if only his authority might have prevailed so far.

"Moreover, I now also do exhort you, my lord king, to endeavour of your wisdom along with the country over which the King of kings and Lord of lords hath given you the sovereignty, to observe in all points those things that agreeth with the unity of the catholic and apostolic Church. For so it cometh to pass that after you have had dominion of a temporal kingdom, the most blessed chief of the apostles will himself gladly open also to you and yours with the rest of the elect the entrance to the heavenly kingdom. The grace of the eternal King keep you in safety, most beloved son in Christ, and grant you longer reign for the peace of us all."

When this epistle had been read in the presence of king Naiton, and many learned men, and carefully translated into the king's native tongue by them that were able to understand it, he much rejoiced at the exhortation thereof, as it is reported; so much that rising from the midst of his nobles that sat about him, he fell upon his knees and gave God thanks that it was vouchsafed him to have such a gift from the land of the English. "And truly," said he, "I knew before too that this was the true celebration of Easter, but now I do so well know the

poris observandi cognosco, ut parum mihi omnimodis videar de his antea intellexisse. Unde palam profiteor, vobisque qui adsidetis praesentibus protestor, quia hoc observare tempus paschae cum universa mea gente perpetuo volo; hanc accipere debere tonsuram quam plenam esse rationis audimus, omnes qui in meo regno sunt clericos decerno." Nec mora, quae dixerat, regia auctoritate perfecit. Statim namque iussu publico mittebantur ad transcribendum, discendum, observandum, per universas Pictorum provincias circuli paschae decennovenales, oblitteratis per omnia erroneis octoginta et quatuor annorum circulis. Adtondebantur omnes in coronam ministri altaris, ac monachi: et quasi novo se discipulatui beatissimi apostolorum principis Petri subditam, eiusque tutandam patrocinio gens correcta gaudebat.

CAP. XXII

Ut Hiienses monachi cum subiectis sibi monasteriis canonicum praedicante Ecgbercto celebrare pascha coeperint.

Nec multo post illi quoque qui insulam Hii incolebant monachi Scotticae nationis, cum his quae sibi erant subdita monasteriis, ad ritum paschae ac tonsurae canonicum Domino procurante perducti sunt. Siquidem anno ab incarnatione Domini septingentesimo sextodecimo, quo Osredo occiso Coenred

reason of keeping his time, that methinketh I had little understanding of these things before. Wherefore I openly declare and protest before you who are here present, that I will henceforth continually with all my people keep this time of Easter; and I decree that all the clergy in my kingdom ought to receive this manner of shaving which we hear to be very reasonable." And without delay he carried out that which he had said by his princely authority. For forthwith the tables of 19 years for Easter were sent to be copied out, learned and observed throughout all the provinces of the Picts, the erroneous tables of 84 years being everywhere blotted out. All servants of the altar and monks had their heads shaven after the figure of a crown; and the country being well reformed was glad that they were as it were reduced to be new disciples of Peter the most blessed chief of the apostles, and were to be kept safe under his protection.[1]

CHAPTER XXII

How the monks of Hy with the monasteries under their jurisdiction began at the preaching of Egbert to keep the canonical Easter.

Not long after the monks of the Scottish nation, which inhabited the island Hy, with those monasteries under their jurisdiction, were brought by the care of the Lord to the canonical custom of Easter and of the tonsure. For in the 716th [2] year of the Lord's incarnation, when Osred was slain and Cenred

[1] As patron saint, Pl.
[2] Earlier, Vol. I, p. 343. Bede gives 715 as the date.

gubernacula regni Nordanhymbrorum suscepit, cum venisset ad eos de Hibernia Deo amabilis et cum omni honorificentia nominandus pater ac sacerdos Ecgberct, cuius superius memoriam saepius fecimus, honorifice ab eis et multo cum gaudio susceptus est. Qui quoniam et doctor suavissimus et eorum quae agenda docebat erat exsecutor devotissimus, libenter auditus ab universis, immutavit piis ac sedulis exhortationibus inveteratam illam traditionem parentum eorum, de quibus apostolicum illum licet proferre sermonem, quod aemulationem Dei habebant, sed non secundum scientiam; catholicoque illos, atque apostolico more celebrationem, ut diximus, praecipuae sollemnitatis sub figura coronae perpetis agere perdocuit. Quod mira divinae constat factum dispensatione pietatis, ut quoniam gens illa quam noverat scientiam divinae cognitionis libenter ac sine invidia populis Anglorum communicare curavit: ipsa quoque postmodum per gentem Anglorum in eis quae minus habuerat, ad perfectam vivendi normam perveniret. Sicut e contra Brettones, qui nolebant Anglis eam quam habebant fidei Christianae notitiam pandere, credentibus iam populis Anglorum et in regula fidei catholicae per omnia instructis, ipsi adhuc inveterati et claudicantes a semitis suis et capita sine corona praetendunt, et solemnia Christi sine ecclesiae Christi societate venerantur.

Susceperunt autem Hiienses monachi, docente Ecgbercto, ritus vivendi catholicos sub abbate

[1] Or bishop. [2] Rom. x. 2. [3] The coronal tonsure.

took the governance of the kingdom of Northumbria, the father and priest [1] Egbert, dearly beloved of God and to be honourably named of me (of whom we have often made mention before), having come unto them out of Ireland was honourably and very joyfully received of them. And being a teacher of a singular good grace and most devout in the practice of those things he taught should be done, he was gladly heard of all, and by godly and constant advertisements did change that tradition established of old of their fathers, touching whom we may pronounce that saying of the apostle,[2] that they had a zeal of God, but not according to knowledge; and he taught them to keep the principal solemnity after the catholic and apostolic manner under the shape of an unending crown.[3] The which it is clear was done by a wonderful disposition of the divine goodness, to the end that, because that nation was forward freely and without envy to communicate to the English people the understanding they had of the knowledge of God, they should themselves also afterward attain to the perfect rule of life in the things wherein they had been lacking, by the help of the English nation. As contrariwise the Britons, which would not disclose to the English that knowledge which they had of the Christian faith, now that the English people believe and are in all ways instructed in the rule of the catholic faith, are themselves still hardened of age, halting astray from their path, and shew heads without a crown, and honour the solemnities of Christ without fellowship in the Church of Christ.

Now the monks of Hy received at the teaching of Egbert the catholic customs of living under abbot

Duunchado, post annos circiter octoginta, ex quo ad praedicationem gentis Anglorum Aidanum miserant antistitem. Mansit autem vir Domini Ecgberct annos tredecim in praefata insula, quam ipse velut nova quadam relucente gratia ecclesiasticae societatis et pacis Christo consecraverat; annoque Dominicae incarnationis septingentesimo vicesimo nono, quo pascha Dominicum octavo kalendarum Maiarum die celebrabatur, cum missarum sollemnia in memoriam eiusdem Dominicae resurrectionis celebrasset, eodem die et ipse migravit ad Dominum, ac gaudium summae festivitatis quod cum fratribus quos ad unitatis gratiam converterat inchoavit, cum Domino et apostolis ceterisque caeli civibus complevit, immo idipsum celebrare sine fine non desinit. Mira autem divinae dispensatio provisionis erat, quod venerabilis vir non solum in pascha transivit de hoc mundo ad patrem; verum etiam cum eo die pascha celebraretur, quo nunquam prius in eis locis celebrari solebat. Gaudebant ergo fratres de agnitione certa et catholica temporis paschalis; laetabantur de patrocinio pergentis ad Dominum patris, per quem fuerant correcti; gratulabatur ille quod eatenus in carne servatus est, donec illum in pascha diem suos auditores, quem semper antea vitabant, suscipere ac secum agere videret. Sicque certus de illorum correctione reverentissimus pater exultavit, ut videret diem Domini: vidit, et gavisus est.

---

[1] The Celts had hitherto refused to celebrate Easter later than April 21.

Dunchad, about 80 years after they had sent bishop Aidan to preach to the English nation. Moreover, Egbert, the man of the Lord, remained 13 years in the aforesaid island which he had consecrated to Christ, with a new shining as it were of the grace of ecclesiastical fellowship and peace; and in the 729th year of the Lord's incarnation, in which the Lord's Easter was kept on the 24th day of April, after he had celebrated the solemnity of mass in remembrance of the same our Lord's resurrection, himself too departed to the Lord on the same day, and the joy of that highest festival which he began with the brethren whom he had converted to the grace of unity, he finished with the Lord and the apostles and all the other citizens of heaven, or rather ceaseth not to celebrate the very same without end. Further, the providence of God's disposition herein was wonderful, that not only did the venerable man pass from this world to the Father upon an Easter, but also when Easter was celebrated upon that day [1] in which Easter was wont never to be celebrated in that place. The brethren therefore rejoiced in their coming to know the certain and catholic time of Easter, and were glad that their father by whom they had been amended was passing to the Lord to be their patron; he also had joy that he was kept in the flesh so long, until he saw his hearers to receive and keep with him that day for Easter which ever before they avoided. And so being now assured of their amendment, the most reverend father rejoiced to see the day of the Lord: he saw it and was glad.[2]

[2] John viii. 56.

CAP. XXIII

Qui sit in praesenti status gentis Anglorum, vel Brittaniae totius.

Anno Dominicae incarnationis septingentesimo vicesimo quinto, qui erat septimus Osrici regis Nordanhymbrorum qui Coenredo successerat, Victred filius Ecgbercti, rex Cantuariorum, defunctus est nono die kalendarum Maiarum; et regni quod per triginta quatuor semis annos tenebat, filios tres, Aedilberctum, Eadberctum, et Alricum reliquit heredes. Anno post quem proximo Tobias Hrofensis ecclesiae praesul defunctus est, vir, ut supra meminimus, doctissimus. Erat enim discipulus beatae memoriae magistrorum, Theodori archiepiscopi et abbatis Hadriani: unde, ut dictum est, cum eruditione literarum vel ecclesiasticarum vel generalium, ita Graecam quoque cum Latina didicit linguam, ut tam notas ac familiares sibi eas, quam nativitatis suae loquelam haberet. Sepultus vero est in porticu sancti Pauli apostoli, quam intro ecclesiam sancti Andreae sibi ipse in locum sepulcri fecerat. Post quem episcopatus officium Alduulf, Berctualdo, archiepiscopo consecrante, suscepit.

Anno Dominicae incarnationis septingentesimo vicesimo nono, apparuerunt cometae duae circa solem, multum intuentibus terrorem incutientes. Una quippe solem praecedebat, mane orientem; altera vespere sequebatur occidentem, quasi orienti simul et occidenti dirae cladis praesagae: vel certe

CHAPTER XXIII

What is the state of the English nation or of all Britain at this present time.

In the 725th year of Christ's incarnation, which was the 7th of the reign of Osric king of the Northumbrians, who had succeeded Cenred, Witred son of Egbert, the king of Kent, died the 23rd day of April; and left 3 sons, Ethelbert, Eadbert and Alric, heirs of his kingdom which he had governed 34 years and a half. And the next year after him Tobias prelate of the church of Rochester died, a man certainly well learned, as we have said before. For he was scholar to two masters of blessed memory, archbishop Theodore and abbot Hadrian: by which occasion, as has been said, beside his knowledge in literature both ecclesiastical and general, he so thoroughly learned the Greek as well as the Latin tongues, that he had them as perfect and familiar as his own native speech. Now he was buried in the side chapel of St. Paul the apostle, which he had built within the church of St. Andrew for his own place of burial. And after him Aldwulf took upon him the office of the bishopric, and was consecrated by Bertwald the archbishop.

The 729th year of the Lord's incarnation there appeared two comets about the sun and struck great terror into the beholders thereof. For one went before the sun at his rising in the morning; the other followed the setting of the sun in the evening, both presaging as it were terrible destruction to the east as well as the west: or, if you will say, one was the forerunner of the coming of day, the other of

una diei, altera noctis praecurrebat exortum, ut utroque tempore mala mortalibus imminere signarent. Portabant autem facem ignis contra aquilonem, quasi ad accendendum adclinem: apparebantque mense Ianuario, et duabus ferme septimanis permanebant. Quo tempore gravissima Sarracenorum lues Gallias misera clade vastabat, et ipsi non multo post in eadem provincia dignas suae perfidiae poenas luebant. Quo anno sanctus vir Domini Ecgberct, ut supra commemoravimus, ipso die paschae migravit ad Dominum: et mox peracto pascha, hoc est, septima iduum Maiarum die, Osric rex Nordanhymbrorum vita decessit, cum ipse regni quod undecim annis gubernabat successorem fore Ceoluulfum decrevisset, fratrem illius qui ante se regnaverat Coenredi regis, cuius regni et principia et processus tot ac tantis redundavere rerum adversantium motibus, ut quid de his scribi debeat, quemve habitura sint finem singula, necdum sciri valeat.

Anno Dominicae incarnationis septingentesimo tricesimo primo, Berctuald archiepiscopus, longa consumptus aetate, defunctus est die iduum Ianuariarum; qui sedit annos triginta septem, menses sex, dies quatuordecim; pro quo anno eodem factus est archiepiscopus, vocabulo Tatuini, de provincia Merciorum, cum fuisset presbyter in monasterio quod vocatur Briudun. Consecratus est autem in Doruuerni civitate, a viris venerabilibus Danihele Ventano, et Ingualdo Lundoniensi, et Alduino Lyccitfeldensi, et Alduulfo Hrofensi antistitibus, die

[1] In the battle of Tours, in which Charles Martel defeated the Saracens in 732. Bede must have added this sentence after the completion of his *History* in 731.

night, to signify that at both times miseries were hanging over mens' heads. Moreover, they held up a firebrand toward the north, ready as it were to set all a-fire; and they appeared in the month of January, and continued about two weeks. At what time the Saracens, like a very sore plague, wasted France with pitiful destruction, and themselves not long after were justly punished [1] in the same country for their unbelief. And in this year the holy man of the Lord, Egbert, as we mentioned before, passed to the Lord on the very day of Easter; and soon, when Easter was over, that is on the 9th day of May, Osric king of Northumbria departed this life, after he had of himself appointed Ceolwulf, brother of king Cenred his predecessor, to succeed him in the kingdom that he governed 11 years. And both the beginning and the course thereafter of Ceolwulf's reign have been full of so many grievous commotions of withstanding troubles, that it may not yet be known what should be written of them, or what end they will severally have.[2]

The 731st year of the Lord's incarnation archbishop Bertwald, worn out with old age, died the 13th of January;[3] having held his see 37 years, 6 months, 14 days; in whose place, the same year, Tatwin of the province of the Marchmen was made archbishop, after he had been priest in the monastery called Bredon. Moreover, he was consecrated in the city of Canterbury by the venerable men Daniel, bishop of Winchester, Ingwald of London, Aldwin of Lichfield, and Aldwulf of Rochester on the 10th

[2] In the year 731 Ceolwulf was taken and shorn and afterwards restored to the throne.

[3] In the Roman Calendar his day is Jan. 9th.

decima Iunii mensis, Dominica; vir religione et prudentia insignis, sacris quoque literis nobiliter instructus.

Itaque in praesenti, ecclesiis Cantuariorum Tatuini et Alduulf episcopi praesunt. Porro provinciae Orientalium Saxonum Inguald episcopus; provinciae Orientalium Anglorum Aldberct et Hadulac episcopi; provinciae Occidentalium Saxonum, Danihel et Fortheri episcopi; provinciae Merciorum, Alduini episcopus; et eis populis qui ultra amnem Sabrinam ad occidentem habitant Valchstod episcopus; provinciae Huicciorum Vilfrid episcopus; provinciae Lindisfarorum Cyniberct episcopus praeest. Episcopatus Vectae insulae ad Danihelem pertinet, episcopum Ventae civitatis. Provincia Australium Saxonum iam aliquot annis absque episcopo manens, ministerium sibi episcopale ab Occidentalium Saxonum antistite quaerit. Et hae omnes provinciae ceteraeque australes ad confinium usque Hymbrae fluminis, cum suis quaeque regibus, Merciorum regi Aedilbaldo subiectae sunt.

At vero provinciae Nordanhymbrorum, cui rex Ceoluulf praeest, quatuor nunc episcopi praesulatum tenent; Vilfrid in Eburacensi ecclesia, Ediluald in Lindisfaronensi, Acca in Hagustaldensi, Pecthelm in ea quae Candida Casa vocatur, quae nuper multi-

---

[1] Bishops of Dunwich and Elmham.
[2] Bishop of Hereford.

day of the month of June, being the Sunday; a man notable for his godliness and wisdom, and also well conversant in Holy Scripture.

Wherefore at this present time Tatwin and Aldwulf are bishops over the churches of Kent. Further, of the province of the East Saxons Ingwald is bishop; of the province of the East English Aldbert and Hadulac are bishops;[1] of the province of the West Saxons Daniel and Forthere are bishops; of the province of the Marchmen Aldwin is bishop; and of that people which dwell beyond the river Severn to the west Wahlstod[2] is bishop; of the province of the Hwiccas Wilfrid[3] is bishop; of the province of the Lindisfaras Cynibert[4] is bishop. The bishopric of the Isle of Wight appertaineth to Daniel bishop of the city of Winchester. The province of the South Saxons continuing now some years without a bishop seeketh for itself the ministry of a bishop from the prelate of the West Saxons. And all these provinces and the other southward provinces as far as the bound of the river Humber, with their several kings, are in subjection to Ethelbald king of the Marchmen.[5]

But of the province of Northumbria, where Ceolwulf is king, four bishops now hold the prelacy; Wilfrid[6] in the church of York, Ethelwald in that of Lindisfarne, Acca[7] in that of Hexham, Pehthelm in that of Whitern, which, for that the number of believing people hath been multiplied, hath been

[3] To be distinguished from Wilfrid II of York; see below.
[4] Bishop of Lindsey.
[5] He is not reckoned as one of the Bretwaldas, II. 5.
[6] Wilfrid II.
[7] Expelled from his see 731.

plicatis fidelium plebibus in sedem pontificatus addita, ipsum primum habet antistitem.

Pictorum quoque natio tempore hoc et foedus pacis cum gente habet Anglorum, et catholicae pacis ac veritatis cum universali ecclesia particeps existere gaudet. Scotti qui Brittaniam incolunt suis contenti finibus nil contra gentem Anglorum insidiarum moliuntur aut fraudium. Brettones, quamvis et maxima ex parte domestico sibi odio gentem Anglorum, et totius catholicae ecclesiae statum pascha minus recte moribusque improbis impugnent; tamen et divina sibi et humana prorsus resistente virtute, in neutro cupitum possunt obtinere propositum: quippe qui quamvis ex parte sui sint iuris, nonnulla tamen ex parte Anglorum sunt servitio mancipati.

Qua adridente pace ac serenitate temporum, plures in gente Nordanhymbrorum, tam nobiles quam privati, se suosque liberos depositis armis satagunt magis accepta tonsura monasterialibus adscribere votis, quam bellicis exercere studiis. Quae res quem sit habitura finem, posterior aetas videbit.

Hic est impraesentiarum universae status Brittaniae, anno adventus Anglorum in Brittaniam circiter ducentesimo octogesimo quinto, Dominicae autem incarnationis anno septingentesimo tricesimo primo: in cuius regno perpetuo exultet terra, et congratulante in fide eius Brittania laetentur insulae multae, et confiteantur memoriae sanctitatis eius.

made as well the see of a bishopric, and hath him for its first prelate.

The nation of the Redshanks beside at this time have both league of peace with the English people, and rejoice in having fellowship with the universal Church in peace and truth. The Scots which inhabit Britain are content to keep their own borders and work no treason or guile toward the English people. The Britons, albeit for the most part of privy grudge they are against the English people and set themselves wrongfully and of lewd manner against the appointed Easter of the whole catholic Church; yet seeing both divine and human power quite withstandeth them, can have their purpose in neither of them; for though they are in some part their own masters, yet for no small part they are brought in subjection to the English.

And seeing there is the pleasantness of peace and quiet times,[1] many of the Northumbrian people, as well noblemen as private persons, laying away their armour are eager rather to have themselves and their children shoren and enrolled under monastical vows, than to practise the pursuits of warfare. And what event this use is like to have, the next age shall see.

Thus for the present standeth the whole state of Britain, about the 285th year since the English came into Britain, but the 731st year since the Lord's incarnation: in Whose everlasting reign let the earth leap for joy, and seeing Britain hath gladness in His faith, let many islands rejoice and sing praise to the remembrance of His holiness.

[1] From external foes, but there were internal troubles.

CAP. XXIV

Recapitulatio chronica totius operis ; et de persona Auctoris.

Verum, ea quae temporum distinctione latius digesta sunt, ob memoriam conservandam, breviter recapitulari placuit.

Anno igitur ante incarnationem Dominicam sexagesimo, Gaius Iulius Caesar, primus Romanorum, Brittanias bello pulsavit, et vicit; nec tamen ibi regnum potuit obtinere.

Anno ab incarnatione Domini 46 Claudius, secundus Romanorum Brittanias adiens, plurimam insulae partem in deditionem recepit; et Orcadas quoque insulas Romano adiecit imperio.

Anno incarnationis Dominicae 167 Eleuther Romae praesul factus, quindecim annos ecclesiam gloriosissime rexit: cui literas rex Brittaniae Lucius mittens, ut Christianus efficeretur petiit, et impetravit.

Anno ab incarnatione Domini 189 Severus imperator factus, decem et septem annis regnavit, qui Brittaniam vallo a mari usque ad mare praecinxit.

Anno 381 Maximus in Brittania creatus imperator, in Galliam transiit, et Gratianum interfecit.

Anno 409 Roma a Gothis fracta: ex quo tempore Romani in Brittania regnare cessarunt.

CHAPTER XXIV

Chronological recapitulation of the whole work; and concerning the Author himself.

But those things which have been related more at large according to the division of the times, I have thought fit to sum up shortly to the intent they may be better had in memory.

In the sixtieth year then before the incarnation of the Lord, Gaius Julius Caesar, first of the Romans, assailed Britain with war and won the victory, and yet could he not for all that gain the kingdom there.

In the year of the Lord's incarnation 46, Claudius coming the second of the Romans into Britain, brought the greater part of the island into subjection; and also added the Orkney Islands to the Roman empire.

In the year of the Lord's incarnation 167 Eleuther, being made prelate of Rome, ruled the Church fifteen years with great glory. To whom Lucius, king of Britain, sent a letter, asking that he might be made a Christian, and was granted his request.

In the year of the Lord's incarnation 189, Severus, being made emperor, ruled seventeen years, and he compassed Britain with a rampart from sea to sea.

In the year 381, Maximus, being made emperor in Britain, crossed the sea into Gaul and slew Gratian.

In the year 409 Rome was brought down of the Goths; from which time the Romans ceased to rule in Britain.

Anno 430 Palladius ad Scottos in Christum credentes a Caelestino papa primus mittitur episcopus.

Anno 449 Marcianus cum Valentiniano imperium suscipiens, septem annis tenuit: quorum tempore Angli a Brettonibus accersiti Brittaniam adierunt.

Anno 538 eclipsis solis facta est xiv kalendas Martii, ab hora prima usque ad tertiam.

Anno 540 eclipsis solis facta est xii kalendas Iulias, et apparuerunt stellae pene hora dimidia ab hora diei tertia.

Anno 547 Ida regnare coepit, a quo regalis Nordanhymbrorum prosapia originem tenet, et duodecim annis in regno permansit.

Anno 565 Columba presbyter de Scottia venit Brittaniam ad docendos Pictos, et in insula Hii monasterium fecit.

Anno 596 Gregorius papa misit Brittaniam Augustinum cum monachis, qui verbum Dei genti Anglorum evangelizarent.

Anno 597 venere Brittaniam praefati doctores, qui fuit annus plus minus centesimus quinquagesimus adventus Anglorum in Brittaniam.

Anno 601 misit papa Gregorius pallium Brittaniam Augustino iam facto episcopo, et plures verbi ministros, in quibus et Paulinum.

Anno 603 pugnatum ad Degsastanae.

Anno 604 Orientales Saxones fidem Christi percipiunt sub rege Sabercto, antistite Mellito.

CHRONOLOGY

In the year 430 Palladius was sent by pope Celstine to the Scots that believed in Christ to be their first bishop.

In the year 449 Marcian, becoming emperor together with Valentinian, reigned seven years: in whose time the English, being sent for of the Britons, came into Britain.

In the year 538 an eclipse of the sun came to pass on the 16th day of February, lasting the first hour till the third.

In the year 540 an eclipse of the sun came to pass the 20th day of June, and the stars appeared for the space of well-nigh half an hour after the third hour of the day.

In the year 547 Ida began to reign, from whom the royal house of the Northumbrian hath its beginning, and he reigned twelve years.

In the year 565 the priest Columba came out of Scotland into Britain to teach the Redshanks, and built a monastery in the island of Hy.

In the year 596 pope Gregory sent Augustine together with certain monks into Britain, to preach the good tidings of the word of God to the English nation.

In the year 597 the aforesaid teachers came into Britain; being about the 150th year after the coming of the English into Britain.

In the year 601 pope Gregory sent in a pall into Britain for Augustine, who was already made bishop, together with more ministers of the word, among whom was also Paulinus.

In the year 603 a battle was fought at Degsastan.

In the year 604 the East Saxons received the faith of Christ, Sabert being king and Mellitus bishop.

Anno 605 Gregorius obiit.

Anno 616 Aedilberct rex Cantuariorum defunctus est.

Anno 625 Paulinus a Iusto archiepiscopo ordinatur genti Nordanhymbrorum antistes.

Anno 626 Eanfled, filia Aeduini regis, baptizata cum duodecim in sabbato pentecostes.

Anno 627 Aeduini rex baptizatus cum sua gente in pascha.

Anno 633 Aeduine rege perempto, Paulinus Cantiam rediit.

Anno 640 Eadbald rex Cantuariorum obiit.

Anno 642 Osuald rex occisus.

Anno 644 Paulinus, quondam Eboraci, sed tunc Hrofensis antistes civitatis, migravit ad Dominum.

Anno 651 Osuini rex occisus, et Aidan episcopus defunctus est.

Anno 653 Middilangli sub principe Peada fidei mysteriis sunt imbuti.

Anno 655 Penda periit, et Mercii sunt facti Christiani.

Anno 664 eclipsis facta: Earconberct rex Cantuariorum defunctus, et Colman cum Scottis ad suos reversus est; et pestilentia venit; et Ceadda ac Vilfrid Nordanhymbrorum ordinantur episcopi.

Anno 668 Theodorus ordinatur episcopus.

Anno 670 Osuiu rex Nordanhymbrorum obiit.

Anno 673 Ecgberct, rex Cantuariorum, obiit; et synodus facta est ad Herutforda praesente Ecgfrido

In the year 605 Gregory died.

In the year 616 Ethelbert, king of Kent, died.

In the year 625 Paulinus was made bishop of the Northumbrians by archbishop Justus.

In the year 626 Eanfled, daughter of king Edwin, was baptized with twelve other on the eve of Whit Sunday.

In the year 627 king Edwin was christened with his nation at Easter.

In the year 633, king Edwin having been killed, Paulinus returned to Kent.

In the year 640 Eadbald, king of Kent, died.

In the year 642 king Oswald was slain.

In the year 644 Paulinus, sometime bishop of York but then bishop of the city of Rochester, passed to the Lord.

In the year 651 king Oswin was slain, and bishop Aidan died.

In the year 653 the Middle Englishmen were instructed in the mysteries of the faith under Peada their prince.

In the year 655 Penda was slain and the Marchmen were made Christians.

In the year 664 an eclipse came to pass: Earconbert, king of Kent, died; and Colman with the Scots returned to his own people; a great plague arose; and Chad and Wilfrid were made bishops of Northumbria.

In the year 668 Theodore was ordained bishop.

In the year 670 Oswy, king of the Northumbrians, died.

In the year 673 Egbert, king of Kent, died; a synod was made at Hertford, king Egfrid being

rege, praesidente archiepiscopo Theodoro, utillima, decem capitulorum.

Anno 675 Vulfheri, rex Merciorum, postquam septemdecim annos regnaverat, defunctus, Aedilredo fratri reliquit imperium.

Anno 676 Aedilred vastavit Cantiam.

Anno 678 cometa apparuit; Vilfrid episcopus a sede sua pulsus est ab Ecgfrido rege; et pro eo Bosa, Eata et Eadhaeth consecrati antistites.

Anno 679 Aelfuini occisus.

Anno 680 synodus facta est in campo Haethfeltha de fide catholica, praesidente archiepiscopo Theodoro: in qua adfuit Iohannes abba Romanus. Quo anno Hild abbatissa in Streanaeshalae obiit.

Anno 685 Ecgfrid rex Nordanhymbrorum occisus est. Anno eodem Hlotheri rex Cantuariorum obiit.

Anno 688 Caeduald rex Occidentalium Saxonum Romam de Brittania pergit.

Anno 690 Theodorus archiepiscopus obiit.

Anno 697 Osthryd regina a suis, id est, Merciorum primatibus, interempta.

Anno 698 Berctred dux regis Nordanhymbrorum a Pictis interfectus.

Anno 704 Aedilred, postquam triginta unum annos Merciorum genti praefuit, monachus factus, Coenredo regnum dedit.

Anno 705 Aldfrid rex Nordanhymbrorum defunctus est.

Anno 709 Coenred rex Merciorum, postquam quinque annos regnabat, Romam pergit.

present, and archbishop Theodore being president: a synod right profitable, of ten articles.

In the year 675, Wulfhere, king of the Marchmen, when he had reigned seventeen years, died and left the government to his brother Ethelred.

In the year 676 Ethelred laid waste Kent.

In the year 678, a comet appeared: bishop Wilfrid was put out of his see by king Egfrid; and Bosa, Eata and Eadhed were consecrated bishops in his stead.

In the year 679 Alfwin was slain.

In the year 680 a synod was made in the plain of Heathfield touching the catholic faith, archbishop Theodore being president: whereat John the Roman abbot was present; in which year Hild abbess at Whitby died.

In the year 685 Egfrid, king of the Northumbrians, was slain. The same year Lothere, king of Kent, died.

In the year 688 Cadwald, king of the West Saxons, went from Britain to Rome.

In the year 690 archbishop Theodore died.

In the year 697 queen Osthryth was murdered by her own nobles, to wit those of the Marchmen.

In the year 698 Bertred, the king's captain of the Northumbrians, was slain by the Picts.

In the year 704 Ethelred, after he had reigned thirty-one years over the nation of the Marchmen, became a monk and gave up his kingdom to Cenred.

In the year 705 Aldfrid, king of the Northumbrians, died.

In the year 709 Cenred, king of the Marchmen, having reigned five years, went to Rome.

Anno 711 Berctfrid praefectus cum Pictis pugnavit.

Anno 716 Osred rex Nordanhymbrorum interfectus, et rex Merciorum Ceolred defunctus; et vir Domini Ecgbert Hienses monachos ad catholicum pascha et ecclesiasticam correxit tonsuram.

Anno 725 Victred rex Cantuariorum obiit.

Anno 729 cometae apparuerunt, sanctus Ecgberct transiit. Osric mortuus est.

Anno 731 Berctuald archiepiscopus obiit. Anno eodem Tatuini consecratus archiepiscopus nonus Doruuernensis ecclesiae, Aedilbaldo rege Merciorum quintumdecimum agente annum imperii.

Haec de Historia Ecclesiastica Brittaniarum, et maxime gentis Anglorum, prout vel ex literis antiquorum, vel ex traditione maiorum, vel ex mea ipse cognitione scire potui, Domino adiuvante digessi Baeda famulus Christi et presbyter monasterii beatorum apostolorum Petri et Pauli, quod est ad Viuraemuda et Ingyruum.

Qui natus in territorio eiusdem monasterii, cum essem annorum septem, cura propinquorum datus sum educandus reverentissimo abbati Benedicto, ac deinde Ceolfrido; cunctumque ex eo tempus vitae in eiusdem monasterii habitatione peragens, omnem meditandis Scripturis operam dedi: atque inter observantiam disciplinae regularis et quotidianam cantandi in ecclesia curam, semper aut discere, aut docere, aut scribere dulce habui.

In the year 711 Bertfrith the reeve did battle with the Picts.

In the year 716 Osred, king of the Northumbrians, was slain, and Ceolred, king of the Marchmen, died; and the monks of Hy were brought of Egbert, the man of the Lord, to the catholic observance of Easter and right manner of ecclesiastical tonsure.

In the year 725 Witred, king of Kent, died.

In the year 729 comets appeared, the holy Egbert passed away, and Osric died.

In the year 731 archbishop Bertwald died. The same year was Tatwin consecrated ninth archbishop of the church of Canterbury, in the fifteenth year of the reign of Ethelbald king of the Marchmen.

This much concerning the Ecclesiastical History of Britain, and especially of the English nation (so far as I could learn either from the writings of the ancients, or by tradition of my elders, or by my own knowledge), has by the Lord's help been brought into order by me, Bede, the servant of Christ and priest of the monastery of the blessed apostles Peter and Paul, which is at Wearmouth and Jarrow.

Who being born in the territory of the same monastery, when I was 7 years of age, was delivered up by the hands of my kinsfolk to be brought up of the most reverend abbot Benedict, and afterward of Ceolfrid; and from that time spending all the days of my life in the mansion of the same monastery, I have applied all my diligence to the study of the Scriptures; and observing the regular discipline and keeping the daily service of singing in the church, I have taken delight always either to learn, or to teach, or to write.

Nonodecimo autem vitae meae anno diaconatum; tricesimo gradum presbyteratus, utrumque per ministerium reverentissimi episcopi Iohannis, iubente Ceolfrido abbate, suscepi.

Ex quo tempore accepti presbyteratus usque ad annum aetatis meae quinquagesimum nonum, haec in Scripturam sanctam meae meorumque necessitati ex opusculis venerabilium patrum breviter adnotare, sive etiam ad formam sensus et interpretationis eorum superadicere curavi.

" In principium Genesis, usque ad nativitatem Isaac, et iectionem Ismahelis, libros iv.

" De Tabernaculo, et vasis eius, ac vestibus sacerdotum, libros iii.

" In primam partem Samuhelis, id est, usque ad mortem Saulis, libros iii.

" De aedificatione Templi, allegoricae expositionis sicut et cetera, libros ii.

" Item in Regum librum xxx. quaestionum.

" In Proverbia Salomonis, libros iii.

" In Cantica Canticorum, libros vii.

" In Isaiam, Danihelem, duodecim Prophetas, et partem Hieremiae, distinctiones capitulorum ex tractatu b. Hieronymi excerptas.

" In Ezram et Neemiam, libros iii.

" In Canticum Habacum, librum i.

" In librum beati patris Tobiae, explanationis allegoricae de Christo et Ecclesia, librum i.

" Item, Capitula lectionum in Pentateuchum Mosi, Iosue, Iudicum.

" In libros Regum, et Verba dierum.

Further, in the 19th year of my life I was made deacon; in my 30th year I took the degree of the priesthood, both which orders I received by the hand of the most reverend bishop John, at the commandment of Ceolfrid my abbot.

And from the time that I took the priesthood until the 59th year of my age, I have employed myself upon Holy Scripture, for my own need and that of my brethren, briefly to note and gather from what the venerable fathers have written, and in addition thereto to expound after the manner of their meaning and interpretation these following works:—

On the beginning of Genesis as far as the birth of Isaac and the casting forth of Ishmael, 4 books.

Of the tabernacle and his vessels, and of the vestments of the priests, 3 books.

On the first part of Samuel, that is to say, as far as the death of Saul, 3 books.

Of the building of the temple, of allegorical exposition, as also the rest, 2 books.

Likewise on the book of Kings, 30 questions.

On the Proverbs of Solomon, 3 books.

On the Song of Songs, 7 books.

On Isaiah, Daniel, the twelve prophets, and part of Jeremiah, divisions of chapters drawn from the treatise of the blessed Jerome.

On Ezra and Nehemiah, 3 books.

On the Song of Habakkuk, 1 book.

On the book of the blessed father Tobias, 1 book of allegorical exposition concerning Christ and His Church.

Likewise chapters of readings on the Pentateuch of Moses, Joshua and Judges.

On the books of Kings and Chronicles.

"In librum beati patris Job.

"In Parabolas, Ecclesiasten, et Cantica Canticorum.

"In Isaiam Prophetam, Ezram quoque, et Neemiam.

"In Evangelium Marci, libros iv.

"In Evangelium Lucae, libros vi.

"Omeliarum Evangelii libros ii.

"In Apostolum quaecumque in opusculis sancti Augustini exposita inveni, cuncta per ordinem transscribere curavi.

"In Actus Apostolorum, libros ii.

"In Epistolas vii Catholicas, libros singulos.

"In Apocalypsin sancti Iohannis, libros iii.

"Item, Capitula lectionum in totum Novum, Testamentum, excepto Evangelio.

"Item, Librum Epistolarum ad diversos: quarum de sex aetatibus saeculi una est; de mansionibus filiorum Israel, una; una de eo quod ait Isaias: 'Et claudentur ibi in carcerem, et post dies multos visitabuntur'; de ratione Bissexti, una; de Aequinoctio, iuxta Anatolium, una.

"Item, de historiis Sanctorum; Librum vitae et passionis sancti Felicis Confessoris de metrico Paulini Opere in prosam transtuli.

"Librum vitae et passionis sancti Anastasii, male de Graeco translatum, et peius a quodam imperito emendatum, prout potui, ad sensum correxi.

"Vitam sancti patris, monachi simul et antistitis, Cudbercti, et prius heroico metro, et postmodum plano sermone descripsi.

On the book of the blessed father Job.

On the Proverbs, Ecclesiastes, and the Song of Songs.

On the Prophet Isaiah, also Ezra and Nehemiah.

On the Gospel of Mark, 4 books.

On the Gospel of Luke, 6 books.

Of Homilies on the Gospels, 2 books.

On the Apostle whatsoever I have found expounded in the writings of St. Augustine, hath all been by me diligently written down in order.

On the Acts of the Apostles, 2 books.

On the Seven Catholic Epistles, 1 book on each Epistle.

On the Revelation of St. John, 3 books.

Likewise Chapters of readings on all the New Testament, except only the Gospel.

Likewise a book of Epistles to divers persons: whereof one is of the six ages of the world: one of the halting-places of the children of Israel, one of the words of Isaiah: "And they shall be shut up in the prison, and after many days they shall be visited"; one of the reason of Leap Year; one of the Equinox, after Anatolius.

Likewise of the histories of the Saints; a book of the life and passion of St. Felix, confessor, hath been by me translated into prose after the work in metre of Paulinus.

The Book of the life and passion of saint Anastasius, which was ill translated from the Greek, and worse amended by some unskilful person, I have corrected to the sense as well as I was able.

I have written first in heroic verse, and afterwards also in prose the Life of the Holy Father Cuthbert, monk as well as bishop.

" Historiam abbatum monasterii huius, in quo supernae pietati deservire gaudeo, Benedicti, Ceolfridi, et Huaetbercti in libellis duobus.

" Historiam Ecclesiasticam nostrae insulae ac gentis, in libris v.

" Martyrologium de natalitiis sanctorum martyrum diebus; in quo omnes quos invenire potui, non solum qua die, verum etiam quo genere certaminis, vel sub quo iudice mundum vicerint, diligenter adnotare studui.

" Librum Hymnorum, diverso metro, sive rhythmo.

" Librum Epigrammatum heroico metro, sive elegiaco.

" De Natura rerum, et de Temporibus libros singulos.

" Item, de Temporibus librum unum maiorem.

" Librum de Orthographia, alphabeti ordine distinctum.

" Item, librum de Metrica arte; et huic adiectum alium de Schematibus sive Tropis libellum, hoc est, de figuris modisque locutionum, quibus Scriptura sancta contexta est."

Teque deprecor, bone Jesu, ut cui propitius donasti verba tuae scientiae dulciter haurire, dones etiam benignus, aliquando ad te fontem omnis sapientiae pervenire, et parere semper ante faciem tuam.

Explicit Domino iuvante liber quintus Historiae Ecclesiasticae Gentis Anglorum.

The History of the abbots of this monastery, wherein I with joy do serve the divine goodness, to wit of Benedict, Ceolfrid, and Huetbert, in 2 books.

The Ecclesiastical History of our island and nation, in 5 books.

The Martyrology of the birth days of the holy martyrs, in which I have with all diligence endeavoured to set down all those whom I could find, not only on what day, but also by what manner of contest, and under whom as judge they overcame the world.

A Book of Hymns in divers sorts of metre or rhythm.

A Book of Epigrams in heroic or elegiac verse.

Of the Nature of things and of the Times, one book apiece.

Likewise of the Times another greater book.

A Book of Orthography divided in the order of the alphabet.

Also a book of the Art of Poetry; and added thereto another book of Figures and Tropes, that is to say, figures and modes of speech in which the Holy Scriptures are veiled.

And I beseech Thee, merciful Jesus, that to whom Thou hast of Thy goodness given sweetly to drink in the words of the knowledge of Thee, Thou wilt also vouchsafe in Thy lovingkindness that he may one day come to Thee, the fountain of all wisdom, and stand for ever before Thy face.

Here endeth by the help of the Lord the 5th book of the Ecclesiastical History of the English Nation.

LIVES OF THE ABBOTS AND LETTER TO EGBERT

INCIPIT VITA SANCTORUM ABBATUM MONASTERII

IN

UYRAMUTHA ET GYRUUM, BENEDICTI, CEOLFRIDI, EOSTERUINI, SIGFRIDI,

ATQUE

HUAETBERCTI,

AB EIUSDEM MONASTERII PRESBYTERO ET MONACHO BAEDA COMPOSITA

1. RELIGIOSUS Christi famulus Biscopus cognomento Benedictus, aspirante superna gratia, monasterium construxit in honorem beatissimi apostolorum principis Petri, iuxta ostium fluminis Vyri ad aquilonem, iuvante se ac terram tribuente venerabili ac piissimo gentis illius rege Ecgfrido: idemque monasterium annis sedecim, inter innumeros vel itinerum vel infirmitatum labores, eadem qua construxit religione, sedulus rexit. Qui ut beati papae Gregorii verbis, quibus cognominis eius abbatis vitam glorificat, utar: "Fuit vir vitae venerabilis, gratia Benedictus et nomine, ab ipso pueritiae suae tempore cor gerens senile, aetatem quippe moribus transiens, nulli

---

[1] An unusual name, which comes, however, in a genealogy of the kings of Lindsey. He is also called Biscop Baducing.

[2] At the beginning of Book II. of the *Dialogi*.

BEGINNETH THE LIFE OF THE HOLY ABBOTS OF THE MONASTERY

IN

WEARMOUTH AND JARROW, BENEDICT, CEOLFRID, EOSTERWINE, SIGFRID,

AND

HWAETBERT

SET IN ORDER OF BEDE PRIEST AND MONK OF THE SAID MONASTERY

1. Biscop [1] surnamed Benedict, a devout servant of Christ, being favoured of heavenly grace, built a monastery in honour of the most blessed Peter, chief of the apostles, by the mouth of the river Wear, on the north side, Egfrid the venerable and right godly king of that nation aiding him with a grant of land; and amid innumerable travails of journeyings or sicknesses Biscop diligently ruled the said monastery for 16 years with that same devotion wherewith he did build it. And that I may use the words of the blessed pope Gregory,[2] where he extolleth the life of an abbot that had Biscop's surname: "He was a man of venerable life, Benedict in grace and in name, having the heart of a man of ripe age even from the time of his boyhood, for in the ways of his life he was beyond his years and

animum voluptati dedit." Nobili quidem stirpe gentis Anglorum progenitus, sed non minori nobilitate mentis ad promerenda semper angelorum consortia suspensus. Denique cum esset minister Osvii regis et possessionem terrae suo gradui competentem illo donante perciperet, annos natus circiter viginti et quinque fastidivit possessionem caducam, ut adquirere posset aeternam: despexit militiam cum corruptibili donativo terrestrem, ut vero Regi militaret, regnum in superna civitate mereretur habere in perpetuum: reliquit domum, cognatos et patriam propter Christum et propter Evangelium, ut centuplum acciperet, et vitam aeternam possideret: respuit nuptiis servire carnalibus, ut sequi valeret Agnum virginitatis gloria candidum in regnis caelestibus: abnuit liberos carne procreare mortales, praedestinatus a Christo ad educandos ei spirituali doctrina filios caelesti in vita perennes.

2. Dimissa ergo patria Romam adiit, beatorum apostolorum quorum desiderio semper ardere consueverat, etiam loca corporum corporaliter visere atque adorare curavit; ac[1] patriam mox reversus, studiosius ea quae vidit ecclesiasticae vitae instituta, diligere, venerari, et quibus potuit praedicare non desiit. Quo tempore Alchfridus supradicti regis Osvii filius et ipse propter adoranda apostolorum limina Romam venire disponens, comitem eum eiusdem itineris accepit. Quem cum pater suus ab

[1] for *ad*, Pl.

---

[1] With Wilfrid in 653.

gave not his heart to any pleasure." He was come of noble lineage among the English, but being no less noble of mind he was lifted up to be deserving of the company of angels for evermore. In brief, when he was thane to king Oswy and received of his hand a gift of land suitable to his degree, being at the time about 25 years of age, he disdained the perishable possession that he might obtain one that was eternal; he despised earthly warfare with its reward that decayeth, that in warfare for the true King he might be vouchsafed to have a kingdom without end in the heavenly city; he forsook home, kinsfolk and country for Christ's sake and the Gospel's, that he might receive an hundredfold and have everlasting life; he refused to be in the bonds of carnal wedlock, in order that in the glory of virginity he might follow the Lamb without spot in the kingdom of heaven; he would not beget mortal children by carnal generation, being foreordained of Christ to bring up for Him by spiritual instruction sons to be immortal in the heavenly life.

2. So, leaving his native land he went to Rome,[1] and set himself also to visit and worship in the body the places where are the bodies of the blessed apostles, with love of which he had ever been kindled; and by and by having returned home he never ceased diligently to love, honour, and proclaim to all whom he might those rules of ecclesiastical life which he saw at Rome. At which time Alchfrid, son of the aforesaid king Oswy, being also himself minded to visit Rome for the purpose of worshipping at the churches of the blessed apostles, took Biscop for his companion in the same journey. But when his father recalled him from his purpose in the said

intentione memorati itineris revocaret, atque in patria ac regno suo faceret residere, nihilominus ipse ut bonae indolis adolescens, coeptum confestim explens iter, summa sub festinatione Romam rediit, tempore cuius supra meminimus beatae memoriae Vitaliani papae; et non pauca scientiae salutaris quemadmodum et prius hausta dulcedine, post menses aliquot inde digrediens ad insulam Lyrinensem, ibidem se monachorum coetui tradidit, tonsuram accepit, et disciplinam regularem monachi voto insignitus debita cum sollicitudine servavit: ubi per biennium idonea monasticae conversationis doctrina institutus, rursus beati Petri apostolorum principis amore devictus, sacratam eius corpore civitatem repedare statuit.

3. Nec post longum adveniente nave mercatoria, desiderio satisfecit. Eo autem tempore miserat Ecgbertus Cantuariorum rex de Brittania electum ad episcopatus officium virum nomine Vyghardum, qui a Romanis beati Gregorii papae discipulis in Cantia fuerat omni ecclesiastica institutione sufficienter edoctus; cupiens eum sibi Romae ordinari episcopum, quatenus suae gentis et linguae habens antistitem, tanto perfectius cum subiectis sibi populis vel verbis imbueretur fidei vel mysteriis; quanto haec non per interpretem, sed per cognati et contribulis viri linguam simul manumque susciperet.

---

[1] This must have been added by an annotator, for the *Ecclesiastical History* was written after this treatise. Vitalian's date is 657–672.

[2] In a group of islands off Cannes.

[3] The third visit.

[4] *Eccl. Hist.* iii. 29.

journey and caused him to remain in his own country and kingdom, none the less Biscop, being a young man of virtuous nature, forthwith finished the journey which was begun, and hastened with great speed to return to Rome in the days of pope Vitalian of blessed memory, whom we named before;[1] and on this, as also on the visit he made before, having enjoyed abundantly the delights of wholesome learning, he departed thence after a few months and came to the island of Lérins,[2] where he joined the company of monks, received the tonsure, and having the mark of the vow of a monk he kept the rule of discipline with all due care; but after being for two years trained in the learning that belongeth to monastical conversation, he was once more overcome of the love he bore toward blessed Peter, the chief of the apostles, and determined once again to visit the city hallowed of his body.

3. And not long after, by the coming of a merchant vessel he had his wish.[3] Now at that time Egbert, king of Kent, had sent from Britain a man named Wighard[4] which had been chosen for the office of bishop, and had been well instructed in all ecclesiastical usage by the Roman scholars of the blessed pope Gregory in Kent; and Egbert desired to have him ordained bishop at Rome, so that having a prelate of his own nation and tongue,[5] he and all the people under him might be the more perfectly instructed whether in the words or mysteries of the faith; insomuch as they would receive these things, not through an interpreter, but by the lips and hand withal of a man that was of their own kin and tribe.

[5] This seems to imply that the Roman priests had not learnt, or only imperfectly learnt, the native language.

Qui videlicet Vighardus Romam veniens, cum cunctis qui secum venere comitibus, antequam gradum pontificatus perciperet, morbo ingruente defunctus est. At vero papa apostolicus, ne legatariis obeuntibus legatio religiosa fidelium fructu competente careret, inito consilio elegit de suis quem Brittanias archiepiscopum mitteret, Theodorum videlicet seculari simul et ecclesiastica philosophia praeditum virum, et hoc in utraque lingua, Graeca scilicet et Latina, dato ei collega et consiliatore viro aeque strenuissimo ac prudentissimo Adriano abbate: et quia venerabilem Benedictum sapientem, industrium, religiosum ac nobilem virum fore conspexit, huic ordinatum cum suis omnibus commendavit episcopum, praecepitque ut relicta peregrinatione quam pro Christo susceperat, commodi altioris intuitu patriam reversus, doctorem ei veritatis quem sedulo quaesierat adduceret, cui vel illo pergenti vel ibidem docenti, pariter interpres existere posset et ductor. Fecit ut iusserat: venerunt Cantiam: gratissime sunt suscepti: Theodorus sedem episcopatus conscendit: Benedictus suscepit monasterium beati Petri apostoli ad regendum, cuius postea praefatus Adrianus factus est abbas.

4. Quod ubi duobus annis monasterium rexit, tertium de Brittania Romam iter arripiens solita prosperitate complevit, librosque omnis divinae eruditionis non paucos vel placito pretio emptos, vel

[1] 669.

[2] Actually the fourth, but the third from Britain.

But when he came to Rome, this Wighard, with all his company that came with him, died of a disease that fell upon them, before he could receive pontifical rank. Whereupon the apostolical pope, unwilling that this godly embassy of the faithful should fail of its due fruit by reason of the death of the ambassadors, took counsel and chose one of his own men, whom he might send to Britain for archbishop, to wit Theodore, a man learned in secular no less than in ecclesiastical philosophy, and that in both languages, Greek that is and Latin, and he gave him for colleague and counsellor a man of no less stoutness of heart and wisdom, the abbot Hadrian: and because he saw that the venerable Benedict would be a prudent, diligent, devout and notable man, he entrusted unto him the bishop whom he had ordained, and all his company, bidding him give up the pilgrimage which he had undertaken for Christ's sake, and in regard of a higher advantage return to his countrymen, bringing the teacher of truth they had earnestly required, to the which teacher he might become interpreter as well as guide, both on the way thither and when he was teaching therein. Benedict did as he was bidden: they came to Kent,[1] and were very gladly received: Theodore ascended the episcopal throne: Benedict took upon him the governance of the monastery of blessed Peter the apostle, whereof the aforementioned Hadrian was presently made abbot.

4. The which monastery when Benedict had ruled for two years, he hastened to make his third[2] journey to Rome; which he carried out with his accustomable success, and brought back many books of all subjects of divine learning, which had been either

amicorum dono largitos retulit. Rediens autem ubi Viennam pervenit, emptitios ibi quos apud amicos commendaverat, recepit. At ingressus Brittaniam, ad regem Occidentalium Saxonum nomine Coynwalh conferendum putavit, cuius et ante non semel amicitiis usus, et beneficiis erat adiutus. Sed ipso eodem tempore immatura morte praerepto, tandem ad patriam gentem solumque in quo natus est pedem convertens, Ecgfridum Transhumbranae regionis regem adiit; cuncta quae egisset ex quo patriam adolescens deseruit, replicavit; quo religionis desiderio arderet, non celavit; quid ecclesiasticae, quid monachicae institutionis Romae vel circumquaque didicisset, quot divina volumina, quantas beatorum apostolorum sive martyrum Christi reliquias attulisset, patefecit; tantamque apud regem gratiam familiaritatis invenit, ut confestim ei terram septuaginta familiarum de suo largitus, monasterium inibi primo pastori ecclesiae facere praeciperet. Quod factum est, sicut et in prooemio memini, ad ostium fluminis Viri ad Aquilonem, anno ab incarnatione Domini sexcentesimo septuagesimo quarto, indictione secunda, anno autem quarto imperii Ecgfridi regis.

5. Nec plusquam unius anni spatio post fundatum monasterium interiecto, Benedictus oceano transmisso Gallias petens, caementarios qui lapideam sibi

bought at a price, or been given him freely of his friends. And when on his way home he was come to Vienne, he there recovered of the friends to whom he had entrusted them the books that he had bought. Whereupon having entered into Britain he was minded to go to Cenwalh king of the West Saxons, of whose friendship he had before had benefit, and received help of his service. But at that same time, Cenwalh being cut off by untimely death, Benedict at length turned his steps to his own people and the land wherein he was born, and came to the court of Egfrid, king of the Transhumbrian region; unto him he rehearsed all the things he had done since the time that he left home in his youth; he openly shewed the zeal for religion which was kindled in him; he discovered to him all the precepts of ecclesiastical and monastical usage which he had learned at Rome or anywhere about, displaying all the divine volumes and the precious relics of the blessed apostles or martyrs of Christ, which he had brought with him; and he found such grace and favour in the eyes of the king that he forthwith bestowed upon him, out of his own estate, seventy hides of land, and bade him build a monastery there in honour of the chief pastor of the Church. The which was built, as I also mentioned in the preface, at the mouth of the river Wear toward the north, in the 674th year from the Lord's incarnation, in the second indiction, and in the 4th year of the rule of king Egfrid.

5. And when not more than a year had passed after the foundation of the monastery, Benedict crossed the ocean to France, where he required, procured, and brought away masons to build him

ecclesiam iuxta Romanorum quem semper amabat morem facerent, postulavit, accepit, attulit. Et tantum in operando studii prae amore beati Petri in cuius honorem faciebat exhibuit, ut intra unius anni circulum ex quo fundamenta sunt iacta, culminibus superpositis, missarum inibi solemnia celebrari videres. Proximante autem ad perfectum opere, misit legatarios Galliam, qui vitri factores, artifices videlicet Brittaniis eatenus incognitos, ad cancellandas ecclesiae porticuumque et caenaculorum eius fenestras adducerent. Factumque est, et venerunt: nec solum opus postulatum compleverunt, sed et Anglorum ex eo gentem huiusmodi artificium nosse ac discere fecerunt: artificium nimirum vel lampadis ecclesiae vel vasorum multifariis usibus non ignobiliter aptum. Sed et cuncta quae ad altaris et ecclesiae ministerium competebant, vasa sancta, vel vestimenta, quia domi invenire non potuit, de transmarinis regionibus advectare religiosus emptor curabat.

6. Et ut ea quoque quae nec in Gallia quidem reperiri valebant, Romanis e finibus ecclesiae suae provisor impiger ornamenta vel munimenta conferret: quarta illo, post compositum iuxta regulam monasterium, profectione completa, multipliciore quam prius spiritualium mercium foenore cumulatus rediit. Primo quod innumerabilem librorum omnis generis copiam apportavit: Secundo quod reliquiarum beatorum apostolorum martyrumque Christi

[1] The fourth from Britain.

a church of stone, after the Roman fashion which he always loved. And in this work, out of the affection he had for the blessed Peter in whose honour he wrought it, he shewed such zeal that within the course of one year from the time the foundations were laid, the roof was put on, and men might see the solemnities of mass celebrated therein. Further, when the work was drawing nigh to completion, he sent messengers to France, which should bring over makers of glass (a sort of craftsman till that time unknown in Britain) to glaze the windows of the church, its side-chapels and clerestory. And so it was done, and they came: and not only did they finish the work that was required of them, but also caused the English people thereby to understand and learn this manner of craft: the which without doubt was worthily meet for the fastening in of church lamps, and for the manifold employments to which vessels are put. Moreover, this devout buyer, because he could not find them at home, took care to fetch from oversea all manner of things, to wit sacred vessels and vestments that were suitable to the ministry of the altar and the church.

6. Further, to the intent he might obtain for his church from the boundaries of Rome those ornaments also and writings which could not be found even in France, this diligent steward made a fourth [1] journey thither (after he had well ordered his monastery according to the rule), and when he had brought it to an end, he returned laden with a more abundant gain of spiritual merchandise than before. First, because he brought home a vast number of books of every kind: Secondly, because he procured a plentiful grace of the relics of the blessed apostles and martyrs

abundantem gratiam multis Anglorum ecclesiis profuturam advexit: Tertio quod ordinem cantandi, psallendi atque in ecclesia ministrandi iuxta morem Romanae institutionis suo monasterio contradidit, postulato videlicet atque accepto ab Agathone papa archicantore ecclesiae beati apostoli Petri et abbate monasterii beati Martini Iohanne, quem sui futurum magistrum monasterii Britannias Romanum Anglis adduceret. Qui illo perveniens, non solum viva voce quae Romae didicit ecclesiastica discentibus tradidit; sed et non pauca etiam literis mandata reliquit, quae hactenus in eiusdem monasterii bibliotheca memoriae gratia servantur. Quartum, Benedictus non vile munus attulit, epistolam privilegii a venerabili papa Agathone cum licentia, consensu, desiderio, et hortatu Ecgfridi regis acceptam, qua monasterium quod fecit ab omni prorsus extrinseca irruptione tutum perpetuo redderetur ac liberum. Quintum, picturas imaginum sanctarum quas ad ornandum ecclesiam beati Petri apostoli quam construxerat detulit; imaginem videlicet beatae Dei genetricis semperque virginis Mariae, simul et duodecim apostolorum, quibus mediam eiusdem ecclesiae testudinem, ducto a pariete ad parietem tabulato praecingeret; imagines evangelicae historiae quibus australem ecclesiae parietem decoraret; imagines visionum apocalypsis beati Iohannis, quibus septentrionalem aeque parietem ornaret, quatenus intrantes ecclesiam omnes etiam literarum ignari, quaquaversum intenderent, vel semper amabilem Christi sanctorumque

---

[1] Became pope 678.
[2] Vol. II. p. 99,
[3] In view probably of the controversies with Wilfrid.

of Christ to be profitable to many English churches: Thirdly, because he introduced into his monastery the order of chanting, singing, and ministering in church according to the manner of the Roman usage, having indeed asked and obtained of pope Agatho [1] leave to bring to the English in Britain a Roman teacher for his monastery, to wit John,[2] archchanter of the church of the blessed apostle Peter and abbot of the monastery of the blessed Martin. The which John coming thither, not only by the word of his lips delivered what he had learned at Rome to his scholars of ecclesiastical things, but also left good store of writings which are still preserved for the sake of his memory in the library of the said monastery. Fourthly, Benedict brought a worthy gift, namely, a letter of privilege from the venerable pope Agatho, which he obtained with the leave and consent of king Egfrid,[3] and at his desire and request, whereby the monastery built by him was rendered wholly safe and secure continually from all assault from without. Fifthly, he brought home sacred pictures to adorn the church of the blessed apostle Peter built by him, namely, the similitude of the blessed mother of God and ever Virgin Mary, and also of the 12 apostles, with the which he might compass the central vault of the said church by means of a board running along from wall to wall; similitudes of the Gospel story for the adornment of the south wall of the church; similitudes of the visions in the Revelation of the blessed John for the ornament of the north wall in like manner, in order that all men which entered the church, even if they might not read, should either look (whatsoever way they turned) upon the gracious countenance of Christ and His saints,

eius, quamvis in imagine, contemplarentur aspectum; vel Dominicae incarnationis gratiam vigilantiore mente recolerent; vel extremi discrimen examinis, quasi coram oculis habentes, districtius se ipsi examinare meminissent.

7. Igitur venerabilis Benedicti virtute, industria ac religione, rex Ecgfridus non minimum delectatus, terram quam ad construendum monasterium ei donaverat, quia bene se ac fructuose donasse conspexit, quadraginta adhuc familiarum data possessione, augmentare curavit; ubi post annum missis monachis numero ferme decem et septem, et praeposito abbate ac presbytero Ceolfrido, Benedictus consultu immo etiam iussu praefati Ecgfridi regis, monasterium beati Pauli apostoli construxit, ea duntaxat ratione, ut una utriusque loci pax et concordia, eadem perpetuo familiaritas conservaretur et gratia: ut sicut verbi gratia, corpus a capite per quod spirat non potest avelli, caput corporis sine quo non vivit nequit oblivisci, ita nullus haec monasteria primorum apostolorum fraterna societate coniuncta aliquo ab invicem temptaret disturbare conatu. Ceolfridus autem hic, quem abbatem constituit Benedictus, a primis instituti monasterii prioris exordiis adiutor illi per omnia strenuissimus aderat, et cum eo tempore congruo Romam discendi necessaria simul et adorandi gratia adierat. Quo tempore etiam presbyterum Eosteruinum de monasterio beati Petri eligens abbatem, eidem monasterio regendi

[1] Jarrow.

though it were but in a picture; or might call to mind a more lively sense of the blessing of the Lord's incarnation, or having, as it were before their eyes, the peril of the last judgment might remember more closely to examine themselves.

7. So king Egfrid, being greatly delighted with the virtue, industry and godliness of the venerable Benedict, and seeing that his former gift was well bestowed and bringing forth fruit, was minded to enlarge the grant of land that he had made him for the building of the monastery, by giving him yet another 40 hides; and hither, a year after, Benedict sent about 17 monks, setting Ceolfrid over them as abbot and priest; and with the advice or rather even by the commandment of the said king Egfrid, he built the monastery [1] of the blessed apostle Paul; on this condition only, that there should be unity of peace and agreement, and that friendship and kindness should continually be preserved the same between the two places; that just as, to make comparison, the body may not be severed from the head whereby it breathes, and the head may not forget the body without which it hath not life, so none should attempt by any means to separate, the one from the other, these monasteries which were joined together in the brotherly fellowship of the two chief apostles. Now this Ceolfrid whom Benedict appointed abbot was from the very beginning of the earlier monastery in all things his most zealous helper, and he had gone with him to Rome at a convenient season, both to receive needful instruction and to worship withal. At the which time also he chose Eosterwine, priest of the monastery of the blessed Peter, for abbot, and set him to be ruler

iure praefecit: ut quem solus non poterat laborem, socia dilectissimi commilitonis virtute levius ferret. Nec ab re videatur cuiquam duos unum monasterium simul habuisse abbates. Fecit hoc frequens illius pro monasterii utilitate profectio, creber trans oceanum egressus incertusque regressus. Nam et beatissimum Petrum apostolum Romae pontifices sub se duos per ordinem ad regendam Ecclesiam constituisse causa instante necessaria tradunt historiae. Et ipse magnus abbas Benedictus, sicut de illo beatus papa Gregorius scribit, duodecim abbates suis discipulis, prout utile iudicavit, sine charitatis detrimento, immo pro augmento charitatis praefecit.

8. Suscepit igitur memoratus vir curam monasterii regendi, nono ex quo fundatum est anno. Permansit in eo usque ad obitum suum annis quatuor, vir nobilis, sed insigne nobilitatis non ad iactantiae materiem, ut quidam, despectumque aliorum, sed ad maiorem, ut Dei servum decet animi nobilitatem convertens. Patruelis quippe erat abbatis sui Benedicti, sed amborum tanta mentis ingenuitas, talis mundanae ingenuitatis fuit pro nihilo contemptus, ut neque iste monasterium ingressus, aliquem sibi prae ceteris ob intuitum consanguinitatis aut nobilitatis honorem quaerendum, neque ille putaret offerendum: sed aequali cum fratribus lance boni propositi iuvenis gloriabatur se regularem per omnia servare disci-

[1] Linus, A.D. 68, and Cletus or Anencletus, A.D. 80.

over the said monastery: to the intent that the burden, which was too great for him to bear alone, might be lightened, when he was helped by the good courage of a beloved fellow-soldier. Nor let any man think it strange that one abbey should have two abbots at the same time. The cause thereof was Benedict's often journeying in the service of the monastery, his frequent departing and uncertain return across the ocean. For history also relates that the most blessed apostle Peter, of necessity laid upon him, appointed two bishops [1] under him in succession at Rome to rule the Church. And the great abbot Benedict himself, as blessed Gregory telleth us of him, set 12 abbots over his disciples, as he judged expedient, neither did he thereby lessen brotherly love but rather enlarged it.

8. The man aforesaid then took over the charge of ruling the monastery in the 9th year from the time it was founded, and he continued therein for 4 years until his death; he was of noble birth, but did not, as is the manner of some, turn the ornament of noble birth to an occasion for boasting and despising other, but, as becometh a servant of God, to a means of greater nobility of soul. He was indeed cousin of his abbot Benedict; but so high was the honourable spirit of them both, so utterly did they look down upon worldly honour as of nothing worth, that the one, when he entered into the monastery, thought it not meet to seek any dignity for himself above the rest in regard of family or noble birth, nor did the other think it should be offered unto him; but of the good purpose of his heart in eating of the same platter with the brethren his boast was to keep the rule of discipline in all things as befitted his youth.

plinam. Et quidem cum fuisset minister Ecgfridi regis, relictis semel negotiis secularibus, depositis armis, assumpta militia spirituali, tantum mansit humilis, fratrumque simillimus aliorum, ut ventilare cum eis et triturare, oves vitulasque mulgere, in pistrino, in horto, in coquina, in cunctis monasterii operibus iocundus et obediens gauderet exerceri. Sed et abbatis regimine graduque assumpto, eodem animo quo prius manebat ad omnes, iuxta id quod quidam sapiens admonet dicens: "Rectorem te constituerunt, noli extolli, sed esto in illis, quasi unus ex illis, mitis, affabilis, et benignus omnibus." Et quidem, ubi opportunum comperiebat, peccantes regulari disciplina coercens, sed magis tamen ingenita diligendi consuetudine sedulus admonens, ne qui peccare vellet, et limpidissimam vultus eius lucem nubilo sibi suae inquietudinis abscondere. Saepe pro curandis monasterii negotiis alicubi digrediens, ubi operantes invenit fratres, solebat eis confestim in opere coniungi; vel aratri gressum stiva regendo, vel ferrum malleo domando, vel ventilabrum manu concutiendo, vel aliud quid tale gerendo. Erat enim et viribus fortis iuvenis, et lingua suavis; sed et animo hilaris, et beneficio largus, et honestus aspectu. Eodem quo fratres ceteri cibo, semper eadem vescebatur in domo, ipso quo priusquam abbas esset communi dormiebat in loco, adeo ut etiam morbo correptus et obitus sui certis ex signis iam praescius,

[1] Ecclus. xxxii. 1.

And albeit he had been thane to king Egfrid, he put away worldly cares once for all, laid down his weapons, took up spiritual warfare only, and continued humble and so wholly like the other brethren that he was glad to winnow and thresh with them, to milk the ewes and cows, and cheerfully and obediently to be employed in the bakehouse, the garden, the kitchen and all the business of the monastery. Moreover, after he had taken on him the governance and rank of abbot, he continued to be of the same mind toward all as he had been before, according to the admonition of a wise man which said: "They have made thee ruler; be not lifted up, but be among them as one of the rest, gentle, courteous and kindly to all."[1] It is true that, when he found it convenient, he would check sinners by the discipline of the rule, but with the natural affection he was wont to shew he would rather diligently admonish them, that none should be willing to sin, and cloud the fair light of the abbot's countenance with the shadow of their own disquietness. Often as he went abroad any whither to look to the business of the monastery, if he found the brethren at work, he would straightway join himself to their labour; either taking the plough handle to guide the furrow, or fashioning iron with the hammer, or shaking the winnowing-fan, or doing some other such thing. For he was a young man, both able for strength and gentle of speech; and beside of a cheerful spirit, a liberal giver, and of a comely presence. He ate of the same food as the rest of the brethren, and always in the same building with them; he slept in the selfsame common abode as he did before he was abbot, insomuch that even when smitten with sickness and already warned with sure tokens of his

duos adhuc dies in dormitorio fratrum quiesceret. Nam quinque reliquos usque ad exitus horam dies in secretiori se aede locabat: qua die quadam egrediens, et sub divo residens, accitis ad se fratribus cunctis, more naturae misericordis osculum pacis eis flentibus ac de abscessu tanti patris et pastoris moerentibus dedit. Obiit autem per nonas Martias, noctu, fratribus matutinae psalmodiae laude vacantibus. Viginti quatuor annorum erat cum monasterium peteret, duodecim in eo vixit annis, septem presbyteratu functus est annis, quatuor ex eis monasterii regimen agebat; ac sic "terrenos artus moribundaque membra relinquens," coelestia regna petivit.

9. Verum his de vita venerabilis Eosteruini breviter praelibatis, redeamus ad ordinem narrandi. Constituto illo abbate Benedictus monasterio beati Petri apostoli, constituto et Ceolfrido monasterio beati Pauli, non multo post temporis spatio quinta vice de Brittania Romam adcurrens, innumeris sicut semper ecclesiasticorum donis commodorum locupletatus rediit; magna quidem copia voluminum sacrorum; sed non minori sicut et prius sanctarum imaginum munere ditatus. Nam et tunc Dominicae historiae picturas quibus totam beatae Dei genetricis, quam in monasterio maiore fecerat, ecclesiam in gyro coronaret, attulit;[1] imagines quoque ad ornandum

[1] Pl.

[1] Cf. Verg. *Aen.* vi. 732. [2] Wearmouth.

approaching death, he still lay for two days in the brethren's dormitory. For during the remaining 5 days, up to the hour of his departing, he bestowed himself in a more private dwelling; and coming out thence on a certain day and sitting in the open, he called unto him all the brethren, and according to the pitifulness of his nature he gave them the kiss of peace, as they wept and lamented for the departure of so good a father and shepherd. He died on the 7th day of March in the night, while all the brethren were employed in the praise of the early singing of psalms. He was 24 years of age when he entered into the monastery; he lived 12 years therein; he discharged the duties of the priesthood for 7 years, 4 of which he spent in the governance of the monastery; and so, "leaving his earthy frame and limbs ready to die,"[1] he went to the kingdom of heaven.

9. But now that thus much hath been given as foretaste touching the life of the venerable Eosterwine, let us return to the course of our story. No long time after Benedict had appointed him abbot over the monastery of the blessed apostle Peter, and Ceolfrid abbot over the monastery of blessed Paul, he hastened from Britain to Rome for the fifth time, and returned enriched as always with a countless number of gifts of advantage to the churches, namely, a great store indeed of sacred books, yet with the wealth, as before, of no lesser a present of sacred pictures. For at this time also he brought with him paintings of the Lord's history, with the which he might compass about the whole church of the blessed mother of God, built by him within the greater monastery;[2] he also displayed, for the

monasterium ecclesiamque beati Pauli apostoli de concordia veteris et novi Testamenti summa ratione compositas exhibuit: verbi gratia, Isaac ligna quibus immolaretur portantem, et Dominum crucem in qua pateretur aeque portantem, proxima super invicem regione, pictura coniunxit. Item serpenti in heremo a Moyse exaltato, Filium hominis in cruce exaltatum comparavit. Attulit inter alia, et pallia duo olosérica incomparandi operis, quibus postea ab Aldfrido rege eiusque consiliariis, namque Ecgfridum postquam rediit iam interfectum reperit, terram trium familiarum ad Austrum Vuiri fluminis, iuxta ostium comparavit.

10. Verum inter laeta quae veniens attulit, tristia domi reperit: venerabilem videlicet presbyterum Eosteruini quem abiturus abbatem constituerat, simul et fratrum ei commissorum catervam non paucam, per cuncta grassante pestilentia, iam migrasse de seculo. Sed aderat et solamen, quia in loco Eosteruini virum aeque reverentissimum ac mitissimum de monasterio eodem, Sigfridum videlicet diaconum, electione fratrum suorum simul et coabbatis eius Ceolfridi, mox substitutum cognovit; virum scientia quidem scripturarum sufficienter instructum, moribus optimis ornatum, mira abstinentiae virtute praeditum, sed ad custodiam virtutum animi, corporis infirmitate non minime depressum, ad conservandam cordis innocentiam nocivo et irremediabili pulmonum vitio laborantem.

adorning of the monastery and church of the blessed apostle Paul, paintings shewing the agreement of the Old and New Testaments, most cunningly ordered: for example, a picture of Isaac carrying the wood on which he was to be slain, was joined (in the next space answerable above) to one of the Lord carrying the cross on which He likewise was to suffer. He also set together the Son of Man lifted up on the cross with the serpent lifted up by Moses in the wilderness. Amongst other things he also brought home two palls all of silk of exceeding goodly workmanship, with the which he afterward purchased from king Aldfrid and his counsellors (for Egfrid after his return he found had now been killed) three hides of land south of the river Wear, near the mouth.

10. But in the midst of the gladness that he brought in his coming, he found sorrowful tidings at home: to wit, that the venerable priest Eosterwine (whom at the point to go away he had appointed abbot), as well as no small number of the brethren committed to his charge, had already departed this world of a pestilence which was everywhere raging. Yet was there comfort too, because he found that Sigfrid the deacon, a man as meek as he was reverend, had been by and by appointed in the room of Eosterwine out of the said monastery, being chosen thereto both of the brethren as well as of his fellow-abbot Ceolfrid. He was a man well instructed in the knowledge of the Scriptures, adorned with excellent virtues, endowed with a wonderful gift of abstinence, albeit he was grievously hampered in safeguarding the powers of his mind with bodily sickness, being sore troubled to keep the innocency of his heart by reason of a noisome and incurable malady of the lungs.

11. Nec multo post etiam Benedictus ipse morbo coepit ingruente fatigari. Ut enim tantam religionis instantiam etiam patientiae virtus adiuncta probaret, divina utrumque pietas temporali aegritudine prostravit in lectum; ut post aegritudinem morte devictam perpetua supernae pacis et lucis quiete refoveret. Nam et Sigfridus, ut diximus, longa interiorum molestia castigatus diem pervenit ad ultimum. Et Benedictus per triennium languore paulatim accrescente tanta paralysi dissolutus est, ut ob omni prorsus inferiorum membrorum factus sit parte praemortuus, superioribus solum sine quorum vita vivere nequit homo, ad officium patientiae virtutemque reservatis; studebant in dolore semper Auctori gratias referre, semper Dei laudibus fraternisve hortatibus vacare. Agebat Benedictus advenientes saepius ad se fratres de custodienda quam statuerat regula firmare: "Neque enim putare habetis," inquit, "quod ex meo haec quae vobis statui decreta indoctus corde protulerim. Ex decem quippe et septem monasteriis quae inter longos meae crebrae peregrinationis discursus optima comperi, haec universa didici, et vobis salubriter observanda contradidi." Bibliothecam quam de Roma nobilissimam copiosissimamque advexerat, ad instructionem ecclesiae necessariam, sollicite servari integram, nec per incuriam foedari, aut passim dissipari praecepit.

11. And not long after, Benedict also himself began to be distressed with an attack of sickness. For in order that the virtue of patience might be added to give proof beside of their great zeal for religion, the mercy of God caused them both to be cast into bed of a temporal malady; to the end that after sickness had been conquered of death, He might refresh them with the abiding rest of heavenly peace and light. For both Sigfrid, chastened (as I have said) with the long trouble of his inward parts, drew to his end, and Benedict was so weakened during three years with the ailment of a creeping palsy, that he was utterly dead in all the lower part of his body, the upper parts alone (without life in which a man may not remain alive) being preserved for the exercise of the virtue of patience; and both of them endeavoured in the midst of their pain to give continual thanks to their Maker, and to be ever occupied with the praise of God and the encouragement of their brethren. Benedict set himself to strengthen the brethren, that ofttimes came unto him, in the observance of the rule which he had given them: "For ye are not to think," quoth he, "that of my own heart without direction I have set forth the ordinances that I have appointed for you. For all the things I have found most excellent in 17 monasteries, whereunto I came in the travel to and fro of my long and often journeyings, I committed to memory and conveyed to you to keep and profit therefrom." The glorious library of a very great store of books which he had brought with him from Rome (and which in regard of instruction in the Church could not be spared) he commanded to be diligently kept whole and complete, and not marred by neglect, nor broken up and

Sed et hoc sedulus eisdem solebat iterare mandatum, ne quis in electione abbatis, generis prosapiam, et non magis vivendi docendique probitatem putaret esse quaerendam. " Et vere," inquit, " dico vobis, quia in comparatione duorum malorum, tolerabilius mihi multo est totum hunc locum in quo monasterium feci, si sic iudicaverit Deus, in solitudinem sempiternam redigi, quam ut frater meus carnalis, quem novimus viam veritatis non ingredi, in eo regendo post me abbatis nomine succedat. Ideoque multum cavetote fratres semper, ne secundum genus unquam, ne deforis aliunde, vobis patrem quaeratis. Sed iuxta quod regula magni quondam abbatis Benedicti, iuxta quod privilegii nostri continent decreta, in conventu vestrae congregationis communi consilio perquiratis, qui secundum vitae meritum et sapientiae doctrinam aptior ad tale ministerium perficiendum digniorque probetur, et quemcunque omnes unanime charitatis inquisitione optimum cognoscentes elegeritis; hunc vobis accito episcopo rogetis abbatem consueta benedictione firmari. Nam qui carnali," inquit, " ordine carnales filios generant, carnali necesse est ac terrenae suae haereditati carnales terrenosque quaerant haeredes: at qui spirituales Deo filios spirituali semine verbi procreant, spiritualia oportet sint cuncta quae agunt. Inter spirituales suos liberos eum maiorem qui ampliori spiritus gratia sit praeditus aestiment, quomodo terreni parentes

scattered. Moreover, this charge he was constantly wont to repeat to the said brethren, namely, that in the choice of an abbot none of them should think that family kindred should be sought for rather than uprightness of life and doctrine. "And I tell you of a truth," quoth he, "that comparing the two evils, I deem it far more tolerable that all this place where I have built the monastery should be made a wilderness for ever, if God so will, than that my brother after the flesh, whom we know to be walking not in the way of truth, should follow me in the governance thereof as abbot. Therefore, my brethren, be ye always very careful never to choose a father for the sake of his family, nor one from any place outside. But in accordance with the rule of our sometime abbot, the great Benedict, and in accordance with the decrees of our letter of privilege, look ye out with common consent in the assembly of your congregation the man which, by reason of his good life and wise doctrine, shall be shewn better fitted and more worthy than others for the fulfilment of such a ministry, and whomsoever ye shall all with one accord upon loving enquiry judge and choose to be the best: then summon the bishop, and require him to confirm this man with the accustomed blessing to be your abbot. For they," he said, "which beget carnal sons by carnal process must needs seek carnal and earthly heirs for a carnal and earthly inheritance; but they which beget spiritual sons by the spiritual seed of the word, must in all things be spiritual in their doings. Let them then reckon him as the eldest son among their spiritual children, who is thus endowed with more abundant spiritual grace, just as earthly parents are wont to acknowledge their

quem primum partu fuderint, eum principium liberorum suorum cognoscere, et ceteris in partienda sua haereditate praeferendum ducere solent."

12. Neque hoc reticendum, quod venerabilis abbas Benedictus ad temperandum saepe longae noctis taedium, quam prae infirmitatis onere ducebat insomnem, advocato lectore, vel exemplar patientiae Job, vel aliud quid scripturarum quo consolaretur aegrotus, quo depressus in infimis vivacius ad superna erigeretur, coram se recitari iubebat. Et quia nullatenus ad orandum surgere, non facile ad explendum solitae psalmodiae cursum linguam vocemve poterat levare, didicit vir prudens affectu religionis dictante, per singulas diurnae sive nocturnae orationis horas aliquos ad se fratrum vocare, quibus psalmos consuetos duobus in choris resonantibus, et ipse cum eis quatinus poterat psallendo, quod per se solum nequiverat, eorum iuvamine suppleret.

13. At ubi uterque abbas lassatus infirmitate diutina, iam se morti vicinum, nec regendo monasterio idoneum fore conspexit: tanta namque eos affecit infirmitas carnis ut perficeretur in eis virtus Christi, ut cum quadam die desiderantibus eis se invicem priusquam de hoc seculo migrarent videre et alloqui, Sigfridus in feretro deportaretur ad cubiculum ubi Benedictus et ipse suo iacebat in grabato, eisque uno in loco ministrorum manu compositis, caput utriusque in eodem cervicali locaretur, lacrimabili spectaculo, nec tantum habuere virium ut propius posita ora ad

firstborn son as the chief of their offspring, and to consider him to be preferred before the rest, when they divide their inheritance."

12. Nor must I forbear to tell how ofttimes the venerable abbot Benedict in order to abate the weariness of the long nights, when he could not sleep by reason of his grievous malady, would call a reader and have him read to him the story of Job's patience, or some other passage of Scripture, whereby in his sickness he might be comforted and be exalted with a more lively hope to things above out of the depth wherein he was brought down. And because he could in no wise rise to pray, nor without difficulty give utterance or lift up his voice to fulfil the course of the regular psalmody, this wise man, taught of his love of religion, accustomed himself, at the several hours of the daily and nightly prayers, to summon unto him some of the brethren which should sing the appointed psalms antiphonally, that so he himself singing with them so far as he might, should by their aid fulfil what he could not accomplish of himself.

13. But when the two abbots, worn out by long-continued sickness, perceived that they were nigh unto death, and would not be fit to rule the monastery (for so sore lay their bodily sickness upon them, perfecting in them the power of Christ), that one day, when each desired to see and speak with the other, before departing this life, Sigfrid was carried on a stretcher to the chamber where Benedict too was himself laid upon his pallet, and their attendants placing them side by side, their heads were set on the same pillow (a lamentable sight), and albeit their faces were close together they had not strength to

osculandum se alterutrum coniungere possent; sed et hoc fraterno compleverunt officio: inito Benedictus cum eo, cumque universis fratribus salubri consilio, acciit abbatem Ceolfridum, quem monasterio beati apostoli praefecerat, virum videlicet sibi non tam carnis necessitudine, quam virtutum societate propinquum: et eum utrique monasterio cunctis faventibus, atque hoc utillimum iudicantibus, praeposuit patrem; salubre ratus per omnia ad conservandam pacem, unitatem, concordiamque locorum, si unum perpetuo patrem rectoremque tenerent; commemorans saepius Israelitici regni exemplum, quod inexterminabile semper exteris nationibus, inviolatumque perduravit, quamdiu unis iisdemque suae gentis regebatur a ducibus; at postquam praecedentium causa peccatorum inimico ab invicem est certamine diremptum, periit paulisper, et a sua concussum soliditate defecit. Sed et Evangelicam illam monebat sine intermissione recolendam esse sententiam, quia "omne regnum in seipso divisum desolabitur."

INCIPIT LIBELLUS SECUNDUS

14. Igitur post haec revolutis mensibus duobus primo, venerabilis ac Deo dilectus abbas Sigfridus, pertransito igne et aqua tribulationum temporalium, inductus est in refrigerium sempiternae quietis,

---

[1] So that Benedict, Eosterwine and Ceolfrid were all related to one another and of noble birth.

bring them near to kiss each other; yet even this they brought to pass with the help of the brethren. Then Benedict, after wholesome counsel held with Sigfrid and all the brethren, summoned abbot Ceolfrid whom he had set over the monastery of the blessed apostle Paul, being his kinsman [1] not in the bond of the flesh so much as in fellowship of virtue; and all the rest agreeing and deeming it most expedient, he appointed him father over both monasteries; for he judged it best in every way for the maintenance of the peace, unity and agreement of the two places that they should continually have one father and governor; oftentimes recounting the example of the kingdom of Israel, which could not ever be driven from its boundaries by foreign nations, and remained without hurt, so long as it was ruled by one and the same leader from its own nation; but when afterward on account of its former sins the people became enemies to one another and were parted asunder with contention, it gradually perished and fell to ruin from its former stability. He likewise bade them unceasingly remember the Gospel precept,[2] which says that "every kingdom divided against itself shall be brought to desolation."

BOOK II

14. So when after these things two months had gone by, in the first place Sigfrid the venerable abbot, beloved of God, was brought into the refreshment of eternal rest through the fire and water of temporal tribulation, and entered into his home in

[2] Matt. xii. 25.

introiit in domum regni coelestis, in holocaustis perpetuae laudationis reddens sua vota Domino, quae sedula labiorum mundorum distinctione promiserat: ac deinde adiunctis aliis mensibus quatuor, vitiorum victor Benedictus et virtutum patrator egregius, victus infirmitate carnis ad extrema pervenit. "Nox ruit hibernis algida flatibus": dies illi mox sancto[1] nascitura aeternae felicitatis, serenitatis et lucis. Conveniunt[2] fratres ad ecclesiam, insomnes orationibus et psalmis transigunt umbras noctis: et paternae decessionis pondus continua divinae laudis modulatione solantur. Alii cubiculum in quo aeger, animo robustus egressum mortis et vitae expectabat ingressum, non deserunt. Evangelium tota nocte pro doloris levamine, quod et aliis noctibus fieri consueverat, a presbytero legitur; Dominici corporis et sanguinis sacramentum hora exitus instante pro viatico datur; et sic anima illa sancta longis flagellorum felicium excocta atque examinata flammis luteam carnis fornacem deserit, et supernae beatitudinis libera pervolat ad gloriam. Cuius egressui victoriosissimo, neque ab immundis spiritibus aliquatenus impediendo vel retardando, etiam psalmus qui tum pro eo canebatur, testimonium dat. Namque fratres ad ecclesiam principio noctis concurrentes, psalterium ex ordine decantantes, ad octogesimum tunc et secundum cantando pervenerant psalmum, qui habet in capite: "Deus quis similis erit tibi?" Cuius totus hoc resonat textus, quod inimici nominis Christi sive carnales sive spirituales, semper Ecclesiam Christi, semper

[1] for *sancta*, Pl. [2] for *convenerunt*, Pl.

---

[1] Source of quotation unknown. [2] Psalm xii. 6.

the kingdom of heaven, paying unto the Lord in sacrifices of continual praise the vows he had promised with often parting of clean lips; and when 4 more months were passed, Benedict, the conqueror over sin and glorious worker of righteousness, being conquered of bodily weakness came to his end. "The night falls chilly with winter blasts";[1] but for that holy man is soon to rise the day of everlasting happiness, peace and light. The brethren assemble at the church, and sleeplessly pass the dark hours in prayers and psalms: lightening the burden of their father's departure with the unceasing melody of praise to God. Other abide in the chamber, where Benedict, sick in body but strong in mind, was looking for his passage from death and his entry into life. All that night, as was the custom to be done other nights too, the Gospel is read aloud of a priest to comfort his pain; as the hour of his departure is at hand, the sacrament of the Lord's body and blood is given him for his voyage provision; and so this holy soul, searched and tried with the slow flames of profitable chastisement, leaveth the furnace of earth[2] in the flesh, and flieth in deliverance to the glory of heavenly bliss. And to his departure in great triumph, which might not be let or hindered in any way of evil spirits, witness is borne also by the psalm which at that time was being sung for him. For the brethren, hurrying together to the church at nightfall, sang through the psalter, and had at that time reached the 82nd psalm which has for its title "Lord, who shall be like unto Thee?" of the which psalm thus is the whole meaning, that the enemies of the name of Christ, whether they be carnal or ghostly, do strive to break up and destroy always

animam quamque fidelem disperdere ac dissipare conentur; sed e contra ipsi confusi et conturbati, sint perituri in seculum, enervante illos Domino, cui non est quisquam similis, qui est solus altissimus super omnem terram. Unde recte dabatur intelligi coelitus dispensatum, ut talis diceretur psalmus ea hora qua exiret de corpore anima, cui iuvante Domino nullus praevalere posset inimicus. Sextodecimo postquam monasterium fundavit anno, quievit in Domino confessor, pridie iduum Ianuariarum, sepultus in ecclesia beati apostoli Petri; ut quem degens in carne semper solebat amare, quo pandente ianuam regni caelestis intrabat, ab huius reliquiis et altari post mortem nec corpore longius abesset. Sedecim ut diximus annos monasterium rexit, primos octo per se sine alterius assumptione abbatis; reliquos totidem viris venerabilibus et sanctis Eosteruini, Sigfrido et Ceolfrido abbatis se nomine, auctoritate, et officio iuvantibus; primo quatuor annos, secundo tres, tertio unum.

15. Qui et ipse tertius, id est, Ceolfridus industrius per omnia vir, acutus ingenio, actu impiger, maturus animo, religionis zelo fervens, prius, sicut et supra meminimus, iubente pariter et iuvante Benedicto, monasterium beati Pauli apostoli septem annis, fundavit, perfecit, rexit; ac deinde utrique monasterio, vel sicut rectius dicere possumus, in duobus locis posito uni monasterio beatorum apostolorum

the Church of Christ and always every faithful soul; but contrariwise they themselves shall be confounded and dismayed and perish everlastingly, their strength being weakened of the Lord, to Whom there is none like, Who only is the highest over all the earth. Whence it was rightly understood to be disposed from heaven that such psalm should be said in the hour when his soul was leaving his body, against whom, the Lord being his helper, no enemy might prevail. In the 16th year after he had founded the monastery, this confessor fell asleep in the Lord, on the 12th day of January, and was buried in the church of the blessed apostle Peter; so that after death his body lay not far from the relics and the altar of him whom, whiles he was in the flesh, he ever loved, and who opened for him the door of entry into the kingdom of heaven. For 16 years, as we have said, he ruled the monastery; the first 8 of himself without appointment of a second abbot beside; the last 8 with the venerable and holy Eosterwine, Sigfrid and Ceolfrid to aid him with the title, authority, and office of abbot; the first during 4 years, the second during 3 years and the last during one.

15. And he that was third of these, namely Ceolfrid, a man diligent in all things, of quick understanding, not slothful in business, ripe in judgment and fervent in religious zeal, did first, as too we have said before, at the behest as well as with the help of Benedict found, complete and govern the monastery of the blessed apostle Paul for a space of 7 years; and after for 28 years did wisely govern over both monasteries, or, as we might say more truly, over the single monastery

Petri et Pauli, viginti et octo annos sollerti regimine praefuit; et cuncta quae suus predecessor egregia virtutum opera coepit, ipse nec segnius perficere curavit. Siquidem inter cetera monasterii necessaria quae longo regendi tempore disponenda comperit, etiam plura fecit oratoria; altaris et ecclesiae vasa, vel vestimenta omnis generis ampliavit; bibliothecam utriusque monasterii, quam Benedictus abbas magna coepit instantia, ipse non minori geminavit industria: ita ut tres pandectes novae translationis, ad unum vetustae translationis quem de Roma attulerat, ipse super adiungeret; quorum unum senex Romam rediens secum inter alia pro munere sumpsit, duos utrique monasterio reliquit: dato quoque Cosmographorum codice mirandi operis, quem Romae Benedictus emerat, terram octo familiarum iuxta fluvium Fresca ab Aldfrido rege in scripturis doctissimo in possessionem monasterii beati Pauli apostoli comparavit; quem comparandi ordinem ipse, dum adhuc viveret, Benedictus cum eodem rege Aldfrido taxaverat, sed priusquam complere potuisset obiit. Verum pro hac terra postmodum, Osredo regnante, Ceolfridus, addito pretio digno, terram viginti familiarum in loco qui incolarum lingua Ad Villam Sambuce vocatur, quia haec vicinior eidem monasterio videbatur, accepit. Missis Romam monachis tempore beatae[1] recordationis Sergii papae, privilegium ab eo pro tuitione sui monasterii instar illius

[1] Pl.

---

[1] A name transferred from the Justinian Code to the books of the Old and New Testament. The new translation is the Latin translation by Jerome.

[2] Unidentified.

[3] Perhaps at the mouth of the Wansbeck.

of the blessed apostles Peter and Paul situated in two different places; and all the notable works of righteousness begun by his predecessor, these Ceolfrid was as ready to endeavour to complete. For beside all other things needful for the monastery, which his long rule thereof taught him should be provided, he built many chapels; he multiplied the vessels of the church and altar, and all kinds of vestments; the library of either monastery, which abbot Benedict had been so instant to begin, was of him with no lesser diligence doubled: insomuch that he added 3 pandects [1] of the new translation to the single copy of the old which he had brought from Rome; and one of these, when he went back in his old age to Rome, he carried with him amongst other things for a present, but two he bequeathed to the two monasteries. Moreover, in exchange for the manuscript, most excellent for workmanship, of the Cosmographers, which Benedict had bought at Rome, he procured from king Aldfrid, a man well learned in the Scriptures, 8 hides of land beside the river Fresca,[2] for the possession of the monastery of the blessed apostle Paul; and this manner of procuring the land had been fixed by the estimation of Benedict, whilst he still lived, with the said king Aldfrid, but he died before he could complete it. But somewhat later under king Osred, Ceolfrid, paying a fit price in addition, exchanged this piece of land for 20 hides in the place which is called of the inhabitants At the Township Sambuce,[3] because this land was seen to be nearer the said monastery. Having sent monks to Rome in the days of pope Sergius of blessed memory, Ceolfrid obtained from him a privilege for the protection of the monastery,

quod Agatho papa Benedicto dederat, accepit: quod Brittanias perlatum, et coram synodo patefactum, praesentium episcoporum simul et magnifici regis Aldfridi subscriptione confirmatum est, quomodo etiam prius illud sui temporis regem et episcopos in synodo publice confirmasse non latet. Temporibus illius tradens se monasterio beati Petri apostoli, quod regebat, veteranus ac religiosus, et in omni tam seculari quam scripturarum scientia eruditus Christi famulus Vuitmer, terram decem familiarum quam ab Aldfrido rege in possessionem acceperat, in loco villae quae Daldun nuncupatur, eidem monasterio perpetuae possessionis iure donavit.

16. At ubi Ceolfridus post multam regularis observantiae disciplinam quam sibi ipsi, pariter ac suis,[1] pater providus ex priorum auctoritate contribuit; post incomparabilem orandi psallendique sollertiam, qua ipse quotidianus exerceri non desiit; post mirabilem et coercendi improbos fervorem, et modestiam consolandi infirmos; post insolitam rectoribus et escae potusque parcitatem, et habitus vilitatem; vidit se iam senior et plenus dierum non ultra posse subditis ob impedimentum supremae aetatis, debitam spiritualis exercitii vel docendo vel vivendo praecipere formam; multa diu secum mente versans, utilius decrevit, dato fratribus praecepto, ut iuxta sui statuta privilegii iuxtaque regulam sancti abbatis

[1] for *suus*, Pl.

---

[1] Dalton and Dawdon are places near Sunderland.

like that which pope Agatho had granted to Benedict; and this being brought to Britain and made known before the synod was confirmed by the subscription of the bishops there present as well as by that of the noble king Aldfrid, in the manner in which, as is well known, the former privilege was publicly confirmed in a synod by the king and bishops of its time. It was in king Aldfrid's time that Witmer, an aged and devout servant of Christ, skilled in all secular learning as well as in knowledge of the Scriptures, giving himself to the monastery of the blessed apostle Peter (which Ceolfrid then ruled) made over to the same monastery 10 hides of land for a continual possession, granted to him for a possession by king Aldfrid and situate in the township called Dalton.[1]

16. But Ceolfrid, after long discipline in observance of the rule which the father had providently given of the authority of men of former time for the profit of himself and his followers; after displaying a diligence which might not be equalled in prayer and chanting, wherein he ceased not to exercise himself daily; after shewing marvellous zeal in restraining the froward, and sobriety in comforting the weak; after practising an abstinence in food and drink and a poverty of dress rare among rulers; perceived that, being now old and full of days, he could no longer, on account of the hindrance of his great age, either by precept or example, require of them which were subject to him the due pattern of spiritual practice; after much pondering a long time in his heart, he judged it better to enjoin the brethren, in accordance with the decrees of their privilege and the rule of the holy abbot Benedict, to choose out

Benedicti, de suis sibi ipsi patrem qui aptior esset eligerent, et ipse beatorum apostolorum ubi iuvenis cum Benedicto fuerat Romae loca sancta repeteret: quatenus et ipse ante mortem aliquamdiu seculi curis absolutus, liberius sibimet secreta quiete vacaret; et illi sumpto abbate iuniore, perfectius iuxta aetatem magistri quae vitae regularis essent instituta servarent.

17. Obnitentibus licet primo omnibus, et in lacrimas singultusque genua cum obsecratione crebra flectentibus, factum est quod voluit. Tantaque erat proficiscendi cupido, ut tertia die ex quo fratribus secretum sui propositi aperuit, iter arriperet. Timebat enim quod evenit, ne priusquam Romam pervenire posset, obiret; simul devitans, ne ab amicis sive viris principalibus quibus cunctis erat honorabilis, eius coepta retardarentur, et ne pecunia daretur illi a quibusdam, quibus retribuere pro tempore nequiret; hanc habens semper consuetudinem, ut siquis ei aliquid muneris offerret, hoc illi vel statim vel post intervallum competens, non minore gratia rependeret. Cantata ergo primo mane missa in ecclesia beatae Dei genetricis semperque virginis Mariae et in ecclesia apostoli Petri, pridie nonas Iunias, quinta feria, et communicantibus qui aderant, continuo praeparatur ad eundum. Conveniunt omnes in ecclesiam beati Petri, ipse thure incenso et dicta oratione ad altare, pacem dat omnibus, stans in

of their number a fitter man to be their father, and determined himself to revisit the holy places of the blessed apostles at Rome, where in his youth he had been with Benedict: to the end that before his death he might both himself have for a season a respite from the cares of the world, and freedom to remain privily with himself in peace apart; and that the brethren, having taken a younger man for abbot, might in accordance with the age of their new master keep with greater perfection the usages that belonged to the life of their rule.

17. Although at first all withstood him and knelt before him with sobs and tears and oft-repeated prayers, it was done as he willed. And so eager was he to set out, that he hastened to begin his journey the third day after he had declared his secret purpose to the brethren. For he had fear, as indeed it came to pass, lest he should die before he might reach Rome; and wished withal to avoid that his undertaking should be hindered of his friends or the principal men with all whom he was held in honour, and lest money should be given him of some whom he could not at once repay; for his constant habit was, if any man made him a gift, that he would recompense it either at once or after a meet interval, with no less a favour. So, after mass had first been sung in the morning in the church of the blessed mother of God, the ever Virgin Mary, and in the church of blessed Peter, on the 4th day of June, being the 5th day of the week, all who were present having made their communion, he straightway prepared to go. All assemble in the church of blessed Peter, and Ceolfrid having himself lighted the incense and said the prayer at the altar, standing

gradibus, thuribulum habens in manu: hinc fletibus universorum inter letanias resonantibus, exeunt; beati Laurentii martyris oratorium, quod in dormitorio fratrum erat obvium, intrant; vale dicens ultimum, de conservanda invicem dilectione, et delinquentibus iuxta Evangelium corripiendis, admonet; omnibus, siquid forte deliquissent, gratiam suae remissionis et placationis offert; omnes pro se orare, sibi placatos existere, si sint quos durius iusto redarguisset, obsecrat. Veniunt ad litus; rursum osculo pacis inter lacrimas omnibus dato, genua flectunt; dat orationem, ascendit navem cum comitibus. Ascendunt et diacones ecclesiae cereas ardentes et crucem ferentes auream, transit flumen, adorat crucem, ascendit equum et abiit, relictis in monasteriis suis fratribus numero ferme sexcentorum.

18. Illo autem abeunte cum sociis, redeunt ad ecclesiam fratres, se ac sua Domino fletibus et oratione commendant: et post non grande intervallum, completa horae tertiae psalmodia, rursum conveniunt omnes; quid agendum sit consulunt; orando, psallendo, et ieiunando patrem citius a Deo quaerendum decernunt; monachis beati Pauli, fratribus videlicet suis, per eorum quosdam qui aderant, necnon et suorum aliquos, quod decreverunt, pandunt. Assentiunt et illi, fit utrorumque animus unus, omnium corda sursum, omnium levantur voces ad Dominum.

on the steps with the censer in his hands, giveth them all his peace: from thence they go forth, the sound of weeping that all made being heard in the midst of the litanies, and enter the chapel of the blessed martyr Laurence, which stood opposite in the brethren's dormitory; and bidding his last farewell, he warneth them to preserve mutual love and to correct offenders in accordance with the Gospel; he offereth to all who may have offended, the grace of his forgiveness and good-will; he beseecheth all to pray for him and to be reconciled to him, if there were any whom he had rebuked with more harshness than he should. They come to the shore; again he giveth the kiss of peace to all amidst their tears; he prayeth and goeth aboard the ship with his company. The deacons of the church also embark, bearing lighted tapers and a golden cross; he crosseth the river, adoreth the cross, mounteth his horse and departed, leaving in his monasteries brethren to the number of about 600.

18. And as he departed with his company, the brethren return to the church, and with tears and prayers commend themselves and their belongings to God; and after no long interval, having finished the psalms of the third hour, they all again assemble; they consider what should be done; they determine with all speed to ask for a father from God with prayer and singing of psalms and fasting; they discover their determination to the monks of blessed Paul, which were their brethren, through some of them which were present, as well as through some of their own company. These also agree, both monasteries are of one mind, the hearts of all and the voices of all are lifted up unto the Lord. At

Tandem die tertia, veniente Dominico pentecosten, conveniunt omnes qui erant in monasterio beati Petri in concilium, adsunt et de monasterio beati Pauli seniorum non pauci. Fit una concordia, eadem utrorumque sententia. Eligitur itaque abbas Huaetbertus, qui a primis pueritiae temporibus eodem in monasterio non solum regularis observantia disciplinae institutus, sed et scribendi, cantandi, legendi ac docendi fuerat non parva exercitatus industria. Romam quoque temporibus beatae memoriae Sergii papae accurrens, et non parvo ibidem temporis spatio demoratus, quaeque sibi necessaria iudicabat, didicit, descripsit, retulit; insuper et duodecim ante haec annos presbyterii est functus officio. Hic igitur electus abbas ab omnibus utriusque praefati monasterii fratribus, statim assumptis secum aliquibus fratrum, venit ad abbatem Ceolfridum cursum navis qua oceanum transiret expectantem: quem elegerant abbatem nuntiant: Deo gratias, respondit, electionem confirmat, et commendatoriam ab eo epistolam apostolico papae Gregorio deferendam suscepit: cuius, memoriae causa, putavimus etiam in hoc opere versus aliquot esse ponendos.

19. "Domino in Domino dominorum dilectissimo, terque beatissimo papae Gregorio, Huaetbertus humilis servus vester, abbas coenobii beatissimi apostolorum principis Petri in Saxonia, perpetuam in Domino salutem.

"Gratias agere non cesso dispensationi superni examinis, una cum sanctis fratribus qui mecum in his locis ad inveniendam requiem animabus suis

length on the third day, at the coming of Pentecost Sunday, all the monks of the monastery of blessed Peter met in council, and of the elders of the monastery of blessed Paul not a few. All are of one mind and both have the same opinion. And so Hwaetbert is chosen abbot, which had not only been taught from earliest childhood in that same monastery the rule of regular discipline, but was also very diligently practised in the arts of writing, chanting, reading and teaching. He too in the days of pope Sergius of blessed memory hastened to Rome, and after tarrying there no small time, learned, copied and brought home all things that he judged needful for himself; moreover, he had also discharged the office of the priesthood for 12 years before. Having therefore been chosen abbot by all the brethren of the two aforesaid monasteries, he straightway took with him some of the brethren and came to abbot Ceolfrid, which was waiting for a ship to take him across the ocean: they inform him whom they had chosen abbot; he answereth: "Thanks be to God," confirmeth the election, and receiveth from Hwaetbert's hands a letter of recommendation to be delivered to the apostolical pope Gregory: some passages whereof we have also thought fit to set down in this work by way of record.

19. "To the most beloved lord in the Lord of all lords, the thrice blessed pope Gregory, Hwaetbert your humble servant, abbot of the monastery of Peter the most blessed chief of the apostles, which is in Saxony, continual health in the Lord.

"I together with the holy brethren which in this place desire with me to bear Christ's most pleasant yoke, to the end they may find rest for their souls, cease

suavissimum Christi iugum portare desiderant, quod te nostris temporibus tam glorificum electionis vas regimini totius ecclesiae praeficere dignatus est, quatinus per hoc quo ipse impleris lumen veritatis et fidei, etiam minores quosque affatim iubare suae pietatis aspergeret. Commendamus autem tuae sanctae benignitati, dilectissime in Christo pater et domine, venerabiles patris nostri dilectissimi canos, Ceolfridi videlicet abbatis, ac nutritoris tutorisque nostrae spiritualis in monastica quiete libertatis et pacis. Et primum quidem gratias agimus sanctae et individuae Trinitati, quod ipse etsi non sine maximo nostro dolore, gemitu, luctu, ac prosecutione lacrimarum a nobis abiit; ad suae tamen diu desideratae quietis gaudia sancta pervenit: dum ea quae iuvenem se adiisse, vidisse atque adorasse semper recordans exultabat: etiam senio defessus beatorum apostolorum devotus limina repetiit. Et post longos amplius XL. annorum labores curasque continuas, quibus monasteriis regendis abbatis iure praefuit, incomparabili virtutis amore quasi nuper ad conversationem vitae caelestis accitus, ultima confectus aetate, et prope iam moriturus, rursus incipit peregrinari pro Christo, quo liberius prisca sollicitudinum secularium spineta, camino spirituali fervens compunctionis ignis absumat. Deinde etiam vestrae paternitati supplicamus, ut quod nos facere non meruimus, vos erga illum ultimae pietatis seduli munus expleatis: pro certo scientes quia etsi vos

not to give thanks to the ordinance of the heavenly judgment, for that it hath vouchsafed to appoint you who are so glorious a vessel of election for the governance of the whole Church in our time, in order that by means of this light of truth and faith wherewith ye are filled, He might shed abundantly the light of His love also on all which are of less account. Now, most beloved father and lord in Christ, we commend to your holy grace the venerable grey hairs of our most beloved father, the abbot Ceolfrid, the nurse and guardian of our spiritual freedom and peace in monastical quietness. And first of all we give thanks to the holy and undivided Trinity that, albeit he has himself departed from us to our exceeding grief amid sighing, lamentation and shedding of tears, yet he hath attained the holy joys of the rest so long desired of him: seeing that even in the weariness of old age he hath devoutly again sought to come to those churches of the blessed apostles, which he remembered with joy to have visited, seen, and worshipped in the time of his youth. And after the long travail of more than 40 years, and the continual cares he had in ruling the monasteries over which he was made abbot, being as it were newly summoned for his unequalled love of virtue to the conversation of heavenly life, in his extreme old age and even now at the point to die, he is beginning again to be a pilgrim for Christ's sake, that so the burning fire of repentance may the more readily consume in the spiritual furnace the former thorns of worldly cares. Next we further entreat your paternity carefully to perform for him the last office of compassion, which we have not been thought worthy to render, being well assured that, albeit his

corpus habetis ipsius, et nos tamen et vos Deo devotum eius spiritum sive in corpore manentem, sive carneis vinculis absolutum, magnum pro nostris excessibus apud supernam pietatem intercessorem habemus et patronum." Et cetera, quae epistolae sequentia continent.

20. Reverso autem domum Huaetberto, advocatur episcopus Acca, et solita illum in abbatis officium benedictione confirmat. Qui inter innumera monasterii iura quae iuvenili sagax solertia recuperabat, hoc in primis omnibus delectabile et gratificum fecit; sustulit ossa Eosteruini abbatis, quae in porticu ingressus ecclesiae beati apostoli Petri erant posita; necnon et ossa Sigfridi abbatis ac magistri quondam sui, quae foris sacrarium ad meridiem fuerant condita, et utraque in una theca sed medio pariete divisa recludens, intus in eadem ecclesia iuxta corpus beati patris Benedicti composuit. Fecit autem haec die natalis Sigfridi, id est, undecimo kalendarum Septembrium, quo etiam die contigit mira Dei providentia, ut venerandus Christi famulus Vuitmer, cuius supra meminimus, excederet, et in loco ubi praedicti abbates prius sepulti fuerant, ipse qui eorum imitator fuerat, conderetur.

21. Christi vero famulus Ceolfridus, ut supradictum est, ad limina beatorum apostolorum tendens, priusquam illo pervenisset, tactus infirmitate diem clausit ultimum. Perveniens namque Lingonas circa horam diei tertiam, decima ipsius diei hora migravit ad

body is with you, yet we as well as you have in his Godfearing spirit (whether abiding in the body or set free from the bonds of the flesh) a mighty intercessor and advocate on behalf of our transgressions before the heavenly mercy." And hereon followeth the rest of the letter.

20. Now on Hwaetbert's return home, bishop Acca was summoned, of whom he was confirmed in the office of abbot with the accustomable benediction. Among the privileges without number, which with the wise exercise of his youthful diligence he recovered for the monastery, this was especially pleasant and grateful to all; he took up the bones of abbot Eosterwine, which had been laid in the porch of entry to the church of the blessed apostle Peter, and also the bones of his sometime master, abbot Sigfrid, which had been buried without the sanctuary toward the south, and placing both in one box (but divided by a middle partition) he laid them within the same church beside the body of the blessed father Benedict. Now this he did on Sigfrid's birthday, that is, on the 22nd day of August, on which day it also happened, by the wonderful providence of God that Witmer died, the venerable servant of Christ, of whom we have already spoken, and there where the aforesaid abbots were already buried, he which had been their follower was himself interred.

21. But Ceolfrid, the servant of Christ, as has been said before, was smitten of sickness as he was hastening to the churches of the blessed apostles, and ended his last day before he arrived there. For reaching Langres about the third hour of the day, he departed to the Lord the 10th hour of the selfsame day, and on the morrow he was buried honour-

Dominum, et crastino in ecclesia beatorum Geminorum martyrum honorifice sepultus est, non solum Anglis genere qui plusquam octoginta numero in eius fuerant comitatu, sed et illius loci accolis pro retardato tam reverendi senis desidero, in lacrimas luctusque solutis. Neque enim facile quisquam lacrimas tenere potuit, videns comites ipsius partim patre amisso coeptum iter agere; partim mutata intentione qua Romam ire desiderant, domum magis qua hunc sepultum nuntiarent reverti; partim ad tumbam defuncti inter eos quorum nec linguam noverant, pro inextinguibili patris affectu residere.

22. Erat autem quando obiit annorum septuaginta quatuor, presbyterii gradu functus annis quadraginta septem, abbatis officium ministrans annis triginta quinque, vel potius annis quadraginta tribus, quia scilicet a primo tempore quo Benedictus in honore beatissimi apostolorum principis suum coepit condere monasterium, ipse illi comes individuus, cooperator et doctor regularis et monasticae institutionis aderat. Cui ne prisci morem rigoris, vel aetatis, vel infirmitatis, vel itineris unquam minueret occasio; ex die quo de monasterio suo profectus abiit usque ad diem quo defunctus est, id est, a pridie nonas Iunias usque ad septimum kalendarum Octobrium diem, per dies cxiv, exceptis canonicis orationum horis, quotidie bis psalterium ex ordine decantare curavit; etiam cum ad hoc per infirmitatem deveniret, ut equitare non valens feretro caballario veheretur, quotidie missa

ably in the church of the blessed Twin martyrs, amidst the tears and lamentations, not only of the Englishmen who to the number of more than 80 had been in his company, but also of the inhabitants of that place grieving that so reverend an old man had been hindered of his desire. Nor indeed was it easy for any man to restrain his tears, when he saw some of Ceolfrid's companions go on the way they had begun, without their father, and other change their purpose of desiring to come to Rome, and rather return home where they might report his burial; while yet other, out of their undying love for their father, remained by the tomb of the dead man in the midst of a people whose language they did not understand.

22. Now at the time of his death he was 74 years of age, 47 of which he had spent in the priest's office, 35 in the discharge of an abbot's duties, or rather 43, because indeed from the first time in which Benedict began to build the monastery in honour of the most blessed chief of the apostles, Ceolfrid was not divided from his company, and was his helper and fellow teacher of the regular and monastical life. And that no occasion either of age or sickness or travel should ever abate the practice of the strictness ordained of old, from the very day he set out to depart from his monastery until the day on which he died, namely, from the fourth day of June until the 25th day of September, for 114 days he had the psalter sung twice daily in due order, not reckoning the canonical hours of prayer; and even when he was grown so weak that he could no longer ride, but had to be carried in a horse-litter, after mass had been sung, he daily made to God

cantata salutaris hostiae Deo munus offerret, excepto uno, quo oceanum navigabat, et tribus ante exitum diebus.

23. Obiit autem septimo kalendarum Octobrium die, anno ab incarnatione Domini septingentesimo sextodecimo, feria sexta, post horam nonam, in pratis memoratae civitatis: sepultus in crastinum ad austrum eiusdem civitatis miliario primo in monasterio Geminorum, astante ac psalmos resonante exercitu non parvo tam Anglorum qui cum eo advenerant, quam monasterii eiusdem vel civitatis incolarum. Sunt autem Gemini martyres in quorum monasterio et ecclesia conditus est, Speusippus, Eleusippus, Meleusippus qui, uno partu matris editi, eadem ecclesiae fide renati, simul cum avia sua Leonilla, dignam loco illi sui martyrii reliquere memoriam, qui piam etiam nobis indignis et nostro parenti opem suae intercessionis et protectionis impendant.

the offering of the saving Host, save only one day, when he was on the ocean, and the three days before his death.

23. Now he died on the 25th day of September in the 716th year of the incarnation of the Lord, on the 6th day of the week, after the 9th hour, in the fields belonging to the afore-named city; and he was buried on the morrow toward the south of the said city at the first milestone, within the monastery of the Twins, in the presence of a great host, not only of the English which had come with him, but also of the brethren of the said monastery, and of the inhabitants of the city, which all sang psalms. Now these Twin martyrs in whose monastery and church he was buried, are Speusippis, Eleusippus, and Meleusippus, which were delivered at one birth and born again in the same faith of the Church, together with their grandmother Leonilla; and they left behind them a memorial of their martyrdom worthy of the spot, and may they bestow even upon us unworthy and upon our father the pitiful help of their intercession and protection!

VENERABILIS BAEDAE
EPISTOLA AD ECGBERCTUM ANTISTITEM

1. Dilectissimo ac reverentissimo antistiti Ecgbercto Baeda famulus Christi salutem.

Memini te hesterno dixisse anno, cum tecum aliquot diebus legendi gratia in monasterio tuo demorarer, quod hoc etiam anno velles, cum in eundem devenires locum, me quoque, ob commune legendi studium, ad tuum accire colloquium. Quod si ita, Deo volente, posset impleri, non opus esset tibi haec per literas scripta dirigere; cum possem liberius ore ad os loquens, quaeque vellem, sive necessaria ducerem, secreta tibi allocutione suggerere. Verum quia hoc ne fieret, superveniens, ut nosti, corporis mei valitudo prohibuit: agere tamen quod potui, erga dilectionem tuam fraternae devotionis intuitu, curavi, mittendo videlicet per literas quod corporaliter veniendo per collocutionem nequiveram. Precorque te per Dominum, ne harum apices literarum arrogantiae supercilium esse suspiceris, sed obsequium potius humilitatis ac pietatis veraciter esse cognoscas.

2. Exhortor itaque tuam, dilectissime in Christo antistes, sanctitatem, ut gradum sacrosanctum quem tibi Auctor graduum et spiritualium largitor charis-

---

[1] Brother of Eadbert, king of Northumbria, and was placed in a monastery by his father Eata, while yet an infant. He became bishop of York in 734 and in 735 received the pall and became archbishop. This letter seems to have been Bede's last work, about 30 years, as he says, after king Aldfrid's death, which took place in 705.

THE VENERABLE BEDE'S EPISTLE TO BISHOP EGBERT

1. To the most beloved and most reverend bishop Egbert,[1] Bede, the servant of Christ, greeting.

I remember that last year,[2] when I tarried with you for some days in your monastery for the purpose of study, you said that on your coming to the same place this year, you would invite me there again, that we might study and take counsel together. And if so it might have been fulfilled of the will of God, there would have been no need for me to write this letter unto you: for speaking face to face I could have set before you in private conference more freely all that I wished or thought it necessary to say. But albeit, as you know, a visitation of bodily sickness hath hindered this from coming to pass, yet out of regard to the brotherly devotion in me to meet your affection, I have endeavoured to do what I might by writing in a letter that which I could not communicate in bodily presence. And I implore you, in the name of the Lord, not to suspect the characters of this letter to shew a wilful arrogance, but to know that they do truthfully offer the service of humility and love.

2. Wherefore, O bishop dearly beloved in Christ, I exhort your holiness that you be mindful with holiness of practice and teaching to maintain the holy dignity with which the Author of all dignity

[2] 733.

matum committere dignatus est, sacrosancta et operatione et doctrina confirmare memineris. Neutra enim haec virtus sine altera rite potest impleri: si aut is qui bene vivit docendi officium negligit, aut recte docens antistes rectam exercere operationem contemnit. Qui autem utrumque veraciter agit, profecto talis servus adventum Domini sui gratulabundus expectat, sperans se citius auditurum. "Euge serve bone et fidelis, quia super pauca fuisti fidelis, supra multa te constituam: intra in gaudium Domini tui." Si quis vero, quod absit, gradu episcopatus accepto, nec seipsum a malis actibus bene vivendo, nec subditam sibi plebem castigando, vel admonendo corrigere curat: quid huic veniente Domino, hora qua non sperat, eventurum sit, evangelica manifeste sententia declarat, qua dicitur ad inutilem servum: "Eiicite in tenebras exteriores, ibi erit fletus et stridor dentium."

3. Ante omnia sane tuae sanctae paternitati suadeo, ut ab otiosis te confabulationibus, obtrectationibus, ceterisque linguae indomitae contagiis pontificali dignitate coerceas: divinis autem eloquiis ac meditationibus scripturarum linguam simul et mentem occupes, et maxime legendis beati Pauli apostoli epistolis ad Timotheum et Titum, sed et verbis sanctissimi papae Gregorii, quibus de vita simul et vitiis rectorum sive in libro Regulae Pastoralis seu in homeliis Evangelii multum curiose disseruit, ut

---

[1] Matt. xxv. 21. [2] The laity of the diocese.
[3] Matt. xxv. 30.

and the Giver of spiritual gifts hath vouchsafed to put in your keeping. For neither of these virtues may duly be fulfilled apart from the other: if either the man of good life neglect the office of teacher, or the bishop which teacheth rightly despise the practice of good works. But such a servant as veritably doeth both these things, assuredly awaiteth His Lord's coming with thankfulness, and hopeth shortly to hear the words:[1] "Well done, good and faithful servant: because thou hast been faithful over a few things, I will set thee over many things: enter thou into the joy of thy Lord." But if, which God forbid, anyone, having taken the dignity of bishop, doth not endeavour either to reform himself from evil courses by right living, or by punishment or warning to amend the people[2] that is subject unto him: what shall befall this man, when his Lord cometh in an hour that he looketh not for, is plainly declared in the word of the Gospel where it is said to the unprofitable servant:[3] "Cast ye him into outer darkness: there shall be weeping and gnashing of teeth."

3. Above all things I beseech you well, holy father, to keep yourself with the worthiness that becometh a bishop from idle gossip and slander and all the other plagues of an unruly tongue; but employ both lips and mind with divine discourses and study of the Scripture, and especially with reading the epistles of the blessed apostle Paul to Timothy and Titus, and, moreover, the words of the most holy pope Gregory, wherein he hath very diligently dealt with both the life and offences of rulers, whether in his book of Pastoral Care or in his homilies on the Gospel; that your speech, being always seasoned with the

sermo tuus semper sapientiae sale conditus, eminentior vulgari locutione, ac divino auditui dignior elucescat. Sicut enim indecens est, si vasa altaris sacrosancta vulgaribus unquam usibus ac vilibus profanentur officiis, ita perversum omni modo ac miserum est, si is qui ad consecranda in altari dominica sacramenta ordinatus est, nunc quidem eisdem conficiendis sacramentis Domino famulaturus assistat, nunc egressus ecclesiam ipso ore eisdemque manibus quibus paulo ante sacra tractaverat, repente frivola loqui vel agere Dominum offensurus incipiat.

4. Ad custodiendam linguae vel operis munditiam, cum lectione divina, etiam societas eorum qui Christo fideli devotione famulantur, plurimum iuvat. Ut si quando vel lingua lascivire, vel operatio prava mihi subrepere coeperit, mox sociorum fidelium manu ne cadere valeam sustenter. Quod cum omnibus Dei famulis sibimet ita prospicere utillimum sit, quanto magis illi gradui qui non suimet tantummodo curam agere, sed etiam erga commissam sibi ecclesiam necesse habet studium salutis impendere; iuxta illum qui dixit, "praeter ea quae extrinsecus sunt, instantia mea quotidiana, sollicitudo omnium ecclesiarum. Quis infirmatur, et ego non infirmor? Quis scandalizatur, et ego non uror?" Quod non ita loquor, quasi te aliter facere sciam, sed quia de quibusdam episcopis fama vulgatum est, quod ipsi ita Christo serviant, ut nullos secum alicuius religionis aut continentiae viros habeant: sed potius

---

[1] 2 Cor. xi. 28, 29.

salt of wisdom, may shine forth above the communication of the multitude, and be more worthy of the hearing of God. For as it is unseemly that the holy vessels of the altar should ever be defiled with mean and common use, so it is utterly wrong and lamentable that he who hath been ordained to consecrate the Lord's sacrament upon the altar should at one moment stand to serve the Lord in the celebration thereof, and the next moment pass straight from the church and begin to sin against the Lord, by using for vain speech or act the very same lips and hands with the which a little before he had been occupied with holy things.

4. Beside sacred study, the company also of men which serve Christ with faithful devotion is of great help in keeping pure lips and clean hands. Wherefore, if at any time my tongue begin to wax wanton, or corrupt dealing to creep into my heart, I may presently be saved, lest I should fall, by the hands of faithful companions. And as it is very expedient for all the servants of God thus to look to themselves, how much more is it so for that degree which is bound not only to beware of itself, but also to be zealous for the safety of the church committed to its charge; according to him which said:[1] "Beside those things which are without, that which cometh upon me daily, the care of all the churches. Who is weak, and I am not weak? Who is offended, and I burn not"? Now I do not say this as though I should know you to be acting otherwise, but because it is commonly reported of some bishops that they in such wise serve Christ, that they have none about them which are men of any godliness or temperance; but rather men which are given up to

qui risui, iocis, fabulis, commessationibus et ebrietatibus, ceterisque vitae remissioris illecebris subigantur, et qui magis quotidie ventrem dapibus, quam mentem sacrificiis coelestibus pascant. Quos tua sancta auctoritate si alicubi repereris velim corrigas, moneasque illos tales suae conversationis diurnae sive nocturnae testes habere, qui et actione Deo digna et exhortatione congrua prodesse populis, ac spiritale ipsorum antistitum opus iuvare sufficiant. Lege enim Actus Apostolorum, et videbis, referente beato Luca, quales secum comites apostoli Paulus et Barnabas habuerint, quid etiam ipsi, ubicunque devenissent, operis egerint. Statim namque ut civitates vel synagogas ingressi sunt, verbum Dei praedicare, et per omnia disseminare curabant. Quod etiam te, dilectissimum mihi caput, sagaciter cupiam, ubicunque potes implere. In hoc namque officium a Domino electus, in hoc consecratus es, ut verbum evangelizes virtute magna, praebente tibi auxilium ipso Rege virtutum Domino nostro Jesu Christo. Quod ita rite perficies si, ubicunque perveneris, mox collectis ad te eiusdem loci incolis, verbum illis exhortationis exhibueris, simul et exemplum vivendi una cum omnibus qui tecum venerint quasi caelestis militiae ductor ostenderis.

5. Et quia latiora sunt spatia locorum, quae ad gubernacula tuae dioecesis pertinent, quam ut solus per omnia discurrere, et in singulis viculis atque agellis verbum Dei praedicare, etiam anni totius

laughter, jesting, tales, revellings, drunkenness and the other allurements of dissolute living; which daily rather feed their belly with feasts than their mind with heavenly sacrifices. Of the which sort if you find any anywhere, I would have you amend them with your holy authority, and admonish them to provide such witnesses of their conversation by day and night as, through conduct worthy of God and exhortations agreeing thereto, may be able to profit the people and further their own spiritual work as bishops. For read the Acts of the Apostles, and you will see from the report of blessed Luke, what sort of companions the apostles Paul and Barnabas had with them, and what sort of work also they themselves did wherever they came. For, as soon as they entered into cities and synagogues, they endeavoured to preach and spread abroad everywhere the word of God. And this, my beloved friend, I wish you also to execute wisely, wherever you are able. For to this duty were you chosen of the Lord, to this were you consecrated, namely, to preach the Gospel with great power by the enabling help of our Lord Jesus Himself, the King of powers. And this you will rightly perform if, wherever you come, you presently gather together unto you the inhabitants of the said place, and offer them the word of exhortation, at the same time holding up, with all your company, the example of good living, like a true captain in the heavenly warfare.

5. And because the region over which the governance of your diocese extendeth is too wide for you to pass through it everywhere yourself alone and preach the word of God in the several villages and homesteads, even within the full course of a year, it

emenso curriculo, sufficias, necessarium satis est, ut plures tibi sacri operis adiutores adsciscas, presbyteros videlicet ordinando, atque instituendo doctores, qui in singulis viculis praedicando Dei verbo, et consecrandis mysteriis caelestibus, ac maxime peragendis sacri baptismatis officiis, ubi opportunitas ingruerit, assistant. In qua videlicet praedicatione populis exhibenda, hoc prae ceteris omni instantia procurandum arbitror, ut fidem catholicam quae apostolorum symbolo continetur, et Dominicam orationem quam sancti Evangelii nos Scriptura edocet, omnium qui ad tuum regimen pertinent, memoriae radicitus infigere cures. Et quidem omnes qui Latinam linguam lectionis usu didicerunt, etiam haec optime didicisse certissimum est: sed idiotas, hoc est, eos qui propriae tantum linguae notitiam habent, haec ipsa sua lingua discere, ac sedulo decantare facito. Quod non solum de laicis, id est, in populari adhuc vita constitutis, verum etiam de clericis sive monachis qui Latinae sunt linguae expertes fieri oportet. Sic enim fit, ut coetus omnis fidelium quomodo fidelis esse, qua se firmitate credendi contra immundorum spirituum certamina munire atque armare debeat, discat: sic, ut chorus omnis Deo supplicantium quid maxime a Divina clementia quaeri oporteat, agnoscat. Propter quod et ipse multis saepe sacerdotibus idiotis haec utraque, et symbolum videlicet, et Dominicam orationem in linguam Anglorum translatam obtuli. Nam et sanc-

---

[1] *σύμβολον*, the watchword or sign by which soldiers of the Christian army recognise one another, Pl.

[2] Anglo-Saxon versions of the Creed and Lord's Prayer are extant, but not in the Northumbrian dialect.

is very necessary that you should take unto you many helpers in the holy work; to wit, by ordaining priests and appointing teachers, which in every village shall aid you with preaching the word of God and consecrating the heavenly mysteries, and especially with performing the rite of holy baptism, when occasion shall arise. And in setting forth this preaching to the people I think that above all else you must endeavour with all diligence to see that the catholic faith which is contained in the Apostles' Creed,[1] and the Lord's Prayer, which is taught us in the Scripture of the Holy Gospel, be rooted deeply in the memory of all which belong unto your rule: It is true that it is most sure that these things have become perfectly known to those who have been taught to read the Latin tongue; but do you cause them to be known and constantly repeated in their own tongue by those that are unlearned, that is, by them who have knowledge only of their proper tongue. And this should be done, not only as touching the laity, that is to say, them which are still established in the life of the world, but also as touching the clergy or monks which are ignorant of the Latin tongue. For by this means it cometh to pass that the whole body of believers shall learn how they should believe, and fortify and arm themselves by steadfast belief against the assaults of unclean spirits: by this means it cometh that the whole band of them that worship God shall understand what most they are bound to seek of the Divine mercy. For the which reason I have myself too ofttimes given to unlearned priests both these things, to wit, the Creed and the Lord's Prayer translated into the English tongue.[2] For this the

tus antistes Ambrosius hoc de fide loquens admonet, ut verba symboli matutinis semper horis fideles quique decantent, et hoc se quasi antidoto spiritali contra diaboli venena quae illis interdiu vel noctu astu maligno obicere posset, praemuniant. Orationem vero Dominicam saepius decantari ipsa etiam nos consuetudo sedulae deprecationis ac genuum flexionis docuit.

6. Quod si haec ut suggerimus in regendis pascendisque Christi ovibus tua pastoralis auctoritas perfecerit, dici non potest quantum tibi supernae mercedis apud Pastorem pastorum in futuro praeparaveris. Quanto enim rariora huius sacratissimi operis in episcopis nostrae gentis exempla reperis, tanto altiora singularis meriti praemia recipies; utpote qui populum Dei per crebram symboli vel orationis sacrae decantationem ad intellectum, amorem, spem, fidem, et inquisitionem eorundem quae decantantur caelestium donorum, paterna pietate ac sollicitudine provocatum accenderis. Sicut e contrario si commissum tibi a Domino negotium minus diligenter compleveris, pro retentione talenti cum servo nequam et pigro partem es recepturus in futuro: maxime si temporalia ab illis commoda requirere atque accipere praesumpseris, quibus nulla caelestis beneficii dona rependere probaveris. Cum enim Dominus mittens ad evangelizandum discipulos dixisset: "Euntes

---

[1] *De Virginibus*, iii. 4, 20.

holy bishop Ambrose,[1] speaking concerning the faith, doth advise, that the words of the Creed should ever be repeated of all the faithful at matins, and that they should arm themselves as with a kind of spiritual antidote against the poison which the devil with malicious cunning casteth before them by day and night. Moreover, we ourselves too have been taught more often repetition of the Lord's Prayer by our own custom of constant supplication and bending of the knees.

6. Wherefore if, as we set before you, of your pastoral authority you shall bring these things to pass in the ruling and feeding of Christ's sheep, it cannot be told how great a heavenly recompense you will have laid up to receive hereafter at the hands of the Shepherd of shepherds. For the fewer examples that you find of this most hallowed work among the bishops of our nation, the higher will be the reward of singular well-doing which you shall obtain; as being one which stirred up of fatherly love and affection hath enkindled God's people, through frequent repetition of the Creed and the Lord's Prayer, to understanding, love, hope, faith, and searching after the heavenly gifts therein rehearsed. Just as contrariwise, if you are careless in perfecting the business committed to you of the Lord, you shall hereafter have your portion with the wicked and slothful servant in recompense for keeping back the talent: especially if you have been bold to ask for and receive temporal benefits from those upon whom you have not thought good to bestow any gifts of the heavenly bounty. For when the Lord, in sending out His disciples to preach the Gospel, had said: " And as ye go, preach, saying

autem praedicate dicentes quia appropinquat regnum coelorum": paulo post subiunxit, dicens: "Gratis accepistis, gratis date; nolite possidere aurum, neque argentum." Si ergo illos gratis Evangelium praedicare iussit, neque aurum vel argentum, vel aliquid pecuniae temporalis ab eis quibus praedicabant accipere permisit: quid rogo illis qui his contraria gerunt periculi immineat?

7. Attende quid gravissimi sceleris illi commiserint qui et terrena ab auditoribus suis lucra diligentissime requirere, et pro eorum salute aeterna nihil omnino praedicando, vel exhortando, vel increpando, laboris impendere contendunt. Sollicite atque intentione curiosa, antistes dilectissime, perpende. Audivimus enim, et fama est, quia multae villae ac viculi nostrae gentis in montibus sint inaccessis ac saltibus dumosis positi, ubi nunquam multis transeuntibus annis sit visus antistes, qui ibidem aliquid ministerii aut gratiae caelestis exhibuerit; quorum tamen ne unus quidem a tributis antistiti reddendis esse possit immunis: nec solum talibus locis desit antistes qui manus impositione baptizatos confirmet, verum etiam omnis doctor qui eos vel fidei veritatem vel discretionem bonae ac malae actionis edoceat, absit. Sicque fit, ut episcoporum quidam non solum gratis non evangelizent, vel manus fidelibus imponant; verum etiam, quod gravius est, accepta ab auditoribus suis pecunia, quam Dominus prohibuit, opus verbi quod dominus iussit exercere contemnant:

---

[1] Matt. x. 7–9.

that the kingdom of heaven is at hand ";[1] a little after he added: " Freely ye have received, freely give: provide neither gold nor silver ": If then He bade them preach the Gospel freely, and did not suffer them to take either gold or silver, or any temporal profit, from those unto whom they preached; what peril, I ask, should threaten them that do the contrary?

7. Consider the very grievous sin committed by them that are most diligent to seek earthly profit from their hearers, but yet strive not to spend any labour at all in preaching or exhortation or reproof to win their eternal salvation. Weigh this carefully and with heedful attention, my beloved bishop. For we have heard, and it is common report, that there are many hamlets and steadings of our nation, lying amongst inaccessible mountains and bosky valleys, where in the passing of many years no bishop hath been seen, which should perform some ministerial act or bestow some heavenly grace; and yet that not one of them may be exempted from paying tribute[2] to the bishop; and that such places are not only without a bishop to confirm the baptized by the laying on of hands, but also without any teacher to instruct them either in the true faith or in the difference between right and wrong. Hence it cometh to pass, that some bishops not only do not preach the Gospel freely or lay their hands upon the faithful, but also (which is yet more grievous) by taking from their hearers the money which the Lord forbade, despise to do the work of the word which He commanded:

[2] What the dues were Bede does not say. The laws of Ini speak of Church-scots to be paid at Martinmas, under penalty, Pl.

quum Deo dilectus pontifex Samuel, longe aliter fecisse omni populo teste legatur. "Itaque conversatus," inquit, "coram vobis ab adolescentia mea usque ad diem hanc, ecce praesto sum, loquimini de me coram Domino, et coram Christo eius, utrum bovem alicuius tulerim, an asinum, si quempiam calumniatus sum, si oppressi aliquem, si de manu cuiusquam munus accepi; et contemnam illud hodie, restituamque vobis." Et dixerunt: "Non es calumniatus nos, neque oppressisti, neque tulisti de manu alicuius quippiam." Cuius innocentiae ac iustitiae merito, inter primos populi Dei duces et sacerdotes annumerari, atque in precibus suis superno auditu atque alloquio dignus existere meruit, dicente Psalmographo: "Moyses et Aaron in sacerdotibus eius, et Samuel inter eos qui invocant nomen eius; invocabant Dominum et ipse exaudiebat eos, in columna nubis loquebatur ad eos."

8. Si autem aliquid utilitatis fidelibus conferri manus impositione, qua Spiritus Sanctus accipitur, credimus et confitemur: constat e contrario, quod haec ipsa utilitas eis quibus manus impositio defuerit, abest. Cuius nimirum privatio boni ad quos amplius quam ad ipsos respicit antistites, qui illorum se promittunt esse praesules, quibus spiritalis officium praesulatus exhibere aut negligunt aut nequeunt? Cuius totius facinoris nulla magis quam avaritia causa est. Contra quam disputans apostolus, in quo Christus loquebatur, aiebat: "Radix omnium malo-

---

[1] 1 Sam. xii. 3, 4.
[2] Psalm xcix. 6, 7.
[3] 1 Tim. vi. 10.

although we read that Samuel the high priest beloved of God acted far otherwise by the testimony of all the people.[1] "Wherefore having walked before you," he saith, "from my childhood unto this day, behold, here I am: witness against me before the Lord and before His Anointed, whether I have taken any man's ox or ass, if I have defrauded any, if I have oppressed any, if I have received a bribe at any man's hand: and I will repent it this day and make restitution to you." And they said: "Thou hast not defrauded us, nor oppressed us, neither hast thou taken aught of any man's hand." And by the deserving of his innocency and righteousness he was thought worthy to be reckoned among the foremost leaders and priests of the people of God, and to have hearing and speech from above when he prayed, as saith the Psalmist:[2] "Moses and Aaron among his priests and Samuel among them that call upon His name; they called upon the Lord and He heard them, in the pillar of cloud He spake unto them."

8. Now if we believe and confess that some advantage is conveyed to believers by the laying on of hands, whereby the Holy Spirit is received: it is contrariwise plain that this selfsame advantage is lacking to them unto whom the laying on of hands is not granted. And who without doubt are to give account for this withholding of benefit more than those very bishops, which either omit or are unable to exercise the office of spiritual governance over them whose governors they promise to be? And of all this evil-doing nothing is more cause than greed. Contending against the which the apostle in whom Christ spake, said:[3] "The love of money is the

rum est cupiditas." Et rursum: "Neque avari," inquit, "regnum Dei possidebunt." Quum enim antistes dictante amore pecuniae maiorem populi partem, quam ulla ratione per totum anni spatium peragrare praedicando aut circuire valuerit, in nomen sui praesulatus assumpserit, satis exitiale et sibimet ipsi, et illis quibus falso praesulis nomine praelatus est, comprobatur concinnare periculum.

9. Haec tuae sanctati, dilectissime antistes, paucis de calamitate qua nostra gens miserrime laborat insinuans, obsecro sedulus, ut haec quae perversissime agi conspicis, quantum vales ad rectam vitae normam revocare contendas. Habes enim, ut credo, promptissimum tam iusti laboris adiutorem, regem videlicet Ceoluulfum, qui et pro insita sibi dilectione religionis, quicquid ad regulam pietatis pertinet, firma protinus intentione adiuvare curabit, et maxime illa quae tu quum sis propinquus illius amantissimus bona coeperis, ipse ut perficiantur opitulabitur. Quapropter velim solerter illum admoneas, ut in diebus vestris statum nostrae gentis ecclesiasticum in melius quam hactenus fuerat instaurare curet. Quod non alio magis ut mihi videtur potest ordine perfici, quam si plures nostrae genti consecrentur antistites, exemplumque sequamini legislatoris, qui quum solus iurgia ac pondus Israeliticae plebis sustinere non posset, elegit sibi divino adiustus consilio, et consecravit septuaginta seniores quorum ope atque consilio impositum

[1] 1 Cor. vi. 10. [2] Cousin.

root of all evil." And again:[1] "The covetous," he saith, "shall not inherit the kingdom of God." For when a bishop moved of the love of money hath taken under title of his prelacy more people than he can by any means within the space of one year pass through and preach unto, or go about and visit, he is plainly shewn to be the cause of a peril which shall be right ruinous both to himself and to those over whom he hath been preferred with the false title of prelate.

9. In speaking thus in few words, beloved bishop, to your holiness touching the calamity under which our nation so miserably suffereth, I earnestly entreat you to strive with all your might to call back to the right rule of life such things as you plainly see to be most corruptly done. For you have, as I believe a most ready helper for this righteous travail in king Ceolwulf, which out of the love of religion engrafted in him will endeavour forthwith of strong purpose to further whatsoever appertaineth to the rule of godliness, and especially will of himself forward the accomplishment of the good work which you, being his well-beloved kinsman,[2] have begun. Wherefore I would have you admonish him carefully that in this your day he shall endeavour to bring the ecclesiastical life of our nation into a better state than heretofore. And I see none other way whereby this may better be brought about than by consecrating more bishops for our people, following the example of the lawgiver, who, when he could not by himself endure the burden of the strifes of the people of Israel, with the help of the divine counsel, chose out for himself and consecrated 70 elders, by whose aid and counsel he might more

sibi onus ferre levius posset. Quis enim non videat quanto sit melius tam enorme pondus ecclesiastici regiminis in plures, qui hoc dispertitum facilius ferant, dividi, quam unum sub fasce quem portare non possit opprimi. Nam et sanctus papa Gregorius, quum de fide nostrae gentis quae adhuc futura et conservanda erat in Christo ad beatissimum archiepiscopum Augustinum missis literis disputaret, duodecim in ea episcopos, postquam ad fidem venirent, ordinandos esse decrevit; in quibus Eburacensis antistes, accepto a sede apostolica pallio, metropolitanus esse deberet. Quem profecto numerum episcoporum velim modo tua sancta paternitas, patrocinante praesidio piissimi ac Deo dilecti regis praefati, solerter implere contendat, quatenus abundante numero magistrorum, perfectius ecclesia Christi in his quae ad cultum sacrae religionis pertinent, instituatur. Et quidem novimus quia per incuriam regum praecedentium donationesque stultissimas factum est, ut non facile locus vacans ubi sedes episcopalis nova fieri debeat, inveniri valeat.

10. Quapropter commodum duxerim, habito maiori concilio et consensu, pontificali simul et regali edicto, prospiciatur locus aliquis monasteriorum ubi sedes episcopalis fiat. Et ne forte abbas vel monachi huic decreto contraire ac resistere tentaverint, detur illis licentia, ut de suis ipsi eligant eum qui episcopus

---

[1] *Eccl. Hist.*, i. 29.

[2] The northern sees were founded in connection with monasteries, Pl.

easily bear the weight that was laid upon him. For who cannot see how much better it is for so vast a burden of ecclesiastical governance to be shared among a number which can bear it more readily when thus distributed, than for one man to be overwhelmed beneath a load which he cannot carry? For the holy pope Gregory too in a letter[1] that he wrote to the most blessed archbishop Augustine concerning the keeping of the faith of our people in Christ, before it had been yet received of them, appointed that, as soon as they were come to the faith, 12 bishops should be there ordained, among whom the bishop of York was to be metropolitan, receiving his pall from the apostolic see. And I could truly be content now that your holy paternity, with the protection of the help of the aforesaid most godly king beloved of God, shall diligently endeavour to complete this number of bishops, in order that through an increase in the number of its masters, the Church of Christ may be more perfectly furnished in the things which appertain to the worship of our holy religion. All the same we know that by reason of the neglect of former kings and the exceeding folly of their grants, a void place may not easily be found wherein the see of a new bishopric shall be made.

10. Wherefore I should deem it convenient if, after holding a greater council and obtaining its consent, by an edict of the bishop as well as of the king, some place belonging to the monasteries be looked for, where the see of a bishopric may be had.[2] And lest perchance the abbot and monks make endeavour to withstand and resist such a decree, let them have leave themselves to choose

ordinetur, et adiacentium locorum quotquot ad eandem dioecesim pertineant, una cum ipso monasterio curam gerat episcopalem: aut si forte in ipso monasterio qui episcopus ordinari debeat inveniri nequeat, in ipsorum tamen iuxta statuta canonum pendeat examine, qui de sua dioecesi ordinetur antistes. Quod si hoc, ita ut suggerimus, Domino adiuvante, perfeceris, facillime etiam, ut arbitramur, hoc obtinebis, ut iuxta decreta sedis apostolicae Eboracensis ecclesia metropolitanum possit habere pontificem. Ac si opus esse visum fuerit, ut tali monasterio, causa episcopatus suscipiendi, amplius aliquid locorum ac possessionum augeri debeat, sunt loca innumera, ut novimus omnes, in monasteriorum ascripta vocabulum, sed nihil prorsus monasticae conversationis habentia: e quibus velim aliqua de luxuria ad castitatem, de vanitate ad veritatem,[1] de intemperantia ventris et gulae ad continentiam et pietatem cordis synodica auctoritate transferantur, atque in adiutorium sedis episcopalis quae nuper ordinari debeat assumantur.

11. Et quia huiusmodi maxima et plurima sunt loca, quae, ut vulgo dici solet, neque Deo neque hominibus utilia sunt, quia videlicet neque regularis secundum Deum ibidem vita servatur, neque illa milites sive comites secularium potestatum qui gentem nostram a barbaris defendant possident: si quis in eisdem ipsis locis pro necessitate temporum sedem episcopatus constituat, non culpam praevaricationis

[1] for *temperantiam*, Pl.

---

[1] This shews that Egbert was not yet archbishop of York when Bede wrote this letter.

one of their number to be ordained bishop and have the episcopal charge over all the places adjoining, which appertain to the same diocese, as well as over the said monastery: or, if it shall happen that in the said monastery none can be found meet to be ordained bishop, yet in accordance with the ordinances of the canons let it still rest with them to settle upon enquiry who from their diocese shall be ordained bishop. And if, with the Lord's help, you do this as we do signify, you will, as we think, very easily obtain that the church of York may have its metropolitan pontiff,[1] in accordance with the decrees of the apostolic see. And if, in order to maintain a bishopric, it shall be found necessary that such a monastery receive some farther increase of territory or possessions, there are, as we all know, innumerable places reckoned under the name of monasteries which yet have no mark at all of monastical life and conversation: of the which I would have some brought over, by authority of the synod, from wantonness to chastity, from vanity to verity, from greed and gluttony to continence and godliness of heart, and used for the furtherance of the episcopal see which is newly to be established.

11. And because there are very many large places of this sort which, as it is commonly reported, are serviceable neither to God nor man, to wit, because neither is the regular life according to God kept in them, nor do they have in them soldiers or thanes of the secular powers to defend our nation from barbarians:[2] if anyone, to meet present needs, set up the see of a bishopric in these same places, he shall not be held to come under guilt of transgression,

[2] Such as the Picts.

incurrere, sed opus virtutis magis agere probabitur. Quomodo enim in peccatum reputari potest, si iniusta principum iudicia recto meliorum principum examine corrigantur: ac mendax stilus scribarum iniquorum discreta prudentium sacerdotum sententia deleatur ac redigatur in nihilum, iuxta exemplum sacrae historiae, quae tempora regum Iudae a David et Salomone usque ad ultimum Zedechiam describens, nonnullos quidem in eis religiosos, sed plures reprobos extitisse designat, vicibusque alternantibus nunc impios bonorum qui ante se fuerant facta reprobare, nunc e contrario iustos impiorum qui se praecesserant gesta nociva, prout iustum erat, iuvante se Dei spiritu, per prophetas sanctos ac sacerdotes omni instantia correxisse; iuxta illud beati Esaiae praecipientis atque dicentis, " Dissolve obligationes [1] violentarum commutationum. Dimitte confractos in remissionem, et omnem conscriptionem iniquam disrumpe." Quo exemplo, tuam quoque sanctitatem decet cum religioso rege nostrae gentis, irreligiosa, et iniqua priorum gesta atque scripta convellere, et ea quae provinciae nostrae, sive secundum Deum, sive secundum seculum sint utilia, prospicere: ne nostris temporibus vel religione cessante, amor timorque interni deseratur inspectoris, vel rarescente copia militiae secularis, absint qui fines nostros a barbarica incursione tueantur. Quod enim turpe est dicere, tot sub nomine monasteriorum loca hi qui monasticae vitae prorsus sunt expertes in suam

[1] for *colligationes*, Pl.

---

[1] Isai. lviii. 6.

but rather to be performing a virtuous act. For how can it be reckoned sinful if the unrighteous judgments of some princes be amended with the right judgment of better princes, and the lying pen of unjust scribes be blotted out and brought to naught by the sober utterance of wise priests; after the example of sacred history which, in setting forth the times of the kings of Judah from David and Solomon down to the last king Zedekiah, declareth that, while some among them were religious, yet many more were reprobate, and that succeeding one another in turn, at one time the wicked did reject the acts of the good which had been before them, whereas at another time contrariwise the just, as was right, with the help of the spirit of God, by the means of the holy prophets and priests, did zealously correct the harmful doings of their unrighteous predecessors; according to that bidding of the blessed Isaiah which saith:[1] "Loose the bonds of exchanges made by force. Set free them that are oppressed, and tear up every unjust record of agreement." Following which example, it beseemeth your holiness also, with the help of the devout king of our nation, to tear in pieces the ungodly and unrighteous acts and charters of former princes, and to provide such things as may benefit our province, whether according to God or according to this world: lest either religion die out in our day and with it be laid aside the love and fear of the inward overseer, or else the number of our secular armies diminish and there be none to defend our coasts from the invasion of barbarians. For though it is a shame to speak of, yet, as you yourselves very well know, these men, which are utterly ignorant of the monastical life, have made

ditionem acceperunt, sicut ipsi melius nostis, ut omnino desit locus, ubi filii nobilium aut emeritorum militum possessionem accipere possint: ideoque vacantes ac sine coniugio, exacto tempore pubertatis, nullo continentiae proposito perdurent, atque hanc ob rem vel patriam suam pro qua militare debuerant trans mare abeuntes relinquant; vel maiore scelere atque impudentia, qui propositum castitatis non habent, luxuriae ac fornicationi deserviant, neque ab ipsis sacratis Deo virginibus abstineant.

12. At alii graviore adhuc flagitio, quum sint ipsi laici et nullius vitae regularis vel usu exerciti, vel amore praediti, data regibus pecunia, emunt sibi sub praetextu monasteriorum construendorum territoria in quibus suae liberius vacent libidini, et haec insuper in ius sibi haereditarium edictis regalibus faciunt ascribi, ipsas quoque literas privilegiorum suorum quasi veraciter Deo dignas, pontificum, abbatum et potestatum seculi obtinent subscriptione confirmari. Sicque usurpatis sibi agellulis sive vicis, liberi exinde a divino simul et humano servitio, suis tantum inibi desideriis laici monachis imperantes deserviunt: imo non monachos ibi congregant, sed quoscunque ob culpam inobedientiae veris expulsos monasteriis alicubi forte oberrantes invenerint, aut evocare monasteriis ipsi valuerint; vel certe quos

[1] Cf. *Hist. Abb.* § 11. [2] Renegade monks.

subject unto them so many places under the name of monasteries, that there is no place at all where the sons of nobles, or of soldiers which have ended their service, can find a possession; and accordingly when they have reached man's estate they continue in idleness and unmarried, without any purpose of abstinence; and for this reason either pass oversea and leave their native land for which they ought to fight, or with yet greater sin and shamelessness they which have no purpose of chastity abandon themselves to fornication and lust, and refrain not even from the virgins dedicated to God.

12. But there are others guilty of yet more grievous sin; which, albeit themselves laymen and neither accustomed to any rule of religious life nor having any love thereof, give money to kings and, under pretence of founding monasteries, buy for themselves lands where they may more freely have opportunity for their lust, and these beside they get assigned unto them by royal edicts for an hereditary possession,[1] and procure too even letters of their privileges (as if such were truly worthy of God) with confirmation of the hands of pontiffs, abbots and the powers of the world. And thus they take possession of plots of land or villages, and henceforth are quit of service to God as well as man, and being laymen exercise lordship over monks therein, and are obedient only to their own lusts: nay, rather, it is not monks that they assemble there, but either any such as having been driven out of true monasteries for the sin of disobedience, they chance to find wandering to and fro, or those whom they themselves have power to entice from their houses;[2] or else at any rate those of their own following

ipsi de suis satellitibus ad suscipiendam tonsuram promissa sibi obedientia monachica invitare quiverint. Horum distortis cohortibus, suas quas instruxere cellas implent, multumque informi atque inaudito spectaculo, iidem ipsi viri modo coniugis ac liberorum procreandorum curam gerunt, modo exsurgentes de cubilibus quid intra septa monasteriorum geri debeat, sedula intentione pertractant. Quin etiam suis coniugibus simili impudentia [1] construendis, ut ipsi aiunt, monasteriis loca conquirunt, quae pari stultitia cum sint laicae, famularum se Christi permittunt esse rectrices. Quibus apte convenit illud vulgi proverbium: quia vespae favos quidem facere cum [2] possint, non tamen in his mella, sed potius venena thesaurizent.

13. Sic per annos circiter triginta, hoc est, ex quo Aldfrid rex humanis rebus ablatus est, provincia nostra vesano illo errore dementata est, ut nullus pene exinde praefectorum extiterit qui non huiusmodi sibi monasterium in diebus suae praefecturae comparaverit, suamque simul coniugem pari reatu nocivi mercatus astrinxerit: ac praevalente pessima consuetudine ministri quoque regis ac famuli idem facere sategerint. Atque ita ordine perverso innumeri sint inventi, qui se abbates pariter et praefectos sive ministros aut famulos regis appellant, qui etsi aliquid vitae monasterialis ediscere laici non experiendo sed audiendo potuerint, a persona tamen illa ac professione quae hanc docere debeat, sunt fun-

[1] for *imprudentia*, Pl. [2] sp. Pl.

---

[1] Jerem. v. 30.

whom they may bring to receive the tonsure with promise of monastical obedience to themselves. With these perverse companies they fill the cells that they have built, and (a wonderful and horrible thing to behold!)[1] the very same men are at one time occupied with their wives and begetting of children, and at another, rising from their beds, they diligently set themselves to be occupied with necessary business within the bounds of the monasteries. Nay, with like shamelessness they even seek out places, as they themselves say, for founding monasteries for their wives, which with equal folly, albeit they are but lay women, suffer themselves to become rulers of the handmaids of Christ. To the which the common proverb fittingly applieth: that wasps, though they may indeed build cells, yet do they not store up honey but rather poison therein.

13. Thus for about 30 years, from the time, that is, when king Aldfrid was taken away from the affairs of men, our province hath been distracted with this perverse madness; so that from that day there hath been scarce a single reeve which hath not during the time of his office provided for himself a monastery of this sort, and at the same time bound his wife in the like guilt of mischievous traffic; and the force of this vile custom continuing, the thanes also and servants of the king have been very forward to follow the same. And so from a corruption of due order very many have been found, which call themselves alike abbots, reeves, and thanes or servants of the king, and which, albeit being laymen they might have learned something of the monastical life by hearsay if not of experience, yet are utterly without part in the character or pro-

ditus exsortes. Et quidem tales repente, ut nosti, tonsuram pro suo libitu accipiunt, suo examine de laicis non monachi, sed abbates efficiuntur. Sed quia praefatae virtutis nec notitiam probantur habere nec studium, quid his aliud quam evangelica convenit maledictio illa, qua dicitur : " Caecus si caeco ducatum praestet, ambo in foveam cadunt? " Quae nimirum caecitas posset aliquando terminari, ac regulari disciplina cohiberi, et de finibus sanctae ecclesiae cunctis pontificali ac synodica auctoritate procul expelli, si non ipsi pontifices magis huiusmodi sceleribus opem ferre atque astipulari probarentur: qui non solummodo huiusmodi decreta iniusta iustis infringere decretis non curant, verum suis potius subscriptionibus, ut praefati sumus, confirmare satagunt: eadem ipsis philargyria dictante, ad confirmandum male scripta, qua emptores ad comparandum huiusmodi monasteria coacti.

Multa quidem adhuc tibi possem de his et huiusmodo praevaricationibus quibus nostra provincia miserrime vexatur, his intimare literis, si non teipsum nossem haec eadem certissime cognovisse. Nam neque haec ita scripsi, quasi certissime te ea quae antea nescires essem docturus, sed ut te amica exhortatione commonerem, ea quae optime noveras errata diligenti prout vales instantia corrigere.

14. Et iam iamque te multum deprecor atque obtestor in Domino, ut commissum tibi gregem sedulus ab irruentium luporum improbitate tuearis:

[1] Matt. xv. 14.

fession whose duty is to teach it. It is true such men, as you know, receive the tonsure suddenly of their own pleasure, and of their own judgment are turned from laymen, not merely into monks but into abbots. But being found to have neither knowledge nor love of the aforesaid virtue, what else is fitly said of them but that curse pronounced in the Gospel:[1] "If the blind lead the blind, do not both fall into the ditch?" Which blindness surely might be brought within bounds and checked with regular discipline, and driven from the borders of the holy Church by the authority of bishop and synod, if the bishops themselves were not found rather to help and consent to this kind of wickedness: the which not only take no pains to overthrow unjust decrees of this sort with just ones, but are forward, as we said, rather to confirm them by the writing of their own hands: the same covetousness moving them to confirm the evil agreements, as compelleth the buyers to establish monasteries of this sort.

There are yet many things I could have told you in this letter concerning these and the like transgressions with which our province is most miserably distressed, did I not know that you are yourself fully aware of them. Nor have I written what I have, as though I were going to make you assured of such things as you did not know before, but in order to warn you by a friendly exhortation to amend, with all the zeal and care you can command, the misdeeds of which you very well know.

14. And again and again I fervently pray and beseech you in the Lord, zealously to guard the flock committed to your charge from the ravening wolves which fall upon it; and to remember that

teque non mercenarium, sed pastorem constitutum esse memineris, qui amorem summi Pastoris solerti ovium ipsius pastione demonstres, proque eisdem ovibus, si ita res poposcerit, cum beato apostolorum principe animam ponere paratus sis. Precor sollicite praecaveas, ne cum idem princeps apostolorum ceterique fidelium gregum duces in die iudicii maximum suae pastoralis curae fructum Christo obtulerint, tuarum aliqua pars ovium inter haedos ad sinistram Iudicis secerni, atque in aeternum cum maledictione mereatur ire supplicium: quin potius ipse tunc eorum numero merearis ascribi, de quibus ait Esaias: "Minimus erit inter mille, et parvulus inter gentem fortissimam." Tui namque est officii diligentissime prospicere, quid in singulis monasteriis tuae parochiae recti, quid perversi geratur: ne vel abbas regularum inscius aut contemptor, vel abbatissa minus digna famulorum famularumve Christi praeponatur examini, nec rursum provisioni[1] spiritualium magistrorum contemptrix et indisciplinata contumacium auditorum turba resultet; maxime quia, sicut vulgo fertur, dicere estis soliti, quod non ad regum curam, non ad aliquorum saeculi principum causam, sed ad vestram tantummodo antistitum inquisitionem atque examen, quid in singulis monasteriis agatur pertineat, nisi forte in monasteriis quilibet in ipsos principes peccasse comprobetur. Tui, inquam, est officii procurare ne in locis Deo consecratis diabolus sibi regnum usurpet, ne pro pace discordia, pro pietate iurgia, pro sobrietate ebrietas, pro charitate

[1] for *praevisioni*, Pl.

---

[1] Isai. lx. 22.

you are appointed to be no hireling but a shepherd, proving your love of the great Shepherd by your careful feeding of His sheep, and ready, if need be, to lay down your life for the sheep, as did the blessed chief of the apostles. I pray you earnestly to beware lest, when that same chief of the apostles and the other leaders of faithful flocks offer to Christ in the day of judgment the fruits of their pastoral care, some part of your sheep be found deserving to be set aside with the goats on the left hand of the Judge, and go under a curse into everlasting punishment; but may you rather deserve to be numbered with those of whom Isaiah speaketh:[1] "The least shall be among a thousand, and a little one among a mighty nation." For it is your duty most diligently to examine what is done aright and what is done amiss in the several monasteries of your diocese: that there be no abbot which doth not know, or which despiseth rules, or unworthy abbess, set over the company of the servants or handmaids of Christ, or again that no scornful and unruly crowd of rebellious hearers rise up against the ordering of their spiritual masters; especially because you the bishops, according to common report, are wont to say, that the examination and enquiry into what appertaineth to be done in the several monasteries belongeth not to the charge of kings nor to the cause of any of the princes of the world, but to yourselves alone, unless perchance anyone within the monastery be found to have offended against the princes themselves. It is your duty, I say, to take heed that in places consecrated to God the devil seize not the rule for himself, lest discord instead of peace, strife instead of godliness, drunkenness

et castitate fornicationes et homicidia sibi sedem vindicent: ne apud te inveniantur aliqui, de quibus merito quaeratur ac dicatur: "vidi impios sepultos, qui cum adviverent, in loco sancto erant, et laudabantur in civitate, quasi iustorum operum."[1]

15. Eorum quoque qui in populari adhuc vita continentur solicitam te necesse est curam gerere, ut sicut in primordio huius epistolae praemonuimus, sufficientes eis doctores vitae salutaris adhibere memineris, et hoc eos inter alia discere facias, quibus operibus maxime Deo placere, a quibus se debeant qui Deo placere desiderant abstinere peccatis, qua cordis sinceritate in Deum credere, qua divinam clementiam supplicantes debeant devotione precari, quam frequenti diligentia signaculo se Dominicae crucis suaque omnia adversum continuas immundorum spirituum insidias necesse habeant munire, quam salutaris sit omni Christianorum generi quotidiana Dominici corporis ac sanguinis perceptio, iuxta quod ecclesiam Christi per Italiam, Galliam, Africam, Graeciam, ac totum Orientem solerter agere nosti. Quod videlicet genus religionis, ac Deo devotae sanctificationis tam longe a cunctis pene nostrae provinciae laicis per incuriam docentium quasi prope peregrinum abest, ut hi qui inter illos[1] religiosiores esse videntur, non nisi in natali Domini et epiphania et pascha sacrosanctis mysteriis communicare praesumant, cum sint innumeri innocentes et castissimae

[1] sp. Pl.

---

[1] Eccles. viii. 10.

instead of temperance, fornication and murder instead of charity and chastity claim to have their dwelling therein; and that there be not found among you any of whom it may be deservedly enquired and said:[1] "I saw the wicked buried, who in their lifetime were in the place of the holy, and were praised in the city as though they were men of just works."

15. You must needs also give careful heed to those who are still retained in the life of the world, remembering, as we forewarned you in the beginning of this letter, to provide for them sufficient teachers of wholesome living, and causing them among other things to learn with what works they ought to please God, and from what sins they which desire to please Him must refrain, with what singleness of heart they must believe in God, with what devoutness they must approach in prayer the Divine mercy, with what often diligence they are bound with the sign of the Lord's cross to fortify themselves and all that belongs to them against the unceasing wiles of unclean spirits, how wholesome for every sort of Christian man it is to receive daily the Lord's body and blood, according to the custom which, you know, is closely followed by the Church of Christ throughout Italy, France, Africa, Greece and all the East. The which form of piety and devout sanctification to God is, through the neglect of their teachers, so far out of use and as it were foreign to almost all the laymen of our province, that those among them which seem to be more religious do not presume to communicate in the holy mysteries save on the day of the Lord's Nativity, on the Epiphany, and on Easter Day; albeit there are great numbers of innocent boys and

conversationis pueri ac puellae, iuvenes et virgines, senes et anus, qui absque ullo scrupulo controversiae, omni die Dominico, sive etiam in natalitiis sanctorum apostolorum, sive martyrum, quomodo ipse in sancta Romana et apostolica ecclesia fieri vidisti, mysteriis caelestibus communicare valeant. Ipsi etiam coniugati, si quis sibi mensuram continentiae ostendat, et virtutem castitatis insinuet, idem et licenter possint, et libenter facere velint.

16. Haec tibi, sanctissime antistes, et tuae dilectionis intuitu et generalis gratia utilitatis breviter adnotare studui, multum desiderans multumque exhortans, ut gentem nostram a vetustis abstrahere cures erroribus, et ad certiorem et directiorem vitae callem reducere satagas: et si sunt aliqui cuiuslibet gradus sive ordinis viri, qui bona tua coepta retinere atque impedire conentur, tu tamen propositum sanctae virtutis, supernae memor retributionis, ad firmum usque finem perducere contendas. Scio namque nonnullos huic nostrae exhortationi multum contradicturos, et maxime eos qui seipsos illis facinoribus a quibus te prohibemus, esse sentiunt irretitos: sed meminisse te decet apostolicae responsionis, quia "obedire oportet Deo magis quam hominibus." Mandatum quippe est Dei: "Vendite quae possidetis, et date eleemosynam." Et: "Nisi quis renuntiaverit omnibus quae possidet, non potest meus esse discipulus." Traditio autem moderna quorundam est, qui se Dei famulos esse profitentur, non solum possessa non vendere, verum

[1] Acts v. 29.
[2] Luke xii. 33.

girls, youths and maidens, old men and women of pure life and conversation, who without any cause of debate might partake of the heavenly mysteries every Lord's Day and also on the birthdays of the holy apostles and martyrs, as you yourself have seen done in the holy and apostolic church of Rome. Yea, even married folk, if anyone would shew them measure of continence, and impart to them the virtue of purity of life, might both lawfully and would gladly do the same.

16. These things, most holy bishop, both out of regard for your affection and for the sake of the common advantage, I have been careful to write unto you in few words, of my great desire and earnest exhortation that you endeavour to deliver our nation from errors of long season, and be forward to bring it back to a more sure and straighter way of life; and if there be some men, of whatsoever rank or degree, which shall set themselves to let and hinder your good beginning, do you nevertheless, remembering your heavenly recompense, strive to hold fast unto the end your holy and virtuous purpose. For I know that there are some which will vehemently withstand this exhortation of ours, especially those who feel that they are themselves entangled in such evil doing from which we would restrain you; but it becometh you to remember the apostolical answer,[1] that "we ought to obey God rather than men." For it is God's commandment: "Sell that ye have and give alms."[2] And: "Unless a man give up all that he hath, he cannot be My disciple." But a new tradition is made of certain men which, professing themselves to be servants of God, not only do not sell what they have, but also get

etiam comparare non habita. Qua ergo fronte audet quisquam ad servitium Domini accessurus, vel ea quae in saeculari vita habuerat retentare, vel sub praetextu vitae sanctioris illas quas non habuerat congregare divitias: cum etiam apostolica sit notissima censura, quae Ananiam et Sapphiram hoc facere molientes, non ullo poenitentiae vel satisfactionis remedio corrigere, sed ipsa statim mortis ultricis acceleravit damnatione punire?[1] Et quidem illi non aliena colligere, sed sua incongrue retinere maluerunt. Unde manifeste patet, quam longe abstiterit animus apostolorum a suscipiendis pecuniarum acquisitionibus, qui sub illa proprie regula Domino serviebant: "Beati pauperes, quia vestrum est regnum Dei": et e contra, partis sinistrae proposito nihilominus instituebantur exemplo: "Vae vobis divitibus, quia habetis consolationem vestram." An forte errasse ac mendacium scripsisse putamus apostolum, cum nos admonens dicebat: "Fratres, nolite errare"; statimque subtexuit: "Neque avari, neque ebriosi, neque rapaces regnum Dei possidebunt." Et iterum: "Hoc autem scitote, quod omnis fornicator, aut immundus, aut avarus, aut rapax, quod est idolorum servitus, non habet haereditatem in regno Christi et Dei." Cum ergo apostolus avaritiam et rapacitatem idolatriam manifeste cognominet, quomodo putandum est eos errasse, qui vel subscriptioni avari mercatus, rege licet imperante,

[1] for *puniri*, Pl.

---

[1] Luke vi. 20, 24. [2] 1 Cor. vi. 9, 10.

them possessions that they have not. With what face then durst a man which would approach the service of God either retain the wealth which he had in his secular life, or heap up such wealth as he had not before under the pretence of a more holy life: seeing too the judgment of the apostles is well known, which, when Ananias and Sapphira devised to do this, forbare to rectify them with any remedy of penance or making amends, but swiftly punished them with sentence of immediate death to avenge their sin? Yet these two did not wish to gain the possession of other, but to keep their own otherwise than was agreed. Whence it is manifest how far it was from the mind of the apostles to make gain of money, serving the Lord as they did especially under the rule:[1] "Blessed are ye poor, for yours is the kingdom of heaven": and contrariwise they were none the less instructed by the example set up of the adverse side: "Woe unto you that are rich, for ye have received your consolation." Or are we to think that the apostle was deceived and wrote a lie when he wrote for our warning:[2] "Brethren, be not deceived"? immediately adding thereto: "Neither the covetous, nor drunkards, nor extortioners shall inherit the kingdom of heaven." And again:[3] "But know ye this, that no whoremonger, nor unclean person, nor covetous man, nor extortioner, who is an idolater, hath any inheritance in the kingdom of Christ and of God." When, therefore, the apostle openly calleth avarice and covetousness, idolatry, how ought we to consider them to be deceived, who have either withheld their hand from subscription to covetous traffic, albeit

[3] Ephes. v. 5.

manum subtraxerint, vel ad eradendas inutiles scripturas ac subscriptiones eorum, manum apposuerint?

17. Et quidem miranda est temeritas stultorum, vel potius deflenda miseria caecorum, qui cum sine ullo respectu superni timoris, passim ea quae apostoli et prophetae afflatu sancti spiritus scripserunt, rescindere ac nihili pendere probantur: illud e contra, quod ipsi vel similes ipsorum instinctu avaritiae vel luxuriae scripserunt, quasi sanctum ac divinitus cautum eradere atque emendare formidant, in morem, ni fallor, ethnicorum, qui contempto Dei cultu ea quae ipsi sibi de corde suo finxerunt ac fecerunt, numina venerantur, timent, colunt, adorant, et obsecrant, Dominica illa insectatione dignissimi, qua Pharisaeos cum suas deuteroses Legi Dei praeponerent, redarguit, dicens: "Quare et vos transgredimini mandatum Dei propter traditionem vestram?" Qui si etiam chartas protulerint in defensionem concupiscentiarum suarum adscriptas, ac nobilium personarum subscriptione confirmatas; tu nunquam precor Dominicae sanctionis obliviscaris, in qua dicitur, "Omnis plantatio quam non plantavit Pater meus caelestis eradicabitur." Et certe a te discere vellem, sanctissime antistes, Domino protestante atque dicente, quia, "lata porta et spatiosa via est quae ducit ad perditionem, et multi sunt qui intrant per eam: cum angusta porta et arcta via sit, quae ducit ad vitam, et pauci sint qui inveniant

[1] δευτέρωσις, the word used by the Greek fathers to translate the Hebrew *Mischna*, and applied to the scribal tradition, Pl.

commanded of the king, or have set their hand to the blotting out of these vain writings and subscriptions?

17. And wonderful truly is the rash folly, or rather lamentable and wretched blindness, of those who without any regard to the fear of heaven are shewn everywhere to abolish and make light of what the apostles and prophets have written by inspiration of the Holy Spirit: yet, on the other hand, shrink from blotting out and correcting what they themselves or men like them have written at the prompting of greed or luxury, as though it were a holy thing and one given of divine ordinance, the which men are, if I mistake not, like the heathen who, despising the worship of God, reverence, fear, worship, adore and supplicate those deities which they have made and fashioned for themselves out of their own imagination, and altogether deserve the rebuke with which our Lord reproved the Pharisees, when they preferred their own traditions [1] to the Law of God, saying: [2] "Why do ye also transgress the commandment of God for the sake of your tradition?" And if further they shall bring forward charters drawn up for the protection of their lusts, and confirmed by the subscription of noble persons; do not you, I beseech you, ever forget the Lord's ordinance which saith: [3] "Every plant which My heavenly Father hath not planted, shall be rooted up." And verily I would fain learn of you, most holy bishop (seeing the Lord declareth and saith: [4] "Wide is the gate and broad is the way which leadeth to destruction, and many there be which go in thereat: because strait is the gate and narrow is the way which leadeth unto life, and few there be

[2] Matt. xv. 3. [3] Matt. xv. 13. [4] Matt. vii. 13, 14.

eam": quid de eorum vita vel salute aeterna confidas, qui toto vitae suae tempore per latam portam et spatiosam viam incedere noscuntur, et ne in minimis quidem rebus voluptati suae vel corporis vel animi causa supernae retributionis obsistere vel repugnare curabant: nisi forte per eleemosynas, quas inter concupiscentias quotidianas ac delicias pauperibus dare videbantur, criminibus absolvi posse credendi sunt, cum manus ipsa et conscientia quae manus offerat Deo, munda a peccatis esse debeat et absoluta; aut certe per mysteria sacrosanctae oblationis, quibus ipsi dum viverent indigni extiterant, per alios iam mortui redimi posse sperandi sunt. An forte illis permodica culpa videtur esse concupiscentiae? De qua paulo latius disputem. Haec Balaam virum prophetiae spiritu plenissimum a sorte sanctorum fecit extorrem, Achan communione anathematis polluit ac perdidit, Saul regni infulis nudavit, Giezi prophetiae meritis privavit ac perpetuae leprae peste cum suo semine foedavit, Iudam Iscariotem de apostolatus gloria deposuit, Ananiam et Sapphiram, de quibus praediximus, monachorum collegio indignos etiam corporis morte mulctavit, et, ut ad superiora veniamus, haec angelos a caelo deiecit, et protoplastos a Paradiso perpetuae voluptatis expulit: et si nosse vis, hic est ille triceps

---

[1] Masses for the dead.

[2] The communism of Acts iv. 32 being regarded as monastical.

that find it"): what confidence you have of the eternal life and salvation of those who are known to be walking all the days of their life through the wide gate and in the broad way, and who not even in the smallest matters endeavoured to withstand and fight against the pleasure of either body or mind for the sake of recompense in heaven: unless perchance we are to believe that they can be absolved from their offences by the alms which in the midst of their daily lust and enjoyments they were seen to bestow upon the poor, although the hand itself and the conscience which reacheth forth the hands to God ought to be purified and set free from sin; or unless we are at least to hope that when they are now dead they can be ransomed by other through the mysteries of the holy oblation,[1] of the which in their lifetime they had shewn themselves unworthy. Or perchance the sin of lust seemeth to them a light one. Of which matter let me discuss more fully. It was this that made Balaam, a man filled with the spirit of prophecy, to be shut out from the inheritance of the saints, that defiled and ruined Achan for being partaker in the accursed thing, that stripped Saul of his kingly crown, that took from Gehazi the due reward of prophecy and polluted him and his seed with the plague of continual leprosy, that brought down Judas Iscariot from the glory of the apostleship, that rendered Ananias and Sapphira, of whom we have already spoken, unworthy of the company of monks,[2] and punished them beside with bodily death, and, to go to higher things, it was this that cast down the angels from heaven, and drove our first parents from the Paradise of everlasting delight. And, if you would know, this is

inferorum canis, cui fabulae Cerberi nomen indiderunt, a cuius rabidis dentibus nos prohibens Iohannes apostolus ait: " Carissimi, nolite diligere mundum, neque ea quae in mundo sunt. Si quis diligit mundum, non est caritas Patris in eo. Quoniam omne quod in mundo est, concupiscentia carnis est, et concupiscentia oculorum et superbia vitae, quae non est ex Patre, sed ex mundo est." Haec contra virus avaritiae breviter sunt dicta. Ceterum si de ebrietate, commessatione, luxuria, et ceteris huiusmodi contagionibus pari ratione tractare voluerimus, epistolae modus in immensum extenderetur.

Gratia te summi Pastoris ad pastionem ovium suarum salutiferam perpetuo conservet incolumem, dilectissime in Christo antistes. Scripta Nonas Novembris, indictione tertia.[1]

[1] Date added, Pl.

that three-headed dog of the lowest pit, to which fables have given the name of Cerberus, from the rage of whose teeth the apostle John warneth us, saying:[1] "Dearly beloved, love not the world, neither the things that are in the world. If any man love the world, the love of the Father is not in him. For all that is in the world, the lust of the flesh, and the lust of the eyes, and the pride of life, is not of the Father, but of the world." Such are the few words we have spoken against the poison of greed. But if I should wish to treat in like manner concerning drunkenness, revellings, wantonness, and all other plagues of this sort, the length of this letter would be beyond measure extended.

May the grace of the chief Shepherd keep you continually in safety, bishop dearly beloved in Christ, for the wholesome feeding of His sheep. Written on the 5th day of November, in the third indiction.

[1] 1 John ii. 15, 16.

TABLE OF KINGS

I. *Kent.*

Ethelbert	*c.* 560
Eadbald	616
Earconbert	640
Egbert	664
Lothere	673
Edric	685
[Anarchy]	686
Witred	690
Eadbert	725

II. *Wessex.*

Ceawlin	560
Cynegils	611
Cenwalch	643
Sexburg	672
Escwin	674
Centwine	676
Cadwalla	685
Ini	688

III. *Essex.*

Sabert	*c.* 600
Sigbert the Little	*c.* 617
Sigbert the Good	before 653
Swidhelm	*c.* 657
Sebbi and Sighere	664
Sigherd and Swefred	694
Offa	*c.* 709

IV. *Northumbria.*

Ethelfrith	593
Edwin	617
Eanfrid in Bernicia Osric in Deira	633
Oswald	634
Oswy in Bernicia Oswin in Deira	641
Oswy	651
Egfrid	671
Aldfrid	685
Eadwulf	705
Osred	706
Cenred	716
Osric	718
Ceolwulf	729

V. *East Anglia.*

Redwald	593
Earpwald	617
Sigbert the Learned	631
Egric	634
Anna	636
Ethelhere	654
Ethelwald	655
Aldwulf	663
Alfwold	713

VI. *Mercia.*

Cearl	606
Penda	626
Peada (under Oswy of Northumbria)	655
Wulfhere	658
Ethelred	675

VI. *Mercia (continued)*—		
	Cenred	704
	Ceolred	709
	Ethelbald	716
VII. *Sussex.*		
	Ethelwalh	*c.* 660

SUCCESSION OF BISHOPS

Cf. Bright, p. 462.

1. *Canterbury.*

Augustine	597
Laurence	605
Mellitus	619
Justus	624
Honorius	627
Deusdedit	655
Theodore	668
Bertwald	693
Tatwin	731

2. *London.*

Mellitus	604
Cedd (bishop of East Saxons)	653
Wini	666
Earconwald	675
Waldhere	*c.* 693
Ingwald	*c.* 704

3. *Rochester.*

Justus	604
Romanus	624
Paulinus	633
Ithamar	644
Damian	655
Putta	669
Cwichelm	676
Gebmund	678

3. *Rochester (continued)*—

Tobias	693
Aldwulf	727

4. *York.*

Paulinus	625
Chad, consecrated	665–6
deposed	669
Wilfrid, consecrated	664
in possession	669
Bosa	678
Wilfrid, restored	686
Bosa, again	691
John	706
Wilfrid II	714?
Egbert	732

5. *Dunwich.*

Felix	631
Thomas	647
Boniface	652
Bisi	669
Acci	673
Aldbert	uncertain

6. *Lindisfarne.*

Aidan	635
Finan	651
Colman	661
Tuda	664
Eata	678
Cuthbert	685
Eadbert	688
Eadfrid	698
Ethelwald	724

7. *Dorchester* or *Winchester*.

Birinus (Dorchester)	635
Agilbert (Dorchester)	650
Wini (Winchester)	662
Lothere (Dorchester)	670
Heddi (Winchester)	676
Aetla (Dorchester)	*c.* 679
Daniel (Winchester)	705

8. *Lichfield*.

Diuma	656
Cellach	658
Trumhere	659
Jaruman	662
Chad	669
Wynfrid	672
Sexwulf	675
Hedda	691
Aldwin	721

9. *Elmham*.

Badwine	673
Hadulac	uncertain

10. *Hereford*.

Putta, possibly	676
Torthere	till 727
Walhstod	till 736

11. *Hexham*.

Eata (with Lindisfarne)	678
Trumbert	681
Eata, again	685
John	687
Wilfrid	706
Acca, expelled	731

12. *Sidnacester* (for *Lindsey*).

Eadhed	678
Ethelwin	680
Edgar	before 706
Cynibert	d. 732

13. *Worcester*.

Bosel	680
Oftfor	692
Egwin	693–4
Wilfrid	717

14. *Leicester*.

Cuthwin	680
[See administered by Wilfrid]	691

15. *Selsey*.

Wilfrid	681–2
Eadbert	709
Eolla	uncertain
[Vacant many years.]	
Sigfrid	723

16. *Sherborne*.

Aldhelm	705
Forthere	709

17. *Whitern, Candida Casa*.

Pecthelm	*c.* 730

INDEX

INDEX

INDEX

INDEX

INDEX

INDEX

INDEX

INDEX

INDEX

INDEX

INDEX